TV Museum

TV Museum
Contemporary Art and the Age of Television

Maeve Connolly

intellect Bristol, UK / Chicago, USA

First published in the UK in 2014 by
Intellect, The Mill, Parnall Road, Fishponds, Bristol, BS16 3JG, UK

First published in the USA in 2014 by
Intellect, The University of Chicago Press, 1427 E. 60th Street,
Chicago, IL 60637, USA

A catalogue record for this book is available from the
British Library.

Cover designer: Stephanie Sarlos
Copy-editor: Richard Walsh
Cover image: Auto Italia LIVE: Double Dip Concession, 2012,
  live broadcast from the ICA, London, as part of the exhibition
  'Remote Control'. Courtesy: Auto Italia South East, London.
  Photograph: Ryan McNamara
Production manager: Tim Mitchell
Typesetting: Contentra Technologies

Print ISBN 978-1-78320-181-5
ePUB ISBN 978-1-78320-245-4
ePDF ISBN 978-1-78320-244-7

Printed and bound by Gomer Press Ltd, UK.

Table of Contents

Acknowledgements

The origins of the project can be traced to *The Glass Eye: Artists and Television* (Dublin: Project Press, 2000), a collection of artists' texts and projects that I co-edited with Orla Ryan. *The Glass Eye* was followed by an exhibition in Dublin, *The Captain's Road*, curated in 2002 with Orla Ryan and Valerie Connor, which presented artworks and events engaging with television in both a suburban home and a workers' social club. My interest in television as an object of artistic and curatorial investigation receded for several years but it was reignited in 2008, when Sarah Cook visited Dublin and spoke to my students at Dun Laoghaire Institute of Art, Design and Technology about *Broadcast Yourself*, the exhibition that she co-curated with Kathy Rae Huffman at Hatton Gallery in Newcastle and Cornerhouse, Manchester. Although *TV Museum: Contemporary Art and the Age of Television* is primarily concerned with artworks, it engages also with practices of curating, exhibition-making and public programming, and seeks to offer a comprehensive account of television's significance in contemporary art, particularly since the early 2000s.

The book incorporates material revised from various journal articles (identified within the text) and conference papers, and I am greatly indebted to the many journal editors, peer reviewers and conference attendees who have helped to shape and inform my research. I have also developed and tested many different elements of this research in seminars with graduate and undergraduate students on art and media programmes, including the MA in Visual Arts Practices (Dun Laoghaire Institute of Art, Design and Technology, Dublin), MA in Curatorial Practice (California College of the Arts, San Francisco), MRes Art: Moving Image at Central Saint Martins (University of the Arts, London) and the Royal Danish Art Academy. In 2012, I was invited to deliver a 'TV Museum' seminar over several months at the Media Faculty of Bauhaus University Weimar, which provided a valuable opportunity to refine the structure of the book. My research has also been sustained through many productive interactions with senior and postgraduate researchers at the Internationales Kolleg für Kulturtechnikforschung und Medienphilosophie (IKKM) at Bauhaus University Weimar, and also with residents at the Zentrum für Kunst und Urbanistik in Berlin.

I would particularly like to thank the following: John Caldwell, Francesco Casetti, Ana Paula Cohen, Benjamin Cook, Valerie Connor, Farrel Corcoran, Tom Dale, Michelle Deignan, Anita Di Bianco, Liam Donnelly, Thomas Elsaesser, Lorenz Engell, Annie Fletcher, Laura Frahm, Alicia Frankovich, Ursula Frohne, Fiona Fullam, Bernard Geoghegan, Tessa

Giblin, Luke Gibbons, Paula Gilligan, Sarah Glennie, Nicky Gogan, Carolina Grau, Melissa Gronlund, Lilian Haberer, Caroline Hancock, Dan Hays, Sinead Hogan, Jane Horton, Daniel Jewesbury, Finola Jones, Jesse Jones, Darin Klein, Mia Lerm Hayes, Alex Martinis Roe, Stephanie McBride, Martin McCabe, Carol McGuire, Bea McMahon, Dennis McNulty, Eoghan McTigue, Leigh Markopoulos, Catherine Morris, Diane Negra, Niamh O'Malley, Paul O'Neill, Volker Pantenburg, Susan Philipsz, Robert Porter, Lucy Reynolds, Orla Ryan, Bernhard Siegert, Mike Sperlinger, Kate Strain, Anne Tallentire, Annette Urban, Huib Haye van der Werf, Helmut Weber and Ian White. This project would never have been possible without the support of colleagues at Dun Laoghaire Institute of Art, Design and Technology, Dublin, and the opportunity for critical reflection afforded by a Research Fellowship (in 2011–2012) as part of the Junior Fellows programme at the IKKM, Bauhaus University Weimar. Vital financial assistance was also provided by the Irish Arts Council/ An Chomhairle Ealaíon in the form of a Project Grant, awarded in 2011.

My sincere thanks are due to the many artists, curators and gallerists who facilitated visits to exhibitions and studios, generously provided access to documentation, production details and images for reproduction, and also to the editors and designers at Intellect Books for their commitment to this project. I am also very grateful to the anonymous peer reviewer of the manuscript, whose generous and insightful comments were incredibly helpful during the revision process, and to Lucy Reynolds for her invaluable editorial guidance. Finally, I want to thank my mother Nora, my sisters Eithne, Aoife, Sinead and Fiona, and my partner Dennis McNulty, for their constant support.

Introduction

Contemporary Art and the Age of Television

W riting in the 1990s, and reflecting upon the museum boom of the previous decade, Andreas Huyssen proposes a possible connection between the prominence of museums and monuments in contemporary culture and the 'cabling of the metropolis' during the 1980s.[1] For Huyssen, the spread of cable television contributed to 'an unquenchable desire for experiences and events', which could only be satisfied by the 'register of reality' carried by museum objects. According to this logic, the material objects that are oldest, and so most distinct from 'soon-to-be-obsolete' commodities, command the greatest presence, carrying the greatest 'memory value' and yielding a 'sense of the authentic' that cannot be matched even by the live television broadcast.[2] In the decades following the museum boom, however, television has itself acquired the status of a 'soon-to-be-obsolete' material object. Furthermore, manifestations of televisual presence—once exemplified by the live broadcast—are now increasingly subject to relativisation and remediation by newer technologies. As a result, it is timely to reconsider the relationship between television and the museum, and to reassess the cultural significance of changes in broadcasting, including those referenced by Huyssen.

There are, however, particular challenges involved in theorising television's altered status as an object of museum memory, as evidenced by two recent accounts of a paradigmatic art installation, Douglas Gordon's *24 Hour Psycho* (1993). In a 2012 publication exploring the borders of cinema, Volker Pantenburg draws attention to television's role as mediating technology in the production of Gordon's work, observing that 'wherever questions of "cinema" seem to be addressed, "film" can just as well mean TV, DVD, or the Internet'.[3] He cites an interview (from 2002) in which Gordon is asked when he first encountered the films referenced in his installations. Gordon responds by recounting his memory of arriving home from a late night shift in a supermarket in the early 1980s and stumbling upon an 'esoteric film series' on Channel 4 television, featuring an array of European and Hollywood auteurs.[4] Noting that the channel had 'just started', Gordon presents it as 'a very important thing: Channel 4 was the only thing on TV at that time of night'. So this memory of television actually concerns a specific moment of innovation in British public service broadcasting. For the first few years of its existence, Channel 4 received an additional public subsidy enabling the development of an experimental approach to the commissioning and scheduling of programmes, aimed at a variety of minority audiences perceived to have been overlooked or marginalised by other public broadcasting services.[5] Significantly, unlike Andy Warhol, who deliberately dissociated himself from the network schedule with its normative assumptions about social and familial life by watching TV shows on tape,[6] Gordon does not describe his relationship with late-night television in the early 1980s in terms of video-enabled 'timeshifting'.[7] Instead he formed part of a larger—albeit unknown—constituency, sharing in the scheduled late-night viewing of esoteric films at a specific moment in the history of British broadcasting. Consequently, it is possible to imagine *24 Hour Psycho* as an exaggerated version of niche broadcasting, in the form of a TV channel showing nothing but Hitchcock's *Psycho*, all day.

24 Hour Psycho also figures prominently within Erika Balsom's analysis of cinema's exhibition in contemporary art. According to Balsom, Gordon sees Hitchcock 'as a kind of hinge between cinema in its classical incarnation and the many transformations to which it has been subjected since its disintegration'.[8] She proposes that *24 Hour Psycho* 'telescopes' two related moments of transition in cinema (involving television and the VCR) while at the same time 'fetishistically overvaluing the director who both emblematized and reflexively interrogated the institution in its classical form'.[9] Balsom also draws upon an interview with Gordon, which specifically concerns the genesis of *24 Hour Psycho*, citing a text relating to the 1996 exhibition *Spellbound: Art and Film*.[10] Again, Gordon recalls watching TV in his family home. But this time the year is 1992 and he is visiting his family for Christmas— traditionally a time when broadcast schedules would feature movie highlights. He describes watching a tape of a TV transmission of *Psycho*, during which his attention was drawn to an erotic detail, in which Norman peers through a hidden peep-hole to watch as Marion undresses. Gordon did not remember seeing this particular detail in the commercial VHS release and he used the remote control to freeze-frame the videotape recording of the televised broadcast to check that the image was 'really there'.

Informed by Gordon's account, Balsom frames *24 Hour Psycho* as a response to the contradictions inherent in the forms of cinephilia enabled by domestic video technology. *24 Hour Psycho,* she argues, 'renders private rituals of image consumption gigantic, taking them back out into the public sphere for examination'. By combining the large-scale projection and modes of collective reception associated with cinema with the practices of copying and altered playback associated with home video, Gordon creates 'a hybrid aggregate that brings into relief the tension between its constituent parts'.[11] For Balsom, the 'public sphere' is very clearly signified by the collective viewing experience of cinema. In contrast, television and video are—by implication—associated with the realm of the individual and the private. There is little doubt that cinema is now seen to function as an important signifier of 'publicness' within contemporary art.[12] Yet, Balsom's account does not allow for the possibility that television, particularly in the idealised version evoked by Gordon's memory of Channel 4, might also signify a type of publicness.

These two versions of the genesis of *24 Hour Psycho* are certainly not in conflict, since they relate to disparate moments in the development of Gordon's practice as an artist. But when considered together they underscore some of the difficulties involved in theorising television as an object of artistic, and cultural, memory. Even though its origins were at least partly shaped by a culturally and historically specific experience of broadcasting, *24 Hour Psycho* has instead come to exemplify *cinema*'s enduring resonance in contemporary art

Above: Douglas Gordon, *24 Hour
Psycho*, 1993.

culture, featuring prominently in a series of thematic exhibitions toward the end of the 1990s, coinciding with cinema's centenary celebrations.[13] These exhibitions formed part of a larger cinematic—or perhaps cinephilic—turn in art practice, which has been extensively theorised by film and art scholars.[14] Yet several artists who were drawn toward histories and memories of cinema during the 1990s also articulated a fascination with television as a cultural form. For example, *24 Hour Psycho* was presented in full as part of *Mobile TV* (1995–1998), a project devised by Pierre Huyghe for transmission on local television in France, which included contributions from Olivier Bardin, Marine Hugonnier and Mélik Ohanian, among many others.[15] TV-themed works were also produced by artists such as Stan Douglas and Dominique Gonzalez-Foerster. Douglas, for example, produced his series of *Monodramas* (1992) for Canadian television and also drew upon the history of broadcasting in gallery installations such as *Hors-champs* (1992) and *Evening* (1994), while Gonzalez-Foerster integrated small portable TV sets into installation works such as *Chambre en Ville* (1996).

To date, however, the televisual has been somewhat overshadowed by the cinematic in theorisations of artists' moving image.[16] Perhaps this relative occlusion speaks to a specific difficulty around television in the art museum, which may be linked to its indeterminate status as simultaneously a material thing, medium, institution and cultural form. Evidently, artists have consistently challenged and expanded normative definitions of cinema and television, through the production of moving image works, devised for theatrical exhibition, broadcast, or gallery presentation. But in addition to functioning as sites of presentation, museums and galleries are also settings in which aspects of cinema and television are evoked, imagined, signified, and to some extent *represented*, through performances, sculptural objects and moving image installations. This task of representation is arguably more straightforward in the case of cinema. Even thirty years after its release, Hitchcock's *Psycho* still clearly signified 'cinema', thus enabling Gordon's work to be read as a response to the remediation of filmic form and cinematic memory by video and television, rather than as an exploration of the televisual image, for example.

In addition, 'Television' is perhaps less readily signified than cinema by iconic content because of its perceived difference from the latter. John Caldwell notes that TV programming, for example, has been routinely framed as subordinate to broadcast 'flow', while television viewing (unlike cinema spectatorship) has been theorised as inherently inattentive. This tendency to emphasise an extreme dualism between film and television—exemplified by Marshall McLuhan's account of 'essential' differences between media—has been particularly unhelpful in understanding contemporary televisual form and consumption, especially with regard to the role of stylisation. Caldwell's own approach, however, offers a counterpoint to what he terms 'the myth of distraction'[17] in relation to television viewing, highlighting the many ways in which television works to attract the audience's attention, through its utilisation of stylistic excess and by rewarding 'discrimination, style consciousness, and viewer loyalty'.[18] He also singles out the 'ideology of liveness' as a further barrier to the analysis of the role of style in the televisual apparatus. Pointing out that the liveness paradigm persisted in phenomenological studies long after live broadcasting ceased

Above: Dynasty Handbag, *E.S.P.
TV presents: Merry Christmas Mary
Boom!,* New York, December 15, 2012.
Courtesy of the artist and E.S.P. TV.

Above: *ESP TV: The Live Live Show,*
Museum of Arts and Design, New
York, April 13, 2013
Courtesy of the artist and E.S.P. TV.

to be the norm, he again notes McLuhan's impact, particularly with regard to the "'all-at-onceness" created by global television's erasure of time and space'.[19]

Caldwell makes the important point that myths of television's 'presentness' were embraced by video artists and activists, many of whom seized upon the 'real-time' experience of video as a means to effect personal and social change.[20] So even though artists and activists often saw themselves as engaged in a social, political or aesthetic critique of television, these critiques did not necessarily counter dominant beliefs about television. Caldwell in fact draws attention to a kind of slippage between television and video, when he notes that qualities of liveness and immediacy were promoted within art discourse as distinctive—even essential—qualities of video, easing the latter's acceptance within 'an art world disciplined by rituals of specificity'.[21] This account resonates with aspects of Martha Rosler's earlier analysis of the 'museumization' of video art in the US context. Charting the end of video's 'utopian moment', Rosler cites curatorial discourses of medium specificity, which helped to obscure important interconnections between histories of art and broadcasting.[22]

If video art's passage into the museum was premised partly upon the cooption of ostensibly televisual presentness, television itself still poses problems of museological categorisation. In one sense, television has been ubiquitous within galleries and contemporary art museums for decades, in the form of the monitors (with or without cathode ray tubes) used to show video works. Yet the apparent ubiquity of TV hardware within art exhibition spaces obscures many problems of defining television as an object of display. In reality, these monitors rarely function as TV receivers and the videos shown on them often have no direct material or economic connection to broadcasting. Even the status of video artworks actually produced for broadcast can be uncertain when they are encountered in the gallery. Do such works constitute 'television' by virtue of their original context of production or distribution, or should they be defined instead as documentation of broadcast events? These uncertainties are amplified by changing modes of production and reception, which complicate the definition 'watching television', since TV consumption is now routinely enabled and (re)mediated[23] by multiple technologies, including online platforms and mobile devices. So while the social space of cinema can be relatively easily evoked in the gallery through timed screenings, raked seating or architectonic installation, the social space of television has arguably become more difficult to stage.

Yet even if television continues to resist representation within the gallery and museum, it continues to attract the attention of artists, curators and public programmers. In fact it would seem that the 2000s actually witnessed both an expansion and an intensification of interest in television. This 'televisual turn' finds its most vivid expression in the proliferation of thematic exhibitions exploring histories and memories of broadcasting (discussed in Chapter One) but it takes many forms, and this study draws attention to many other facets of the televisual in contemporary art practice. In particular, I focus on videos that mimic the form of the TV genres of soaps, sitcoms and serials; projects that deploy reality TV-style production and performance strategies; media works exploring the content or form of broadcast archives; public art projects that draw upon histories and memories of broadcasting; curatorial and institutional practices that borrow from TV genres such as talk shows; and video installations involving professional

Above: Stan Douglas, Installation view
of *Suspiria* at *documenta XI*, Kassel,
Germany in 2002.
Courtesy of the artist and David
Zwirner, New York/London.

television workers as participants and performers. None of these exhibitions and artworks can be readily defined as examples of television, since the vast majority were not devised for broadcast, yet all clearly articulate an engagement with the televisual.

I am especially interested in the definition of the televisual proposed by Lisa Parks, which designates the 'structures of the imaginary/and or epistemological' that have taken shape around television, and refers also to a range of properties often attributed to the medium in critical discourse, such as 'liveness, presence, flow, coverage, or remote control'.[24] Unlike Parks, however, my focus is primarily on those structures of the imaginary that take shape around the televisual within the culture and economy of contemporary art. One such imaginary structure is the notion that art and television somehow exist in an 'oppositional' relation. As both Lynn Spigel and John Wyver have noted in different contexts, histories of art and television have routinely highlighted critique and opposition in place of collaboration and exchange.[25] Wyver, for example, notes video art's early engagement with television, citing a succession of 'privileged moments' from the 1960s and 70s, beginning with the 1968 broadcast (on WDR in Cologne) of *Black Gate Cologne*, a live event staged by Otto Piene and Aldo Tambellini.[26] Noah Horowitz also emphasises the early significance of institutional supports for artists' engagement with video and television, emphasising that these were initially 'typically neither museum- nor gallery-led but undertaken by not-for-profit foundations, public subsidy, and television stations'.[27] Horowitz cites as his examples, the role of various broadcasters in the UK (the BBC, Scottish TV and later Channel 4) and a range of public television and network-affiliated ventures in the US including the artist-in-residence programme at WGBH and experimental television labs at KQED in San Francisco and WNET in New York, established in the late 1960s and early 1970s, long before the development of a market for video art.[28]

Despite these well-known instances of collaboration, however, the relationship between art and broadcasting has tended be framed by artists and critics in terms of opposition. Wyver finds evidence of a 'modernist approach'[29] to television in the discourses of artists and activists, sometimes premised on the assumption that artists possessed a more advanced understanding of the medium's formal characteristics and a more critical perspective on its social and political role than those working in TV. These assumptions could only be made by overlooking significant evidence of television's formal complexities and self-reflexivity, exemplified by figures such as Ernie Kovacs and early sitcoms such as *The Gracie Allen and George Burns Show* and *I Love Lucy* in the 1940s and 50s.[30] In recent years, the notion that artists understand television better than those working in the industry has become increasingly untenable. This might be partly due to changes in television production processes and personnel, since Caldwell notes that during the 1970s and 80s TV personnel became 'more stylistically *and* more theoretically inclined',[31] with the result that, by the early 1990s, primetime television typically involved premeditated (rather than rote) approaches to production. Perhaps as a consequence of these changes, which were articulated in the stylistic excesses theorised by Caldwell, the oppositional dynamic that once shaped the relationship between art and television has been superseded by a different imaginary structure. In this newer framework, (certain forms) of

Above: Stan Douglas, *Suspiria:
Camera 3,* 2002, C-Print mounted
on gatorboard 31 x 41 inches
(78.7 x 104.1 cm).
Courtesy of the artist and David
Zwirner, New York/London.

television production—associated with particular modes of consumption—are celebrated for their textual complexity, stylistic sophistication and reflexivity.

Another imaginary structure is also worth highlighting; the notion that there is an 'age of television', which may or may not have ended. For Milly Buonanno, the age of television (coinciding with the second half of the twentieth century) was marked by television's 'rapid ascent to a leading position in the sphere of information and popular entertainment'.[32] Significantly, she frames this ascent in terms of a series of transitions, which should be periodised differently within disparate cultural contexts. In order to chart these transitions, she draws upon a three-way periodisation offered by John Ellis, beginning with an era of 'scarcity' (limited channels and limited hours of transmission), lasting until the early 1980s in some contexts, followed by a period of 'growth' (wider choice of channels and increased competition for audience ratings) until the 1990s, a decade marked by 'abundance' (diversification of modes of accessing programmes on a variety of platforms and networks, segmentation of the viewing public).[33] Buonanno also adds an important caveat, however, noting that the age of televisual abundance is accompanied by a relative scarcity of content, requiring 'extensive recourse to archive material and old television programmes in order to feed [...] the voracious appetite of a distribution system that is expanding at an enormous rate', with the result that television becomes 'a living museum of itself'.[34]

Buonanno's comment introduces the possibility that the museum—even though it precedes television—has become part of the imaginary of the televisual. By framing television as a *living* museum, and so differentiating it from the mausoleum, Buonanno presumably wishes to avoid the implication that television's third age will be its last. Nonetheless, television's status as the dominant medium of contemporary culture is no longer secure. For example, in the revised version of his influential study *Liveness: Performance in a Mediatized Culture,* originally published in 1999, Philip Auslander highlights the growing dominance of digital media in reconfiguring paradigms of liveness, citing 'an ongoing, unresolved struggle for dominance among television, telecommunications and the internet'.[35] He concludes, however, that television continues to play an important role in shaping the production and reception of live performance, emphasising the extent to which television itself borrowed from theatre in its early years. To this end, he cites Lynn Spigel's observation that television was often promoted as a 'better approximation of live entertainment than any previous form of technological reproduction', because by broadcasting direct to the home it 'would allow people to feel as if they really were at the theatre'.[36] Auslander emphasises that the goal of televised drama was not simply to convey a sense of the theatrical event but rather to 'recreate the theatrical experience for the home viewer through televisual discourse and, thus, to *replace* live performance'.[37] But his account is not premised upon a celebration of the ontological differences between live and mediatised performance. Instead he proposes that liveness is a 'historically contingent concept continually in a state of redefinition',[38] which must be understood through reference to specific cultural contexts.

The televisual turn in contemporary art actually encompasses several collaborative projects engaging with the history of 'live television', including a multi-episode webcast series by London-based Auto Italia South East (discussed in Chapter Seven) and various projects realised by New York-based Scott Kiernan and Victoria Keddie, as E.S.P. TV. In some respects, especially significant in light of Buonanno's account of television as 'living museum', Kiernan and Keddie also engaged with television as a 'living museum', but in a different sense to that suggested by Buonanno's discussion of ever-expanding distribution. This is because E.S.P. TV consciously work with antiquated television production technology and favour distribution systems that are somewhat outmoded, such as local cable, while at the same time making full use of online and social media. Since 2011, Kiernan and Keddie have produced *E.S.P. TV*, a regular television show for Manhattan Neighborhood Network (MNN), public access cable television.[39]

Each episode of the *E.S.P. TV* cable show features a mix of experimental music, video art and performance and is recorded in front of an audience, in various venues,[40] with live green-screening and analogue video mixing. The recordings (taped to VHS) are then edited into half-hour episodes for subsequent cablecast to Manhattan-based viewers, and episodes are posted on the MNN website once they have aired. Keddie and Kiernan also occasionally organise social gatherings when an episode of the show airs on MNN. Significantly, these events can only be held in Manhattan venues with local cable access (not satellite) so they typically take place in various Italian bars and restaurants around New York's Canal St. Area, rather than in galleries. Given their fascination with outmoded television technology, Keddie and Kiernan might appear to reiterate the mythologies critiqued by Caldwell. I would argue, however, that their practice is not premised upon an ontological model of liveness. Instead, through their attenuation of processes of production and transmission, they actually draw attention to the cultural construction and the symbolic value, within an artworld context, of televisual liveness.

Memorialising Television or Legitimating Contemporary Art

Although television no longer seems to function primarily as a target of artistic critique, its precise significance for contemporary artists remains open to question. Reflecting upon developments in art practice during 2010, Mike Sperlinger identified television as a 'focus of serious artistic archaeology', citing various exhibitions and artworks engaging with its history as a cultural form.[41] Colin Perry (writing in early 2011) also acknowledged television's currency for artists, claiming that it has 'once more become a fashionable subject within artistic practice and discourse'.[42] He seems to suggest, however, that the recent televisual turn lacks a historical consciousness. In particular, he argues that activist traditions within British broadcasting have been excluded from 'communal memory and art history', attributing this exclusion to the fact that 'artists have stopped trying to change television'.[43] While I fully agree that artists are no longer primarily concerned with reforming television, I am less convinced that activist traditions have been wholly excluded from art history. Instead it seems to me that television's past as a site of social and political critique is actually of greater interest to artists, curators and art institutions than its future.

It is possible, in my view, to identify a specific moment at which television began to figure prominently as an object of memorialisation and historicisation in contemporary art. Here I am referring to the inclusion of two very different works in *documenta 11*, curated by Okwui Enwezor in 2002. These works are *Handsworth Songs* (1986) by Black Audio Film Collective and *Suspiria* by Stan Douglas (2002). *Handsworth Songs* is an experimental documentary essay on the subject of race and civil disorder in the UK, filmed in Handsworth (a predominantly working class urban area of Birmingham) and London in 1985. Incorporating newsreel and archival material,[44] it offers a counterpoint to mainstream media representations of civil unrest, and was made by Black Audio Film Collective, one of several production groups recognised by Channel 4 as part of its official remit as a public service broadcaster with a mandate to serve minority audiences.[45] By presenting this work in *documenta 11* sixteen years after it was first broadcast, Enwezor clearly identified it as an important point of reference—and a precedent—for later moving image artworks engaging with documentary traditions and issues of identity, race and migration. At the same time, the inclusion of *Handsworth Songs* highlighted the growing importance of the gallery, and attendant decline of public service broadcasting, as a supportive context for the production and distribution of critically engaged documentary practice.

If the inclusion of *Handsworth Songs* recalled an earlier era marked by formal innovation and social critique, then *Suspiria* posed questions about the ontology of television at the close of the analogue era. Responding to the context of Documenta and the history of Kassel (where the Brothers Grimm compiled their typology of fairy tales), Douglas's work takes its title from the 1977 horror film directed by Dario Argento, one of the last 35mm features to be shot in Technicolor. The central character in Argento's film is an American girl terrorized by European witches and the narrative dramatises a confrontation between 'New' and 'Old' worlds, partly through the use of colour, light and music. The theme of the supernatural was amplified in the *documenta 11* installation through the placement of cameras into a purpose-built eighteenth-century ruin (the Octagon, which forms part of the Hercules monument in Kassel), now home to a colony of bats, and through the manipulation of a technical property of the NTSC television system to produce spectral visual effects. As Douglas points out, NTSC was initially a black-and-white system:

> When color was introduced, the standard was not reconfigured but adapted [...] by using the black-and-white picture information (luminance) as a carrier signal over which the color information (chrominance) could be superimposed—the color television system in North America is, in effect, a system of ghosts.[46]

In Douglas's *Suspiria*, scenes drawn from the Grimms's *Fairy Tales* and pre-recorded in Vancouver were superimposed over live images from the cameras inside the Octagon, and the chrominance and luminance signals combined using a computerised video switching system so that the 'oversaturated faces and figures [...] bleed over into their setting', approximating the look of Argento's Technicolor film. Accompanied by a soundtrack that was mixed using the same switching system, the images were transmitted from the Octogon to the Museum Fridericianum by day and to the local television station Hessische Rundfunk at night,[47] generating infinite variations of the fairy stories.

The Hercules monument is clearly a fitting site for an exploration of myth and fairytale, but as a purpose-built ruin it might also be read as an appropriate metaphor for broadcasting, particularly given Max Dawson's observation that television has repeatedly been framed as an incomplete technology, always in need of improvement or repair.[48] My research suggests that Douglas is not the only artist to explore, through strategies of installation and technologies of transmission, a possible correspondence between a monumental architectural structure and the social, cultural or technological form of television. Instead, *Suspiria* (and the inclusion of *Handsworth Songs* in *documenta 11*) should be understood in relation to a broader process of memorialising television, which extends beyond, and yet is posited within, the domain of contemporary art practice. This process has been charted by Amy Holdsworth in a study of television as an object of memory and nostalgia, which includes analysis of cinema, TV programming, broadcasting museums and also installation works by artists such as Gillian Wearing.[49] Holdsworth's research contributes to, and is informed by, broader debates amongst television and media scholars concerning the future of television studies as a field, engaging with issues in preservation, as well as transformations in practices of production, distribution and reception.[50]

Although I draw upon Holdsworth's analysis, my study is more narrowly focused on television as an object of artistic memory (as well as critique and imagination) in contemporary art discourse. Consequently, I am specifically interested in the values that are attached—in art discourse—to television as a once-dominant cultural form, which occupies a contested position in relation to the public sphere. Perry suggests that while television may function as an object of 'voguish nostalgia' for artists and curators, its 'public role' remains largely unexamined.[51] But it remains unclear precisely how this public role might actually be defined or judged by artists or curators, since the relationship between broadcasting, civil society and the state varies hugely across cultural and historical contexts. Television exists in myriad forms and its commercial variant is routinely accused of contributing to the privatisation of culture. For example, art historian David Joselit has emphasised, in his analysis of the relationship between art, activist practice and television, that US network TV actually functions 'against democracy'.[52] The public role assigned to television in any given context is not solely a consequence of actually existing practices of production and reception—it is also partially linked to the ways in which television is *imagined* to function. It is interesting to note, for example, that unfamiliar public broadcasting contexts have served as objects of fascination (even envy) amongst artists and curators, who often imagined that 'foreign' institutions were more supportive of artistic practice than those closer to home.[53]

Even if television's status as a public form is highly contested, this does not preclude it from playing an important role in contemporary art discourse concerning public life. In fact, I argue that artists, curators and institutions continue to engage with television precisely for the purpose of articulating, and sometimes legitimating, contemporary art's *own* contested 'publicness'. This dynamic is especially apparent in artworks produced for the public realm (the focus of Chapter Five) and in curatorial projects and institutional initiatives that borrow from the television talk show (discussed in Chapter Six). In order to understand how TV might possibly play a role in legitimating the publicness of contemporary art, however, it is also necessary to first consider how television's *own* cultural status has altered since the early 2000s. This period has in fact witnessed significant changes, specifically of certain modes of TV consumption, as noted by Michael Z. Newman and Elana Levine. They argue that culturally elevated forms of television, most typically serialised drama, which are often viewed on DVD or as downloads, are routinely dissociated and distinguished from more traditional modes of television viewing.[54] Their analysis poses a number of important questions for any study of the relationship between television and contemporary art culture, in part because they frame the museum as a site for the cultural elevation of popular art forms. Newman and Levine do not, however, engage with the televisual turn in contemporary art and so they overlook the cross-institutional dimension of cultural legitimation.

Memorable Experiences and the Museum Economy

Rather than focusing exclusively on examples of artists' film and video that appropriate from television genres, this study encompasses a range of curatorial projects, performances and public programming initiatives encountered in museums and galleries, which draw upon television talk, current affairs and entertainment shows, and which sometimes emphasise the qualities of liveness and presence traditionally attributed to broadcasting. Although these TV-themed events draw attention to the mediatised quality of everyday life, highlighted by Auslander, they also cannot be understood without reference to the altered context of art institutional production and exhibition. Here I am referring to the fact that art museums (like the providers of goods and services in the retail industry) are increasingly expected to source and secure resources, whether in the form of corporate sponsorship, ticket sales or public subvention, through the creation of 'memorable'[55] visitor experiences.

Artists, curators and institutions have responded to this situation in many different ways. For example, Noah Horowitz charts the rise of 'experiential art'—encompassing performances and other events—across a range of contexts, from museums to art fairs.[56] Art institutions are also increasingly expected to use a range of social media to build and maintain relationships with disparate constituencies, likely to include art professionals, local residents and, in many instances, tourists, who may encounter programming at first hand or remotely. My research suggests that, even though its dominance as a cultural form is now in question, television continues to figure in the promotion and mediation of art institutions as social spaces, most notably through the presentation of performances, discussions and other events to gallery audiences, and in the simultaneous or subsequent webcasting of these presentations.

Art museums have also responded critically to the pressures and expectations generated by the experience economy, as evidenced by the four part exhibition and research project *Play Van Abbe*, realised at the Van Abbemuseum (in Eindhoven, the Netherlands) from November 2009 to August 2011. This project was structured around analysis of the history, role and activities of the museum, and it required multiple visits over a period of two years to be experienced in full.[57] I am especially interested in the fourth and final part, entitled 'The Tourist, the Pilgrim, the Flaneur (and the worker)', which deliberately employed the terminology associated with market research and audience development strategies.[58] Visitors were invited to encounter the exhibition as tourists, pilgrims, flaneurs, or workers— roles developed with the collaboration of an experience designer (a new strategy for the museum). Arriving at the museum, they were presented with a range of role-specific 'tools' and props such as tailored maps, adapted signage and audio guides. These props were also displayed at various points throughout the galleries, so that visitors could potentially shift between roles during their visit, and a number of 'Game Masters' were also available to engage with visitors, providing information on roles and eliciting feedback.[59]

Although *Play Van Abbe* did not specifically explore the relationship between television and contemporary art, it is worth noting that part four included two canonical examples of artists' television by Martha Rosler. The older work, *Semiotics of the Kitchen* (1975), appropriates and parodies the self-consciously pedagogical mode of presentation once common in TV cookery shows, engaging with television as a site of social instruction and tool of self-improvement and so resonating with the 'pilgrim' and 'worker' experiences of the museum. In contrast, *Martha Rosler Reads 'Vogue'* (1982)—devised as a live performance for the Paper Tiger public access cable TV show—articulates a shift toward a less formal and more intimate style of address, in which Rosler plays the role of reader rather than teacher. Although a hint of the pedagogical persists, this work engages the viewer as a consumer, in a manner that is more attuned to the pleasures offered by the role of tourist or flaneur. The exhibition also featured a much newer multi-part work, Oliver Ressler's *What is Democracy?* (2009), an eight-channel video installation consisting of interviews conducted with activists and political analysts, shown on multiple monitors with headphones. With a total running time of 118 minutes, this project has an instructional character, including numerous shots of 'talking heads'. But while Rosler's single-screen videos were modelled after TV shows (and in the case of *Martha Rosler Reads 'Vogue'*, actually devised for broadcast), *What is Democracy?* can be defined as a 'post-broadcast' work, designed to circulate online as well as within gallery contexts.[60] *Play Van Abbe* directly addressed altered expectations and perceptions of the art museum as a space for the production and consumption of memorable experiences, whilst also alluding to the changing form of the 'televisual' within art practice.

Timeframe, Method and Organisation

My study develops a cross-institutional approach to the televisual turn in contemporary art, addressing both important changes within the economy of contemporary art production and exhibition, and significant shifts in practices of television production, distribution and consumption, particularly since the early 2000s. This cross-institutional approach is informed by a range of theoretical positions and methodological frameworks associated with television studies, media theory, art history and (to a lesser extent) curatorial and performance studies. Although I find the work of Bourdieu[61] useful in understanding the production of value at the intersection of art and television economies, I do not employ a specifically sociological framework to analyse contemporary art culture. Instead my research is more directly indebted to theoretical and methodological approaches developed in relation to media production cultures. I am especially interested in the work of John Caldwell because of his attention to the processes and consequences of rapid technological, economic and cultural change in the media industries.[62]

More importantly, for the purposes of my research, Caldwell also highlights the interconnections between reflexive media forms and the cultural practices of production communities, emphasising that reflexivity cannot be explained either in terms of the self-critique that is historically associated with the avant-garde, or dismissed as a marketing technique. Instead, he develops an expansive definition of 'industrial reflexivity' to include 'forms of local cultural negotiation and expression' that are highly significant for 'lived production communities'.[63] While I draw upon many aspects of Caldwell's thinking, there are clearly important differences between the production cultures of art and television, not least the fact that the art 'industry' lacks both a history of unionised labour[64] and a symbolic centre of production to rival Hollywood. While New York and London remain important within the contemporary art economy as symbolic and actual centres of commerce and exchange (with concentrations of major galleries and dealers), there are many supposed 'centres' of artistic production, sometimes valued within art discourse precisely because they are symbolically *dislocated* from the arena of market exchange. It is worth noting that several of the artists referenced in this study, even those with a relatively modest income, cultivate networks of professional affiliation that are national, supranational and global. In order to secure employment (generally in art schools), gain access to grants, scholarships and lucrative public commissions, or take advantage of favourable tax conditions, they might maintain a social or production base in two or more countries. Artists must also manage a geographically dispersed array of professional and social relationships, seeking gallery representation both within and beyond their countries of residence, in order to access different sectors of the market.

These relationships are developed and maintained through regular interactions at events such as art fairs, including Art Basel, and recurrent survey exhibitions such as the Venice Biennale, the Whitney Biennial and Documenta. Not unlike film festivals, these events are often financed by a mix of (supranational, national and municipal) public subvention and corporate sponsorship, and in addition to fulfilling a promotional function they serve as a focal point for the commissioning and sale of artworks, sometimes realised through co-production arrangements. As such it is possible to draw broad parallels between the art context and the forms of public subvention, sponsorship and co-production arrangements common in (European) film and television industries. But although I acknowledge commonalities between art and television economies, my discussion is more specifically concerned with the role played by television and the televisual in the negotiation and articulation of change in contemporary art, with respect to modes of sociality, cultural status and prestige, structures of subvention, strategies of publicity and mediation, and conditions of labour and production.

Before turning to the organisation of the book, one final note about my theoretical framework is warranted. This study makes reference to the formation of public museums as cultural institutions, to the histories and models of public broadcasting, and to the practices of artists and curators working in the public realm. In addition, it engages with theorisations of the public sphere developed by Habermas, which have been extensively interrogated and contested within art and philosophical discourse.[65] It is not my intention, however, to argue for a restoration of the bourgeois public sphere or to endorse Habermas's analysis of the relationship between media and the formation of public culture. Instead, I am primarily interested in the role assigned to, and played by, television and the televisual in the ongoing production of contemporary art as an ostensibly *public* cultural form.

The book is organised into seven chapters and each approaches the concept of a 'TV museum' differently. At the outset, in Chapter One, I engage with the museum as a physical space in which practices of television production and reception can be evoked and materially staged. In Chapter Two I consider how television might function in the museum's operations as a technology of civic reform, education, and governmentality, a theme which I extend in Chapter Three through an analysis of the museum as a social space and site of self-display. Chapters Four and Five shift focus to consider how individual artworks might fulfil a museological function in relation to television, by registering changes in television memory or in the articulation of concepts of public space and culture. Chapter Six examines more direct convergences between art institutions and broadcasting, by focusing on museums and curators as TV producers and presenters. Finally, Chapter Seven considers how changing labour conditions for art and television workers find expression within and beyond the museum, in art reality TV shows and TV-themed artworks.

Each chapter draws together a number of theoretical perspectives, bringing them to bear upon the analysis of five or six artworks or exhibitions realised since 2000, with other relevant examples referenced briefly in the text, or cited in footnotes. In addition, I highlight a number of significant earlier intersections between television, art and curatorial practice, including canonical examples of artists' video and television, influential exhibitions and activist practices of media production since the late 1960s. Some of these historical references may already be familiar to readers with a knowledge of contemporary art, to whom this book is principally addressed, but they serve an important contextualising function in my discussion. In some instances, these earlier works point to enduring concerns in contemporary art, but more often they offer a counterpoint to the televisual currents unfolding in art and curatorial practice during the 2000s. Approximately half of the post-2000 artworks and exhibitions discussed in depth were viewed at first hand, sometimes in more than one context, while others were encountered in a more mediated form, via video documentation and installation images provided by artists, curators and gallerists. It is worth noting that some of the works discussed were designed from the outset to be viewed in multiple and highly mediated forms. This is most notable in the case of live performances filmed for webcasts or reconfigured as installations, and these alternate iterations are referenced where relevant. My discussion is also informed by email exchanges and personal conversations with numerous artists and curators, in addition to reviews, published interviews and other secondary materials.

The focus of Chapter One, 'Sets, Screens and Social Spaces: Exhibiting Television', emphasises television's role in the reconfiguration of spatio-temporal and social relations, as a consequence of its capacity, theorised by Samuel Weber, to bring the distant close and make the proximate appear distant.[66] Artists and curators have been drawn toward the exploration of television's material and social form for many decades, and these concerns are manifest in artworks, actions and exhibitions realised in a range of contexts, since the early 1960s, including private galleries and furniture stores. Some of these works critique the role played by broadcasting in promoting ideologies and practices of material consumption, but my discussion also highlights an alternate vision of television as a distributor of social ambience and atmosphere. Informed by these developments, I argue that artists and curators have often been highly attuned to television's mutability as a material and social form. In the second half of the chapter, I identify a significant shift in practices of exhibiting television, manifest in a new emphasis on memorialisation and 'retrospection', in public museums and galleries since the early 2000s.[67] But I argue that television's prominence as an object of material display in art exhibition spaces also speaks to institutional and cultural anxieties concerning newer modes of sociality associated with the internet. Perhaps to a greater extent than television, these modes resist and evade materialisation in the museum.

Chapter Two, 'Quality Television and Contemporary Art: Soaps, Sitcoms and Symbolic Value', seeks to counter the emphasis on opposition found in many accounts of the relationship between art and television, by examining notions of social distinction and prestige that connect television and the museum. Informed by histories of the museum and broadcasting, in Europe and the US, I highlight the various ways in which both institutions have sought to demonstrate and legitimate their status as 'public'. My discussion draws attention to—and is informed by— the work of several artists who have approached television as a cultural and social resource rather than as an object of reform. In particular, I consider a number of artists' sitcoms, soap operas and serial dramas produced since the mid-2000s, generally for exhibition within gallery contexts. My research suggests that references to television and the televisual continue to fulfil an important role within the cultural economy of contemporary art, in part because it has long functioned as a site for the negotiation and representation of class and cultural difference. Contesting the view that elevated cultural status is bestowed upon certain forms of television in museums, I emphasise both the growing importance of lifestyle-oriented media in the production of symbolic value within the art economy, and the continued significance of the critical interpretation and debate around it as value-generating practices.

Chapter Three, 'Reality TV, Delegated Performance and the Social Turn', explores differences and parallels between television and the museum as sites of non-professional performance, drawing upon histories of broadcasting, video activism and art. My discussion is informed by Claire Bishop's theorisation of the social turn in contemporary art, and also by her analysis of various artworks in which non-professional performers—who appear as themselves—serve as stand-ins for the social body.[68] While acknowledging what Bishop notes as the importance of changing labour practices in relation to the outsourcing or delegation of artistic performance, I argue that the visibility of non-professional performers in art practice should also be understood in relation to developments within the broader context of media production and consumption. In particular, I draw attention to an array of precedents in television genres ranging from civic educational programmes to commercial game shows and reality TV makeover genres. My research suggests that these forms of programming often fulfil implicit, or explicit, pedagogical and even governmental function, which is either reiterated or contested in an array of recent video installations that borrow from television, soliciting the participation of an array of non-professional performers.

Chapter Four, 'European Television Archives, Collective Memories and Contemporary Art', focuses on the work of several artists who have explored the relationship between television and memory, by engaging with the content and form of broadcast archives. The chapter examines various ways of theorising television memory, including approaches that highlight either the destructive and amnesia-inducing quality of the medium or the 'hyper-integrative' character of the media event. Informed by the work of Jerome Bourdon,[69] I argue for a model that can account both for everyday habits and routines that form part of the experience and memory of television, and also for television's altered relationship to other technologies of distribution and storage. The first part of the chapter focuses on a range of works since the 1970s that emphasise television's capacity to shape collective memory, both nationally and globally, often through reference to 'media events'. Many of these works are linked by the use of strategies of re-enactment, historical reconstruction or more self-conscious re-making, sometimes through reference to moments of significant social or political unrest. The second part of the chapter deals with more recent works, realised during the late 2000s, that explore absences, gaps or elisions in collective memory. It considers the re-enactment of broadcast events that failed to generate public discourse at an earlier moment, the archiving of broadcast content that has acquired a second life in social media, and the exploration of interconnections between familial, national and broadcast histories.

Chapter Five, 'Monuments to Broadcasting: Television and Art in the Public Realm', examines the changing significance of television for artists engaging with the public realm through the production of site-oriented works. Many artists were initially drawn toward television as a communications technology with the potential to function as a social connector, but by the mid-1980s the relationship between television and public space was often framed in terms of privatisation and spectacularisation. Since the early 2000s, however, television's 'potential' has acquired a new and different significance for artists, particularly for those working in the European context. Informed by critiques of public space offered by Anna McCarthy and Malcolm Miles,[70] I discuss six site-specific or site-responsive artworks that use histories, theories and technologies of broadcasting to explore the changing form of public space, posing questions about the current form and viability of the public sphere. These projects are notably diverse in form, encompassing sound works, participatory events, sculptural video installations, displays of banners, placards and other protest materials, temporary architectural constructions, and performative actions. I also identify the figure of the 'monument' as an important point of reference for understanding how these disparate works of public art might preserve histories and ideals of broadcasting.

Chapter Six, 'Talk Shows: Art Institutions and the Discourse of Publicness', examines a number of exhibitions, artworks and public programming initiatives realised since the early 2000s, which articulate a recurrent interest in the television talk show as a privileged mode of public discourse. Informed by theorisations of the public sphere and histories of institutional critique, I argue that the daytime talk show has served—and continues to function—as an important cultural reference for curators and artists seeking to chronicle or critique the fragmentation of the bourgeois public sphere. My discussion encompasses talk-show themed exhibitions at European institutions, performative artworks modelled on talk shows and a series of current affairs themed talks developed for the Hammer Museum in Los Angeles. I also consider various US and European examples of 'museum TV', ranging from the cable television shows produced by the Long Beach Museum of Art during the 1980s, to a number of European projects developed during the 2000s in response to the challenges and opportunities presented by niche-oriented commercial television and the internet.

Chapter Seven, 'Production on Display: Television, Labour, and Contemporary Art', focuses primarily on artworks that involve the participation of TV workers, as performers or collaborators. While the activist video makers of the late 1960s and early 1970s often developed 'heterarchical' production practices as a critique of the media industries, many of the artists who have been drawn toward television during the 2000s have developed a more nuanced exploration of television work, attuned to the parallels that might exist between economies of art and television production. The chapter also discusses the representation of artistic production in broadcast television, focusing on an array of art reality TV shows developed for US and UK contexts since the mid-2000s, many of which have been framed as quasi-educational, in part through the involvement of curators and critics as mentors and judges. Informed by cultural industries and production studies research,[71] I highlight interconnections as well as differences between art and television production cultures, including the significant changes which have occurred in professional hierarchies and the growing significance of immaterial and affective labour.

Through these explorations of the interconnections articulated in exhibition practices between contemporary art and the televisual, in the legitimation of specific modes of consumption and performance, as well as in the practices of artists engaging with archives and the public realm, and in curatorial practice and in depictions of labour, I argue that television continues to occupy a central place within contemporary art. In addition to functioning as a central object of critique, exploration and memorialisation in its own right, television also informs the processes through which perceptions of cultural status, models of public space and discourse, practices of cultural memory, and cultures of production are defined, negotiated and legitimated. Consequently, I hope that my examination will yield insights about the televisual that resonate both within the sphere of contemporary art discourse and within the broader context of media and cultural studies.

Chapter One

Sets, Screens and Social Spaces: Exhibiting Television

Above: James Coleman, *So Different …
and Yet*, 1978–80. Video installation.
Performed by Olwen Fouéré and Roger
Doyle. © James Coleman.

If the word 'television' in ordinary usage applies not just to the medium as a whole but, more precisely, to its materialization as the receiving *set*, this emphasizes just how determining the aspect of 'setting' and 'placing' is for a medium that deprives distance as well as proximity of their traditional stability and hence of their power to orient. What is distant is set right before us, close up; and yet what is thus brought close remains strangely *removed*, indeterminably *distant*. And what is traditionally proximate is set apart, set at a distance.

Samuel Weber, *Mass Mediauras: Form, Technics, Media*[1]

[Nam June] Paik's work joins the most ephemeral and the most 'tangible' aspects of television: on the one hand the realtime flow of signals and, on the other hand, the TV-set as a piece of furniture in the private home, the place where machine-time and life-time are integrated. Such concerns seemed to fade from view as video art asserted itself as a specifically artistic medium […] when these concerns re-emerged in the art of the 1990s, they re-emerged not within the framework of video art, but […] in terms of a new artistic interest in inhabited places and social spaces.

Ina Blom, *On the Style Site: Art, Sociality and Media Culture*[2]

Introduction: Exhibiting Television

In a widely-cited analysis, which engages with television as material object, medium and cultural technology, Samuel Weber identifies a complex dynamic of distance and proximity, noting that what is brought close through TV nonetheless remains removed and distant, while what is traditionally close acquires a quality of removal. Significantly, Weber is not solely concerned with practices of television production and reception; he also refers to the ways in which television is materialised, conceptualised and described in language. Even though he refers to 'ordinary' usage of the term *television*, his analysis highlights its slipperiness, tacitly acknowledging the ways in which television actually evades representation, despite (or perhaps because of) its apparent familiarity. Even though Weber does not specifically address the relationship between television and contemporary art, his text is important in illuminating the specific challenges involved in theorising the exhibition of television both within and beyond the museum. In part, this is because Weber's analysis has elicited a valuable critique in the form of Anna McCarthy's argument for a more site-oriented approach to television's material culture and place.

McCarthy situates Weber's analysis in relation to a broader preoccupation with television as a form of 'remote inscription that produces—and annihilates—places: the place of the body, the place of the screen, the place of dwelling'.[3] She acknowledges that 'like all technologies of "space-binding," television poses challenges to fixed conceptions of materiality and immateriality, farness and nearness, vision and touch'. This is because, as she points out, television 'is both a thing and a conduit for electronic signals, both a piece of furniture in a room and a window to an imaged elsewhere, both a commodity and a way of looking at commodities'.[4] Television is framed by McCarthy as analogous to the network. She notes that because of its 'scalar complexity' it can be considered at different scales, which include a close-up on the network's 'terminal point' of the television set, on specific viewing subjects or groups, or attention to what she terms 'centralizing transmissions'.[5] Focusing on one particular level, however, involves neglecting the others and the tensions between them, and it is precisely because of this complexity that, McCarthy argues, television has proved important in philosophical discourse, as an embodiment of the tension between the 'global' and the 'local'. At the same time, however, television's status as a material object is often overlooked, with the result that the television apparatus (as distinct from television's historical association with Fordist processes of standardisation)[6] is routinely conceptualised as an agent and emblem of placelessness, without sufficient attention to the ways in which television is encountered within the multiple spaces of everyday life, such as airports, restaurants, supermarkets and shopping malls.[7] Consequently, McCarthy argues for an examination of television's role in organising 'particular relations of public and private, subjects and others' that characterise everyday places.[8] Informed by McCarthy's approach, this chapter focuses on art galleries, museums and other spaces of exhibition, as specific contexts and places in which television is encountered, and in which its complex materiality, and simultaneous status as thing, conduit for signals, furniture, window, commodity and way of looking at commodities, can become especially pronounced. I also consider how television's mutability, with respect to materiality, cultural status and modes of sociality, has been registered and articulated within art installations and exhibitions, through practices of curation, installation, display and design.[9]

There are many difficulties involved in analysing the particular relations produced by the exhibition of television, not least those involved in actually defining 'television' as an exhibited object. According to Weber, the term *television* is commonly used to signify both the medium and its materialisation in the form of the 'receiving set', and its receptive function is integral to his account of the proximate and distant. Receiving sets have certainly been important in the exhibition of television, perhaps most notably in the case of Nam June Paik's *Exposition of Music—Electronic Television* at Galerie Parnass in Wuppertal, which featured numerous modified TV receivers, tuned to what was then Germany's only television station.[10] The opening hours of the gallery, located in a villa that was also the private home of gallerist Rolf Jährling, had to be altered for the duration of Paik's exhibition, because TV services were then only available in the evening. According to Weber's definition, there are certainly a great many instances in which video monitors are enabled to receive electronic signals—most obviously in works involving closed circuit television. But, despite the importance of Paik's show, it is relatively unusual to encounter functioning television receivers in gallery or museum spaces. In fact 'television' is more likely to be signified by the staging (through arrangements of lighting, furniture and hardware) of viewing environments, often with domestic associations. Significantly, the quasi-domestic setting of Galerie Parnass enabled the modified television sets to be encountered simultaneously as furniture, things and conduits.

The museum and gallery spaces in which television is exhibited also need to be differentiated from the 'everyday places' highlighted in McCarthy's account. In fact, for some theorists, museums are important precisely because of their difference from sites of material display considered more mundane. Andreas Huyssen, for example, values the museum as a space in which to encounter 'objects that have lasted through the ages', differentiating these objects from 'commodities destined for the garbage heap'.[11] In Huyssen's model, the function of the museum is to counter, rather than simply compensate for, the dissolution of material experience attributed to television; to 'expand the ever shrinking space of the (real) present in a culture of amnesia, planned obsolescence and ever more synchronic and timeless information flows'.[12] Huyssen does not consider how exhibitions of artworks engaging with the materiality of television might offer a means of engaging critically with the economic logic of planned obsolescence, or indeed the role played by the museum in this economy.

This brings me to the next challenge involved in theorising the exhibition of television— the fact that its material form is subject to change over time. Here I am referring not just to the displacement of the console as 'receiving set' by newer devices, but also to the fact that displays of television monitors have sometimes featured within, for example, the design of television studios, particularly newsrooms. There are also many other situations, sometimes framed as 'special events', where the technology of broadcasting is placed on display, such as (for example) satellite broadcasting events, in which control rooms, technicians or other elements of the technological apparatus of television are made visible to audiences.[13] These changes are registered, albeit somewhat obliquely, in Weber's account of television. Informed by Walter Benjamin's analysis of the baroque theatre as an allegorical 'court', in which things are brought together only to be dispersed, Weber proposes a parallel between the disordered scenery of baroque allegory and the forms of disorder that characterise television, emphasising that even though television 'tends to unsettle', through its operations of displacement and setting apart, it also 'presents itself as the antidote to the disorder to which it contributes'.[14] To illustrate this point, Weber alludes to the 'infinitely repeated sets of television monitors' favoured in the studio backdrops of global television news networks such as CNN, which, he argues, imply that an integrated whole might somehow emerge out of indefinite repetition.[15] It is possible, however, that television's self-exhibition as 'antidote to disorder' might actually be a stylistic response to the institutional disorder of US broadcasting. Here I am referring to John Caldwell's analysis of stylistic excess in US television during the 1980s, which was partly shaped by the proliferation of new networks, including CNN.[16]

Above: The installation of *The Amarillo News Tapes*, 1980) by Doug Hall, Jody Proctor and Chip Lord, *Broadcast Yourself*, Hatton Gallery, 2008. Photograph by Kevin Gibson, Hatton Gallery, Newcastle for AV Festival 08.

Above: The living room installation
featuring single channel video 'TV spots'
by artists including Ian Breakwell, Chris
Burden and Wendy Kirkup and Pat Naldi
(at the opening), *Broadcast Yourself*,
Hatton Gallery, 2008. Photograph by Kevin
Gibson, Hatton Gallery, Newcastle for AV
Festival 08.

In this chapter, I focus on specific encounters with television as a material object within artworks and exhibitions. But rather than treating galleries and museums as 'everyday' contexts, I consider how the exhibition of television actually articulates a shifting, and sometimes fraught, relationship between the museum and the realm of the everyday. I argue that practices of exhibiting 'television' communicate changes in the form and function of museums, which have historically functioned as social spaces organised around material display. As Tony Bennett has demonstrated, museums developed historically and continue to operate in many instances: as important settings for the ordering of social relations, through processes of classification and categorisation and the integration of objects into narratives of progress and development.[17] These mechanisms are certainly very different from television's own production of order through disorder, as theorised by Weber. Nonetheless, my research suggests that artists and curators have sometimes used their engagement with television to assert the traditional role of the museum or gallery, as institutions of civic education and reform. Through its operations of critique and classification, the museum offers a potential antidote to the framing of television within art discourse as a technology of consumption implicated in the production of cultural or social disorder. Most of the examples that I discuss, however, do not conform to this model. Instead the exhibitions and artworks highlighted in this chapter tend to articulate a reflexive engagement with the historical context of the museum.

Rather than offering a comprehensive survey I identify some significant moments in the exhibition of television, as material object and medium, since the 1960s, focusing particularly on projects that demonstrate the continued significance of Nam June Paik's thinking in relation to sociality, as theorised by Ina Blom. I am also interested in artworks and exhibitions that engage with television as a mutable cultural form, through the reconfiguration of installations over time or through the development of retrospective modes of exhibition-making. Much of this chapter is concerned with theorising this retrospective turn, which emerged toward the end of the 1990s, but which has become particularly pronounced since the early 2000s.[18] My discussion focuses on four exhibitions; *Broadcast Yourself*, curated by Sarah Cook and Kathy Rae Huffman at the Hatton Gallery, Newcastle and Cornerhouse, Manchester (2008), *Changing Channels: Art and Television 1963–1987*, curated by Matthias Michalka at Museum Moderner Kunst (MUMOK) Vienna (2010), *Are You Ready for TV?*, curated by Chus Martinez at Museum d'Art Contemporani de Barcelona (MACBA), Barcelona (2010–2011), and *Remote Control*,[19] curated by Matt Williams at the Institute of Contemporary Arts (ICA), London (2012).

These are just a small selection of the many TV-themed exhibitions realised since 2000 that might be discussed here.[20] Several exhibitions engaging with the contemporary and historical context of artists' television also took place within the US, such as *Broadcast*, co-organized by the Contemporary Museum, Baltimore and Independent Curators International (touring to several venues from 2007–2010) and *Television Delivers People*, curated by Gary Carrion-Murayari at the Whitney Museum, December 12, 2007 – February 17, 2008.[21] The late 2000s also witnessed major touring retrospectives focusing on the work of artists known specifically for their engagement with television during the 1960s, 70s and 80s, including Nam June Paik, Dan Graham, Dara Birnbaum and General Idea.[22] My discussion of the 'retrospective mode' of exhibition-making focuses primarily on shows produced within European public institutions, but my examples are deliberately varied in terms of scale, scope and available resources, ranging from expansive surveys in art museums with important collections, to smaller projects realised by independent curators, and themed shows presented by arts centres without collections.

Homes, Galleries and Social Spaces

According to Ina Blom, Nam June Paik was 'the first to state and exploit artistically the fact that television is, first of all, a controller and producer of time itself', in terms of both free time and machine time, and she emphasises that his work 'explicitly evokes the ecstatic quality of TV as a way of bringing out the dynamics of an affect-based machinery that reorganizes social space'.[23] So while Paik was interested in the material properties of television, he did not envisage the television set as an exclusive 'receiver' of broadcast transmissions to be countered or critiqued. Instead, Blom suggests that Paik saw television as technology with the potential to enable social interaction through affect, and was specifically interested in it as a screen that could function as a light source and distributor of ambience and atmosphere.[24] Paik was not the only artist, however, to place television on display in Germany during 1963. A different perspective on television as material and cultural object was articulated in Konrad Lueg and Gerhard Richter's action *Leben mit Pop—eine Demonstration für den kapitalistischen Realismus* (*Living with Pop—A Demonstration for Capitalist Realism*). Also involving a 'receiving set', this work was presented not at a gallery, but rather in a furniture store (the Berges Möbelhaus in Düsseldorf), where the two artists placed themselves on view, posed among an array of consumer objects that included a television. Writing about the 'politics of memory' in relation to this work, Andrew Weiner notes that the event was timed to coincide with the broadcast of a German television programme historicising the achievements of Konrad Adenaeur, who had recently announced his resignation as Chancellor.[25] Thus, the project drew attention both to the materiality of the TV set as consumer object and to the role played by television in the promotion of Germany's postwar 'economic miracle' or *Wirtschaftswunder*.

If Paik's *Exposition* approached the television receiver as a distributor of ambience, then Lueg and Richter's *Living with Pop* much more clearly emphasised the normative function of broadcasting, through their critique of its role in the production of narratives of national progress. By the late 1970s, however, a different vision of televisual materiality and sociality, which seems more indebted to Paik's exploration of affect, had begun to emerge in the work of artists such as John Chamberlain and Dan Graham. In an essay, originally published in 1986, which explores the multiple intersections between art and design apparent in an array of gallery, showroom and office environments, Dan Graham discusses

SECRET HORROR, 1980
MIKE'S HOUSE, 1982
MICHAEL SMITH

Above: Installation view with works
by Michael Smith, *Changing Channels:
Art and Television 1963–1987*, mumok:
Museum Moderner Kunst, Vienna,
2010. Photo©mumok/Deinhardstein
Courtesy: Michael Smith and Ellen de
Bruijne Projects Amsterdam.

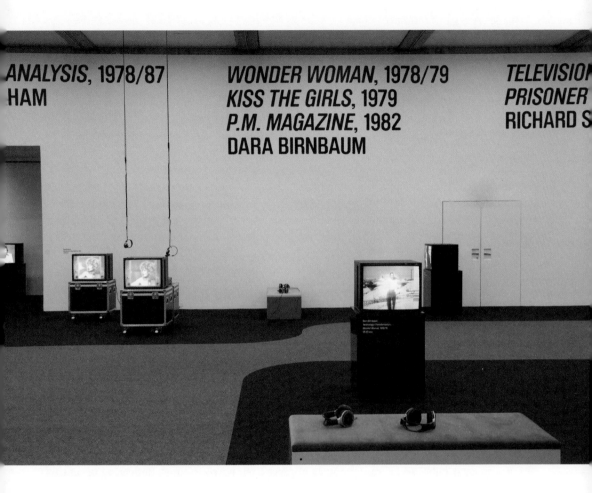

Above: Installation view with works
by Dara Birnbaum, *Changing Channels:
Art and Television 1963–1987*, mumok:
Museum Moderner Kunst, Vienna,
2010. Photo©mumok/Deinhardstein
Courtesy: Dara Birnbaum and Barbara
Gladstone Gallery.

several foam furnishing works by Chamberlain, which serve as functional seating and as a quasi-immersive environments by virtue of their tactile properties. One of these works (the title of which is not specified) was devised as an installation for the lobby of the *Westkunst* exhibition organised by Kasper König at Cologne in 1981. Described by Graham as a 'room-filling, raw foam-rubber couch with television monitors at either end',[26] Chamberlain's *Westkunst* installation was intended to resemble the pay TV-sets then found in the waiting areas of US bus terminals and airports. These monitors played TV commercials, initially suggesting a celebration of consumerism. But on closer inspection they were revealed as a succession of flawed outtakes or 'bloopers', that according to Graham 'revealed, unconsciously, the ideological conventions that determine the advertising industry's artificially constructed version of the American consumer's "dream"'.[27] Chamberlain's *Westkunst* work is significant, in my view, because it signals a move away from the normative model of television as a consumer object situated domestically and marks the emergence of a more expansive vision of televisual materiality and sociality within contemporary art discourse. In particular, *Westkunst* seems to anticipate Anna McCarthy's theorisation of 'ambient television', which highlights its presence within the 'everyday realm' of an array of non-domestic environments, ranging from city streets, to supermarkets, airports and train stations.[28] In Chamberlain's work, television is no longer understood primarily as a conduit between the home and the world outside; instead the televisual forms an integral part of social space.

Graham's own practice during the 1980s also articulated a fascination with changing modes of televisual sociality, responding to the new modes of moving image consumption enabled by home video, as evidenced by *Three Linked Cubes/Interior Design for Space Showing Video* (1986). This structure, with its reflective glass walls, comprises three semi-enclosed spaces, with cushions on the floor as seating and it is designed to be placed in a bright rather than darkened environment, enabling viewers to watch videos, displayed on a small monitor in each 'cube', and simultaneously observe their surroundings. Reflecting upon this work in one of a series of conversations with Benjamin Buchloh (from 1999–2000), Graham frames it as response to the museum as a social space:

> I realized that a museum could be a social space and I fell in love with the empty lobbies, the gift shop, coffee shop, areas where people could relax. So I did work like *Three Linked Cubes/Interior Design for Space Showing Videos* [...] where teenagers could lie on the floor. I think what I did was to discover the tradition of the museum instead of pursuing the stupid idea of Institutional Critique.[29]

Three Linked Cubes does not constitute a display of 'television' in the sense defined by Weber since, like Chamberlain's work, it does not involve a receiving set. But by highlighting video viewing as a social practice and everyday mode of relaxation, Graham was responding to changes in the everyday function of the domestic TV set, which by the 1980s would have been used to view video tapes as well as receive cable or broadcast transmissions.

Above: Installation view, Are
You Ready for TV?, Museu d'Art
Contemporani de Barcelona,
2010–2011.
Photograph: Juan Andrés
Pegoraro.

Above: Installation view of TV studio
environment, *Are You Ready for TV?*,
Museu d'Art Contemporani de Barcelona,
2010–2011.
Photograph: Gunnar Knechtel.

Above: Douglas Davis, *Ménage à Trois*,
1986; installation view, *Are You Ready for
TV?*, Museu d'Art Contemporani
de Barcelona, 2010–2011.
Photograph: Gunnar Knechtel.

Graham's work is also important because it anticipates changes in the social, institutional and physical architecture of the art museum as a site of leisure. According to Blom, during the 1990s, art museums were being transformed into 'facsimiles of ordinary spaces of existence', the inhabitants of which were invited to simply 'be' rather than to 'see'.[30] These changes found expression in the practices of artists such as Dominique Gonzalez-Foerster and Jorge Pardo, whose works unsettled the distinction between exhibition design, architecture and installation, sometimes by devising spaces, environments or structures for viewing or living.[31] Blom reads these developments as evidence of a 'new continuity between home TV and museum video', which involved the enfolding of 'artistic creativity and private life-styling',[32] and she finds evidence of this shift in exhibitions such as *Rooms with a View: Environments for Video*, at Guggenheim Museum Soho in 1997. Curated by John G. Hanhardt and Nancy Spector, this exhibition featured approximately 30 single-channel videos, spanning three decades, by artists such as Bruce Nauman, William Wegman and Pipilotti Rist. The videos were displayed in Graham's *Three Linked Cubes* and in three other viewing environments, designed by Angela Bulloch, Vito Acconci and also (collaboratively) by Jorge Pardo and Tobias Rehberger.

While Blom embraces the fact that, in these viewing spaces, 'the specific video art content was somehow relegated to the status of atmospheric surround'[33] others were more sceptical. *New York Times* reviewer Roberta Smith even implied that the 'content' might be literally damaged by this mode of display, noting that viewers could climb and sit on 'Vito Acconci's jungle gym' (a structure incorporating 12 monitors) 'to the extreme detriment of the tapes being screened'.[34] Rather than embracing the atmospheric surround, exemplified (for Blom) by Paik's work, Smith laments the loss of a clear figure-ground distinction:

Unfortunately, it is nearly impossible to focus on any single video under these conditions, which resemble a somewhat lax and disorganized video sculpture by Nam June Paik. The individual tapes are lost within a whole that is more about entertainment than art, in a gallery that becomes an image-zapped lobby through which visitors pass on their way to quieter surroundings.[35]

The only viewing environment to actually meet with Smith's full approval was Graham's *Three Linked Cubes,* perhaps partly because it pre-existed the exhibition and so constituted a recognisable work in its own right. In this 'room with a view', which situated monitors within a structure of clear and mirrored glass walls, Smith found what appeared to be a familiar critique of television. She noted that the walls of Graham's structure multiplied the 'images of monitors and viewers alike while creating a slight suggestion of surveillance; both effects emphasize the omnipotence—or as the Situationists put it, the spectacle—of television'.[36] So instead of responding to this work as an exploration of leisure and relaxation, or specific changes in modes of video and television consumption, Smith reasserted a very familiar model of the museum as a space in which an ostensibly dominant cultural form (television) could be presented for analysis and critique.[37]

By the late 1990s, however, television's cultural dominance was also being called into question within the gallery, in exhibitions such as *Home Screen Home* at Witte De With, Rotterdam in 1998. This show was guest curated by Michael Shamberg, a filmmaker known for his involvement in video activism during the 1970s. As a journalist for *Time* magazine, Shamberg had reviewed the seminal 1969 exhibition *TV as a Creative Medium*, presented at the Howard Wise Gallery in New York, and was prompted to join forces with two of the exhibiting artists, Frank Gillette and Ira Schneider, after seeing their video installation *Wipe Cycle* (1969).[38] Shamberg became a member of Raindance Corporation, along with Gillette and Schneider, and published the activist manifesto *Guerrilla Television* as a special issue of the journal *Radical Software*, before founding the collective Top Value Television or TVTV.[39] In early 1980s, Shamberg again reinvented himself, this time as a Hollywood producer and director of such films as *The Big Chill* (1983). But he continued to maintain a connection with video art and, just two years before he curated *Home Screen Home*, he actually worked with Dan Graham on the installation *New Design for Showing Video* (1996).

Timed to coincide with the 27th International Film Festival Rotterdam, *Home Screen Home* encompassed a broad range of video works, including activist material from the sixties and seventies, music videos and commercials, by artists and filmmakers such as Joan Jonas, Chris Marker, Antoni Muntadas, Mark Romanek and Martha Rosler. The works were presented in an environment that was designed to reference the exhibition's focus on domestic space as a site for the consumption of video as well as television. Significantly, it also included a number of participants, such as Kathryn Bigelow and Atom Egoyan, much more closely associated with feature filmmaking. The exhibition should be read as a response to changes within the sphere of moving image production and distribution. Shamberg's press release emphasises the 'challenge the Net poses to the conventional exhibition system',[40] thus alluding both to the possible impact of the internet on the contemporary art economy and the implications of online distribution structures (then largely undeveloped) for theatrical film exhibition. The histories of artists' television and video activism therefore, formed just one element in *Home Screen Home* of a much broader exploration of economic, technological and social change.

So far, I have traced changes in the exhibition of television within contemporary art contexts through an analysis of diverse examples of art practice and exhibition-making. These changes are, however, also articulated in the form of a specific installation work that has

Next page: General Idea, *Pilot* (1977); installation view, *Are You Ready for TV?*, Museu d'Art Contemporani de Barcelona, 2010–2011. Photograph: Gunnar Knechtel.

been reconfigured many times since it was first shown. James Coleman's *So Different ... and Yet* (1978–1980), is a single channel video with a running time of approximately one hour. It is centrally concerned with the televisual dynamics theorised by Weber of 'setting in place' and ordering through disorder. Staged and shot in a single take, with minimal in-camera editing, this work resembles an extremely static, dialogue-heavy television play. At the same time, it utilises visual effects that would be out of place in a realist drama. It features two performers (Olwen Fouéré and Roger Doyle) who occupy a setting that, although vaguely domestic, is rendered ambiguous through the use of visual effects to amplify certain colours (blue, red and green), so that the two figures appear dislocated from their environment.[41] Fouéré, seated in the foreground, continually rearranges herself on a couch, pointedly recalling Manet's *Olympia*, while in the background, her companion picks out a series of melodies on a grand piano. Her behaviour suggests that she may be watching television, while remaining conscious of her own image, perhaps as though it is being reflected on a screen. She frequently refers in her dialogue to events that seem to be occurring elsewhere (or have occurred in the past) but the focus of her attention remains elusive. Her status as a coherent subject is also open to question because, as Benjamin Buchloh notes, both she and the male protagonist seem to 'assume the roles of a number of increasingly intertwined and disparate characters within a trivial melodrama'.[42]

Describing the installation of *So Different ... and Yet,* Buchloh refers to a 'singular color monitor [...] displayed in a large white architectural frame, generating a sense of unusual sculptural formality'.[43] But, as Jean Fisher notes, this arrangement is subject to continual alteration. In a contribution to the catalogue accompanying Coleman's 2009 exhibition at the Irish Museum of Modern Art (IMMA)[44], Fisher observes that *So Different ... and Yet* was previously displayed on a monitor in a room fitted with green lighting and a viewing couch (in its second exhibition of 1980), installed in 'an Irish castle renowned for staging medieval banquets'[45] in 1985, shown at the Whitechapel (in 2006) in a set co-designed by Liam Gillick, and subsequently presented as a 'lecture performance' in the exhibition *Un teatre sense teatre* at MACBA (in 2007–2008).[46] Claiming that, 'we, the viewers, are physically included in the set as a "mirror" of the projected image',[47] Fisher reads the continual transformation of *So Different ... and Yet* as an extension of Coleman's critique of the mechanism of scopic desire and, crucially, as a critical engagement with 'increasingly disciplinary technocratic regimes'.[48]

Fisher's analysis suggests that the successive reconfigurations of the apparatus of display signified by the 'set' should be read partly as a commentary on the mutability of the televisual. But in later configurations of this work, the social and physical architecture of the museum becomes increasingly integrated into the 'set' as 'mirror of the projected image'. This quality of integration was particularly evident when *So Different ... and Yet* was shown in 2009, on an outdoor screen temporarily installed at the Irish Museum of Modern Art. The museum's primary location is in the Royal Hospital Kilmainham, a structure built in 1684 as a residence for retired solders, and is loosely modelled after Les Invalides in Paris. At IMMA, Coleman's work was displayed on a huge LED screen in the museum's courtyard, similar in scale and technology to those found at sporting events, concerts or used in outdoor advertising.

The sound was relayed via speakers placed around the courtyard, as well as in the reception area, so the work could be viewed and heard from a variety of vantage points. Viewers could move around the courtyard, approaching the screen to inspect the vast grid of tiny blue, red and green bulbs making up its surface. By entering the courtyard, however, viewers also positioned themselves within an architectural environment organised around the display of power, emphasising the extent to which the public art museum inherits the disciplinary function of older social institutions—quite literally in the case of IMMA. Unlike Blom, and Dan Graham, Coleman does not seem to engage with the museum as a site of relaxation. Instead the installation of *So Different … and Yet* appeared to signal a reassertion of the museum's traditional role in ordering social and material relations. By placing the LED screen on display within the courtyard of the seventeenth-century building, Coleman did not seek to stage the museum as an extension of televisual social space. Instead, the televisual was framed within the architecture of the museum, becoming an object of display.

Television and the Retrospective Mode of Exhibition

Even though television has tended to resist definition and representation in the museum, its status as a dominant cultural form was relatively secure from the 1960s until the 1990s. Since then, however, this status has become increasingly open to question. Responding to this shift, several curators have developed what I term a 'retrospective' approach, employing chronological models of categorisation (sometimes in conjunction with thematic frameworks) to highlight continuities and changes in the relationship between art and television over time. In this section, I compare several examples of the retrospective mode of exhibition-making and consider why the once-dominant cultural form of television might continue to serve as a focus for curatorial and institutional attention. My first example, *Broadcast Yourself*, was co-curated by Sarah Cook and Kathy Rae Huffman, and first presented at the Hatton Gallery in Newcastle, within the context of the 2008 AV Festival,[49] which explores intersections between art, society and technology. The 2008 edition of the festival engaged directly with the spread of Web 2.0 technologies, including social media that enable a form of 'self-broadcasting', and the attendant reconceptualisation of televisual transmission and reception. In keeping with this focus, *Broadcast Yourself* highlighted continuities and differences between social media practices (such as video sharing via YouTube) and artists' use of both broadcasting and various forms of narrowcasting. These issues were explored through the inclusion of canonical works devised for broadcast, including Chris Burden's *TV Commercials* (1973–1977), which features the artist as performer, and Bill Viola's *Reverse Television* (1983/84), which depicts individual TV viewers apparently 'looking back' at television. It also featured newly commissioned works, such as *The Fantasy A-List Generator* (2008) by Active Ingredient (Rachel Jacobs/ Matt Watkins), which consisted of a video booth in which members of the public took on the personality of a celebrity and were interviewed in this role in a live webcast.

In addition to emphasising the continued relevance of older works devised for broadcast or gallery exhibition, Cook and Huffman highlighted commonalities between public art projects produced within disparate cultural contexts. The exhibition included documentation of Kit Galloway and Sherrie Rabinowitz's *Hole in Space* (1980), which created a live video and audio link between passers-by on streets in NY and LA, using satellite television. This work was clearly framed as an important precedent for Shaina Anand's *KhirkeeYaan* (2006), an open-circuit TV system developed in the KhirkeeYann Extension neighbourhood of New Delhi, which used television sets, surveillance security equipment, installed in locations up to 200 metres apart, to enable local network communication and 'conversation'. Both projects were very much in tune with the core focus of *Broadcast Yourself* on artists who 'have challenged the passive relationship viewers have with television by taking control of TV and the way it is both produced and consumed'.[50]

The development of *Broadcast Yourself* was informed both by Cook's research into new media curating and by Huffman's extensive experience of commissioning and exhibiting artists' television, at institutions such as Long Beach Museum of Art. Significantly, in addition to highlighting art historical precedents for 'self-broadcasting', Cook and Huffman also reflected upon the ways in which television has been exhibited, through the re-presentation of earlier curatorial projects involving online media, such as *TV Swansong*. Curated by UK-based artists Nina Pope and Karen Guthrie in 2002, *TV Swansong* consisted entirely of newly commissioned works devised to be experienced as a live webcast on a specific date.[51] By focusing on liveness, the project both proposed a particular understanding of television—aligned with the shared experience of time and space—and suggested that the web might take the place of 'TV' in offering this experience. Reviewing *TV Swansong* for *Frieze* magazine, Dan Fox interpreted the title as a reference to 'television's last gasp, a final act set in the digital heartland of its nemesis, the Internet',[52] before going on to list numerous technical hiccups, suggesting that *TV Swansong*'s embrace of the internet might have been somewhat premature. Cook and Huffman also presented material relating to another curated online project, *56k Bastard Channel TV*, established in 2004 by Reinhard Storz within the context of the Viper Media Festival, Basel Kunsthalle.

Through its inclusion of these earlier curatorial projects, *Broadcast Yourself* both emphasised the growing importance of the web, as a site of artistic production and exhibition, whilst underscoring the continued significance of the gallery as a site for the ordering of relations between art and television. Cook and Huffman also used strategies of installation and design to explore the social and material architecture of the TV studio, through its presentation of *The Amarillo News Tapes* (1980) by Doug Hall, Chip Lord and Jody Procter, produced on a residency undertaken by the artists and organised by Hall at KVII-TV (Channel 7) in Amarillo, Texas in 1979. The three artists worked in collaboration with local news reporters and anchorman Dan Garcia to explore forms of news gathering and presentation practices, with a particular emphasis on theatrical style and ritual. In addition to displaying the video documentation, Cook and Huffman worked with the AV Festival and Cornerhouse to produce a full-size replica of the KVII-TV news desk, spotlit

Above: Installation view of
Remote Control, 2012, Institute of
Contemporary Arts, London, UK.
Photography Mark Blower.

and raised above floor level on a low, carpeted dais. This replica underscored the theatrical quality of the news production and presentation environment, while at the same time clearly differentiating the gallery from the web as an exhibition space.

Broadcast Yourself also incorporated a video display environment, described in documentation as the 'living room installation', featuring a patterned rug, curtains, electrical fire, potted plant, coffee table, couch and CRT television. This space was used to display several single channel works, including Burden's *TV Commercials*, and suggested an attempt to replicate a 'typical' viewing environment from the 1970s. Unlike the reconstruction of the Amarillo news studio, the living room installation vaguely recalled the strategies of display sometimes used in museums of broadcasting[53] to explore television's material culture. Fittingly, the 'living room' served as the viewing environment for a series of videos that included Michael Smith's *It Starts at Home* (1982), made in collaboration with Mark Fischer. In this work, Smith plays 'Mike', a hapless individual who subscribes to cable, and becomes a TV star when his receiver is accidentally transformed into a camera, transmitter and monitor. Even though he fails to recognise that he is 'on TV', Mike's show attracts the attention of numerous viewers, including a mysterious figure called 'Bob' (played by a toupee) who is revealed as a powerful TV producer. As his fame increases, however, Mike is visibly disempowered, and both he and his home are subjected to a series of makeovers initiated by Bob, who dispatches new furniture for the 'set'. While *It Starts at Home* is clearly integral to Cook and Huffman's exploration of continuities between artists' television and social media, it also reiterates the emphasis on materialities of TV production and reception apparent throughout the exhibition.

My next two examples—*Changing Channels: Art and Television 1963–1987* (curated by Matthias Michalka at MUMOK) in 2010 and *Are You Ready for TV?* (curated by Chus Martinez at MACBA) in 2010–2011—are relatively similar in terms of scale and organisational resources, but deploy diverse strategies of exhibition display and design. At MUMOK, Michalka's approach was informed by a long-standing curatorial engagement with the moving image, articulated in earlier exhibitions such as *X Screen* (December 2003—February 2004). Like *Broadcast Yourself*, *Changing Channels* was framed partly as a response to the relativisation of television by newer media but, instead of alluding generally to changes in forms and modes of reception, Michalka specifically drew attention to the reconceptualisation of 'public' and 'private' realms:

> [W]hat was formerly private and public in the domain of television is being completely reassessed via YouTube, live stream and video on demand, and by television on laptop computers and cell phones. This therefore is a good time to [...] take a closer look at the artistic confrontation with television and the aim of renegotiating and transforming the relationship between art and the public.[54]

Taking its title from an issue of *Radical Software* magazine, *Changing Channels* framed the period from the 1960s to the late 80s as the heyday of artists' television, the exhibition focused on the work of artists such as Dan Graham and Dara Birnbaum, Valie EXPORT, David Lamelas, Nam June Paik, Stan Vanderbeek, Wolf Vostell, Andy Warhol and Peter Weibel. Commenting upon the selection criteria,[55] Michalka emphasised the importance of presenting works together that were made both inside and outside museum contexts.

In this respect, the project engaged with television as a site of production and exhibition, which might potentially function as an alternative to the art museum. The exhibition included extensive documentation of Gerry Schum's TV Gallery, in the form of a dedicated study centre, and a comprehensive selection of Warhol's TV-related film and broadcast work, including *Soap Opera*, (1964), *Outer and Inner Space* (1965), *Fashion* (1979–80), *Andy Warhol's T.V.* (1980–1983) and *Andy Warhol's Fifteen Minutes* (1985–87). Although *Changing Channels* was organised thematically, it nonetheless retained a chronological dimension, through the exploration of technical manipulations and political activism in the early and late 1960s, the relationship between art and the public sphere during the 1970s (with an emphasis on works made for broadcast) and an extensive section addressing Warhol's interest in celebrity culture, extending into the 1980s. As with the earlier show *X Screen*, Michalka collaborated with Julie Ault and Martin Beck (artists and founder members of Group Material) on the exhibition design. Large wall graphics and bright colours, recalling the television colour-test palette and alternated with grey and black in the carpeting and seating, were used to produce a cohesive visual environment and to suggest pathways through the galleries. Identical Hantarex monitors were used extensively, with headphones typically located in seats and couches, so that visitors would not be literally 'attached' to screens. The exhibition also featured a number of sculptural installations, by artists engaging with television as a material object, including works by Paik and Vostell.

It is important to note that the admission ticket granted repeat entry to the exhibition, and visitors were able to consult a publication designed (loosely) in the style of a TV guide, in order to plan their viewing. So, in theory at least, *Changing Channels* invited a relatively relaxed mode of return consumption, with the gallery functioning as a media lounge. Yet in a short article reviewing this show (and also previewing *Are You Ready for TV?* at MACBA) writer and curator Kathy Noble responded somewhat negatively to the cohesive exhibition design, exclaiming that 'after many hours of moving from one identical screen to another, my eyes blurred'.[56] Noting the curatorial emphasis on alternative distribution systems, she also suggested that *Changing Channels* might have been more effective if it had actually 'played on a television station', echoing the strategy originally employed by Schum, or had been realised 'on the Internet'. Noble also previewed *Are You Ready for TV?*, framing it as both more 'experimental' in approach than *Changing Channels*, and more specifically concerned with the pedagogical form and function of television. While this is a fair description of the content of the MACBA show, based upon advance publicity information, it is possible that Noble may have been somewhat frustrated by the display strategies used in *Are You Ready For TV?*.

Curated by Chus Martinez with the collaboration of artists Dora García, Johan Grimonprez and Albert Serra, and designed by architect Olga Subirós, *Are You Ready For TV?* developed a particularly expansive approach to the relationship between art, culture and television. It encompassed artworks produced in North and South America as well as Europe, primarily since the 1960s, emphasising the cultural significance of (predominantly public service) television with episodes drawn from a range of philosophical, educational and arts series, such as *Un Certain Regard* (1964–1974), *Civilisation* (1969), *Ways of Seeing* (1972) and *The Shock of the New* (1982). Like *Changing Channels*, *Are You Ready for TV?* highlighted television's importance and never fully realised potential as an exhibition platform that could rival or counter the museum. But while the MUMOK exhibition framed artists and activists as the primary agents in this alternate vision of television, the MACBA show drew attention to experimental and critical currents within television's own production cultures.

Are You Ready for TV? was structured around a series of ten thematic selections, including 'The Empty Podium', exploring the presence of philosophy on French television; 'Dead Air: That Dreaded Silence', featuring works that show aspects of television usually hidden such as *TVTV Looks at the Oscars*, 1976; 'Site-specific Television', featuring canonical broadcast artworks by David Hall amongst others; and 'What's my line?', dealing with themes of mediated identity through reference to the work of Warhol, Judith Barry and Chip Lord. While the overall organisation of this material was less conventionally art-historical than *Changing Channels*, each thematic selection proposed a conceptual framework that might be used to understand the changing relationship between art and television. The vast majority of works included in the show were produced before 2000, but the project did encompass a new multi-part commission by Albert Serra entitled *Els Noms de Crist* (2010). Serra's work was shot in the spaces of the museum, exhibited as an installation and made temporarily accessible online at *TV Web MACBA*.[57] A catalogue for the exhibition was also published online in serialised form.[58]

As with *Changing Channels*, visitors to the MACBA show were presented with a detailed guide, listing the thematic issues explored in each section, in order to plan and manage their viewing. But they were not permitted to use their tickets for repeat admission, despite the considerable volume of material on view. Within the gallery spaces, each of the ten selections was assigned its own specific environment, with works displayed on huge, glass-fronted television monitors, on smaller, flat, touch-screen monitors, with headphones attached, and on monitors embedded in the gallery walls. Lighting and seating arrangements were used in some of these environments to suggest specific modes of sociality, variously associated with the classroom, the television studio and (less obviously) the private home. The overall aesthetic was much more clinical than that of *Broadcast Yourself*, or indeed *Changing Channels*, with extensive use of white plastic chairs throughout. At MACBA, the 'TV studio' environment was quite different from the replica presented in *Broadcast Yourself*, both because it lacked a retro aesthetic and because it did not actually incorporate a studio set. Instead, the banks of raked seating facing the large screen and the prominent suspended lighting alluded more generally to the physical and social architecture of the studio, as a setting in which TV production processes could potentially be observed by an audience.

The large television monitors used throughout *Are You Ready for TV?* also tended to dominate the galleries, and the combination of reflective surfaces and high-contrast lighting found in several environments created significant barriers to viewing, so that visitors seated in front of these screens often could not avoid viewing their own reflected images. This display strategy might seem to suggest a critique of television as 'spectacle', echoing Roberta Smith's reading of *Three Linked Cubes/Interior Design for Space Showing Video* in 'Rooms with a View'. As I have argued, Smith tacitly rejects the model theorised by Blom of the museum as an atmospheric social space, reasserting its traditional role as a site of civic instruction and reform. The design of *Are You Ready for TV?*, which largely excluded cushioned seating, certainly did not emphasise relaxation or comfort. But this does not mean that it reasserted a traditional hierarchical relation between art and television, or necessarily framed the museum as a site of order and critique. Instead, the evocation of the classroom in the design of the MACBA show seemed highly self-conscious, almost parodic, as though questioning whether the museum could legitimately fulfil a pedagogical role in relation to television, while at the same time fully acknowledging television's *own* neglected history of critique and experimentation.

My final example, *Remote Control* at the ICA, was considerably smaller in scale than both the MUMOK and MACBA exhibitions, in terms of the number of works exhibited. It did, however, incorporate an expansive programme of performances and talks, entitled 'Television Delivers People', including several events devised for web streaming. In addition, the show was specifically scheduled to coincide with a significant moment in the history of television broadcasting: the commencement in the London region of the UK's switchover from an analogue to a digital signal. Perhaps as a consequence of this context, *Remote Control* was distinguished by a particularly strong emphasis on technological obsolescence and televisual materiality, both in relation to broadcast infrastructure and TV as a consumer object. This emphasis was especially apparent in the lower gallery, which featured Simon Denny's installation *Channel 4 Analogue Broadcasting Hardware from Arqiva's Sudbury Transmitter* (2012). This hardware did not bear an obvious relationship to 'television' in its consumer form. Instead it consisted of large bank of machinery incorporating dials, gauges and other analogue display devices, contained in various equipment cabinets placed in a row with a number of cabinet doors opened to reveal contents that included circuitry. A gallery information sheet framed this installation as an exploration of 'questions surrounding spatial distribution and ecology', while also noting a visual resemblance between the older hardware and newer technologies that will 'ultimately replace it—namely the vast data storage stacks owned by companies such as Google and Facebook'. In addition to this hardware installation, Denny contributed a wall-mounted sculpture, *Analogue/Digital Transmission Switchover: London* (2012), incorporating a 3D flat-screen television and artificial eyeballs, comically alluding to 'advancements' in television technology.

Designed and curated by Denny in collaboration with ICA curator Matt Williams, further obsolete transmission hardware dominated a section of the lower gallery exhibition and included a series of 18 identical wall-mounted video monitors, each displaying a single channel work produced since the late 1960s. Several of these works were originally devised for broadcast, including Gerry Schum's *Fernsehgalerie/TV Gallery: Land Art* (1968/1969), David Hall's *TV Interruptions* (1971) and *This is a Television Receiver* (1976), and Dara Birnbaum and Dan Graham's *Local TV News Analysis* (1980). Many of these videos are well known—even iconic—examples of artists' television, featured in several of the exhibitions already cited. But, when placed in proximity to Denny's hardware installation, the display proved especially effective in highlighting television's mutable materiality.

Hall's *This Is a Television Receiver* (1976), one of the iconic videos shown at *Remote Control*, was originally commissioned by the BBC, as an unannounced opening work for their special *Arena* video art programme, first transmitted March 10, 1976. At the outset, BBC news presenter Richard Baker delivers a didactic text on illusionism in television production, culminating in the statement 'This is a television receiver.' Using analogue means, the statement was rerecorded several times, so that the image is progressively distorted. As Sean Cubitt points out, as the curvature of the television screen also becomes more apparent,[59] Hall's work emphasises both the material properties of the receiver and its function within a larger institutional formation. Although devised to be viewed on a domestic television receiver, Hall's work is conventionally exhibited in gallery spaces on a museum-standard Hantarex or Sony 'cube' monitor with cathode ray tube (CRT).[60] The wall-mounted monitors used at the ICA to display video works such as *This Is a Television Receiver* were, however, much smaller than standard museum cube monitors and, although they incorporated CRTs, they loosely resembled computer screens commonly used in office environments. Through the presentation of Hall's work on this non-standard monitor, in proximity to the display of obsolete hardware, *Remote Control* drew attention to the contradictions inherent in the display of 'television' in the gallery.

Conclusion: Producing the Museum as Social Space

Since at least the 1960s, art exhibitions have emerged as important spaces in which the changing materiality and sociality of television can be explored, and in which certain aspects of the televisual can manifest physically, and be examined at close quarters. Exhibition visitors routinely encounter sculptural displays of television hardware (including, at times, functioning TV receivers); video works that explore and replicate televisual modes of address; and also replicas of more ambiguous evocations of TV production and reception environments. By exhibiting television, museums and galleries sometimes assert their traditional function as institutions in which order is produced through strategies of display and categorisation, and narratives of progression. In many of the examples I discuss, however, the exhibition of television becomes a means through which artists and curators seem to explore and negotiate changes in the social function and form of art institutions. This approach is especially apparent in the works that I have discussed by artists such as Dan Graham and James Coleman, which demonstrate an engagement with altered practices of moving image consumption both within and beyond the museum.

Furthermore, while television continues to fulfil an important role in the ongoing production of the museum as a social space, it is increasingly framed as an object of cultural memory rather than a focus or platform for social or political reform. The rise of the retrospective mode of exhibiting television, since the early 2000s, articulates this new emphasis on memorialisation, but this curatorial practice can also be read as an indirect response to the growing importance of the internet (and social media) in private and public life. Although television's cultural displacement, and remediation, by newer media technologies has been widely noted,[61] the consequences of this shift for art institutions are still somewhat unclear.[62] Online media may also be even more resistant than television to representation within museums and galleries, because its institutional form continues to be strongly linked to the display and organisation of objects. The internet now constitutes a technically, if not necessarily economically, viable platform for the distribution and exhibition of moving image art works, thus superseding television as an alternative to the museum in this respect.[63] Perhaps more importantly, it is widely promoted as a social space, promising modes of social interaction that surpass even television's historical claim to offer a window upon the world. It is the social aspect of the internet (much more pronounced with the emergence of 'Web 2.0' applications in the 2000s) that arguably presents the greatest challenge to the museum's traditional function.

For this reason, even though they are ostensibly concerned with television, exhibitions such as *Broadcast Yourself, Changing Channels, Are You Ready for TV?* and *Remote Control* can also be read as disparate responses to the challenges that the internet poses for the museum as an institution. Although they constitute diverse responses to this challenge, it is notable that all four exhibitions strongly emphasised the importance of design and installation as a means of encouraging interaction and engagement with moving image works. By incorporating documentation of *TV Swansong*, the curators of *Broadcast Yourself* recognised the web as an important site for the historicisation and remediation of television. But they also asserted the particularity of the gallery as a physical social space, through the production of replicas and display environments, which were intended to resonate with the content and history of artworks, and draw attention to the material culture of domestic television viewing. A more cohesive approach to exhibition design was apparent in *Changing Channels*, intended to encourage visitor interaction with an expansive array of material, including many works devised for broadcast. While the curators of *Are You Ready for TV?* and *Remote Control* utilised the web as a supplementary space of distribution and exhibition, they also worked with architects and artists on a range of design, lighting and installation strategies, with the aim of producing distinctive and memorable viewing environments. In the case of *Remote Control*, the gallery actually served as a setting for the display of television's physical 'remains', in the form of obsolete transmission hardware. This might be interpreted as a gesture of mourning for analogue broadcasting, but it would be more accurate to read it as an assertion of the art museum's importance as a space in which the history and future of television, as a once-dominant cultural form, can be reassessed.

Chapter Two

Quality Television and Contemporary Art: Soaps, Sitcoms and Symbolic Value

By the 1960s, the advertising industry knew that people not only saw through ads, they *enjoyed* their skills of decipherment. The art-house commercial, with its symbolic density and aura of artistic complexity, allowed media literate publics to experience the joy of being sophisticated 'readers'. These commercials talked up to the younger media literate publics by addressing them not as advertising's dupes but as erudite critics of complex texts who could imaginatively travel to the art house while watching TV at home.

Lynn Spigel, *TV by Design: Modern Art and the Rise of Network Television*[1]

The cultural legitimation of television is premised upon a rejection and denigration of 'television' as it has long existed, whether in the form of conventional programming, low-tech viewing (real time, with commercials), or the elite conception of a mass audience too passive or too stupid to watch differently.

Michael Z. Newman and Elana Levine, *Legitimating Television*[2]

Introduction: Opposing Art and Television

Almost since its inception, television has functioned as an object of artistic fascination, a focus for technological and formal experiment, and social critique.[3] Artists have also engaged at various points in important dialogues and collaborations with television producers for many decades, as evidenced by the research of Lynn Spigel, John Wyver and others. Yet, as both Spigel and Wyver have noted, the relationship between art and television has all too frequently been framed in terms of opposition.[4] Citing David Antin's account of this oppositional dynamic, in the canonical text 'Video: Distinctive Features of the Medium' (first published in 1975), Lynn Spigel contests his claim that television grammar developed largely without artists' participation, noting that:

such statements ignore the numerous cross-media exchanges between fine artists, commercial artists, museum curators, and TV producers in the early broadcast era. This view of video as television's 'other' has continued in much of the literature about video so that by now we inherit the distinction TV vs. video (and digital) as a commonsense historical procedure.[5]

Above: Stills from Fiona Macdonald,
Museum Emotions 2003. 106 minutes.
Stereo Digital Betacam.
Courtesy of the artist.

Spigel sets out to uncover television's role in collapsing the divide between 'high' and 'low' culture during the post World War Two period, by serving as a 'vehicle for the widespread dissemination of modern visual forms'.[6] To this end, she highlights the 'common aspirations' shared by artists, designers, advertisers with regard to 'television's potential as cultural form and means of visual expression'[7]—a potential to be realised in part through formal and technological experimentation.

In contrast to Spigel, David Joselit tends to locate television's 'potential' in its network structure. He frames television as the 'first major public medium experienced in private: there are no ticket sales to keep track of, no crowds to count, just anonymous viewers, each in his own home',[8] and he argues that these conditions of anonymity and privacy have helped to transform democratic publics into statistically defined markets.[9] Even though he bemoans television's current compromised form, however, Joselit seems to envisage a future moment when it might yet *become* a genuinely public medium. Somewhat surprisingly, for Joselit, this yet-to-be achieved publicness bears little relation to the history or current formulation of public television, and is instead framed partly as an outcome of criticism, art practice and activism: practices charged with the task of producing 'utopian pathways across the locked-down terrain of television'.[10]

Although Joselit's analysis is premised upon a critique of network television's cultural and institutional dominance, it takes relatively little account of changes in televisual form and consumption. He also does not consider whether the practices of artists and activists might have helped to inform or shape institutional change in commercial television since the 1960s.[11] Spigel's research, by comparison, reveals complex interconnections between advertising and art cinema in the 1960s, in terms of both production and reception, contributing to the development of what she terms the 'art house' TV commercial. These forms of advertising borrowed the aesthetic of New Wave cinema, incorporated psychedelic visual effects, and sometimes even espoused civil rights or anti-war messages. According to Spigel, they resulted from the knowledge of television networks and advertising agencies that activities of 'interpretation' and 'metareflection' were popular with television audiences and that 'media criticism was good for marketing'.[12]

These newer forms of advertising were effective precisely because they solicited the attention of viewers who perceived themselves to be sophisticated, media-literate consumers. A somewhat similar dynamic is noted by John Caldwell in relation to the 'intellectual excess' apparent in several US television shows during the 1980s, such as *Moonlighting* (1985–89) and *thirtysomething* (1987–1991) and subsequently in *Northern Exposure* (1990–1995) and *The Larry Sanders Show* (1992–1998). Often characterised by pronounced intertextuality, these shows rewarded recognition and distinction, justifying the 'college educations that helped produce their quality demographics'.[13] Here Caldwell is referring to the fact that these shows were addressed toward a specific (and commercially valuable) slice of the viewing population and, in pursuit of this demographic, they cultivated prestige. Significantly, Caldwell also draws attention to the emergence, or more accurately, the growing institutional recognition of, new viewing contexts in the early 1990s. He notes that Nielsen Media Research began

Above: Kennedy Browne, *Episode 306: Dallas, Belfast*, 2006. Single channel video loop, 12 minutes. Commissioned by PS², Belfast, as one of the project series *Space Shuttle*. Production still: audition days September 2nd & 3rd 2006 in the Titanic Quarter. Courtesy of the artists.

Above: Kennedy Browne, *Episode 306: Dallas, Belfast*, 2006. Single channel video loop, 12 minutes. Commissioned by PS², Belfast, as one of the project series *Space Shuttle*. Production still: Peter Mutschler closing up the Space Shuttle structure after the day's filming. Courtesy of the artists.

Above: Desirée Holman Composite image, *The Magic Window*, 2007. Three channel video installation.
Courtesy of the artist and Jessica Silverman Gallery.

Above: Desirée Holman, production
still, *The Magic Window*, 2007. Three
channel video installation.
Courtesy of the artist and Jessica
Silverman Gallery.

Above: Phil Collins, *soy mi madre*,
2008,16 mm film transferred to video;
colour, sound; 28 min. Production still,
Mexico City, 2008.
Courtesy of Shady Lane Productions,
Berlin.

to recognise that 'young and active demographic groups, important to advertisers and traditionally thought to be light TV viewers', often engaged in viewing TV outside the types of domestic settings that had traditionally been privileged in the production of ratings.[14]

For several decades, as evidenced by the work of Spigel and Caldwell, television advertisers, producers and rating agencies have sought, through stylistic excess which included a marked intertextuality, to address viewers who perceive themselves as educated and media literate. For Caldwell, the aestheticisation of television forms part of a broader trend in US culture, 'where artistic styles have been suburbanized, proliferated, and mass-marketed to middle-class consumers' and (citing Pierre Bourdieu) he frames the performance of stylistic competence as a means of achieving social power and mobility.[15] Michael Z. Newman and Elana Levine have also engaged with television as a site of distinction, in a 2012 study that addresses television's altered cultural status in the era of media convergence.[16] Within the promotional, journalistic, fan-generated and academic discourses that structure the production and consumption of 'quality television', they note the mobilisation of concepts of authorship, artistic achievement and distinction, derived from the realm of 'art'. The term 'quality television' has been in use for several decades but acquired greater currency in television studies during the 2000s, following the critical success of serialised dramas such as *The Sopranos* (1999–2007), *The West Wing*, (1999–2006), *The Wire* (2002–2008) and *Mad Men* (2007–). More recently, the quality television label has been extended to include comedies such as *30 Rock* (2006–), that differentiate themselves from traditional sitcoms through the use of single-camera shooting rather than a more obviously set-bound multi-camera approach.[17] These shows, which are often promoted as the creations of prominent auteur-producers (known as 'Showrunners') are routinely celebrated for their complex storylines, rich characterisations, high production values and supposed self-reflexivity. It can be argued, however, that self-reflexivity is not actually particular to 'quality television' but rather has become a pervasive characteristic of industrial production culture, leading Caldwell to observe (in 2008) that 'film and television today reflect obsessively back on themselves and invest considerable energy in over-producing and distributing this industrial self-analysis to the public'.[18]

Newman and Levine argue, however, that attributions of quality are linked to changing modes of distribution and consumption, associated with the era of media convergence. Citing the widespread use and promotion of DVDs, DVRs, online video, HDTV and mobile devices,

Next page: Phil Collins, *soy mi madre*,
2008, 16 mm film transferred to video;
colour, sound; 28 min. Production still,
Mexico City, 2008.
Courtesy Shady Lane Productions,
Berlin.

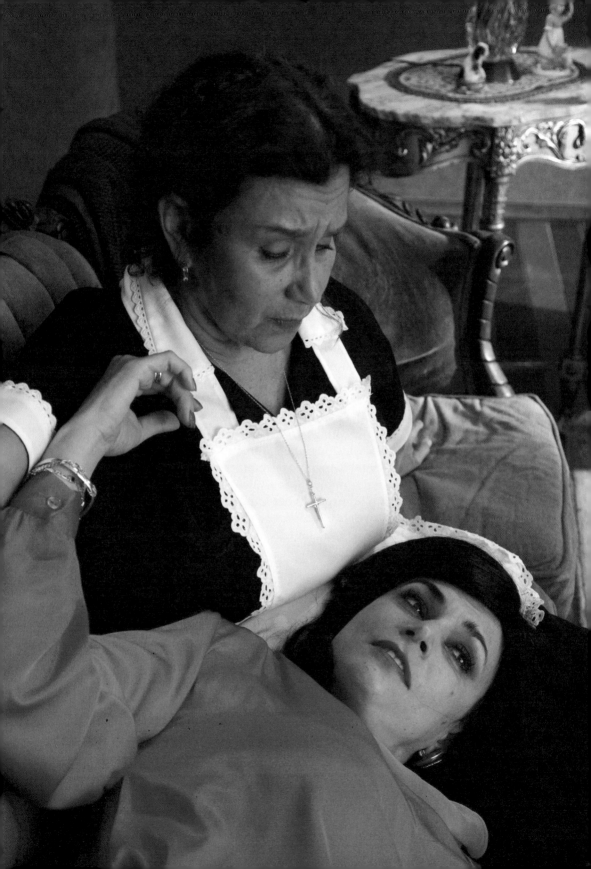

they propose that television is no longer primarily understood as a domestic appliance. Instead, these newer 'technologies of agency' promise liberation from traditional modes of 'watching TV', routinely designated as passive.[19] In addition to highlighting rhetorics of technological innovation, Newman and Levine cite precedents for the cultural elevation of popular arts, through reference to histories of theatre, jazz and photography. They specifically emphasise the legitimating role of 'traditional high art spaces such as museums and concert halls', in conjunction with critical discourses associated with educational institutions such as the university.[20] Yet while Newman and Levine's analysis is persuasive, they do not elaborate upon the role played by art museums in the cultural elevation of television since the 1950s, beyond a fleeting reference to the selection of *The Sopranos* as the first television series to be exhibited in the Museum of Modern Art, New York in 2001.[21] So, just as Joselit relies upon a somewhat fixed conception of television, Newman and Levine seem to rely upon a fixed conception of the museum as an unchanging institution. In addition, by drawing upon Bourdieu's sociological research into notions of cultural capital and distinction, which was primarily conducted in France, they do not consider how the legitimating function and status of the museum might be linked to specific modes of subvention or governance, which vary across European and North American contexts. More importantly, Newman and Levine's analysis cannot explain why many contemporary artists are interested in television genres that do *not* fit current definitions of 'quality', including soaps, telenovelas and multi-camera sitcoms.

In this chapter, I question the notion that museums function as sites for the legitimation, elevation or critique of TV production and consumption. Instead I propose that television increasingly serves as an important resource for artists seeking to engage with a range of social and political issues concerning place, class, cultural, ethnic and sexual difference, which are of relevance not only to practitioners but also to art institutions. While I differentiate between the agendas of artists and institutions, my analysis is informed by the fact that artworks—particularly installations—are routinely developed, even commissioned, for a specific institutional setting, even if they circulate extensively beyond this context. I have also chosen to include works that did not evolve as commissions, which demonstrate that television is an important reference for artists seeking to question the form and symbolic economy of contemporary art culture. The five works discussed in depth are *Museum Emotions* (2003), a multi-part soap opera by Australian artist Fiona Macdonald, *Episode 306: Dallas, Belfast* (2006), a site-specific project by Kennedy Browne (a collaboration between two Irish artists, Sarah Browne and Gareth Kennedy), *The Magic Window* (2007), a three-channel installation by US artist Desirée Holman, *soy mi madre* (2008), a telenovela by the British artist Phil Collins and *Ourhouse* (2010–), a multi-part series by another British artist, Nathaniel Mellors.[22]

Despite the varied nationalities of these artists, many of their works actually reference US-made TV shows, such as *Dallas* (1978–91), *Knots Landing* (1979–1993), *The Cosby Show* (1984–1992), *Roseanne* (1988–1997) and *Melrose Place* (1992–1999). Many of these artists explicitly engage with US television both because it is a privileged site for the negotiation of cultural difference and because it functions as a highly recognisable emblem of globalisation. *Soy mi madre* might seem to differ from the other works discussed, since it explores the production and consumption of Mexican television, but Collins's project, which was commissioned for a US museum, is also concerned with a global television form that is widely exported: the telenovela. Evidently, these are not the first artists to engage with sitcoms, soap operas and the TV series form; Dara Birnbaum, Joan Braderman, Stuart Marshall, Martha Rosler and many others have engaged with popular television formats since the 1970s. But while this earlier generation tended to engage with television as an object of reform or critique, I argue that television actually serves as a cultural resource for Collins, Holman, Kennedy Browne, Macdonald and Mellors.

Although the five works discussed in this chapter were devised primarily for exhibition as installations, the origins of Mellors's multi-part project lie in a short work called *The 7 Ages of Britain Teaser*, which was commissioned by the BBC for broadcast at the beginning of the final episode of a survey of British culture, *The Seven Ages of Britain* (2010), presented by David Dimbleby. Commenting on this broadcast, Colin Perry points out that *The 7 Ages of Britain Teaser* was contextualised by Dimbleby, who described the work as a 'comment on the role of television in modern society', stating: 'Whatever you make of it, it shows how much art has changed in the last hundred years'. For Perry, this type of contextualisation serves to negate strategies of 'criticism, parody and deconstruction'.[23] I would argue, however, that these strategies are no longer of central interest to many contemporary artists precisely because they have pervaded television for many decades.

Museums, Public Television and the Game of Distinction

Before discussing the works of Collins, Holman, Kennedy Browne, Macdonald and Mellors further, it is important to return to the question of how museums and broadcasters have developed as sites of cultural elevation and distinction that must also assert, and legitimate, their own status as 'public'. Newman and Levine cite various art forms that have risen 'to the status of high culture through the separation of audiences by class and by the establishment of institutions such as symphony orchestras and art museums functioning outside of the for-profit commercial sector'.[24] They do not, however, engage with the institutional history or economy of this sector and this type of survey also lies beyond the scope of my own study. Nonetheless, it is important to signal some of the cultural and historical factors that structure practices of culture elevation and social distinction.

As Carol Duncan points out, the history of the museum is marked by a shift in orientation away from the expert connoisseur-viewer, who might have encountered artworks without labels in a privately-owned 'princely gallery' during the eighteenth century and toward the bourgeois citizen, who is instead addressed as a rational subject with the capacity to make aesthetic judgements and so to engage in a process of (self-) transformation.[25] Duncan's research also demonstrates that the museum's role as public institution and ritual site has been configured differently within US and European contexts. Citing the establishment of three important art institutions in the 1870s in three cities where business and banking elites were concentrated (New York, Boston and Chicago), Duncan emphasises that institutions such as New York's Metropolitan Museum, the Boston Museum of Fine Arts and the Art Institute of Chicago were informed by 'the model of the public museum as a ritual that makes visible the ideals of a republican state, frames the "public" it claims to serve, and dramatizes the unity of the nation'.[26] However, she also notes that the US museum model was 'consciously borrowed from Europe'. The founders of these museums often sought to replicate the monumental architecture of their European counterparts, exemplified by the Louvre or National Gallery in London's Trafalgar Square, suggesting that the US institutions were not the products (or the relics) of political opposition. Rather than actually arising out of lived historical struggles for civic power,[27] instead US museums simply *displayed* European style publicness. In addition, while they needed to 'appear inclusive and democratic in order to effectively symbolise community and define national identity',[28] according to Duncan, these newly established institutions asserted their distance from the state by establishing autonomous self-perpetuating boards of trustees, with the aim of keeping these new institutions outside the jurisdiction of 'often hostile city politicians'.[29]

Nonetheless there are commonalities between European and US museums, particularly with regard to the formation of taste cultures since the nineteenth century, in that both aspired to stimulate economic growth by inculcating 'a taste for more artfully designed and internationally competitive goods'.[30] Tony Bennett notes that public museums even served the needs of the department store through 'civilizing programmes' in which female department store sales assistants were sent to exhibitions, in order to acquire 'the principles of taste'.[31] He points out that this notion of the public museum as a utilitarian site of civic formation is difficult to reconcile with the conceptualisation of aesthetic experience underpinning Bourdieu's theorisation of distinction, stating:

> Bourdieu is no doubt right to call attention to the role of the art gallery in producing the pure gaze of aesthetic contemplation. But this needs to be complemented by accounts of the parallel attempts to train the eye of the visitor in a civically utilitarian fashion that also formed—and still do—an important aspect of the practices of public art galleries.[32]

The key issue here is that museums are not simply spaces in which cultural capital is acquired and demonstrated through the exercise of judgement based upon contemplation. Instead they should be understood as relatively flexible and adaptable sites of utilitarian 'training', responsive to the changing demands and requirements of civic society.[33] Bennett is also deeply critical of Bourdieu's concept of the 'habitus', which he argues fails to allow for the possibility of contradiction and differentiation.

The habitus was initially defined by Bourdieu as a 'unitary lifestyle [...] a unitary set of choices of persons, goods, practices'[34] and it served to structure his interpretation of empirical data.

Above: Nathaniel Mellors, *Ourhouse
Episode 1: Games*, 2010. Still from HD
video, duration 34 minutes.
Courtesy the artist; Matt's Gallery,
London, MONITOR, Rome; Galerie
Diana Stigter, Amsterdam. © Nathaniel
Mellors.

Above: Nathaniel Mellors, *Ourhouse
Episode 2: Class*, 2010–11. Still from
HD video, duration 30 minutes.
Courtesy the artist; Matt's Gallery,
London, MONITOR, Rome; Galerie
Diana Stigter, Amsterdam. © Nathaniel
Mellors.

Above: Nathaniel Mellors, *Ourhouse
Episode 3: The Cure of Folly*, 2011. Still
from HD video, duration 33 minutes.
Courtesy the artist; Matt's Gallery,
London, MONITOR, Rome; Galerie
Diana Stigter, Amsterdam. © Nathaniel
Mellors.

Above: Nathaniel Mellors, *Ourhouse Episode 4: Internal Problems*, 2010. Still from HD video, duration 21 minutes 55 seconds.
Courtesy the artist; Matt's Gallery, London, MONITOR, Rome; Galerie Diana Stigter, Amsterdam. © Nathaniel Mellors.

According to this model, symbolic value is always governed by the principles of the habitus, so when 'intellectuals or artists read popular novels, watch Westerns, or read comics, they transform such popular works into props of distinction through *distancing or ironic readings* governed by the organizing principles of the bourgeois aesthetic habitus'.[35] There is no room in Bourdieu's account—as theorised by Bennett—for shared tastes between different class groups, or deviations from the ideal-type of a class habitus.[36] Members of the working class are simply deemed unable to participate as 'players in the field in which the game of distinction takes place',[37] until such time as informal and formal mechanisms of exclusion, in education and elsewhere, are removed. In the meantime, their interests must be represented by intellectuals who can demonstrate socially validating competencies.[38] Bennett's critique of the 'habitus' reflects specific problems for artists working with television genres such as the sitcom or soap that have, at times, been assigned a low cultural status. Following the logic of Bourdieu's analysis (and to some extent the critique of cultural elevation offered by Newman and Levine) the production of an artwork in the style of a soap opera or a multi-camera sitcom could simply be read as a transformation of a 'popular work' into a 'prop of distinction'.

In the case of television, however, it is entirely possible that that a 'popular work' might actually incorporate a 'distancing or ironic reading' of its own form and context. This point is illuminated by Laurie Ouellette's discussion of an episode of the US sitcom *Roseanne* in which the Conner family are chosen to participate in the Nielsen rating system.[39] Initially an enthusiastic participant in the ratings study, Roseanne is angered by the Nielsen representative's assumption that her family is likely to be addicted to commercial television. Suspecting a 'conspiracy' between advertisers and politicians wishing to maintain the social status quo, she resolves to disrupt the ratings by watching only the Public Broadcasting Service (PBS). But, after forcing her family to suffer through 'slow-moving educational documentaries' and 'public lectures "live from Yale"', she relents and gladly switches to a marathon showing of *The Beverly Hillbillies* on a commercial channel.[40] For Ouellette, this episode both illustrates Bourdieu's theorisation of distinction, and 'shows, by example, that "mass appeal" television genres like sitcoms can be meaningful and enlightening',[41] hence demonstrating the types of attributes actually claimed by PBS.

I will return to *Roseanne* later in this chapter, but first it is important to consider how museums and public television both functioned separately and intersected in the production of distinction, well before the convergence era theorised by Newman and Levine. According to Ouellette, public television 'secures cultural distinction—and invites recurring charges of elitism—by defining the public that it exists to serve against a negative image of an indiscriminate mass audience'. Unlike the implicitly discerning viewers of PBS, the 'mass' audience are imagined to be 'glued to uncivilized afternoon talk shows, insipid sitcoms, cops-and-robbers dramas, sensationalistic tabloid news, and formulaic movies-of-the-week'.[42] One of the ways in which PBS articulated its difference from other forms of television was through imported programming, especially British drama, and Ouellette notes the continued importance of *Masterpiece Theater* (1971–). Initially sponsored by Mobil Oil,

Masterpiece Theater has long served as a high-profile vehicle for 'quality' shows, such as *The Forsyte Saga* and *Upstairs, Downstairs*, combining the pleasure of soap opera with 'literary cachet'.[43] The prestige status of the show was initially achieved through the involvement of Alistair Cooke as presenter, already well known to US audiences because of his long-standing association with the Ford Foundation-produced arts programme *Omnibus* (1952–1961).[44] The show's prestige status was also bolstered by promotional strategies such as a series of Mobil-sponsored seminars on *Masterpiece Theater* at the Museum of Broadcasting (now the Paley Center for Media) in 1980.[45] Ouellette notes that these strategies allowed PBS to present 'legitimate drama' in serial form, addressing an audience who wished to view themselves as theatregoers rather than as television soap opera fans.[46]

Rather than simply envisaging public television as a site for the production of distinction and preservation of social privilege, Ouellette specifically frames PBS as a technology of *governmentality* that, like the public museum, is directly implicated in projects of civic and social reform. She notes that the establishment of PBS in the late 1960s was a response both to a perceived decline in cultural standards and to acute conflicts between the demands of the consumer economy and the political order, a recurring issue for the modern democratic capitalist state. It is also important to emphasise that, by this point, television was already well established as a technology of governmentality in the US, in which cultural distinction and patronage played a key role, as evidenced by Anna McCarthy's account of US television in the 1950s.

McCarthy explores the policies and practices of organisations seeking to promote the interdependency of capitalism and democracy, often through sponsored programming, and she argues that television's supposed independence was actually predicated upon an understanding of corporate leaders as 'moral guardians of the interests of the nation'.[47] She emphasises that proponents of the commercial system were especially interested in 'the connotations of *patronage* associated with the idea of sponsorship, positioning sponsors as community institutions bringing culture and learning to mass audiences'.[48] She cites a number of 'prestige' programmes, including *Omnibus* and anthology drama series such as *Goodyear Playhouse* (1951–57) and *Producers Showcase* (1954–57), which enabled corporations to present themselves as public benefactors, not unlike museum trustees. These series were often highly effective in creating a familiar, everyday image of the corporation 'as public servant or citizen', while at the same time invoking more elevated images of patronage by 'donating cultural goods to viewers'[49] in the form of original drama. As Lynn Spigel points out, arts and cultural programming also appealed to *advertisers* because, anticipating the narrowcasting[50] that emerged in subsequent decades, it was perceived to deliver a 'class' rather than 'mass' audience. She states:

> sponsors considered 'class' audiences to have more discriminating tastes than average consumers and to be willing to spend discretionary income on those tastes. In addition, advertisers assumed women associated cultural programs with refinement and family values, and because sponsors knew that women were responsible for the lion's share of

household purchases they wanted to invest in stations that projected an aura of good taste.[51]

While sponsors sought to address more affluent, or aspirational, viewers though arts programming during the 1950s, museums were also becoming interested in the educational and publicity opportunities presented by the medium of television. Since art museums provided a foundational example of sponsored public culture in the US, it is not surprising that institutions such as the Museum of Modern Art began to explore common interests and objectives with commercial broadcasters. Citing MoMA's 'Television Project', an initiative supported by a three-year grant from the Rockefeller Brothers Fund (awarded in 1952), Spigel demonstrates that the museum saw television as a way to teach 'the public how to appreciate, consume and look at art in the age of television'.[52] MoMA officials were specifically interested in using commercial rather than public television, both because they wanted to ensure independence from state education policies which they regarded as insufficiently 'progressive', and also because they were keen to attract the large audiences potentially offered by commercial networks.[53] Spigel also makes the important point that, during this period, commercial television was itself perceived by the museum as an important site of aesthetic experimentation and innovation.[54] So instead of fostering the model favoured in many European contexts, in relation to both public museums and public service broadcasting, where public culture might function as a counterpoint to the realm of commerce MoMA instead promoted art, design, and advertising as highly individualised forms of creativity and experimentation, which celebrated the values of freedom and self-expression imagined to be embodied by the artist and designer.

By contrast, in their account of cultural legitimation, Newman and Levine envisage the art museum as a cultural temple with the power to sacralise and elevate culture by virtue of its symbolic removal from the sphere of commerce. Yet, as I have sought to demonstrate through this short history, the social function of the museum as public institution, whether as a site for the exercise of aesthetic judgement, a setting for more utilitarian processes of 'training', or a context for 'elevation', has clearly altered over time. Like public broadcasters, museums cannot *confer* cultural status unless they maintain and assert their own legitimacy. While US museums have traditionally been dependent upon philanthropy, promoted as offering greater autonomy than state funding, European public museums have relied upon state subvention to assert their autonomy from the marketplace. In recent decades, however, many art institutions in both contexts have become more reliant upon corporate models of governance and financing, which threaten to undercut perceptions of autonomy by drawing attention to the status of art works as financial assets.[55] Art museums in US have become more visibly integrated into the wider cultural economy of leisure and tourism, and must negotiate and articulate their difference from sites of commerce and entertainment in new ways. Within the European context, traditional modes of subvention for public institutions, including museums and broadcasters, have faced an array of challenges, not least those resulting from the 'austerity' regimes established following the credit crisis of 2008.

I am not suggesting here that museums and broadcasters are confronted by a wholly unprecedented crisis of legitimacy as public institutions. Instead I would argue that these institutions are, in fact, continually engaged in the legitimation of their cultural status as 'public'. This status is achieved in many different ways as evidenced by the research of Bennett, Duncan and Ouellette. It might, for example, involve securing forms of subvention that communicate a symbolic distance from the marketplace. Alternatively, or in parallel, museums may specifically seek to present exhibitions or public programmes that function as sites of rational-critical debate, through their exploration of timely social and political issues, as already discussed in Chapter One. Television has of course also functioned in this way, securing a more elevated cultural status though its focus on 'public affairs' in documentary and news genres, but also tackling cultural and social issues in drama, including soaps and sitcoms.

Television's Cultural and Social Relevance

Although they largely overlook PBS, Newman and Levine do acknowledge that notions of 'quality', sometimes specifically aligned with social critique, were mobilised in the US well before the late 1990s. For example, they note various commercially-motivated attempts by television networks, during the 1960s and 70s, to address social issues, 'sometimes in the potentially radical space of the comedy-variety show'.[56] But these attempts at 'cultural relevance' proved less effective in securing critical praise and academic attention than several new sitcoms introduced in the 1970s with the specific aim of reaching more urban and socially liberal viewers. Both *The Mary Tyler Moore Show* (1970–1977), produced for CBS by MTM Enterprises, and M*A*S*H (1972–1983) helped to re-establish television's cultural legitimacy, prefiguring a shift toward more demographically-focused programming.

McCarthy also emphasises the role of independent producers such as MTM and Norman Lear in developing 'socially relevant' sitcoms, such as *The Mary Tyler Moore Show* (1970–1977) and *Maude* (1972–1978), arguing that the positive representation of formerly marginalized social groups in these sitcoms reflects a shift enabled by the development of less episodic and more serialized narratives, which enabled a more expansive emotional range and consequently created an impression of political or social progress. While these modes of representation should not be confused with actual progress, McCarthy makes the point that certain forms of quality television, specifically the 'progressive sitcom', became 'a resource on which journalists, policymakers and media industry' could draw, sometimes as a means of confirming changing social attitudes. According to this framework, the progressive sitcom functioned, at least potentially, as 'a form of public service, raising controversial issues, sparking debate, and bringing hidden assumptions out in the open'.[57] This notion of commercial television as a discursive resource with regard to issues of representation and difference seems especially pertinent to the work of several contemporary artists discussed in this chapter, particularly Macdonald, Kennedy Browne, Collins and Holman.

These newer forms of 'progressive' programming also helped to ensure the continued cultural relevance of television. By the 1980s, the critical and commercial success of the NBC show *Hill Street Blues* (1981–87), which combined elements of the soap opera and police procedural drama, had 'cemented the economic logic behind Quality fare' as a means of ensuring the survival of network television in a multi-channel environment.[58] *Hill Street Blues* actually borrowed stylistically from *The Police Tapes* (1977), an observational drama broadcast on PBS, directed by Alan and Susan Raymond, the same team responsible for *An American Family* (1972). Deirdre Boyle points out that *The Police Tapes* was itself heavily indebted, in terms of subject matter, camerawork and use of dramatisation, to *Officers of the Law* (1976), a documentary made by Minnesota-based video collective University Community Video (UVC), one of several groups to emerge as part of the 'guerrilla television' movement in the late 1960s and early 70s.[59] My intention in referencing this complex genealogy is not simply to demonstrate that activist aesthetics were co-opted by commercial producers, but rather to emphasise the importance of 'critique' as a connection between art, activism and commercial television production.

Jonathan Bignell notes that 'visually distinctive' US television dramas such as *Hill Street Blues*, and subsequently *Homicide: Life on the Street* (1993–99), *NYPD Blue* (1993–2005) and *CSI: Crime Scene Investigation* (2000–) were crucial to the legitimation of commercial US programming as 'quality television' within the British context.[60] He notes that the 1990 (British) Broadcasting Act required the Independent Television Commission (ITC) to apply what it termed a 'quality threshold' when awarding ITV franchises, with the result that companies had to demonstrate a commitment to quality programming associated with high culture, a category then perceived to exclude US imports. But by exhibiting the televisual or tele-literate characteristics understood in terms of 'visual distinctiveness' and stylistic reflexivity, television dramas could present themselves in 'opposition to the mass-audience popular forms such as soap opera and sitcom'.[61] Significantly, Bignell does not interrogate the assumptions around audience that underpin this validation of stylistic reflexivity. Newman and Levine, however, argue that cultural legitimation of certain modes of production and consumption is predicated 'upon a rejection and denigration of "television" as it has long existed', and specifically on the dismissal of conventional programming such as game shows and 'low-tech' modes of viewing, in real time and with commercials.[62]

According to this hierarchy, the viewer of daytime soaps and game shows is denigrated as passive, while the consumer of quality television is depicted as too active, busy and smart to watch advertising. This notion of 'active' consumption is manifest in part through the practices of collecting facilitated by new modes of distribution, as evidenced by Derek Kompare's research on the rise of the DVD series box set, an important platform for serial drama. For Kompare, the DVD box set is integral to the shift from a 'flow' model of distribution (based upon the sale of audiences to advertisers) to a 'publishing' model,[63] which involves the direct sale of a product to consumers. Kompare also makes the important point that blogs and online forums were widely used to refine and promote DVD series box sets of shows such as *The X Files* (initially in the form of individual episodes) in the late 1990s and early 2000s. These DVD releases sought to address connoisseurs and experts through the inclusion of commentaries and supplementary material, recalling the strategies used in PBS programming such as *Masterpiece Theater*. Kompare's analysis demonstrates that symbolic value continues to be produced in the media industries through practices of interpretation and analysis, whether they involve accredited experts or involve online fan communities. Online forums, for example, can be seen to supplement, if not rival, traditional settings such as the university and museum for the attribution of quality. This does not mean an end to museological practices of distinction but rather suggests that symbolic value generated through interpretation and analysis in one context may actually be exchanged elsewhere.

Television as a Cultural Resource in Contemporary Art

Turning now to the work of artists who have engaged with television as a resource, my first example, *Museum Emotions* (2003), utilises the conventions of the soap opera to explore modes of sociality and discourse internal to contemporary art culture. This work was independently produced by Melbourne-based artist Fiona Macdonald, with funding from the Australia Council for the Arts over a three-year period. Like many soap operas, *Museum Emotions* engages with questions of community and locality. But instead of exploring social bonds specific to a particular workplace, family grouping or residential area, it focuses on the Melbourne contemporary art scene. Consisting of nine episodes, each approximately 10–12 minutes, shot on location in various local art spaces, it is described by Macdonald as 'a conceptual soap opera that uses the characterization and dramatic form of mainstream soap-opera and its episodic structure to develop a contemporary art story'.[64] The 'story' unfolds at a slow pace and much of the action takes place at private views of exhibitions, in the offices of commercial galleries, art studios or at a cocktail bar, where artists exchange gossip or pseudo-intellectual commentary on contemporary art and culture.

Several exhibition visitors wear summer clothing, indicating that *Museum Emotions* was shot during the summer months, but the sunny outdoor locations that tend to feature prominently in Australian soaps such as *Neighbours* (1985–) and *Home and Away* (1988–), are wholly absent. Although Macdonald cites US shows such as *Knots Landing* and *Melrose Place*[65] as references in the development of plotlines, she does not attempt to replicate the style of either show. Instead, the episodes are deliberately stylistically diverse; one takes the form of a science-fiction dream sequence, for example, in which a character interacts with an artificial intelligence, while several others incorporate choreographed dance elements, typically unfolding in the background. A degree of this kind of stylistic self-consciousness was also a feature of US television in the 1980s and 90s, as evidenced by Caldwell's analysis of intertextuality and intellectual excess in shows such as *Moonlighting* and *Northern Exposure*. But while Macdonald's 'speaking subjects' frequently ruminate on their anxieties, beliefs and value systems, they do not resemble the psychologically motivated characters typically encountered in television drama. The characters in *Museum Emotions* do not reveal their inner desires through their actions, or through wordless gesture and expressions in the manner of melodrama. Instead they tend to deliver monologues on their intentions and motivations, in the manner of press releases or painstakingly constructed artists' statements.

Rather than reading *Museum Emotions* as an analysis of television, I would argue that it uses aspects of the soap opera to explore the discursive form of contemporary art culture. Some of the plot lines are certainly structured around dilemmas and desires concerning personal relationships, professional ambitions, and broadly similar to those explored in shows like *Melrose Place*. However, the dialogue is loaded with 'art speak', as suggested by the titling of episodes such as 'The Spontaneous Fullness of Being' and 'The body with organs that got left out in the rain'. Several characters discuss the merits of criticality, invoking specific philosophical traditions, sometimes for the purposes of self-promotion, while others espouse esoteric personal ideologies, or adopt self-consciously 'business-like' language. *Museum Emotions* is clearly not intended to function as a documentary, and does not serve an avowedly anthropological function. Nonetheless, it does feature numerous performers and locations that would be familiar to anyone with a knowledge of the Melbourne art scene, and it is arguably this familiarity that Macdonald seeks to undercut through her use of characterisations and plotlines drawn from TV soap opera.

While *Museum Emotions* focuses specifically on the culture of contemporary art, my next example invokes memories of television to explore aspects of urban regeneration that are of significance not only to artists but also residents of Belfast. *Episode 306: Dallas, Belfast* is a 12-minute film by Kennedy Browne (Sarah Browne and Gareth Kennedy) realised within the context of a public art project, entitled *SPACE SHUTTLE*, which took place in Belfast between summer 2006 and spring 2007. Developed by a small artist collective located in the centre of Belfast, *SPACE SHUTTLE* consisted of a 'mobile workstation' in which artists or multidisciplinary groups could engage with aspects of the local environment for one or two weeks.[66] The 'shuttle' was a flexible box that could be easily transported and it was temporarily located at several sites, including the former shipyard where the Titanic was built (an area earmarked for regeneration as the Titanic Quarter). It was also used by Kennedy Browne as a film set in which to produce a 12-minute fiction based on a script devised for an imagined episode of *Dallas*, which was not precisely a remake but rather more loosely based upon themes and plotlines explored in the original series.

Using elements of improvisation, three separate casts enacted three distinct but related re-enactments of this script, which included themes of development, prosperity and choice, perceived as relevant to the Belfast context. The fragment of the show being 're-enacted' is not directly recognizable as a scene from *Dallas*. Instead, it features a discussion taking place in 1987 between the characters JR, Bobby and Carter McKay, centring around a deal that threatens to give 'foreigners' such as 'commies' and 'Arabs' control over Texas assets. *Dallas* was chosen as a reference point in part because, according to the artists, it 'evokes a certain nostalgia in the Irish/UK context, when people used the TV programme as a way to vicariously live the life of JR, Bobby, Sue Ellen et al'.[67] *Episode 306: Dallas, Belfast* both exploits this nostalgic appeal and underscores the dissonance between past and present, and between the real and imagined locations of 'Dallas' and 'Belfast'. While several of the performers wear Stetson hats there is no attempt at verisimilitude—male characters are played by women in two versions of the scene—and the set is clearly recogniseable as a temporary portable structure.

In addition to attracting the attention of reception theorists,[68] *Dallas* figures within Caldwell's account of televisual style. This is partly on account of its use of regional locations, which 'unlike Los Angeles [...] had not been stripped of their particular charms and cultural personalities through overuse and overexposure'.[69] In particular, Caldwell cites the use of wide-angle shots of Dallas locations and architecture in the highly rated episode 'Who Shot J.R.?', which served to 'underscore the economic bed of the narrative'.[70] Although wholly at odds with the spectacle and scale of this TV show, in terms of its aesthetic, Kennedy Browne's video also derives much of its visual impact and conceptual coherency from its pointed use of waterside locations in the Titanic Quarter. The interactions between characters are punctuated by quiet shots of the surrounding cityscape, featuring slowly-passing boats against a skyline littered with cranes, with views of regeneration landmarks such as the Odyssey arena (a sports and entertainment venue built in 2000), as well as the post-industrial port area. So rather than simply opposing 'fantasy' to 'reality', the artists instead draw attention to the ways in which discourses around regeneration, in which the reconfiguration of a former industrial area becomes a centre for leisure, are shaped by desire—for social status and material wealth—and by notions of conspicuous consumption. In *Episode 306: Dallas, Belfast*, the cultural memory and the production history of *Dallas* functions as a resource to explore processes of social, cultural and economic change unfolding in Belfast.

Unlike my previous examples, Desirée Holman's *The Magic Window* (2007) is explicitly framed as an exploration of television history, drawing its title from an early advertisement for television receivers and recalling Lynn Spigel's research on television as a domestic object that was often promoted through promises of transportation to another realm.[71] This three-channel video projection stages an imaginary encounter between two sitcom families: the middle-class Huxtables (from *The Cosby Show*) and the working class Conners (from *Roseanne*). The left and right screens present mock-ups of the domestic environments occupied by each family, while the central screen depicts an empty, neutral space, in which the TV families encounter each other and then merge in a choreographed dance routine, incorporating retro chroma-key visual effects, which play on all three screens. Significantly, rather than directly reediting scenes from *The Cosby Show* and *Roseanne*, Holman relies on costuming, sets and props, including grotesque rubber facemasks, to evoke memories of the characters and their domestic environments.

In terms of their materiality, the facemasks loosely resemble props and materials employed by artists such as Lynda Benglis, with whom Holman has exhibited, and Paul McCarthy, who has explored aspects of the sitcom form in videos such as *Family Tyranny/Cultural Soup* (1987).[72] Depicted in drawings accompanying the moving image installation, that also underscore the sitcom's privileged relationship to consumer culture, Holman's masks draw direct attention to each domestic world through material components such as clothing and furnishings, which function alongside the dialogue and storylines to communicate each family's position with a social hierarchy. In some respects, *The Magic Window* engages with television as a miraculous technology of consumption, recalling Joselit's observation that TV invites us to embrace 'our discipline as consumers', and to lose ourselves in 'a lively world of things', that we mistake for a 'social, even a democratic world in which we "vote" our preferences by buying them'.[73]

The affective qualities of the televisual 'things' signified by the half-remembered sets and props of 1980s sitcoms in Holman's work also cannot be fully dissociated from a more prevailing nostalgia for television's past, manifest in practices of scheduling. Lynn Spigel has theorised the appeal of 'nostalgia networks' which 'amass audiences not only by taking them back in time, but also by promising them a fantastic sense of shared place' such as Nick at Nite and TV Land. She observes how:

> Nostalgia networks transport viewers back to the Brady Bunch's ('oh so 70s') brown and orange kitchen, Mary's Minneapolis newsroom, and Cosby's posh but cozy Brownstone, places that have become an imaginary geography for viewers.[74]

For Spigel, there is a marked difference between conventional network and cable re-runs of these types of shows, often scheduled or 'stripped' so that they occupy the same time slot on each day of the week and the nostalgia networks' careful creation of 'themed flows' that involve repackaging of old TV according to a 'mass camp sensibility' that appeals to viewers who regard themselves 'as somehow more sophisticated and "hip" than the naive audiences of the past'.[75]

Something of this sensibility may be apparent in Holman's work and *The Magic Window* is certainly structured around the production of a 'fantastic [...] shared place', into which viewers can enter, through viewing and remembering. But the fantasy that Holman explores—in which two TV families temporarily merge and become one—is clearly different from that offered by the nostalgia networks, since it speaks to a desire for the dissolution of ethnic and class difference. Holman's work, to a greater extent than that of artists such as Benglis and McCarthy, frames the 1980s sitcom as an important site for the representation of class and ethnic difference, while at the same time tacitly acknowledging the fact that representation of difference is no substitute for social progress. As noted by one reviewer, the ill-fitting masks, combined with the choreography, results in an amplified sense of 'awkwardness [which] highlights the contrivances of the original shows', but Holman does not dismiss these sitcoms as contrived or inauthentic depictions of familial life and instead 'takes seriously [their] attempts at reshaping public notions of race, class, and gender'.[76]

My next example, *soy mi madre* (2008) by Phil Collins, was commissioned for a specific exhibition context, but it has been extensively exhibited elsewhere. It is distinguished by notably high production values for an artwork, matching, if not exceeding, those of the television form that it references. *Soy mi madre*, which translates as 'I am My Mother', is a 28-minute single-screen video work with Spanish dialogue and English subtitles, produced within the context of Collins's residency at the Aspen Art Museum in Colorado. In addition to referencing the form of the Mexican telenovela, it is inspired by Jean Genet's play *The Maids,* which was partly based upon a real-life murder case. The central characters in Collins's drama are Solana and Clarita, a mother and daughter employed as domestic maids by the wealthy couple Sable and Sergeant Sainte. Following a series of self-consciously melodramatic dilemmas and disclosures, Sable is revealed to be the daughter of the older maid, culminating in a dramatic confrontation.

Soy mi madre has been framed as an engagement with the Latino community in Colorado, many of whom come from north-western Mexico and would consequently be familiar with the form of the telenovela. A press release, for a subsequent exhibition at Victoria Miro Gallery in London notes that 'in Aspen itself, this community figures mainly as a non-resident, low-qualified work force, dispersed through a ring of satellite towns from which it commutes daily'.[77] Like soaps, telenovelas share many stylistic features with theatrical and film melodrama, in terms of performance style, dramatic themes and use of music, but unlike most US soaps they are often programmed in primetime slots and are very strongly marked by closure. Broadcast each weekday for a period ranging from two months to two years, they progress toward a definitive conclusion, in which the 'good' characters are often rewarded and the 'evil' ones are punished. Telenovelas also routinely circulate beyond their original context of production, via exports for broadcast in other countries or DVD sales, so they are fully embedded within global media flows.[78] While telenovelas have been celebrated by some theorists for their potential to articulate the concerns and experiences of women, Adriana Estill has argued that the production of the commercial broadcaster Televisa sometimes reiterate unstated ethnic hierarchies in Mexican society through casting, so that members of social elites were played by lighter skinned actors, while also propagating an idealised model of the nation, in which 'good people (honest, caring communities of lower class people) will always win out'.[79] Estill further emphasises that 'this narrative invests a great proportion of the Mexican population with moral and social power, in order to compensate them for not having financial power'.[80]

In many respects, *soy mi madre* is faithful to the telenovela form and style. Shot on film in Mexico City rather than in Aspen, it was produced with the involvement of celebrated television designers, accomplished screenwriters and well-known Mexican actors, in addition to two performers drawn from the 'local transsexual-prostitute community'.[81] But in other respects, Collins deviates from the conventions of the traditional telenovela as identified by Estill, because his central characters are all revealed to be in some way false or unreliable. More importantly, the characters are played by a continually changing succession of actors, drawing attention to ethnic difference, most notably in the scene where Sable accuses her maid (and half-sister) Clarita of being 'an Indian, a knacker, a scrubber'. This approach to casting forms part of Collins's broader deployment of defamiliarisation techniques. At one point, for example, the camera briefly follows the actress playing the part of Solana as her scene ends and she leaves the set. Rapidly shedding the character of the maid, she assumes the pose of an imperious actress, greeted by an assistant bearing a glass of water.

The movement of the camera at this point also reveals the presence of other crew members, tracks and camera equipment, framed by curtains, as though literally 'backstage'.

It might be argued that, by fusing aspects of the telenovela form with 'high-cultural' sources such as Jean Genet's *The Maids* in the production of an artwork for a museum context, Collins is contributing to a process of 'cultural elevation' analogous to that theorised by Newman and Levine. But an analysis of the commissioning context points toward a different form of symbolic exchange. Aspen Art Museum is a non-collecting institution, reliant on a mix of private and corporate benefactors, including wealthy local residents, and Collins's project was developed within the context of a newly-established Artist in Residence programme, created specifically to engage a larger community.[82] This programme can be understood in terms of the ongoing legitimation of institutional publicness theorised in histories of the museum and broadcasting. Crucially, however, Collins does not bring representatives of the Colorado Mexican community into the museum, as participants in the production of an artwork. Instead, he proposes and involves a much more geographically dispersed, and highly mediated, community that confounds conventional institutional requirements for demographic diversity. So, in this instance, it is both the globalised economy of television distribution and the specific form and history of the telenovela that serves as an artistic resource.

My final example, Nathaniel Mellors's multi-part drama *Ourhouse* (2010–), differs from the works already discussed both because it is more ambitious in scale (to date, four of the planned six episodes have been completed and the shortest episode is 24 minutes) and encompasses a sculptural aspect.[83] As already noted, Macdonald, Kennedy Browne and Holman draw upon traditions of television that are clearly located in the past, directly referencing sitcoms and dramas produced in the 1970s, 80s and 90s. Like Collins, however, Mellors engages with the serialised drama, a genre that is still very much alive. Certain aspects of *Ourhouse*, most notably the mix of horror and absurd dark humour, are somewhat reminiscent of the work of showrunner Alan Ball, best known for *Six Feet Under* (2001–05) and *True Blood* (2008–). But in terms of style, the most important televisual precedent for Mellors's surreal storytelling can be found in an earlier example of quality television, *Twin Peaks* (1990–91).[84]

Ourhouse is set in a large but extremely dilapidated English country mansion, home to the Maddox-Wilson family. The central characters are an overbearing patriarch, Charles 'Daddy' Maddox-Wilson, his glamorous and much younger wife 'Babydoll' (played by Gwendolyn Christie),[85] adult sons 'Truson' and 'Faxon', his brother 'Uncle Tommy', and the only member of staff apparently employed by the family, an Irish gardener called 'Bobby'. Much of the action takes place within domestic and rural settings exist in a somewhat unsettling spatial relation to each other, despite the fact they appear mundane, and familiar from an array of British sitcoms. In addition, the relationships between characters, and their motivations, cannot be explained in terms of psychologically-motivated desires. Instead, the drama is structured around the mysterious effects produced by the sudden and unexplained arrival, in *Ourhouse Episode 1: Games* (2010), of a large middle-aged man incongruously dressed in casual sportswear. The family fail to recognise his human status, instead labelling him 'The

Object' or 'Thingy', and this problem of naming signals a breakdown of language, which is somehow linked to the nocturnal activities of The Object, who is seen—in *Ourhouse Episode 2: Class* (2010–2011)—ingesting academic texts such as E.P. Thompson's *The Making of the English Working Class* (1963).

As the drama unfolds, the texts and images consumed by The Object serve to dictate the course of the narrative. So, for example, after The Object is seen devouring books on Flemish painting in *Ourhouse Episode 3, The Cure of Folly* (2011), several strangers appear on the estate and proceed towards the manor in search of the 'stone of madness'. As the narrative unfolds, it becomes apparent that they are intent on re-enacting the scene depicted in Hieronymus Bosch's *The Extraction of the Stone of Madness* (1494), a painting sometimes interpreted as a representation of false knowledge. Unlike the dream or fantasy sequences found in shows such as *Six Feet Under*, disruptions in causality and spatial logic remain unexplained in *Ourhouse*, as evidenced in a scene from *Episode 2: Class* which features absurd dialogue between two characters, where a TV set seems to enable two-way communication. In addition to the central enigma surrounding The Object, there are several subplots concerning interfamilial dynamics and class tensions, such as those explored via Babydoll's alternately abusive and flirtatious relationship with Bobby, which help to create a plausible story world invested with a degree of depth. So even though the overall narrative logic may be absurd, the quality of the performances, script-writing, cinematography and design means that *Ourhouse* remains constantly engaging and at times even narratively compelling.

Through the interactions between Babydoll and Bobby, *Ourhouse* reiterates the emphasis on television as site for the articulation of cultural and class difference apparent in works such as *The Magic Window* and *soy mi madre*. But unlike Holman and Collins, Mellors also seems to use certain aspects of TV-style serialisation as a resource in the production and distribution of this work. Significantly, *Ourhouse* was not commissioned by a single institution. Instead, it was realised with the support of British and Dutch art agencies and organisations, (including Arts Council England and The Mondriaan Foundation, Netherlands Fonds BKVB, Nederlands Filmfonds), with specific episodes commissioned for particular exhibition contexts, such as De Haalen, Harlem and the *British Art Show 7*. Although the episodes were not actually 'premiered' in sequence (Episode 4 seems to have been completed or at least shown before Episode Three), the multi-episode structure nonetheless serves as a highly effective means of promoting a moving image work across an array of geographically dispersed exhibition contexts.[86]

Conclusion: Television and Symbolic Value in Contemporary Art

Throughout this chapter I have sought to counter the recurrent emphasis on opposition in many accounts of the relationship between art and television, by focusing on notions of prestige and processes of legitimation that connect television and the museum. While Newman and

Levine tend to envisage art museums as arbiters of cultural taste with the power to bestow status and distinction, my research instead suggests that contemporary art institutions must continually assert and demonstrate their *own* legitimacy as public institutions. So although strategies of legitimation are indeed relevant to any understanding of how television and the televisual art are valued within the cultural economy of contemporary art, art institutions do not primarily serve as contexts for the elevation of television. Instead, I have argued that symbolic value is produced through forms of *exchange* between the two, which can no longer be understood through reference to traditional cultural hierarchies.

In an analysis of the relationship between the art market and celebrity culture, Isabelle Graw specifically contests Bourdieu's view (articulated in *The Rules of Art*) that symbolic and market value are 'relatively independent of each other'.[87] She notes the historically important role played by 'symbol-bearers' such as art historians, critics, and curators. Even if they deny their role in this process, these privileged producers of knowledge certainly contribute to the generation of symbolic—and consequently market—value.[88] But she also points out that, in recent decades, lifestyle and fashion magazines have begun to rival established symbol-bearers in the designation of contemporary art's symbolic value.[89] She finds evidence of this in the prevalence of lists in art and lifestyle publications, in which critics rank their favourite artists or exhibitions.[90] These modes of publicity meet the demand for clear hierarchies, but rarely offer any reflection on criteria for inclusion or exclusion. As her analysis makes clear, value is not simply bestowed by museums, but rather produced through a complex and fluid exchange of publicities, involving art institutions and lifestyle-oriented media.[91] If this logic is extended to the analysis of artists' sitcoms, soap operas and serial drama, it is possible to see that references to television and the televisual fulfil an important role within the art economy, both because television signifies 'popular art' and because it has functioned as a site for the negotiation of cultural difference for many decades.

I have argued that, in diverse ways, the artists discussed in this chapter all engage with television as a resource, rather than approaching it as a medium or cultural object in need of reform. While Fiona Macdonald's *Museum Emotions* uses strategies of scripting and staging drawn from television soap opera to articulate the discursive character of a familiar contemporary art culture, Kennedy Browne's *Episode 306: Dallas, Belfast* draws upon the cultural memory of a show that exemplified consumption, and exploited the aesthetic appeal of the regional, in order to explore the ideology of regeneration. Desirée Holman's *The Magic Window* is equally explicit in its mobilisation of cultural memory, but more specifically focused on fantasies of social progression through representation. In the most recent works discussed, *soy mi madre* and *Ourhouse*, the artists match the industrial values of commercial television by employing strategies of outsourcing production or by integrating resources from many different agencies. For Phil Collins and Nathaniel Mellors, television is valuable not simply as a consequence of its cultural and social relevance in an earlier moment, but because it continues to change, yielding new strategies for the production and distribution of contemporary art.

Chapter Three

Reality TV, Delegated Performance and the Social Turn

It is quite curious that the first films ever made by Louis Lumière show workers leaving the factory. [...] A brilliant installation by Harun Farocki makes clear where the workers leaving the factory are headed. Farocki collected and installed different cinematic versions of *Workers Leaving the Factory*, from the original silent version(s) by Louis Lumière to contemporary surveillance footage. Workers are streaming out of factories on several monitors simultaneously: from different eras and in different cinematic styles. But where are these workers streaming to? Into the art space, where the work is installed.

Hito Steyerl, 'Is a Museum a Factory?'[1]

[R]eality TV is a symptom of a broader privatization of civic discourse and governance in U.S. political culture. Indeed, the genre's contemporary excesses—first born [...] from a perceived scarcity of production resources—speak to the excesses of privatized citizenship, a traumatic experience often expressed in the language of suffering and tears by those who are cast to play out the contemporary dramas of civic life on the reality TV screen.

Anna McCarthy, *The Citizen Machine*[2]

Introduction: from the Factory to the Museum

In this chapter I focus on performances in front of the camera, in artworks and television, by people who do not generally perceive themselves as artists or professional actors. These performers, who may or may not be paid, appear both 'as themselves' and, in many instances, as the representatives of a specific social demographic. Rather than focusing on the conditions of labour encountered by these art and television workers, I am interested in the symbolic value generated through their visible involvement as performers. My discussion is informed by Claire Bishop's analysis of 'delegated performance' in contemporary art,[3] but while Bishop develops an art historical genealogy, I focus on differences and continuities between art and television production as sites of non-professional performance. Consequently I draw upon theories and histories of US and British television, developed by Anna McCarthy, Laurie Ouellette and Su Holmes among others, and upon the work of a range of thinkers, including Tony Bennett, Hito Steyerl and Thomas Elsaesser, who have engaged with how museums and galleries function as spaces of training for practices of display and emulation.

Tony Bennett's work has been especially important in understanding the 'exhibitionary architecture' of the nineteenth century, which included not only public museums but also arcades and department stores. This architecture did not simply enable the inspection of objects, it also allowed for 'the visitors to be the objects of each other's inspection—scenes in which, if not a citizenry, then certainly a public displayed itself to itself in an affirmative celebration of its own orderliness in architectural contexts which simultaneously guaranteed and produced that orderliness.'[4] More recently, Bennett has theorised the public museum of the late twentieth century as a 'civic laboratory' that seeks to produce a measurable 'civic yield', in the form of 'learning outcomes, improved visitor attentiveness, increased accessibility, social cohesion or greater cross-cultural understanding',[5] focusing particularly on the role played by displays of material objects in the achievement of these outcomes.

In this chapter I focus on galleries as privileged sites for the display of mediated images of performance, often in the form of large scale video projections, the materiality of which may be understated or even disavowed. Numerous commentators have noted the prevalence of moving image works within museums and galleries since the 1990s, with some drawing attention to the pervasiveness of projected images in particular. George Baker, for example, has observed that the prevalence of projections 'floating like restless ghosts'[6] throughout contemporary art spaces in recent decades might be somehow linked to the forms of abstraction generated by finance capitalism.[7] Art criticism, he suggests, cannot propose a 'social explanation' for the rise of the 'projected image' in the gallery precisely because 'the social forces subtending this shift have become increasingly unrepresentable'.[8] Here, Baker is referring to an array of social and economic developments associated with the shift from productive to post-productive capitalism, including the increased importance of the stock market and land speculation, the radical alteration of urban formations, systematic unemployment, capital flight and disinvestment, and the necessity of the market 'crash'. I find many aspects of Baker's analysis persuasive, yet it could be argued that the social forces he describes actually find expression not solely in the pervasiveness of the projected image. They can also be identified in the emergence of video installation as the privileged point of intersection in the gallery between the modes of self-display that are associated with production and those concerned with the consumption of art. Here I am referring both to the self-display of those who 'perform themselves' on screen, and to the place of the gallery as a privileged site for the public performance of the labour of consumption by its visitors.

In a provocative and compelling analysis of the art museum as factory, Hito Steyerl highlights the forms of labour routinely performed by exhibition visitors. Noting that several former factories (as well as former churches, train stations, etc.) have been transformed into exhibition spaces, Steyerl goes on to describe the work of moving image consumption now

Next page: Pierre Huyghe, *Mobil TV*
(Mobile TV), 1995. View of the exhibition
Aperto at Nouveau Musée/Institut d'art
Contemporain, 1995. Collection Institut
d'art Contemporain, Rhône-Alpes © Adagp,
Paris © Droits réservés.

often performed in these spaces, citing 'crowds' of people 'bending and crouching in order to catch glimpses of political cinema and video art', sometimes grappling with poor projection and sound.

Although she differentiates this crowd, as 'multitude'[9] from the 'mass' of the factory (and the cinema), Steyerl argues that the labour of consumption is often publicly invisible, primarily because museums, like factories, are subject to surveillance. Crucially, however, she argues that the crowd as multitude does acquire a kind of articulation in the gallery through what she terms the 'cinematic politics' of exhibitions such as *documenta 11*, curated by Okwui Enwezor. Noting that Enwezor was criticised for presenting numerous and often lengthy moving image works, making it impossible for any one individual to view the exhibition in full, Steyerl reads such criticism as a tacit acknowledgement of the fact that instead of addressing the traditional bourgeois subject, who aims to 'master' the show, *documenta 11* required a 'multiple gaze, which is no longer collective, but common'.[10] This multiple subject, Steyerl argues, is 'interpellated' by the museum-as-factory, precisely through the displacement, or absence, of the gaze of the bourgeois sovereign spectator.

Steyerl also identifies another example of visibility through absence, in the form of Harun Farocki's multi-channel installation, *Workers Leaving the Factory in Eleven Decades* (2006). On a row of monitors this installation presents side by side multiple scenes of workers exiting through factory gates and doorways, ranging from the Lumière version(s) to contemporary surveillance footage. Consequently, this work exhibits the (non)representation of labour while at the same time formally suggesting the spill over of labourers into the museum. Although her analysis is highly persuasive, Steyerl's focus on absence and invisibility, and attention to the labour of consumption may actually work against an acknowledgement of other labourers who actually constitute a highly visible (albeit mediated) presence in art museums. Here I am referring to the many moving image artworks that feature images of ostensibly 'ordinary' people, who appear both as performers and as themselves. Pervading contemporary art spaces, these images depict forms of labour that, despite their ubiquity, elude conventional modes of political and social organisation. In addition, while exhibited in ways particular to contemporary art, these representations of labour resonate with modes of non-professional performance that have become commonplace in various forms of (primarily reality) television, discussed in more detail below

Delegated Performance in Contemporary Art

Claire Bishop has proposed the term *delegated performance* to describe a range of artworks involving either live or mediated performance, realised since the 1990 by artists such as Santiago Sierra, Tino Sehgal, Jeremy Deller and Annika Eriksson. She is interested in performances where—in her view—'authenticity' is 'relocated from the *singular* body of the artist to the *collective* authenticity of the social body'.[11] This social body is figured through the involvement of performers who are required 'to *perform themselves*' and in the process

Above: Superflex, *superchannel.org*,
Coronation Court, Superchannel
Studio in Liverpool. Tenants producing
internet TV, (c. 2001–2002).
Courtesy of Superflex.

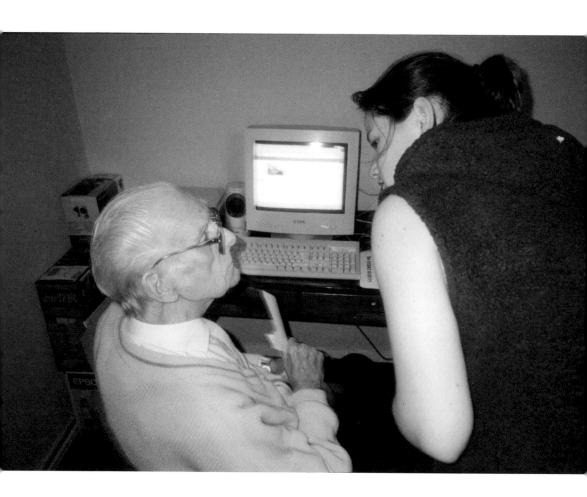

Above: Superflex, *superchannel.org*,
Coronation Court/George chatting to
the viewers (c. 2001–2002).
Courtesy of Superflex.

'to signify a larger socio-economic demographic, for which they stand as an authentic metonymic fragment'.[12] As examples of mediated performance, she cites Artur Zmijewski's *Singing Lesson 1* (2001), which features a group of deaf students singing in public, and Phil Collins's *The World Won't Listen* (2005–2007), a trilogy depicting fans of *The Smiths* in Bogota, Istanbul and Indonesia singing to a karaoke soundtrack of their favourite band's songs.

While Bishop does not frame these works as representations of labour precisely, she does highlight an altered economy of artistic production since the 1990s. She notes that, while artists working with performance in the 1960s and 70s often used their own bodies to produce work quickly and cheaply, delegated performance tends to be more costly and is often realised—in its live form—within contexts such as art fairs where its publicity value can be maximised.[13] She also offers an art historical genealogy, citing several live works realised in Argentina in the 1960s, which emphasised the social specificity of the performers. These works include Oscar Masotta's happening, *To Capture the Spirit of an Image* (1966), in which 'twenty, elderly, lower middle class people were paid to stand [for an hour] in a storage room, in front of an audience, and be subjected to fire extinguishers, a high-pitched deafening sound, and blinding white light',[14] and Oscar Bony's *La Familia Obrera (The Worker's Family)* (1968), which comprised an Argentine family (a man, woman and child) sitting on a platform in an exhibition space.[15] Although she notes the importance of these precedents, Bishop reserves the notion of delegated performance for works realised since the 1990s, because she seeks to emphasis the connections between artistic 'delegation' and work practices involving subcontracting and outsourcing—practices that enable corporations to profitably divest themselves of responsibilities for their workers' welfare. Differentiating between artistic and corporate strategies, Bishop goes on to argue that the 'best' examples of outsourced or delegated artistic performance are 'constructed situations' that are not tightly controlled, and tend to maximise rather than minimise risk, in contrast to conventional wisdom within the domain of corporate outsourcing. Ultimately, however, it is difficult to determine if she regards delegated performance as a critical response to the rise of corporate outsourcing or simply a concurrent development.[16]

Bishop also identifies reality television as one of the 'dominant modes of mediatic representation against which these [delegated performance] works so frequently battle'[17] and she is one of the few theorists to consistently acknowledge the importance of reality TV in understanding the 'social turn' in contemporary art. In her introduction to an anthology of writings on participation, for example, Bishop alludes to artists who 'intervene critically in participatory forms of mass media entertainment', citing Phil Collins's *The Return of the Real* (2005–2007) and Matthieu Laurette's *The Great Exchange* (2000).[18] Elsewhere, in an *Artforum* article on the social turn, exploring a 'surge of artistic interest in collectivity, collaboration and direct engagement with specific social constituencies',[19] she discusses numerous works devised for broadcast or webcast contexts, including the Danish group Superflex's internet TV station *tenantspin*, (developed in collaboration with residents of a Liverpool high-rise housing estate in 1999), the film of *The Battle of Orgreave* (2001) directed by Mike Figgis, which documents a reenactment organised by Jeremy Deller, and Lincoln Tobier's *Radio L*

Above: Apichatpong Weerasethakul,
Haunted Houses (Thai Version) 2001,
60 minutes, digital, 4.3, stereo, colour.
Scripted from two episodes of the
TV series Tong Prakaisad, Channel 5,
Bangkok.
Courtesy of the artist.

Above: Apichatpong Weerasethakul,
Haunted Houses (Thai Version) 2001,
60 minutes, digital, 4.3, stereo, colour.
Scripted from two episodes of the
TV series Tong Prakaisad, Channel 5,
Bangkok.
Courtesy of the artist.

Above and Next pages: Artur Żmijewski, *Repetition*, 2005. Installation, single channel video, 39.17 min., color, sound Ed. of 3 + 1 AP + 1 EP Courtesy the artist & Galerie Peter Kilchmann, Zurich.

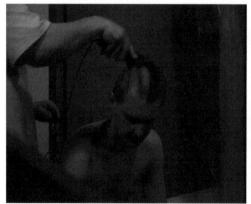 

d'A (2002), realised with residents of Aubervilliers, outside Paris. However, Bishop's short texts do not claim to develop a comparative analysis of contemporary art and television as participatory forms, or address the continuities and differences between modes of mediated performance commonly found in contemporary art and television.

In this chapter, I examine changing modes and economies of non-professional performance in commercial and public television, and argue that histories of television are important in understanding modes of mediated performance that are now commonplace in contemporary art. I begin with a discussion of US educational television during the 1950s, focusing on programmes that use role-play by non-professionals to model and teach civic attributes. I turn to entertainment shows during the same period, produced by commercial and public service broadcasters in the US and UK, which were organised around personal disclosures of hardship and suffering. Sometimes dismissed as a form of 'misery TV', these shows typically required participants to compete for prizes, with the winner determined by the studio audience. I also address how political, regulatory and technological developments during the 1960s and 70s shaped the emergence of video art and activist practices, resulting in new modes and contexts of non-professional performance, and examine the proliferation of reality TV genres from the late 1980s onward. Through my analysis of these examples, I demonstrate that television has frequently functioned as a site in which non-professional performers have served as 'authentic' metonymic fragments of the social body, in the roles of citizens, deserving poor, community members or litigants.

Informed by these histories, I consider several contemporary artworks in which non-professional performers appear as themselves and also in other guises; as residents, villagers, experimental subjects, acting students and consumers. I am not presenting these as examples of 'delegated performance'. Rather, I am interested in the more general use of non-professionals, as a means of signifying a fragment of the social body. Emblematic of the 'social turn' theorised by Bishop, my first two examples are Pierre Huyghe's collaborative television station *Mobile TV* (1995–97), realised in several French cities, and the *tenantspin* web TV project produced by Superflex. I then turn to four video installations realised since the early 2000s, with non-professionals as performers, including Apichatpong Weerasethakul's *Haunted Houses* (Thai Version) (2001), featuring the residents of a Thai village as the characters of a television soap opera, Artur Żmijewski's *Repetition* (2005), a re-enactment of the controversial 'Stanford prison experiment' conducted by social psychologist Philip Zimbardo in 1971, and Gillian Wearing's video installation *Bully* (2010), produced in conjunction with a feature-length documentary (*Self Made*) in which non-professional performers are trained as method actors. My final example, *This Unfortunate Thing Between Us* (2011) was realised by Phil Collins as a performance for German television and theatre, and invites television viewers to purchase and enact a series of 'experiences'. But it also exists as a video installation, in various configurations, furnished to suggest a quasi-domestic viewing situation.

When encountered as artworks in gallery contexts, these four video installations do not demand very particular physical and social interactions—in the manner of some

Above: Gillian Wearing, *Self Made*,
2010. Colour film with sound, 84 min.
© the artist, courtesy Maureen Paley,
London.

'participatory' artworks. Importantly, however, the status of the performers as non-professionals (and hence as a possible stand in for the social body) is generally made explicit, either through the content of the work, or through the provision of contextualising material. Through my discussion of these four installations,[20] I explore how the mediated performances of non-professionals encountered in the gallery might differ from the modes of performance that have become commonplace in television.

Citizens and Sufferers: From Civic Education to 'Misery TV'

In *The Citizen Machine*, a study of 'governing by television in 1950s America', Anna McCarthy considers the importance of what she terms 'wooden acting' in a little-known public affairs television series called *Soap Box*, broadcast live on the St. Louis station KETC in 1955. She focuses on an episode of the show, sponsored by the city's Parent-Teacher Association and devised as a response to the impending desegregation of state elementary schools, which featured role-playing scenarios with parents and teachers taking on the roles of obvious 'character types', in order to explore 'community concerns about integrated classrooms'.[21] Noting that the show was conceived and presented not as 'rote entertainment nor the passive reception of a civics lesson', but rather as a 'form of active democratic involvement',[22] McCarthy situates it in relation to a much larger array of programming practices, often supported by philanthropic foundations as a means of involving citizens in practices of self-governance. She notes that the use of prepared role-play instead of unscripted discussion might appear to signal a fear of conflict concerning the issue of racial integration, but points out that the strategy of 'hypothetical conversation' was actually widely used in the postwar era, by 'social scientists, philanthropists and opinion researchers, as well as grassroots reformers and activists', whose aim was to support the workings of democracy.[23]

Crucially, *Soap Box* also included other elements, such as expert advice and group discussion, meaning that those engaged in the role play scenarios did not simply perform themselves, but rather played a dual role, both as stock characters and as 'themselves'. As McCarthy's analysis makes clear, the awkward mannerisms of the participant ensured that they would not be mistaken for professional actors and so their real task was not to convince in the roles of blustery father or patient teacher, but rather to effectively model the behaviour of *citizens*. Public affairs programmes such as *Soap Box*, however, occupied a relatively marginal position within the TV schedules and there were many other roles assigned to the non-professional performer in US television during the 1950s. In a different context, for example, McCarthy has discussed the use of candid camera techniques in short films made by Allen Funt for the 1950s arts programme *Omnibus*, which implicitly encouraged more responsible forms of citizenship through observation of everyday behaviour.[24] She points out that Funt's use of documentary was also of particular interest to social psychologists such as Stanley Milgram and Philip Zimbardo, and she notes that Zimbardo actually worked with Funt on the production of several classroom films.

By this point, audience participation and personal disclosure were already commonplace within commercial broadcasting, as evidenced by several shows in which contestants competed for sponsored prizes by making their private difficulties public. Amber Watts has analysed a number of shows featuring 'individuals disclosing real-life troubles on-air in the hope of receiving some reward in return',[25] including *Queen for a Day*, which first appeared on radio in 1945 and then on daytime television, from 1956 until 1964. In addition, she notes that *Strike it Rich* (1947–58) and *High Finance* (1956–57), both broadcast in primetime, and the daytime show *The Big Payoff* (1951–59), all combined disclosure with quiz or game elements. Recordings of *Queen for a Day*, which now circulate on YouTube, suggest that it was characterised by a relatively upbeat tone, staged in a studio furnished to resemble a very brightly lit ballroom. The host, contestants and audience members were smartly dressed and the women's stories were punctuated by sponsorship messages, sometimes presented in the form of helpful advice, such as a sequence explaining how to make coffee, relayed via quasi-dramatic scenarios set in an idealised domestic world.

Despite this cheery tone, Watts notes that the women chosen to compete for the 'crown' were often in genuine need of assistance, and many had experienced sudden hardship as a result of bad luck, such as loss of job or an accident or death in the family. At the end of the show, the audience would vote with applause-o-meter for the most deserving contestant to be granted her request, along with thousands of dollars worth of other consumer goods. So in order to secure a reward for their suffering the contestants needed to appear *deserving*, and in addition the solution to their problems had to be found in consumer goods. Watts emphasises that even though the TV show coincided with a postwar era of prosperity, many viewers would have had memories of deprivation, and so were susceptible to anxieties concerning security and stability.[26] Through the contestant's narratives of hardship, luxury goods could be presented as a source of security in case of future need, such as the washing machine one woman requested in order to take in laundry while her husband was out of work.[27]

There is a tendency to think of these so-called 'misery' shows as a distinctively American phenomenon, but ordinary people also told stories of suffering on the BBC show *Is This Your Problem?* (1955–57), analysed by Su Holmes. This programme was launched in the same month that the public service monopoly ended with the arrival of ITV, and it seems to have developed within the context of a renegotiation of the relationship between BBC and its broadcaster, involving a redrawing of the boundaries between public and private spheres. As is often the case with live broadcasts from this era, no recordings survive, but Holmes's analysis draws upon production notes, scripts, reviews, correspondence and a trailer inviting BBC viewers to write in with their problems.[28] The trailer features an aerial shot of a city (presumably London) that dissolves to images of roads and streets, single houses, and finally a curtained window with a light behind it, while (in voiceover) a woman asks if there might be hidden problems—that television might resolve in some way. Holmes also emphasises that this period was marked both by awareness of an increasingly privatised society and by the full establishment of the Welfare State, which 'effectively legalized state intervention

Above: Gillian Wearing, *Bully*, 2010
Colour video for projection with sound,
7 min 55 sec. © the artist, courtesy
Maureen Paley, London.

Above: Phil Collins, *This Unfortunate Thing Between Us*, 2011. Still from a live TV broadcast, 60 min. Sharon Smith and Susanne Sachsse. Courtesy Shady Lane Productions, Berlin.

into family life'.[29] Instead of offering consumer goods as a solution to viewers' problems, *Is This Your Problem?* offered the advice of a (male) expert panel which included a doctor, a university vice chancellor, and a representative of the clergy.[30] The situation of the person seeking help would generally be introduced by the female presenter, in friendly terms, as a contrast to the supposedly 'objective' advice offered by the panel.

Unlike *Queen for a Day, Is This Your Problem?* did not include a studio audience and, instead of a ballroom, the set resembled the pseudo-domestic environments often found in talk shows.[31] Nonetheless, the show was regarded by some viewers as invasive and inappropriate for British television. Holmes describes one edition, featuring an 'unmarried mother' who had asked for her identity to be disguised. This resulted in a 'titillating aesthetic framework, potentially inciting the viewer's curiosity when its intention was actually to block their gaze',[32] prompting some viewers to criticise the programme as sensational. *Is This Your Problem?* clearly struggled to find a televisual means to actually represent those it proposed to help, signalling a fundamental resistance to its goal of making 'hidden' problems visible. Yet its very existence, albeit within a different broadcasting context, during the same period as *Soap Box* and *Queen for a Day* indicates that even in the mid-1950s a wide range of roles were envisaged for, and assigned to, non-professionals appearing in front of the camera. Holmes's analysis also indicates that these roles served the needs of broadcasters, particularly during period of institutional, political or economic or change, when the very notion of 'public service' was being redefined.

Political, Technological and Institutional Change: New Roles for Non-professionals

By the early 1960s, the civic projects theorised by McCarthy had declined, partly as a consequence of regulatory changes enabling commercial programming to be considered a public service.[33] This was the period of the often-cited speech by Newton Minow likening television in the US to a 'vast wasteland' and castigating the failure of the broadcast networks to act in the public interest.[34] The decade was marked by changes in broadcasting and communications policy, eventually leading to the establishment of PBS, and also to new requirements for locally-originated programming on Community Antennae cable television (CATV). In a persuasive analysis of the these political shifts, Thomas Streeter notes the emergence of an 'odd alliance' established in support of cable technology, including '1960s media activists, traditional liberal groups, industry lobbyists and Republican technocrats'.[35] Streeter also identifies a utopian belief in the ostensibly 'new' technology of cable, which was viewed by some as a means of defusing social unrest. As evidence of this, he cites the report of the President's Task Force on Communications Policy, published in 1969, which 'vaguely but enthusiastically suggested that cable television, by allowing minorities and disaffected groups an outlet to express themselves and to communicate with the nation, might reduce their feelings of alienation and thus help solve the "problem" of the social unrest [...] sweeping American society in 1968, particularly the unrest in black ghettoes'.[36]

If cable television was promoted as a potentially more inclusive distribution technology, then video was also emerging during this period as a focus of utopian aspiration amongst artists and activists, in part because it was associated with qualities of immediacy and liveness. According to John Caldwell, 'video artists and electronic politicos alike embraced the liveness myth as a key to radical video production', with many claiming that the 'real-time' experience of video could, by changing habitual ways of seeing, 'alter both personal experience and social practice'.[37] Aspects of this thinking persist even today, in accounts of seminal video installations such as Frank Gillette and Ira Schneider's *Wipe Cycle* (1969). This work consisted of a bank of nine monitors and a closed-circuit video camera recording live images of viewers leaving an escalator, and approaching the gallery entrance. Following a time-delay these images appeared on the monitors, intercut with pre-recorded segments that were intended to evoke memories or associations with television. For David Joselit, *Wipe Cycle* functions as a successful attempt 'to represent and to pluralize the monolithic "information" of network TV through a spectator's unexpected encounter with her or his own act of viewing'.[38] In a contribution to the catalogue for the *Changing Channels* exhibition in 2010, Joselit suggests that disparate image streams merge in *Wipe Cycle* so that the visitor is imaginatively confronted with their own image as a television viewer, He also argues that 'closed-circuit works of video art are structurally identical to cable access tv', noting that although *Wipe Cycle* and other closed-circuit video installations 'were intended to introduce circuits of video feedback within the controlled environment of the gallery, they also served as a blueprint for guerrilla television's response to the centralization of commercial television through the production of politically engaged documentaries on cable, or what Gillette describes as a symbiotic feedback between receiving and broadcasting'.[39]

Throughout the 1970s, numerous activist groups, including Videofreex, Raindance Corporation and Top Value Television (TVTV), embraced technologies of video and cable television, sometimes with the aim of circumventing network distribution. Deirdre Boyle has chronicled the rise and fall of several media activist groups during this era, differentiating between those who (like TVTV) aimed to 'reform' television from within, and more community-oriented media producers such as Broadside TV.[40] Founded by Ted Carpenter, and based in Johnson City, Tennessee, Broadside was supplying up to six hours per week of locally-produced programming to cable providers by the early 1970s, so that

Next page: Phil Collins, *This Unfortunate Thing Between Us*, 2011. Performance in two parts broadcast live on German public television. 15 & 16 September 2011, Hebbel am Ufer, Berlin/ZDFkultur. Production still. Photo: Ivana Kličković. Courtesy Shady Lane Productions, Berlin.

they could fulfil the regulatory requirements of the Federal Communications Commission (FCC). Broadside TV tapes frequently included documentary coverage of local cultural activities, as well as an interview-based oral history series, often prominently featuring local residents communicating their cultural and historical knowledge. Carpenter's approach was informed both by the Challenge for Change programme which the National Film Board of Canada developed in the late 1960s, and by the regional philosophy of the Highlander Center, established in Appalachia in the 1930s as 'an out-growth of the folk-school movement',[41] but his emphasis on the visible participation of non-professionals also recalls the civic televisual projects theorised by McCarthy.

In Broadside TV tapes, local orientation was manifest through the participation of local presenters and performers, who appeared both as themselves and as the representatives of a specific (local) demographic. Boyle also notes that Carpenter evolved a range of strategies to build and maintain the trust of those appearing on screen. He would gather material produced within related social contexts, show prospective interviewees this material, encouraging them to respond on camera, and record them unobtrusively by using a monitor rather than looking through a viewfinder.[42] The rapid playback enabled by video was also clearly crucial to the development of trust in this production process, as interviewees could easily and quickly review the recordings and request changes or moderate their own approach if needed. Ultimately, the revolution in production and distribution advocated by the guerrilla television groups of the 1970s did not unfold as hoped, partly as a consequence of regulatory changes.[43] Yet videotapes made by and featuring non-professionals had become a staple of commercial television by the late 1980s in the form of shows such as *America's Funniest Home Videos* (1989–), described by Deirdre Boyle as 'a perversion of guerrilla television'.[44] MTV's *The Real World*, structured around the daily experiences of a group of 'housemates' (including several aspiring singers, actors or models) was also launched in 1992 and it included a diary-like section in which participants spoke directly to the camera about their experiences, paralleling the 'confessional' tone that characterised the new generation of daytime television talk shows emerging in the 1990s, including *Ricki Lake* (1993–2004) and *Jerry Springer* (1991–).

Laura Grindstaff has argued that these confessional talk shows 'presaged the reality-programming trend of the next century by relying on "real" people as talent and incorporating emergent notions of audience interactivity via live studio audiences, phone-in response lines, and web-based fan sites'.[45] These shows tended to be characterised by 'outrageous' guests, unruly audiences and sensational discussion topics, sharply contrasting with what Grindstaff describes as 'the "nice" days of *Donahue*, in which well-heeled middle-class guests debated whether families should adopt black children'.[46] It has been argued that television and radio talk shows potentially provide a forum for the articulation of forms of social experience that occupy a marginal position within, or are entirely absent from, the public sphere.[47] But such a reading is difficult to reconcile with Grindstaff's analysis of the confessional daytime genre, in a study tellingly entitled *The Money Shot*, which is informed by direct experience of working behind the scenes.

Like the 'misery TV' shows of the 1950s, confessional talk shows often feature stories of personal hardship. Importantly, however, participants are not encouraged to present themselves as deserving of support, in order to win the approval of the studio audience and secure a sponsored prize. Instead, other modes of behaviour are likely to be cultivated by the producers of these shows. Informed by the research of sociologist Arlie Hochschild in relation to the 'emotional labour'[48] expended by workers in service industries, as well as her own direct experience of working on these types of productions, Grindstaff highlights various strategies used to manage the forms of self-expression around which talk shows are structured. She notes that, through their own performance of emotional labour, workers were routinely required to manage the responses of the talk show guests, ensuring that strong emotions would be visible on screen at the appropriate moment.[49]

The work of both Grindstaff and Hochschild has also informed David Hesmondhalgh and Sarah Baker's study of young television researchers involved in the production of a British talent-based reality show (broadcast in 2007) featuring a mix of amateur and semi-professional performers.[50] Workers on this talent show were guided in their interactions with performers, and 'instructed by the series producer to elicit the strongest possible versions of the emotions that the contestant is feeling', making sure that these emotions would be displayed not just on stage but also 'in the contributor's walk on to the stage (trepidation, nervousness, excitement) and the post-performance chat in the green room (joy, disappointment, frustration, anger)'.[51] As this description makes clear, the contestants are expected to comport themselves as aspiring, professional 'talent', as well as displaying the emotional responses that signify their ordinariness.

It is possible, however, that at least some talent show performers can draw either upon formal training or prior experience of appearing in front of a live audience: resources not available to most of the 'ordinary people' appearing on confessional talk shows. Bishop's analysis of delegated performance identifies 'MTV and reality shows such as *Pop Idol*'[52] as emblematic of the dominant modes of mediatic representation contested by 'delegated performance'. But like MTV music videos, reality TV productions such as *The Real World* and *Pop Idol* generally feature actual or aspiring professional performers. Consequently I would argue that the confessional talk show is a much closer analogue to the 'constructed situations' that Bishop describes in contemporary art, because they routinely require non-professionals to signify their authenticity by performing both as themselves *and* as representatives of marginalised social groups.

Some theorists of reality television have identified very specific linkages between performance and changing technologies of governmentality. McCarthy, for example, links the rise of reality-based programming in the US to a reconfiguration of the relation between the 'mass' and the individual. She notes that the conception of the 'abstract individual' that often underpinned the civic projects of the Cold War era has now given way to 'singularizing personifications that stand both for political constituencies (moms, soccer and hockey; Joes, six-pack and plumber) and consumer segments'[53] so that the concept of *lifestyle* becomes central to practices of citizenship. But rather than emphasising a radical break with the older

Above: Phil Collins, *This Unfortunate Thing Between Us*, 2011. Performance in two parts broadcast live on German public television. 15 & 16 September 2011, Hebbel am Ufer, Berlin/ZDFkultur. Production still.
Photo: Ivana Kličković. Courtesy Shady Lane Productions, Berlin.

model of the 'self-governing' subject, articulated in the civic projects of the 1950s, McCarthy finds some evidence of continuity:

> Although reality TV's voyeuristic promise of civic therapy is easy to dismiss as so much gimmickry, there are nevertheless some uneasy overlaps between its visions of self-help and those of the social reformers who cast 'ordinary people' to act out therapeutic race relations in the civic programmes [of the 1950s].[54]

She is especially critical of reality shows that advocate personal transformation in place of political or economic critique, citing *Judge Judy* (1996–) as a prominent outlet for moralism in television.[55] But before turning to *Judge Judy*, and to the specific roles assigned to those who perform themselves as 'litigants' in her television courtroom, it is worth considering how the history of reality TV, and its precursors, might relate to the availability of actual social supports.

Amber Watts makes the point that *Queen for a Day* went off the air in 1964—a year that witnessed the launch of the 'Great Society' programmes (which included Medicare), increased welfare benefits and also the passing of the Civil Rights Act through congress. She argues that the return of misery-style reality television four decades later coincided with cuts to Medicare and welfare introduced under the George W. Bush administration in 2004. Watts is specifically referring here to shows such as Miracle Workers (2006), *Supernanny* (2005–2011) and *Extreme Makeover: Home Edition* (2004–) that seek to 'transform real Americans in real need—be it of medical, economic, psychological, or behavioural support— into healthy, attractive, and financially stable citizens'.[56]

These shows generally include some form of expert advice or service, sometimes coupled with provision of consumer goods. As with the early audience participation shows, the message is aimed at the audience as well as the contestants and Watts emphasises that, by 'focusing on the perils of financial and material instability', these forms of reality TV encourage viewers to be self-sufficient, while at the same time 'diverting potential sympathy into consumerist fantasy'.[57]

Laurie Ouellette and James Hay also note parallels between *Queen for a Day* and newer forms of 'charity TV' in the US, but they argue that 'today's charitable interventions are much more extravagant and prolific, appearing on network and cable channels during daytime and primetime hours'.[58] They also make the point that these interventions are now likely to be more specialised, often taking place outside the TV studio, involving professional helpers and experts who go 'on location'. More importantly, they emphasise that 'TV's foray into the helping culture is now more intensely aligned with the rationalities of deregulation and welfare reform'.[59] Elsewhere, Ouellette has examined the neo-liberal agenda running through reality-style programming from *Survivor* and *Big Brother* to courtroom shows such as *Judge Judy*, which appeared on US television in 1996, in advance of the specific welfare cutbacks highlighted by Watts.[60] While TV shows with simulated courtroom settings have been a feature of US television since the 1950s, *Judge Judy* was the first to exploit 'real cases and real people', initially featuring actual litigants who were recruited in small-claims courts and offered travel expenses and court fees to present their cases on television. As Ouellette points out, (Judge) Judy Sheindlin came to prominence during the 1990s for her 'tough love' rhetoric[61] and actually presents her show as a public service. Similar claims are, Ouellette notes, made by another TV judge, who frames the courtroom-based reality genre as an *antidote* to the excesses of television soap opera:

> America's been looking at soap operas for going on 50 some years, and they legitimize the most back-stabbing, low-down, slimeball behavior. That's gotten to be acceptable behavior [...] We find ourselves confronted with a lot of soap-opera behavior in our courtrooms.[62]

It seems highly probable, however, that the litigants in *Judge Judy*, like the guests on many daytime talk shows, are chosen and coached by producers precisely so that they will display 'back-stabbing, low-down, slimeball behaviour'.

In Sheindlin's courtroom, excessive displays of emotion are solicited simply so that they can be publicly punished, as the litigants are forbidden to speak or move freely and must respond only when addressed. Litigants are also subjected to comments upon their appearance, deportment, character and personal history, generally presented without context or evidence. Much of the show's dramatic impact, as suggested by the content of clips circulating on YouTube, derives from these types of (carefully managed) confrontations, in which a litigant fails to adhere to these 'courtroom' rules, attempts to defend themselves and is berated into submission by Sheindlin. So while *Judge Judy* ostensibly demands obedience and passivity, it also derives much of its entertainment value from displays of unruliness, which are also being 'judged'. The most valuable performers, and the most 'authentic' (in terms of their relation to the larger social body) are those who appear to struggle with the role of litigant, and the disciplinary constraints of the TV courtroom.

Mediated Performances and Social Bodies in Contemporary Art

If the 1990s witnessed the pervasive presence of non-professionals as performers in television, across an array of new and established genres, then the same decade was marked by a growing emphasis on the social aspects of media production and consumption, manifest in the activities of artists, curators and institutions.[63] Galleries and museums, in addition to hosting and housing artist-designed environments for viewing and relaxing, facilitated the establishment of temporary sites and stations of television production, such as Pierre Huyghe's *Mobile TV*. First realised in 1995 as part of the exhibition *Aperto* at the Nouveau Musée/Institut d'art Contemporain de Villeurbanne,[64] this project involved the creation of a local television channel, which transmitted interviews (including several with members of local associations), documentation of artworks and 'short actions' by Huyghe and other artists. *Mobile TV* was subsequently realised in several other contexts, including presentations at Le Magasin, Grenoble and Le Consortium, Dijon, with the involvement of additional collaborators, exemplifying the 'interest in collectivity, collaboration and direct engagement with specific social constituencies' noted by Bishop.[65]

As it involved the extension of the museum's programming activities beyond the physical space of the gallery, and into the realm of local broadcasting, Huyghe's project seems somewhat indebted to the techno utopian discourses associated with cable television and video in the 1970s, albeit in a muted form. The Dijon version incorporated a six-programme contribution by the artist Olivier Bardin, entitled *Une télé pour la télé (A Television for Television)* (1996), which actually emphasised television's *lack* of interactivity. Reflecting upon this work in a 2009 interview with Huyghe and Hans Ulrich Obrist, Bardin notes that for each of the six programmes, he 'invited young people into the studio individually, asking them to create a live half-hour broadcast which would take account of […] the real-time transmission to viewers who could see us, but with whom interaction was, by definition, impossible'.[66] Yet even if this work emphasised the limits of television as social connector, an emphasis on televisual 'real time' persists, with Bardin claiming that time is 'the necessary condition to understand the full complexity of the images of others'. This is because, he argues, 'if we initially perceive individuals as objects, when they first declare themselves on show, we then need time to recognise them as subjects'.[67]

However, it is important to note that *Mobile TV* was *not* framed through reference to histories of video activism, even if Bardin's approach was partly premised upon the ontological specificity of televisual 'real time'. In contrast, the Danish artists group Superflex strongly emphasised the connective potential of internet TV, promoting their project 'Superchannel' (established in 1999) as 'a network of local studios used by people and communities as a discussion forum, presentation medium and a physical gathering place'.[68] In 2000 Superflex were commissioned to work with a group of residents, many of them older people, living in a high-rise housing estate in Liverpool, which was undergoing a redevelopment process.[69] This initiative was supported by the Foundation for Art & Creative Technology (FACT) and subsequently launched under the new name *tenantspin*, resulting in the production of 180 'live one-hour webcasts in 2001–2002', exploring issues such as 'rent increases, resident participation and technology, landlords, demolition, the built environment, high rise living, regeneration and beans on toast'.[70]

The collaboration between Superflex and the *tenantspin* group generated considerable interest in national media and artworld contexts; resulting in a BBC-commissioned radio programme called 'SuperBlock' which was transmitted nationally on Radio 3. The group also contributed to exhibitions such as *Open Source Art Hack* (New Museum of Contemporary Art, New York) and *Demo Station no 4* (2003) by Rirkrit Tiravanija at Ikon Gallery in Birmingham,[71] and it has continued to function as an important model for theorists and practitioners engaging with community television.[72] Yet even though this project is clearly informed by the history of activist community media, the participants and funders were not necessarily motivated by radical social or political critique. It is worth noting that, although originally scheduled for refurbishment, the building where *tenantspin* originated was demolished instead, prompting Superchannel programme manager Alan Dunn to note in 2004 that *tenantspin* 'was never going to be powerful enough to reverse or challenge a budgetary decision'.[73] By 2006, Superflex's involvement had come to an end, but *tenantspin* continues to exist as a community media organisation co-managed by FACT and Arena Housing, a 'social landlord' responsible for 14,000 properties across the North West of England. In its revised form, *tenantspin* encompasses several strands, including the commissioning of artists to work in a collaborative context, and the provision of community training opportunities such as blogging, web casting, public speaking and filmmaking. Group members also continue to produce issue-based webcasts, framed by FACT organisers as 'the heart of tenantspin and its original ambition to act as a public sphere, a place to create communal moments around an idea or subject'.[74]

Yet as a prominent exemplar of community media production, *tenantspin* is also implicated in governmental discourses of social and civic reform. Although it was formed in the wake of an already-agreed change in housing provision and management, which had involved consultation with local residents, it functioned as a model of 'civil renewal'. This point is clearly made by arts policy researcher Emily Keaney, who praises *tenantspin* as a communication of civic pride.[75] Keaney also emphasises that participation in arts projects can be helpful in the development of vocational skills, which can in turn make individuals more 'employable' or encourage them to become active in volunteering. In this account, *tenantspin* is valued for its potential to cultivate civic responsibility and establish a new, and implicitly client-based, relationship between the state and its public. So, although there are significant differences between the institutional and political contexts of British public art in the early 2000s and US educational television in the 1950s, the history of *tenantspin* suggests that non-professional television performers and producers still play an important role within governmental processes of civic education.

As already noted, *Mobile TV* and *tenantspin* were devised to be encountered, by some constituencies at least, outside the physical space of the gallery as local television transmissions or webcasts. Now, however, I turn to four video installations that are generally exhibited in gallery settings, even if one (*This Unfortunate Thing Between Us*, by Phil Collins) originated as a televised theatre performance. All four installation works also share an emphasis on the scripting of performance, with the artist typically taking on the role of director and, in some instances, appearing on screen as the orchestrator of the 'constructed situation' (Żmijewski) or in the more conventional role of film director (Wearing). My first example, *Haunted Houses* (Thai Version) (2001) is the work of the Thai artist and filmmaker, Apichatpong Weerasethakul, who maintains a double practice, moving between feature films and gallery installations. Apichatpong often works with the same predominantly non-professional actors on features and installations, frequently using rural areas in the Khon Kaen Province of Thailand as locations. *Haunted Houses* (Thai Version), a single channel video work commissioned for the seventh international Istanbul Biennial, was also shot in this rural area, using ten private homes as 'sets', with the residents as actors.[76] The hour-long script is derived from two episodes of a very popular TV soap series entitled *Tong Prakaisad*, broadcast by Royal Thai Army Television, Channel 5, Bangkok, and as the title perhaps suggests, *Haunted Houses* explores the notion that the homes of these residents are somehow 'haunted' by the soap opera characters.

In structuring this work, Apichatpong uses a strategy reminiscent of the surrealist 'exquisite corpse', casting multiple performers in the same role, an approach similar to that employed in his earlier feature *Mysterious Object at Noon* (2000). Playing characters such as 'The General', 'the Lady' and 'Miss Dara', the village residents perform a sequence of melodramatic scenarios, involving familiar soap opera themes of love, betrayal, loss and jealousy. The same fragments of the script, and the same awkwardly performed gestures, seem to recur as the action shifts from one home to the next. There is an obvious disjunction between the lavish lifestyles evoked by the soap opera dialogue and the domestic environments inhabited by the village residents. For example, scenes referring to a car are enacted in relation to substitute objects. So, for example, a moped is replaced by a trailer filled with wood) in one scene, prompting the laughter of actors and those observing the performances. Yet *Haunted Houses* does not offer a critique of television soap opera or the modes of consumption with which it is conventionally associated. Instead it develops a more open-ended exploration of village life, utilising the framework of the soap, incorporating glimpses of the countryside beyond the houses, while the sound of the TV show can be heard in the background. These non-professional performers are certainly playing themselves, and also standing in for a specific, rural, demographic, but they are also adhering to a script and they interact with each other almost entirely through the dialogue and gestures of characters in *Tong Prakaisad*. In this way they seem to perform themselves most vividly as avid consumers of television, symbolically distancing this work from *tenantspin*, in which high-rise residents are cast in the role of internet TV producers.

My next example, Artur Żmijewski's *Repetition* (2005), is a single-screen recording of a re-enactment of the Stanford prison experiment, framed in press material (published for the Venice Biennale) as a logical and 'natural' extension of Żmijewski's interest in playing the role of 'laboratory scientist, arranging quasi-therapeutic situations'.[77] While Apichatpong's performers work with scripted dialogue and gestures, the participants in *Repetition* are presented with a 'constructed situation' that is not fully scripted, but rather determined by a set of rules, which replicate those employed in an infamous social-psychological experiment. Philip Zimbardo's original study was intended to support strategies for prison reform, and involved a group of volunteers, filmed by multiple cameras, who played the roles of 'inmates' and 'guards' in an environment that simulated the architecture of a prison. Due to run for two weeks, the experiment was stopped after six days because participants started to exhibit pathologically sadomasochistic behaviour. Interestingly, while Zimbardo's research has been discredited within most academic contexts, McCarthy notes that he has established a new area of expertise, as 'a commentator on, and even a consultant to, [...] reality TV programs'.[78]

Shot over seven days, but with a running time of just under 40 minutes, *Repetition* is heavily edited to produce a sense of narrative tension and imply progression towards a dramatic climax. Perhaps more importantly, it prominently features Żmijewski on screen, in several sequences where he seems both ready and willing to interfere with the rules of his experiment. One of the first shots features a 'prisoner' (later identified as number 433) apparently screaming as he clutches the bars of his cell, followed by onscreen text detailing the fact that the original experiment had to be halted early. So from the outset, it seems apparent that at least one participant in Żmijewski's reenactment has experienced some sort of crisis. *Repetition* is also replete with references to the quasi-scientific aesthetic of *Big Brother*, shot with a mix of hand-held and fixed cameras suggesting surveillance technology with frequent onscreen textual references to the passage of time. It also features edited interviews with prospective participants conducted in advance of the experiment, concerning their education, previous occupations and motivation, analogous to those used in a range of reality genres. While most participants are attracted solely by the payment, the man who will later be assigned number 433 claims to be motivated by 'curiosity', clearly signalling his difference from the group.

As the action unfolds, *Repetition* employs standard reality TV-style strategies of characterisation and narrativisation; on 'Day 3' prisoners are shown rehearsing the rules in response to prompts from the guards, but by Day 4, prisoner 433 is already refusing to answer and this precipitates a slow but steady collapse in the authority of the guards. Instead of standing back to observe these events, Żmijewski repeatedly intervenes and alters the experimental conditions, discharging some of the guards and making another the 'warden', responsible for management and implementation of 'full corporal discipline'. On Day 5 Żmijewski reappears and demands that the warden must ensure that prisoners' heads are shaved, prompting further resistance and on 'Day 7' the prisoners are told that they can no longer use the toilets, prompting a mass withdrawal and a sudden, though not unexpected, end to the experiment. The closing sequence cuts between the final day and two informal interviews conducted by Żmijewski one month later. The first features Pawel Moczydlowski, listed as 'consultant to the experiment, former head of prisons in Poland', who comments that 'a warden who identifies with the role of the guard at a certain point becomes a beast'. The second interview is with the participant who was (re)cast as the prison warden, and he pointedly reminds the artist of his responsibility for the outcome of the project. Through these strategies, Żmijewski seems to foreground his own questionable motivations as producer of the work, thus making explicit his own desire to achieve a sensational outcome, equal to the infamy of Zimbardo's experiment. In a sense, by drawing attention to his own role as artist Żmijewski acknowledges the impossibility of repeating the experiment. But on a more basic level, the strategies used in the casting, shooting and editing of his work are difficult to differentiate from those employed in reality TV genres, apart from one important detail. The man cast as 'prisoner no. 433' delivers a much less convincing performance of 'himself' than many of the unruly 'real life' litigants who enter the courtroom of *Judge Judy*.

To an even greater extent than *Repetition*, Gillian Wearing's single screen installation *Bully* (2010), which was produced in parallel with her documentary feature *Self Made* (2010), draws upon the formal strategies found in reality TV, particularly the 'makeover' genre.

Self Made records a training process in method acting, undertaken by seven participants (two women and five men) recruited in response to an advertisement; 'Would you like to be in a film? You can play yourself or a fictional character. Call Gillian'. It is framed as an exploration of the relationship between personal experience and professional skill in the Stanislavski 'Method' acting tradition, widely associated with the Actor's Studio. Much of the training takes place in a grim, windowless room where the participants are guided by Sam Rumbelow, an acting teacher credited as a Creative Consultant, who explains that they will learn to use their history and 'humanity' as actors. Rumbelow is a fascinating figure in his own right, skilfully and sensitively navigating very complex emotional territory as he guides his new students through a series of exercises that become gradually more ambitious, involving props, sound effects and supporting performances by professional actors. But *Self Made* cannot be described as a documentary about method acting as it does not examine the specific use by professional performers of techniques such as improvisation and 'sense memory'. Furthermore, it offers no contextual information about the history of the Method or its difference from other models of training.

Wearing seems interested in, but does not directly address, the fact that the excavation and exploitation of personal histories to trigger an emotional response on cue might overlap or conflict with techniques used in psychotherapy. The latter point is important because a significant number of the participants disclose traumatic events (abandonment, bullying, domestic abuse) in the course of their training and one man even outlines his plans for killing himself, naming a specific date. There are several moments, particularly the exercise in which James, a former victim of bullying, directs actors in a restaging of a traumatic scenes from his past, where the training seems specifically devised to produce a therapeutic effect. These memories of trauma are also played out in *Bully*, an eight-minute work devised for gallery exhibition,[79] which is shot in a different space, again without windows but much larger (and more intimidating) than the main rehearsal room of *Self Made*. James again directs a scenario based upon incidents from his past under Rumbelow's supervision, this time overseeing and 'casting' a much larger number of performers in the roles of bullies, victim and witnesses. As the action unfolds, James both instructs the other participants and slips frequently out of his role as director of the exercise, adopting an accusatory tone toward the bullies and witnesses, and in these moments he plays 'himself' as the authentic victim.

Bully is edited to suggest a single take of the acting exercise, but the structure of *Self Made* is much closer to that of a reality TV makeover show, incorporating carefully-managed revelations of the participants' personal histories and motivations. Wearing also appears in several sequences focused on the making of the short films through which the performers demonstrate their newfound skills. Filmed outside the training environment on location these sequences also emphasise Wearing's technical and creative expertise, through the visible presence of (another) crew and production equipment. Unlike Żmijewski, however, she is rarely depicted interacting with the performers and instead Rumbelow acts as her stand in. So while *Repetition* draws attention to the ethical problems inherent in Żmijewski's restaging of the Stanford prison experiment, *Self Made* seems to sidestep the issues raised by the creation of a constructed situation in which vulnerable individuals mine their memories of trauma, apparently without the support of a therapist. Finally, although the 'training' framework strongly suggests participants will benefit personally or professionally from their involvement in the project, the only participant whose stated occupation actually involves self-display (Jerome, identified as a model) recedes from view shortly after the introductory sequence. Perhaps Jerome simply dropped out of the project, but it is also possible that, as a quasi-professional performer, his involvement was less symbolically valuable than that of the other participants.

My final example *This Unfortunate Thing Between Us* (2011) by Phil Collins, originated as a theatre performance and simultaneous broadcast on the German digital channel ZDFkultur, televised over two nights from the Hebbel am Ufer theatre in Berlin.[80] The work presents its TV and theatre audiences with a question, posed by a woman whose image appears intermittently on a large video screen hanging above the stage, repeatedly asking (in German) 'What is this unfortunate thing between us?'. For those seated in the theatre, this question could be read as a reference to the large cameras positioned on the stage or even to the screen itself, which drew attention away from the physical performance towards its mediated image; and for those viewing on television the question might also signify the physical distance separating them from the audience in the theatre, and from each other. But the 'thing' referenced in this question might also be commodification, since 'TUTBU TV' took the form of a shopping channel with presenters selling individual experiences in place of mass-produced goods.

There were several products on offer, ostensibly tailored to the desires of the German viewing public, available for the bargain price of €9.99 each, with a special discount of €7.99 for the unemployed, pensioners and students. On the first night of the performance, the 'experiences' for sale were demonstrated by actors in the hope of tempting prospective customers. So a 'Stasi-style interrogation' was followed by a 'historical porn scene' set in the Victorian era and, finally, a death-bed scene in a modern hospital, in which the dying person could express 'dissatisfaction and resentment', rather than reconciling with family members. On the second night, these three experiences were again presented on stage, but this time with the three purchasers in the leading roles. In the group interview that concluded the second night all of the customers appeared to express satisfaction but throughout the performance they seemed somewhat dislocated, perhaps overwhelmed by their chosen experiences. Even the young bearded man who found himself costumed as a maid, being eagerly undressed by willing sexual partners in the historical porn scene, seemed slightly removed from the action. Unlike Wearing in *Self Made*, however, Collins does not attempt to delve into their individual motivations as participants and instead their involvement in the project is premised upon the notion that these particular 'experiences' would appeal to most Germans.

This Unfortunate Thing Between Us responds, albeit indirectly, to developments within the European broadcasting landscape, which have prompted concerns over the future of the televisual public sphere amongst media theorists.[81] As already noted, the project involved the temporary transformation of ZDFkultur into a shopping channel, but the identity of this station (a digital service offered by a publicly-funded broadcaster) was already in flux. Originally known as ZDFtheaterkanal, it initially focused on live arts such as dance, opera and cabaret but in May 2011 (just four months before the televising of *This Unfortunate Thing Between Us*) it was rebranded as ZDFkultur, with a much more expansive definition of the arts, including games and pop music.[82] So the project coincided with, and might be said to articulate, a moment of crisis in German digital broadcasting, and in this sense it recalls the stylistic changes theorised by Caldwell in US network TV during the 1980s.[83] The cross-institutional production process also required Collins to negotiate some of the contradictions that arise when notions of publicness historically associated with theatre are transposed to the realm of broadcasting. These contradictions became apparent in the televising of the historic porn scene, which was edited (by a live TV director on duty in the transmission van) to exclude some of the action from below the waist.[84]

The experience of viewing *This Unfortunate Thing Between Us* in the theatre also produced a strong awareness of the hierarchy of viewing positions existing within the auditorium itself. Despite the sometimes obstructive presence of the cameras on stage, most of the audience in the theatre could view the full bodies of the actors as well as the televised version of the scene. But those seated very close to the stage—or indeed participating in the action—did not have this doubled vantage point. This hierarchy situates Collins's work in relation to a much earlier tradition of self-referential moving image production, theorised by Thomas Elsaesser through reference to the 'Rube Film'.[85] The character of the Rube, appearing in films such as Robert Paul's *The Countryman's First Sight of the Animated Pictures* (1901), remade by Edwin S. Porter for Edison as *Uncle Josh at the Moving Picture Show* (1902), is generally an inexperienced viewer who mistakes the onscreen action for reality, disrupts the screening and is sometimes punished by the projectionist. Noting that these films have often been interpreted as didactic parables aimed at rural or immigrant viewers, Elsaesser argues that they instruct audiences not 'by way of [...] negative example, shaming and proscription, but rather, by a more subtle process of internalized self-censorship'. Accordingly, discipline is imposed specifically by allowing audiences to 'enjoy their own superior form of spectatorship, even if that superiority is achieved at the price of self-censorship and self-restraint'.[86]

This internalisation of discipline operates within the context of a much larger 'civilizing' process that cinema 'both supports and exacerbates': a shift from proximity by touch toward a combination of distance and proximity.[87] Another important site of this civilizing process is, of course, the museum, and Elsaesser concludes by noting that video and installation works from the 1960s and 1970s, by artists such as Anthony McCall, Dan Graham, Malcolm Le Grice and Andy Warhol, 'manage to trap spectators in time-delay mirror mazes and have them catch themselves in cognitive loops'. He further suggests that these works enable or involve forms of 'learning' in which spectators take on new roles, as 'users, visitors, witnesses, players and [...] especially as Rubes'.[88] It may seem somewhat perverse to connect *This Unfortunate Thing Between Us* with the Rube film, because Collins actually *does* offer the spectator (viewing on the first night of the show) the opportunity to enter the fantastical world depicted on screen. But it is precisely by entering the stage area that the viewer loses the ability to observe the mediation of their image for a television audience, with the result that the non-professionals joining the cast initially appear to be 'unfortunate' Rubes, who have failed to grasp the full implications of the transaction.

Yet, as Elsaesser's formulation makes clear, the primary role of the Rube is to encourage self-discipline amongst *other* viewers and *This Unfortunate Thing Between Us* seems to embrace and perhaps complicate this disciplinary scenario, by introducing the possibility that those seated in the auditorium might also be Rubes. The customers who joined the actors on stage were indeed genuine television viewers, chosen from a large number who phoned in on the first night of ZDFkultur transmission. But for those seated in the auditorium on the second night—presented with the results of patently unreliable 'research' supposedly revealing the inner desires of Germans—there was no way to verify the non-professional status of these performers. Consequently, any sense of superiority achieved by the theatre audience on the basis of their detachment or self-restraint was steadily and comically eroded, to the point that it became difficult to determine exactly who or what might really be 'unfortunate'.

These disciplinary dynamics operate differently in the installation version of the work, which features recordings of the two broadcasts, shown in separate spaces, sometimes installed in small caravans. Collins has also presented the videos (at Void Gallery in Derry, in 2012–13) as projections in adjoining gallery spaces furnished—with couches, carpeting, standard lamps, and kitsch ornaments in wooden sideboards—to suggest two living rooms decorated during the 1970s or 80s. There was no attempt at Void to precisely replicate the domestic setting of broadcast reception, since the installations did not include TV monitors. Instead, there was an obvious dissonance between the use of video projection and the slightly antiquated furnishing, suggesting a somewhat self-conscious staging of familial domesticity, in which the sexually explicit content of 'TUTBU TV' was clearly out of place. This exhibition strategy (which also involved the restriction of entry to over-18s) underscored the difference between the home and gallery as sites of 'television' viewing, implicitly framing the gallery as a setting in which social norms of TV production and reception could be suspended.

Conclusion: the Social Turn and the Historical Context of Institutional Change

As evidenced by the histories cited in the first half of this chapter, non-professionals have performed themselves on television since at least the 1950s, and have served as a focus of interest for video activists and artists for almost as long. But it may also be that the visible participation of non-professionals becomes especially important when broadcasting and art institutions are required to legitimate or renegotiate their relationship to the public sphere. Within the history of broadcasting, these moments have included the arrival of commercial competition in British television in the mid-1950s, the establishment of PBS in the US in the late 1960s, the expansion of public access in cable television during the 1970s, and the refining of niche-oriented digital television services by European public broadcasters. Meanwhile, in the art context, Bishop's research emphasises the prevalence of non-professional performers in artworks during the 1960s and 70s, long before the 'social turn' of the 1990s. In addition to outlining the continuities apparent in the roles assigned to these performers within the disparate modes of art and television production, my discussion has explored the parallels between game shows, talk shows, reality TV genres and theatres, museums and galleries as sites of 'training' and labour.

It is important to note that film and 'quality' television consumption also incorporate a training dimension, as evidenced by Thomas Elsaesser's analysis of the 'DVD-enabled' feature, which rewards multiple viewings, and 'responds to the conditions of distribution, reception, consumption, cinephilia, connoisseurship, and spectatorship appropriate for the multi-platform film'.[89] Citing a Deleuzian model, in which control takes the place of discipline, Elsaesser states that 'media consumption has become part of the "affective labor" required in modern ("control") societies, in order to properly participate in the self-regulating mechanisms of ideological reproduction, for which retraining and learning are now a lifelong obligation'.[90] His analysis resonates with Steyerl's account of the art museum as a successor to the factory and a privileged setting for the labour of consumption, but it perhaps more clearly emphasises the intersection between participation and training in contemporary culture.

This intersection is apparent in several of the examples of contemporary art practice discussed in this chapter, even if it is sometimes disavowed. While Superflex's *tenantspin* clearly drew upon activist traditions of community media production, it has also been celebrated by policy theorists as a successful example of civic education. Wearing's film *Self Made* and installation *Bully* are both explicitly structured around a process of training, which is ostensibly focused on Method acting but is actually premised upon a quasi-therapeutic process of self-transformation. These works also place considerable emphasis on processes of display and demonstration, with learners often depicted in the role of viewers as well as participants, through the use of reaction shots. Like Wearing, Żmijewski reiterates the reality TV structure of transformation through self-knowledge, but *Repetition* actually addresses the differences between models of discipline and control through the continual reconfiguration of the rules, particularly that of the reluctant 'warden' who uses negotiation to resolve conflict.

Of all the projects discussed in this chapter, the works by Apichatpong Weerasethakul and Phil Collins are the most directly focused on the consumption of television, and both involve non-professional participants who reveal little of themselves, beyond the fact that they are television viewers. Unlike Wearing's trainee Method actors, who must evolve the content of dramatic scenarios from their own histories, or Żmijewski's subjects, whose reactions are ostensibly the focus of the social-psychological experiment, Apichatpong and Collins's performers are provided with scripted characters to inhabit. It could be argued that, to an even greater extent than the other examples, through its original form as a televised performance broadcast from a theatre over two consecutive nights, *This Unfortunate Thing Between Us* strongly emphasises qualities of liveness and immediacy. But in place of the rhetoric of transformation espoused by advocates of video as technology of immediacy and liveness, Collins explores through his interactions with viewers as consumers, the mysterious and yet apparently enduring appeal of televisual self-exploitation.

Chapter Four

European Television Archives, Collective Memories
and Contemporary Art[1]

The spectator must be led to remember, with even a bit of nostalgia, those moments which are preeminently televisual—the explosion of the *Challenger*, the assassination of John F. Kennedy (the footage of which was replayed again and again during the time of the recent twenty-fifth anniversary of the event). What is remembered in these nostalgic returns is not only the catastrophe or crisis itself, but the fact that television was there, allowing us access to moments which always seem more real than all the others.

Mary Ann Doane, 'Information, Crisis, Catastrophe'[2]

Fear that television, the professed medium par excellence for the production of vanishing acts, will itself inevitably disappear might be seen to lead towards an increased obsession with television memory and the nostalgia for television past. Anxieties about television and even television studies, therefore, might be seen to run parallel to present anxieties regarding history and memory in general.

Amy Holdsworth, *Television, Memory and Nostalgia*[3]

Introduction: Artists and Television Archives

In a recent article exploring the archiving of television in the US, Lynn Spigel reflects upon Andy Warhol's practice of taping TV shows during the last decade of his life. She notes that his collection of recordings, which includes shows such as *Father Knows Best* and *Celebrity Sweepstakes*, has been preserved not because of its content but because it was assembled by a 'unique collector'.[4] For Spigel, the somewhat arbitrary nature of 'Andy's Archive' underscores the fact that television's preservation continues to be partly dictated by issues of context, offering an important counterpoint to the 'fantasy of total accumulation'[5] fuelled by the internet and the proliferation of storage technologies. These opposing visions of the archive offer a starting point from which to consider how a younger generation of artists, who have experienced this proliferation during their lifetime, might approach the relationship between television, history and memory.

This chapter focuses primarily on three moving image artworks (all realized since 2009) that engage with European television archives and share a concern with absences, gaps or elisions in collective memory. The three works are *Haukka-Pala (A-Bit-to-Bite)* (2009) by Laura Horelli (born 1976, in Helsinki), *Theta Rhythm*, (2010) by Bojan Fajfrić (born 1976, in Belgrade) and *19:30* (2010–ongoing) by Aleksandra Domanović (born in 1981, Novi Sad).

Above: Stan Douglas, Installation view of *Evening* (1994) at The Renaissance Society at the University of Chicago in 1995. Courtesy the artist and David Zwirner, New York/London.

All works incorporate television material broadcast either before or during the 1980s and sourced many years later from the archives of national broadcasters. *Haukka-Pala* consists entirely of re-edited clips of a children's TV show, presented by Horelli's mother in 1984 and 1986 on the Finnish public television channel TV2. *Theta Rhythm* is structured around the 8th session of the Central Committee of the Communist League of Serbia (September 23 and 24, 1987), which was broadcast live on the state television channel, Radio-Television Belgrade and was attended by Fajfrić's father. *19:30* is much more expansive in terms of the broadcast material and institutional contexts it references, and more loosely linked to the artist's familial experience. The project initially focused on idents (introductory graphic and music sequences) for evening news broadcasts on Jugoslavenska Radiotelevizija over several decades, beginning in 1958, but now includes idents for evening news programmes from television stations based in Bosnia and Herzegovina, Croatia, Kosovo, Macedonia, Montenegro, Serbia, Slovenia and Vojvodina.

These three works are typically exhibited in gallery contexts; *Haukka-Pala* consists solely of a single video work, usually displayed on a 4.3 television monitor (sometimes known as a 'box' monitor), *Theta Rhythm* is a single screen video projection shown either on its own or together with contextualizing texts and research videos, while Domanović's project encompasses video, collaborative performance events and an online archive of broadcast material. Versions of these works have also been shown in film festivals but all three artists seek to operate primarily within the contemporary art economy, offering works for sale via private galleries and sourcing grants and commissions from publicly funded agencies, museums and other art institutions. It is also worth noting that these artists do not live in their countries of origin and are instead currently based in urban centers for contemporary art production and exhibition; Horelli and Domanović in Berlin, and Fajfrić in Amsterdam. All three belong to a generation that experienced varied shifts in the political economy of broadcasting during the 1980s and early 1990s, which subtly (or radically) altered the role and function of television in the public sphere. For both Domanović and Fajfrić, memories of television are bound up with particularly dramatic and violent transformations in the public sphere. This is because changes in the form of broadcasting coincided with the break-up of Former Yugoslavia, and are intrinsically linked to the articulation of its conflicting claims regarding national identity and statehood.

Clearly, however, Domanović, Fajfrić and Horelli are not the first generation of artists to address the relationship between television, history and memory, or the first to employ strategies of re-enactment or reconstruction. Several possible precedents might be cited, perhaps most notably T.R. Uthco and Ant Farm's, *The Eternal Frame* (1975), which explores media images, and also memories, of the assassination of President Kennedy. *The Eternal Frame* begins with an excerpt from the Super-8 footage shot by Abraham Zapruder, a bystander on the parade route who recorded the only film of Kennedy's assassination. Based upon this footage, T.R. Uthco and Ant Farm members staged a re-enactment of the assassination at Dealey Plaza in front of unwitting spectators who are interviewed about their responses. Despite the obviously irreverent casting of Doug Michels as Jackie Kennedy,

Above: Stefanos Tsivopoulos,
Untitled (The Remake) 2007, video still,
HDV transferred to Bluray.
Courtesy: the artist.

Above: Stefanos Tsivopoulos,
Untitled (The Remake) 2007, video still,
HDV transferred to Bluray.
Courtesy: the artist.

Above: Gillian Wearing, *Family History*, 2006. Video for projection, 35 min 32 sec; 16mm film transferred to DVD for monitor, 2 min 52 sec. © the artist, courtesy Maureen Paley, London.

Above: Gillian Wearing , *Family History*, 2006. Video for projection, 35 min 32 sec; 16mm film transferred to DVD for monitor, 2 min 52 sec. © the artist, courtesy Maureen Paley, London.

several bystanders interviewed by the artists react to the simulation as though they were viewing a recording rather than a performance. Others seem more attuned to differences between what they see and what they recall, describing their memories of watching television coverage of the aftermath of the assassination. Perhaps most surprisingly, several bystanders assume that the re-enactment is actually an official form of ceremonial remembrance.[6]

The Eternal Frame also explores the role of mediation in political culture, alluding to intersections between celebrity and contemporary art in sequences featuring the 'Artist-President', a hybrid figure modelled after John F. Kennedy, who extols the significance of the media image.

The Eternal Frame develops a critique of media spectacle that is structured around the televisual mediation, and touristic consumption, of a specific historical event, which had occurred more than a decade before its production. In contrast, *Videograms of a Revolution* (1992) by Harun Farocki and Andrei Ujică, reconstructs a historical narrative of a more recent event—the Romanian revolution of December 1989—and focuses more explicitly on the sphere of news production. This work examines the physical, institutional and symbolic role of television during a process of radical political and cultural change and is constructed solely from material shot by professional crews and amateur videographers during the revolution in December 1989. In the course of an uprising against the Ceaușescu government, demonstrators occupied the television station in Bucharest and broadcast continuously for 120 hours, transmitting statements of revolutionary intent and solidarity, appeals for support and information about the search for Ceaușescu and his family, followed by his capture, a televised trial and execution. As Eva Kernbauer has noted,[7] Farocki and Ujică's film was in part a response to debates surrounding the authenticity of the televised images, especially those of victims and of the execution, and the film attempts to reconstruct a historical narrative of the revolution and its mediation, by combining broadcast material with footage of negotiations and preparations inside the television station. Rather than producing a simple chronology, Farocki and Ujică instead emphasise the extent to which the ideals and objectives of the revolutionaries were ambivalently articulated through the form of the television transmissions.[8]

Stan Douglas has also explored the changing role and form of television during a period of significant social unrest, in *Evening* (1994). But unlike Farocki and Ujică, Douglas deals with events that had occurred decades earlier. *Evening* work is a three channel video installation, which examines the transformation of television news in the US at the end of the 1960s, informed by newspaper reports and television footage relating to the Chicago-area television

Next page: Laura Horelli, *Haukka-Pala /*
[A-Bit-to-Bite], 2009. Installation view.
Courtesy the artist and Galerie Barbara
Weiss, Berlin.

station WLS. Owned by ABC, this low-rated station was one of the first to introduce a new approach to the presentation of television news, known as 'Happy Talk', involving a greater focus on human interest stories, banter between co-anchors and changes in vocal delivery, including the use of a energetic upbeat tone. These changes generated higher ratings and were widely imitated across the US. Douglas's installation presents evening news programmes by three (fictionalised) Chicago-area network affiliates on two specific 'news days' January 1, 1969 and January 1, 1970. While 'WAMQ' and 'WCSL' have made the transition to Happy Talk by the 1970s, 'WBMB' adheres to the traditional 'paternal' model. The arrangement of speakers allows the viewer to focus on one 'station' or to experience a polyphonic soundtrack, which aims to 'underline repetitions and differences'[9] between the treatment of the main news stories covered on these two dates; the ongoing Vietnam war, the Chicago Seven Trial, and the first inquest into the assassination of Black Panther Deputy Chairman Fred Hampton.

Douglas interprets the introduction of Happy Talk as a response to problems posed for television by ongoing social and political conflicts, such as those highlighted by the US Civil Rights Movement. He reads it as 'a hysterical response to the news of the late sixties, with the conflicting demands of station owners, television advertisers, and audiences' and specifically as a means of offering 'closure [...] by *theatrical* rather than editorial means'.[10] Television had played a key role in publicising the Movement's activities, demands and leaders during the 1960s and Douglas notes that news coverage initially helped to make 'local conflicts national and, later, international issues'. But, he notes, the forms of coverage and publicity offered by network news ultimately helped to undermine the credibility of those seeking radical social change, so that by the close of the decade their demands were being presented as 'unreasoned'.[11]

The switch to Happy Talk was widely reported at the time, but it is only in recent years that media historians and theorists have actually begun to closely examine the motivations (and the political beliefs) of the researchers who contributed, as news consultants, to the formulation and implementation of these changes. Craig Allen notes that many news consultants who advised broadcasters during this period were sociologists with experience of working in academic contexts, and who were often deeply committed to a class-based analysis. Some of them sought to contest the view that the US was a 'classless society' and, informed by studies of social stratification, they questioned the idea that there was only one public to be served by broadcast news.[12] When these consultants examined the ratings for television news, they were 'baffled that broadcasters felt they were providing public service with newscasts that appealed only to the 25% of viewers with college degrees'.[13] They regarded changes in the form and delivery of television news, then still heavily indebted to the newspaper form, as a way to address a broader demographic and so produce a true 'public service'. Not surprisingly, broadcasters were relieved to be 'unburdened of the idea that public service meant small, unprofitable audiences' and happy to discover that, by 'fitting news to the largest groups',[14] they could increase profits and still meet their public service obligations.

Above: Laura Horelli, *Haukka-Pala /
[A-Bit-to-Bite]*, 2009. Still from color
video with sound. 28 minutes.
Courtesy the artist and Galerie Barbara
Weiss, Berlin.

There are several other factors, however, which contributed to the changing form of television news during this period. For example, Allen and Douglas both cite various innovations in broadcast technology, such as the greater availability of pictorial content on film and tape, believed by consultants to broaden the appeal of news. Significantly, Allen also points out that the some of the findings informing the transition toward Happy Talk, during the late 1960s, were based upon audience research relating to memories of television coverage of Kennedy's assassination and subsequent events. He notes that several viewers recalled being 'captivated' not only by the events they were witnessing on screen but also by the experience of seeing newscasters communicating as 'real people'.[15] So the transformations in news mediation explored in *Evening* are founded, in part, on research relating to *memories* as well as perceptions and expectations of television.

Douglas's work seems to anticipate a renewal of interest in reconstruction on the part of contemporary artists.[16] More recently, in *Untitled (The Remake)* (2007), Stefanos Tsivopoulos has used reconstruction to critique aspects of Greek news broadcasting during the era of the dictatorship, while also developing an exploration of the material culture of television production in an earlier era.[17] Commissioned for the inaugural Athens Biennale in 2007, this work is a 14-minute single-channel video projection that incorporates archive footage of nationalistic spectacles apparently involving elements of historical re-enactment.[18] It also features a reconstruction of television news presenters preparing for a broadcast, observed by a cameraman in a newsroom dating from the 1960s, equipped with cameras, lights and studio set-ups drawn from the collection of the Museum of Television in Athens.[19] The video opens with a black and white graphic sequence incorporating fragments of classical columns and a montage of ceremonial military events with the Acropolis visible in the background, ending with scenes of a huge crowded stadium. The transition to the reconstruction begins with a series of highly formal close-ups in muted colour, slowly tracking from left to right, past an array of antiquated lights and cameras, filmed against a background of dark grey drapes. Wider shots reveal an initially empty television studio equipped with black and white monitors, and displaying more archival fragments in the form of a montage that seems to be *about* television. This incorporates shots of male and female presenters preparing for a broadcasting, camera operators and also monitors displaying what appear to be images of the first 1969 moon landing, thus providing a sense of orientation in time but also generating a kind of televisual *mise-en-abyme*.

Tsivopoulos's camera then begins a reverse movement, tracking back from right to left and revealing a studio now populated by living camera operators and two young

Next page: Laura Horelli, *Haukka-Pala / [A-Bit-to-Bite]*, 2009. Still from color video with sound. 28 minutes. Courtesy the artist and Galerie Barbara Weiss, Berlin.

Above and Next pages: Bojan Fajfrić, *Theta Rhythm*, 2010. Courtesy of the artist.

newscasters, costumed in accordance with the fashions of the sixties, going through the same rituals of preparation: applying make-up, shuffling papers. Although the 'newscasters' in the reconstruction can be seen to speak, there is no diegetic sound, only slow abstract electronic music punctuated from time to time by a tone that suggests a synchronisation signal used in film or television production. The flickering images of the moon landing, now more visible on the studio monitors, pass unnoticed in the background; in contrast to the countless dramatic narratives where these same images serve as the focus of attention for large groups (families, strangers, co-workers), acting as shorthand for a shared cultural memory mediated and structured by television. Gradually a different televisual memory, associated with the classical past rather than the technological future, emerges as the focus of Tsivopoulos's attention. The remainder of *Untitled (The Remake)* oscillates between shots of the newscasters and a further montage of archive footage depicting a series of military festivities. The parades include young men and women costumed to evoke Greece's classical past, with the men bearing shields and spears. While these 're-enactments' are superficially similar to out-takes from a Hollywood 'sword and sandal' epic from the 1960s, the presence of floodlights and the serious expressions of the participants reveal these scenes to be propaganda. They formed part of the regular parades of *Polemiki Areti* (translated as Arm's Virtue) that were presented as *Theamata* (spectacles) for mass consumption at the Panathinaiko Stadium in Athens during the era of the military dictatorship (1967–1974). The neutral expressions and mechanical gestures of the 'newscasters' also provide a stark contrast to the emotive imagery of mass spectacle, hinting at the complicity of broadcasters in the perpetuation of nationalistic fictions.

For Tsivopoulos, these spectacles serve as a point of connection between the dictatorship established in Greece in 1936, and which made extensive propagandistic use of radio and theatre, and the later military regime that took hold following a coup d'état in 1967. This latter event occurred only months after the establishment of two Greek television stations—one run by the national broadcaster (ERT) and the other run by the military (YENED). Through its exploration of propagandistic spectacle, *Untitled (The Remake)* underscores television's historical role—within the Greek context and elsewhere—as a site for the exercise and display of political power, emphasising the extent to which broadcasting can function as an arm of the state. The structure of Tsivopoulos's work clearly locates this model of broadcasting in Greece's past. But the highly aestheticised presentation of antiquated cameras, lights and other objects, now part of a museum collection, might also be read as an allusion both to television's displacement by newer media, and to its uncertain future as a public cultural form in many European contexts.

While there are important differences between *The Eternal Frame, Videograms of a Revolution, Evening* and *Untitled (The Remake)*, all four works engage with television as a *news* medium, focusing on direct address as a distinctive feature of televisual form, integral to the medium's widely promoted attributes of liveness and immediacy. The newer works discussed in this chapter, by Horelli, Domanović and Fajfrić, also encompass an engagement with direct address and television news. But I argue that, through their explorations of the relationship between television, history and memory, these three artists question television's historical status as a public cultural form, by drawing attention to elisions and gaps in television memory. Importantly, rather than focusing on television's mediation of major political and social events, Horelli, Domanović and Fajfrić use practices of re-editing, re-enacting and re-mixing to investigate archival fragments that wholly failed to achieve the status of 'media events'. *Haukka-Pala*, *Theta Rhythm* and *19:30* also situate television within the context of other technologies of media storage, retrieval and distribution, ranging from diaries to media-sharing websites. So these artists are responding, in part, to television's relativisation, and remediation, by newer (and older) media.[20] Before addressing the form of these works more closely, however, it is necessary to more clearly specify how television memory has been theorised.

Television, Memory and Media Events

According to Jerome Bourdon, the relationship between television and memory has tended to be understood in two main ways. He identifies 'a destructive model, and a hyper-integrative model based on a single program type: media events'.[21] In the destructive model, television is aligned with 'forgetting', produced by the continual replacement of one 'big story' after the next, while in the 'integrative, media-event-based model, television is seen as a major instrument in the shaping of collective memory, especially national, and sometimes global'.[22] It is also possible to complicate the distinction between destructive and integrative models through reference to Mary Ann Doane's widely-cited theorization of 'catastrophe' as an integral component of television's temporal form. Citing television coverage both of the assassination of John F. Kennedy and of the events marking the 25th anniversary of the assassination, Doane argues that 'what is remembered in these nostalgic returns is not only the catastrophe or crisis itself, but the fact that television was there, allowing us access to moments which always seem more real than all the others'.[23] While Doane emphasizes the commercial logic underpinning television's orientation toward commemoration, Daniel Dayan and Elihu Katz have theorized the media event primarily in terms of a renewal of social connections between familial and national groups.[24] They argue that live television coverage of 'ceremonies' ranging from the traumatic to the celebratory (including state funerals, the Olympics and royal weddings) serve as occasions for shared viewing and for the production of collective memory.

But to what extent is the concept of the media event actually relevant to my discussion, and to the archived material explored in the three artworks I have cited? Both *Haukka-Pala* and *19:30* refer to pre-recorded material (children's programming and idents) that form a routine component of broadcast schedules, so cannot be readily identified as media events. *Theta Rhythm* is structured around the live broadcast coverage of the 8th session of the Central Committee of the Communist League of Serbia, the outcome of which helped to ensure

Above: Aleksandra Domanović, *19:30*,
2010/11. HD video, colour, sound;
11 mins Edition of 5 + 2 AP. Courtesy
of the artist and Tanya Leighton,
Berlin.

Slobodan Milošević's rise to power. But the 1987 broadcast did not involve an interruption of scheduled programming and is not presented in Fajfrić's account as a significant occasion for the type of collective viewing characteristic of a media event. In fact, the central concern of *Theta Rhythm* is how the meeting and its outcome *failed* to resonate publicly at the time of broadcast. So while the concept of the media event may inform understanding of these works, these artists are more interested in the absences or failures that characterize the relationship between television and collective memory.[25]

All three artists assert a direct, even intimate, connection to the content of television archives, which is both familial and national. But at the same time they also explore a sense of temporal distance or dislocation, through their focus on the experience of encountering, or re-encountering, broadcast material many years after it was first transmitted. So the development of *Theta Rhythm* begins with the artist's uncertain and possibly imagined memory of seeing his father on television in the 1980s and culminates with a dramatization of his father's recollections of the day of the broadcast. Horelli's work centres around her encounter as an adult with archived footage of a TV show that featured her (now deceased) mother as a presenter. Only *19:30* is explicitly framed through reference to the artist's own memories of television viewing and, significantly, Domanović recalls hearing the music signalling the start of the TV news, rather than actually watching the broadcasts.

In order to fully understand the forms of remembering explored in these three artworks it is necessary to look beyond the integrative and destructive models critiqued by Bourdon, toward his own 'less radical' account of television memory, based upon empirical research conducted in France in 1993. Bourdon frames French television as broadly representative of European public service broadcasting during this period, which, by comparison with US television, had a 'different pace', with less emphasis on drama in news programming, and was 'more likely to be domesticated into daily routines'.[26] Bourdon also notes that French audiences reported watching about 16 hours of television a week (roughly equivalent to 140 minutes a day), and that much of this viewing took place within 'collective family circumstances',[27] which might include the extended family.

While there are commonalities between the consumption of French, Finnish and Yugoslav television during this period, there are also some important differences. A study of public broadcasting in Finland (published in 1989) noted that Finns tended to watch only 100 minutes of television per day, and even less during the summer months. More importantly, it identified a highly intellectual, activist approach on the part of the Finnish national broadcasting company YLE, informed by a socialist (even distinctly Marxist) critique of cultural imperialism, in which television was very consciously conceived as a means 'to preserve and enhance the uniqueness of Finnish culture'.[28] This led to a strong emphasis on didactic informational programming on the YLE stations TV1 and TV2, which was still somewhat apparent in the late 1980s, despite growing commercial competition.[29] Even though the range of programming choices increased in the following decades, enabling the viewer's experience of television to become more private, a later study of social uses of television in Finland (based on data sets from 1996 and 2005) concluded that elements of collective viewing remained important in Finnish television culture, concluding that 'most people want scheduled programs from television to experience "old-fashioned communality" in the digital era'.[30]

The history of broadcasting in former Yugoslavia is clearly more complex, both because of the interconnections between the broadcasters in the various republics prior to the break-up of Yugoslavia and because of the central role played by media in the development and articulation of nationalism before and during the conflicts of the early 1990s. Writing in 2005, Zala Volcic notes that initially 'mass media in general and broadcasting in particular served the socialist goal of the creation of a sense of the Yugoslav national community', and were controlled by the League of Communists of Yugoslavia. So even if the media were relatively 'unconstrained'[31] by comparison with other Communist states, broadcasting could not be defined in terms of a Reithian model of public service. By the late 1980s each Yugoslav republic had its own television station, with a system for the sharing of productions, and this period also marked a shift toward a more overtly nationalist discourse. In the case of the Slovenian station TVS, Volcic notes that 'Slovenians started to be daily reproduced as nationals, through a whole complex of beliefs, assumptions, habits, images, logos, representations and practices'[32] and more specifically 'programmes such as the evening news at 7.30 pm were transformed into shows with a new national focus'.[33] The work of both Domanović (who was born in Novi Sad, Serbia but grew up in Slovenia) and Fajfrić should then be understood within the context of a significant transformation in the form and experience of national broadcasting during the 1980s.

Turning to the model developed by Bourdon, it is possible to organize television memory into four main categories. In addition to 'media events', they include 'wallpaper' memories (relating to habits and routines rather than actual viewing), 'flashbulb' memories that have proved especially traumatic, and 'close encounters'—memories of 'real-life' interactions between viewers and television personalities. This framework seems especially pertinent to my analysis precisely because it encompasses analysis of memories not defined by *viewing*. The 'wallpaper' category underscores the importance of recurrent, and often collective, habits and practices in relation to television, sometimes aligned with (and perhaps contributing to) a sense of the home as a 'safe' place. Television is therefore positioned in relation to a whole range of predominantly domestic 'clocking' activities that involve 'sequencing and the setting of frequency, duration and scheduling',[34] through which the world itself is domesticated, a process that is enhanced by television's serial form and the presence of familiar figures such as TV hosts and newscasters.

In different ways, Horelli, Fajfrić and Domanović are attuned to the temporal rhythms of broadcasting and to these processes of domestication. A focus on scheduling is especially apparent in *19:30*, which takes its title from the regular start time of evening news broadcasts. But Horelli's re-editing of *Haukka-Pala* also responds to the fact that children's television programmes typically occupy a fixed position within daily and weekly schedules, and are likely to be remembered within the context of everyday domestic routines. These routines are potentially highly normative, as demonstrated by Paddy Scannell's research into the

Above: Aleksandra Domanović, *19:30*,
2010/11. HD video, colour, sound;
11 mins Edition of 5 + 2 AP. Courtesy
of the artist and Tanya Leighton,
Berlin.

temporal order of British public service broadcasting.[35] The notion of 'close encounters' might also be relevant to the work of Horelli and Fajfrić, although this is a more tenuous connection. Bourdon notes that this experience is marked by 'a sense of transgression', because 'a bridge is built between two realms that usually cannot be connected'.[36] *Haukka-Pala*, which includes voiceover narration by Horelli, could be said to engage in a process of bridge-building, but in this instance the transgression involves the linking of two realms that are separated in time, rather than perceptions of the ordinary and the extraordinary that (in Bourdon's account) separate everyday life from television. An even more pronounced transgression occurs in Fajfrić's work, because he plays the part of his own father in a historical reconstruction, which incorporates the archived material.

Television, Memory and Material Culture

In recent years, analysis of the relationship between television and memory has also expanded to engage more fully with the issue of materiality. In a study that focuses primarily (although not exclusively) on the British context, Amy Holdsworth identifies 'an increased obsession with television memory and the nostalgia for television past'.[37] She is not wholly dismissive of this nostalgic current, however, and instead finds self-reflexive approaches to the representation of television viewing (in which television is conceived as visual medium and material object) in contemporary art, cinema and television. I am especially interested in Holdsworth's account of a two-channel moving image installation by British artist Gillian Wearing, entitled *Family History* (2006). *Family History* was originally devised for presentation in two 'show homes' located in the UK cities of Reading and Birmingham, and presented in conjunction with Wearing's solo exhibition at the (publicly-funded) IKON Gallery in Birmingham.

Wearing's installation consists of two videos, one of which is presented in the style of a chat-show, hosted by Trisha Goddard (a familiar figure on UK daytime television) and featuring an interview with Heather Wilkins. Now middle-aged, Wilkins became known to British television viewers during the 1970s for her participation as a teenager in the BBC television series *The Family* (1974), an observational-style documentary inspired by *An American Family* (1972).[38] The other video component of Wearing's installation is much shorter and presented in an adjoining room of the exhibition space. It features a young girl (described in the press release as 'a young Wearing lookalike'), seated in a domestic living room decorated to suggest the 1970s. The girl watches scenes of conflict drawn from *The Family*, featuring the teenage Heather, and she comments (in conversation with an off-screen interviewer) briefly upon her experience of viewing. Both videos, despite their different running times, end with a slow zoom out that reveals the 1970s living room to be a set, situated (like the TV chat show environment) in a television studio.

Holdsworth emphasizes the importance of Wearing's work in understanding the material and sensory processes through which memory is made, noting the differences between the forms of domesticity on display in the 1970s living room set, the TV chat show set and the 'show home' environment of the exhibition:

> the revealed structure of the set [...] highlights a pattern of reflections; through the simulated past/present of the adjoining 'sets', one a reconstruction and the other a retrospective, the project interrogates the making of memory within television's various living rooms.[39]

Like many of the other examples cited by Holdsworth, *Family History* certainly does develop a self-reflexive approach to the representation of domestic viewing. But this work also presents Wearing's viewing experience not only as somehow distinctive (because it contributed to her development as an artist) but *also* as representative of a larger cultural experience.

Family History was promoted as an explicitly autobiographical work in the publicity surrounding its presentation in Birmingham (where *The Family* was shot) and Reading (where Wearing grew up). At the same time, Wearing's experience is very firmly situated within the context of a larger narrative of collective viewing, through Trisha Goddard's interview with Heather, which explores memories of the production process, Heather's doubled experience as both viewer and participant, and the problems that resulted from the celebrity status bestowed upon the Wilkins family. This celebrity status is illustrated through the inclusion of clips showing throngs of photographers at the wedding of Heather's eldest sister, which might itself be regarded as a 'media event'. So even if Wearing's project develops a critique (through the mimicry of the chat show format) of television's tendency toward nostalgia, *Family History* also mobilizes notions of collectivity in ways that seem to authorize the artist's memory of television. Consequently, it emphasizes continuities and convergences between individual and collective experience, in contrast to the insistence on failures, absences and gaps in television memory evident in *Haukka-Pala*, *Theta Rhythm* and *19:30*.

Failures and Gaps in Television Memory: *Haukka-Pala, Theta Rhythm* and *19:30*

In 2009, *Haukka-Pala* was exhibited at the Venice Biennale as part of an exhibition of works by Finnish, Danish, Swedish and Norwegian artists, entitled *The Collectors*, curated by the artist duo Elmgreen and Dragset. The selection of Horelli's work as part of a national presentation might seem to signal an official endorsement of *Haukka-Pala*, as an exploration of Finnish cultural history. But Elmgreen and Dragset adopted as self-consciously disruptive position in relation to norms of national representation, by staging the Nordic and Danish pavilions as luxurious villas, emphasizing parallels between the Biennale and a commercial Expo. Visitors to the exhibition were invited to imagine the pavilions as home to imaginary occupants (including an art collector) and presented with often darkly humorous glimpses into these occupants' lives. *Haukka-Pala* seemed somewhat out of place in this lavish setting, perhaps because the onscreen image of domesticity offered by children's public service broadcasting in the mid-1980s was so clearly at odds with the images of aspirational living conjured elsewhere in the exhibition. But the very inappropriateness of the viewing environment may also have served to intensify the emotional affect of the work.

The *Haukka-Pala* television show, which promoted healthy eating and also incorporated references to traditional customs, was written and presented by Horelli's mother Helena (a nutritionist) during the years shortly before her death. Horelli re-edits several episodes of the show, adding a voiceover commentary (in Finnish, subtitled in English) and excerpts from the diaries that her mother kept during her early twenties, which are presented in yellow text on screen. At various points, Finnish dialogue between Helena and her co-presenter—a puppet dog called Ransu—is audible and English subtitles are again provided. Some of these onscreen exchanges prompt memories of Horelli's own childhood so, for example, a reference to peas in one dialogue calls to mind a memory of picking weeds from her father's pea fields. But at other moments, she adopts a more analytical role as narrator and viewer, slowing the video image so that fragments of her mother's gestures can be examined more closely.

One reviewer reads the extension of these gestures through time-stretching as both an 'act of reduction' and a way of bringing her mother temporarily to life, serving 'to animate her, to conjure her'.[40] The same reviewer points out that 'by investigating her own experience as if it were a paradigm [Horelli] produces works that are formally and strategically intelligent, and which constitute much more than a retelling of one individual's experiences'. This 'paradigmatic' dimension is apparent when Horelli reflects on her own experience of viewing the tapes for the first time; she recognized her mother's laughter but thought she seemed strange and unfamiliar 'from the front'. This comment, while communicating a personal response, also draws attention to the mode of address commonly employed in educational television, news programming and (in an earlier era) continuity announcements, whereby the presenter faces the camera and addresses viewers directly or implicitly, through dialogues with a co-presenter.

Horelli also comments on formal distinctions between disparate forms of direct speech, which are placed in relation to each other through the interplay between voiceover, video and diary extracts. So the work embraces the televisual fiction of the shared 'here and now', while also differentiating between practices of scripted and natural speech, and activities of remembering and storytelling, viewing and reviewing. By weaving together the content of the programme and her own memories of family life, Horelli also highlights normative aspects of Finnish children's television. For example, when her mother explains to the viewers that it is good to eat with friends once a day, Horelli explains that her own family always ate dinner together at 5 pm and, noting that Ransu recently celebrated his thirtieth year on Finnish television, she draws attention to the continued significance of children's television in asserting social and domestic norms, whether national or familial.

While Horelli focuses on a broadcast genre that typically lacks overt political content, Bojan Fajfrić's *Theta Rhythm* is concerned with television coverage of political party meetings and conferences. As already noted, this work is a reconstruction of a specific day in September 1987, focusing on the daily routine of Fajfrić's father, who at that time worked as an administrator for Belgrade's City Committee. The day's events included a meeting of the Central Committee of the Communist League of Serbia, the outcome of which contributed to the rise of Slobodan Milošević. The session was broadcast live on national television and Fajfrić's father was one of several people in attendance to be caught sleeping on camera during the lengthy and protracted meeting. Fajfrić emphasizes, however, that the act of falling asleep was barely noticed at the time as it was a relatively common occurrence in these meetings:

> At the time when Milošević was fighting for power, the sessions and meetings were endless. His strategy was to allow anybody attending the meeting to speak about anything vaguely connected to the subject of the renewal of the Communist Party without time limit […] so the majority of the participants would vote *yes* without formulating their critical judgment just to be able to go home.[41]

Fajfrić notes that the specific session during which his father fell asleep was later recognized by historians as 'a symbolic turning point that led to the rise of nationalism and wars in former Yugoslavia.' His father, who opposed the politics of Milošević, subsequently left the political administration in 1990 to begin a new career based on his hobby of horse-riding.

For Fajfrić, the innocent act of falling asleep is a metaphor for the failure of his father's generation to alter the course of history, and the fact that this specific image entered the historical record makes it possible to conceptualize other possible outcomes—even if only imaginatively. So *Theta Rhythm* constitutes an attempt to identify and visualize a specific moment when the course of historical events might have been altered, and the title of the work refers to brainwave activity observed during certain states of sleep and wakefulness, and associated with memory and learning, introducing a quasi-scientific framework. Shot on HD cam, with production values and an attention to period detail that matches the standard of much commercial television, the reconstruction features a central performance by Fajfrić in the role of his father, complete with a convincingly retro haircut and suit. As already noted, the practice of reconstruction has become relatively commonplace in contemporary art in recent years, but Fajfrić's work is distinctive because his film incorporates archived broadcast footage, and this footage has been altered. At a key moment historical accuracy gives way to fictionalization as Fajfrić uses compositing technology to insert his own image into the archive footage, recalling film narratives such as *Zelig* (1983) or *Forrest Gump* (1994), but also underscoring the fact that the images of the Belgrade meeting were *not* viewed as 'iconic'.

Theta Rhythm also includes an ambiguous sequence in which Fajfrić (playing his father) is seen riding a racehorse on a track, costumed as a jockey. Photographed at sunrise, these shots are much more obviously dramatic and arresting than the preparations for the party meeting or the archive material. Appearing in fragmentary form, precisely at the intersection between sleep and wakefulness, these scenes are both fantastical and highly compelling, suggesting either powerful memories or desires that were subsequently to be fulfilled by Fajfrić's father following his change of career. Through this juxtaposition of the dramatic and mundane, *Theta Rhythm* explores the difficulty of recognizing and representing significant moments in the flow of history, demonstrating that significance can be subjective and that the public time of broadcasting intersects with other temporalities, including the unfolding of a career and a family history. In some respects, Fajfrić's strategy of reconstructing a specific date recalls aspects of Stan Douglas's *Evening*. But while Douglas chooses two 'news days' (January 1, 1969 and January 1, 1970) one year apart in order to highlight changing modes of television news presentation, Fajfrić's choice is dictated by a specific historical event. Douglas's project is also much more indebted to historical and archival research and his installation employs a comparative structure to make these findings explicit.

Fajfrić does draw to some extent upon historical research in the staging of his reconstruction, but the dream-like quality of his work articulates its debt to memory, in the form of his father's recollections. When this work is shown as a looped moving image installation, the transition from evening to morning is especially ambiguous, inviting reflection upon the boundaries between sleep and wakefulness as well as between past and present. For this reason the work is perhaps more suited to a gallery context than a cinema screening, as suggested in one review of the Oberhausen International Short Film Festival 2011.[42] But *Theta Rhythm* has been shown extensively at festivals and Fajfrić has sought to preserve aspects of the looped form in the festival edit of the work, by incorporating opening and closing scenes that are very similar.

Domanović's ongoing project *19:30* has an even more fluid form, encompassing videos, performances and online explorations of the graphical and musical form of idents preceding evening news broadcasts. Reviewing the work within the context of the exhibition *Free* at the New Museum, New York, Karen Rosenberg identified it as representative of the 'intense desire for communal experience', articulated in the show as a whole.[43] Encompassing the production of multiple artworks, in various media, the core of *19:30* is a publicly accessible archive in the form of an online collection of image and audio files. Domanović lived through the break-up of former Yugoslavia and her interest in television was shaped by childhood memories of hearing the title music that announced evening news broadcasts on television every evening at 7.30 pm, at which point adult activity and street life would pause, particularly during the war years.[44] This title music was usually instrumental, often produced with electronic technology, and typically devised to induce a sense of urgency and intensity. As an adult, Domanović's interest in this material (and her own memory of television) was prompted by subsequent events—specifically her encounter with fragments of this music that had, during the 1990s, been remixed by techno DJs and music producers, acquiring a kind of second life online through YouTube etc. When she realised that this material was largely overlooked in academic media studies, Domanović set about researching it with the support of a grant from Rhizome.

Initially focusing solely on the music used in news idents she later expanded her analysis to include the visual elements of the sequences, which tended to have high production values by comparison with other national TV productions, generally incorporating sophisticated animation and graphics. Domanović has now built a collection of research material by personally visiting broadcasters all over former Yugoslavia, and this material is accessible in an online 'chronology'.[45] Reflecting on her research process, she notes the limited resources available to some broadcasters and points out that access to archived material in these contexts is often dependent upon personal connections, the intervention of cultural agencies, or payment of commercial fees, as title sequences constitute a potential source of income for these broadcasters.

But even though she has sought to systematically gather, organize and contextualize elements of broadcasting history, Domanović does not solely identify with the custodial role of archivist. She is instead committed to making this material available for reconfiguration by others, broadly in keeping with the ethics of open source programming, and she contributes to its after-life by collaborating with DJs on live performances and parties, developing ongoing remixes of sound and image files, elements of which are incorporated into her video installations and single screen works. The live performance events, which are sometimes staged within the programmes of major exhibitions, are especially interesting because (unlike gallery installations) they create the conditions for a self-consciously collective experience of this material. It is possible—though by no means clear—that these performances could also elicit shared memories of television in ways that might echo some of the social and discursive functions attributed to media events. But Domanović makes no attempt to mimic the temporal rhythms and routines of broadcasting and instead her performances and parties emphasize and exploit the pronounced dislocation of these archival fragments from the television schedule.

Conclusion: Television, Memory and Publicness

It might be argued that, in seeking to assemble, organize and preserve fragments of broadcast history, Domanović's project forms part of a broader nostalgic current within contemporary culture, echoing the fascination with television's impending disappearance noted by Holdsworth in television, cinema, art and academic discourse.[46] More specifically, Domanović, Fajfrić and Horelli seem to be grappling with some of the same questions highlighted in media studies concerning television's shifting role within public life. John Caughie, for example, laments the loss of the 'public space' offered by culturally prominent television in an earlier era, citing the reception of the 1966 BBC television play Cathy Come Home, while also reflecting upon 'television's part in the waning of the public sphere, its complicity in the performance of a subject which is constantly in play'.[47] Here Caughie is referring to the limitations not only of television but of television studies, and specifically with forms of theorising that (by virtue of their focus on the play of difference) are 'ill-equipped to imagine a different television, one which escapes the "relentless spectacle of the present"'.[48]

But for artists such as Domanović, Fajfrić and Horelli, television's imagined 'publicness' does not exist either in an idealized past or in a utopian moment that is yet to come. In contrast, television's status as public cultural form is presented as open to question and subject to processes of continual redefinition. These processes encompass the re-enactment of broadcast events that failed to generate public discourse at an earlier moment (Fajfrić), the development of archival resources that serve as a focus for social gathering and media sharing (Domanović) and the exploration of the role played by children's television in mediating between public and private realms (Horelli). So rather than imagining television a cultural form to be contested or invaded in the interests of producing a public medium, these artists consider the many different ways in which publicness might be temporarily manifested—or contested—through practices of remembering. I have argued that Bourdon's framework, and particularly his concept of 'wallpaper memory', is more relevant to these works than 'destructive' or 'hyper-integrative' notions of memory, because it emphasizes how practices of remembering television may be linked to everyday habits and routines. All three artists share a focus on these routines—evident in Domanović's attention to broadcast schedules, in Fajfrić's re-enactment of a televised event from a participant's perspective, and in Horelli's interweaving of her mother's public speech with diary entries. But they also communicate a relationship to television memory, and to broadcast archives, that emphasizes temporal dislocation.

These works articulate a distinct sense of detachment both from the moment of transmission and also from the everyday habits and routines that may have shaped the experience of television at that moment. They also propose a model of the archive that is at odds with conventional institutional formations, typically organized around the storage and management of content, including 'iconic' footage that can be used to signify collectivity for the purposes of critique or nostalgia. Instead of treating broadcast archives simply as a repositories of programme content, Domanović, Fajfrić and Horelli draw upon archived material to question how memories of television are structured and mediated by technologies of storage. Through strategies of re-mixing, re-enacting, and re-editing, their work seeks to communicate, and indeed share, an experience of television founded upon temporal dislocation rather than recollection. So they do not work toward the production of an ideal archive conceived in terms of the total accumulation of programme content, but instead draw attention to precisely those aspects of the experience and memory of television that resist conventional archival storage and preservation.

Chapter Five

Monuments to Broadcasting: Television and Art in the Public Realm

Public space is lent an aura of democracy in debates on urban design by a notion that it is where people of different classes, races, and genders mix informally. I understand how it comes to be defended in the face of the encroachment of privatized space in the mall, the business park, and the gated apartment compound. But it was never, I suggest, a site of democracy, always a site in which power was performed by those who held it through processions, public executions, and the siting of public monuments which construct historical narratives to lend present regimes an illusion of being a logical culmination of a history.

Malcolm Miles, 'Critical Spaces: Monuments and Changes'[1]

The effects of television's presence in places other than the home are not reducible to 'the privatization of public space', as some might argue. This is because public spaces are not purely and self-evidently public; they are, like every other cultural space, characterized by particular configurations of public and private. Indeed what makes the public/private division such a major category of social power is the fact that it is dynamic and flexible, varying from place to place.

Anna McCarthy, *Ambient Television: Visual Culture and Public Space*[2]

Introduction: Defining the Public Realm

In this chapter I explore how artists have drawn upon histories, memories or perceptions of broadcasting when engaging with the changing form of public space through site-oriented artworks. Produced in a variety of British and German contexts since the early 2000s, I focus on six artworks which incorporate a site-specific or site-responsive element, and also involve the exploration of cultural histories and, in most instances, technologies of radio or television. The six works discussed are *You Are Not Alone* (2009) by Scottish artist Susan Philipsz; *Radio Ballet* (2003) by the Hamburg-based collective LIGNA; *Küba* (2005), by Turkish artist Kutluğ Ataman; *State Britain* (2007) by British artist Mark Wallinger; *Bataille Monument* (2002) by Swiss artist Thomas Hirschhorn; and *Was ist Öffentlichkeit?* (2004) (What is Publicness?) by Danish artist Katya Sander. These projects are notably varied in form, encompassing sound installations, participatory events, sculptural video installations, displays of banners, placards and other protest materials, temporary architectural constructions and performative actions.

Rather than focusing solely on works commissioned by public art agencies, which are informed and mediated through reference to institutional definitions of public space, I have chosen to include examples that call the very definition of the 'public realm' into question. Some of these works were presented in spaces that are routinely publicly accessible, even if their status as public spaces is open to question, such as the main train station in Leipzig, Germany (LIGNA) and the Duveen Galleries of Tate Britain (Wallinger). Others were installed in spaces that are generally less publicly accessible, because they are spaces of work or private residence, such as a disused postal sorting office in central London (Ataman), the headquarters of a public service broadcaster in Berlin (Philipsz), the residential village built for the 1972 Munich Olympics (Sander) and a social housing complex outside the centre of Kassel, Germany (Hirschhorn).

I argue that, when considered together, these projects provide evidence of the fact that broadcasting, especially in its public service form, continues to operate as an important, albeit contested, signifier of publicness in European contemporary art culture.[3] Some of these artists work with histories and technologies of broadcasting precisely because they seek to question the development and current status of the democratic public sphere and understand broadcasting as fulfilling an integral role in this social and political formation.[4] Whether as an ideal or actually existing cultural form, public broadcasting continues to be valuable for some—but by no means all—of these artists, because it offers a symbolic counterpoint to the securitisation and closure of spaces previously understood as public.[5]

It is important to emphasise that none of the six contemporary works discussed in this chapter actually involved the display of television receivers or monitors in straightforwardly public spaces. Two of the projects (Philipsz, LIGNA) actually focused on radio rather than television and the installations by Sander and Wallinger were devised for gallery contexts. Ataman's installation does incorporate an array of antiquated receivers but, in the version of the work I discuss, the setting for the installation was a disused postal sorting office, which had not previously been publicly accessible. Hirschhorn's project incorporated a temporary television studio, which included monitors but, as I will argue, both the location and mediation of *Bataille Monument* posed questions about its public accessibility. Consequently these works are very different from earlier public art initiatives (commissioned by organisations such as the Public Art Fund in the US and Artangel Trust in the UK) engaging with the public realm. Here I am referring primarily to the prominent use of outdoor screens by curators and artists seeking to critique the privatization of culture and public space, such as the

Next page: Susan Philipsz, *You Are Not Alone*, 2009.
Photography: Nick Ash.

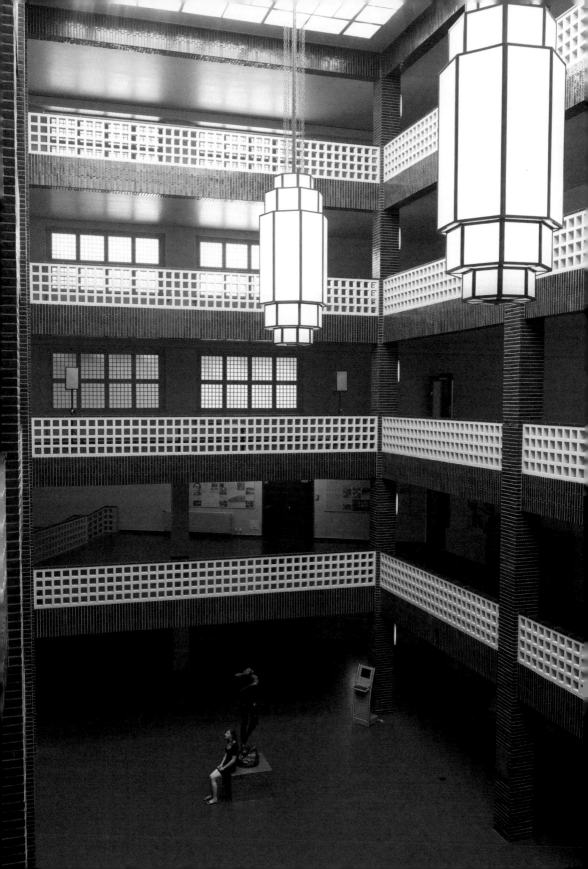

Above: Susan Philipsz, *You Are Not Alone*, 2009.
Photography: Nick Ash.

Spectacolour lightboards located in Times Square and Piccadilly Circus during the 1980s.[6] Although the computerised lightboards used for advertising purposes in the 1980s cannot be precisely described as *television*, spectacularised urban spaces such as Times Square are nonetheless distinctively 'televisual' in character.[7]

The televisuality ascribed to these environments, according to Anna McCarthy, is partly a function of value judgements that align television with the privatisation of public space; one which 'is very frequently characterized by journalists and academics alike in singular terms: as the privatization of public space, as a contaminant polluting the polis, bombarding us with images, destroying the pristine space of the public sphere'.[8] McCarthy also suggests that theorists of urban architecture sometimes bemoan the fact that US cities are becoming 'like television', and she identifies in these statements a sense of 'mourning and nostalgia for the mythic architectural ideals of the eighteenth century'.[9] Countering this nostalgia, she argues against an idealistic notion of 'public space as a polis under siege'. Perhaps more importantly, for the purposes of my own analysis of television and art in the European public realm, McCarthy insists upon the dynamism and flexibility of 'public/private divisions',[10] noting that cultural spaces are configured differently from place to place. She is especially attentive to television's role in the 'visual and bodily constitution of the subject as a citizen'[11] in an array of public and quasi-public spaces. But cultural histories also play a role in the shaping and articulation of 'public/private' divisions in the spaces of everyday life, and for artists and curators working within European contexts, television is not necessarily understood in opposition to the public sphere. Instead histories and technologies of radio and television tend to be intertwined in complex ways with ideals of the public sphere, to the extent that broadcasting (especially in its public service form) may actually function, like the idealised 'polis', as an object of 'mourning and nostalgia'.

As I have noted, the 1980s witnessed a widespread use of outdoor advertising screens on the part of European and US artists and curators, evident of a shared interest in critiquing the spectacularisation of public space. But the more recent works I cite at the outset articulate a very different approach to the relationship between television and the public realm. Many of the artists invoke histories and memories of broadcasting through their approach to site (Philipsz, Sander), strategies of display and installation (Ataman), and use of radio and television production or distribution (LIGNA, Hirschhorn, Wallinger). While these later works may articulate diverse visions of 'publicness', they tend to share a concern with values and objectives that have historically been claimed by public service broadcasters with regard to the promotion of civil society, the production or maintenance of social bonds, and the representation of minority views and interests. Some of these projects draw either explicitly or obliquely upon these ideals, in order to articulate a specific concept of the public realm, or to question the continued significance and viability of these ideals. Rather than simply reiterating the social and political objectives of public service broadcasting, however, many of them pose questions about their continued viability within the contemporary cultural economy.

These artworks do not function as monuments to broadcasting in a traditional sense, as they were not devised to fulfil a commemorative function. Nevertheless, I argue that

Above: LIGNA, *Radio Ballet*, Leipzig
Hauptbahnhof, 2003.
Courtesy of the artists.

Above: LIGNA, *Radio Ballet*, Leipzig
Hauptbahnhof, 2003.
Courtesy of the artists.

the notion of the 'monument' is useful in thinking about how they engage with the public sphere, often consigning it irrevocably to the past. In a widely-cited theorisation of the differences between history and memory, Pierre Nora argues that there are 'no longer *milieux de mémoire*, real environments of memory' and instead only 'lieux' or 'sites' of memory.[12] In Nora's formulation, the presence of a monument, as a material trace, actually articulates the *absence* of an older form of shared memory. Of the six works in my selection, the projects by Ataman, Hirschhorn and Wallinger involved the greatest emphasis on the production and display of 'material traces'; only the installation of Philipsz's work at Haus des Rundfunks (Broadcasting House) in Berlin made use of an already existing connection between the object of memorialisation and the site of the 'monument'. Nonetheless, I argue that the figure of the monument persists as a point of connection between all six projects.

It is also worth reiterating the fact that none of these works were devised for public squares or parks, traditionally important settings for monuments and memorials,[13] and spaces which, as Malcolm Miles argues, are 'lent an aura of democracy in debates on urban design by a notion that it is where people of different classes, races, and genders mix informally'. Miles notes that public space is often 'defended in the face of the encroachment of privatized space in the mall, the business park, and the gated apartment compound',[14] even though, as he points out, civic amenities such as public squares only rarely function as sites of 'democratic determination' (outside the context of insurrection). Instead they are more typically 'sites of power's display', and have long served this function, as the scene of processions, public executions and as the setting for triumphalist public monuments. Public service broadcasting has also fulfilled similar functions through the televising of events such as royal weddings and state funerals. Therefore, while city squares may seem especially precious as public spaces in the face of encroaching privatisation, public museums and broadcasters may also serve as symbolic counterpoints to the privatisation represented by commercial media.

As already noted, like public squares and monuments, the art museum is a site of 'power's display' but one whose historical association with the establishment of democratic political formations may nonetheless make it valuable, in specific cultural contexts, as a monument to publicness. According to Carol Duncan, unlike public art museums in the US, European institutions such as the Louvre in Paris and the National Gallery in London can be understood as *monuments* commemorating a triumph over the principle of aristocratic privilege.[15] The founding of public service broadcasters in most European contexts, and specifically in the UK and Germany, where the six works discussed in this chapter were exhibited, certainly did not signify a triumph over aristocratic privilege, and cannot be likened to the opening of the Louvre collection to the public. In fact the British Broadcasting Corporation, which succeeded the privately-owned British Broadcasting Company in 1927, founded (in 1922) by the British General Post Office and various telecommunications companies, was actually formed with a Royal Charter. Crucially, however, the BBC was structured so that it would explicitly function independently of government and business interests. It could also be argued that the arrival of commercial competition in the form of ITV in 1955 served to

Above: LIGNA, *Radio Ballet*, Leipzig
Hauptbahnhof, 2003.
Courtesy of the artists.

underscore the particularity of public service broadcasting, requiring the BBC to both renegotiate and more clearly articulate its identity *as* a public institution.[16] While it is not my intention here to revisit the history of British broadcasting, there is little doubt that the principles of the BBC, which serves to inform and educate as well as entertain, in the interest of sustaining civil society and citizenship, have shaped perceptions of broadcasting as a signifier of publicness.

Media Activism and Monuments to Postmodernity

Before turning to the analysis of the six recent works that serve as the focus of this chapter, it is important to note that broadcasting has also functioned as an important point of reference for US artists working in the public realm in the 1970s and 1980s. Some of these artists often adopted an explicitly activist agenda, as evidenced by the 'guerrilla television' movement,[17] but others were more specifically interested in media policy. For example, Liza Bear and Keith Sonnier produced two tapes, *Send/Receive I* and *Send/Receive II* (both 1977), combining policy analysis alongside practical demonstration of new technologies of broadcasting. Part one of *Send/Receive* functions as a kind of 'bulletin', with onscreen text, references to news items and information on groups such as the Public Interest Satellite Association (PISA), then engaged in lobbying the Federal Communications Commission (FCC) for access to satellite technology. The second part features documentation of communications experiments conducted by the artists, in conjunction with NASA-affiliated scientists. This included a transmission from 'the New York Earth Station of the Send Receive Satellite Network', and incorporated imagery of dancers transmitted from different sources, synchronised so that they appeared to be in harmony.

There are evident parallels in terms of content and form between the *Send/Receive* tapes and the earlier work of Nam June Paik, and also with the initiatives developed by artists such as Otto Piene and Aldo Tambellini at the Center for Advanced Visual Studies in MIT, established by Gyorgy Kepes in 1967.[18] Liza Bear's subsequent work, however, was even more focused on policy critique and reportage in its examination of communications policy issues, ranging from satellite to cable franchising, as evidenced by *Towards a New World Information Order* (1979). A survey of the *Communications Update* series Bear produced with Dee Dee Halleck for NYC cable, this tape includes a report on a UNESCO conference, held in Nairobi, Kenya, on the global information divide, drawing parallels between natural resources campaigns and communications imbalances, framing the radio spectrum as a natural resource.[19]

If Bear's approach was marked by a move away from formal experimentation and toward policy activism, then other artists continued to envisage broadcasting as a technology that could be used to enhance social connectivity because of its supposedly inherent qualities of liveness and immediacy. Kit Galloway and Sherrie Rabinowitz, for example, developed The Satellite Arts Project in 1977 with support from the National Endowment for the Arts,

NASA and the Corporation for Public Broadcasting. As Lisa Parks has noted, this was one of several intersections between art practice and satellite technology during the 1970s and it involved the production of live transmissions of performance art featuring bodies that were separated in space but visually joined through the use of satellite technology. For Parks, this type of 'media-performance art [...] imagines itself not only as a struggle over representation but as synonymous with the satellite apparatus—as part of the satellite's potential for the global circulation of signals'.[20] In other works, Galloway and Rabinowitz's work is indicative of a mode of activist media art that, while framed as critique of actually existing communications practice, simultaneously argues for the social and communicative potential of new technologies.

Aspects of this potential were realised, albeit temporarily, in Galloway and Rabinowitz's *Hole in Space* (1980), which was produced with support from the NEA and sponsors such as Western Union, General Electric and Wold Communications. Promoted as 'A Public Communications Sculpture', it took the form of a live satellite feed between a window in The Broadway department store located in Century City shopping mall, LA and a window at the Lincoln Center in New York. Mounted video cameras, microphones and wall-sized screens were installed at each location, enabling people to watch and communicate with others on the opposite coast in real time over three evenings between November 11–13, 1980. Gloria Sutton notes that widespread coverage in mainstream news media generated public interest in the project, prompting family and friends to congregate at the two screen locations on the final evening of the link.[21] As it was presented without sponsor logos, credits or explanatory text, Galloway and Rabinowitz's project was described by some commentators as a 'free videophone',[22] combining elements of the practical and the quasi-fantastical, and fulfilling a futuristic vision of two-way or interactive communication via 'television'. Unlike many of the groups associated with the 'guerrilla television' movement, who sought to democratise media production and distribution, *Hole in Space* seems to have addressed a public already composed of media users. It presented these users with a technologically advanced service (the 'videophone'), offered in space that was both free and publicly-accessible and, in the case of the Lincoln Center, traditionally associated with public culture. At the same time, *Hole in Space* established a symbolic equivalence between 'public' and commercial spaces, by creating a telecommunications link between an institution historically associated with urban renewal through culture, such as the Lincoln Center, and a long-established department store adjoining a shopping mall, in the case of The Broadway.

Hole in Space was just one of several art projects produced in the late 1970s and early 1980s to be sited in heavily-trafficked commercial centres in the US and Europe. Billboards and computerised lightboards located in thoroughfares such as Times Square in New York and Piccadilly Circus in London also functioned as prominent sites for the location of temporary public artworks, many of them supported through sponsorship.[23] The majority of these works were temporary initiatives, curated by non-profit arts agencies (such as the Public Art Fund, or Creative Time in the US, and Artangel in the UK). By the late 1980s, artists such as Dara Birnbaum were also being commissioned by commercial entities to

Above: Mark Wallinger, *State Britain*,
2007. Mixed media installation,
5.7 x 43 x 1.9m approximate.
Copyright the artist, courtesy Anthony
Reynolds Gallery, London.
Photo by Dave Morgan.

Above: Mark Wallinger, *State Britain*, 2007. Mixed media installation, 5.7 x 43 x 1.9m approximate. Detail, installation at Tate Britain, 2007. Copyright the artist, courtesy Anthony Reynolds Gallery, London.

Above: Thomas Hirschhorn, *Bataille Monument*, 2002. Documenta11, Kassel.
Photo: Werner Maschmann
Courtesy Gladstone Gallery, New York and Brussels.

Above: Thomas Hirschhorn,
Bataille Monument, 2002.
Documenta11, Kassel.
Photo: Werner Maschmann
Courtesy Gladstone Gallery,
New York and Brussels.

produce permanent time-based installations for inclusion within commercial environments. Located in the Rio shopping mall, Atlanta, Birnbaum's *Rio Videowall* (1989) consisted of a grid of 25 video monitors which integrated live news feeds from the Atlanta-based Cable News Network (CNN) with pre-recorded material and footage of shoppers drawn from surveillance cameras. Superficially, Birnbaum's project might seem to resemble *Hole in Space*, embracing technological innovation and 'potential'. But Anna McCarthy's analysis of *Rio Videowall* suggests that it should be understood somewhat differently, as a pointed, albeit subtle, critique of the consumer-driven economy of urban redevelopment.[24]

Noting that the mall was located in a relatively poor neighbourhood close to downtown Atlanta, and built on empty land that had been cleared as part of an earlier urban renewal process, McCarthy states that by the late 1980s this area had been targeted for commercial and residential development aimed at young urban professionals. Birnbaum's work, which was selected through a juried national competition sponsored by the mall's developer, was commissioned as 'an "attraction" that would draw visitors to the mall', forming part of a festive entertainment environment. Birnbaum actually regarded the work, as McCarthy points out, as 'a political statement about the geographic instability and multiplicity of everyday experience in consumerism's visual culture', intending it to serve as a critique of the policies of land-use shaping urban development and also of malls as a 'vanguard, mediatized spaces'.[25] The pre-recorded footage, to be integrated through a computer-based keying system with the live feeds from CNN and of shoppers in the mall, actually showed the site before the mall was built: 'a grass slope sparsely dotted with trees'. McCarthy suggests that this 'lackluster plot of ground could be anywhere', emphasising that Birnbaum did not romanticise the history of the neighbourhood, but rather 'called the "truth" of this landscape into question'.[26]

Visiting the mall in 1993, prompted by descriptions of Birnbaum's work, McCarthy was interested in the possibility that *Rio Videowall* could reveal 'Rio's complexity as a *place* in the sense of the term proposed by Doreen Massey: not a romantic, timeless sense of communal, ecological belonging but rather a dynamic expression of general space-time relations on all scales as they appear in one particular physical site'.[27] Yet the project's effectiveness as a critique of consumerism clearly depended upon the commercial success of the mall, and the presence of throngs of shoppers whose movements would shape the interplay between live and pre-recorded material on the screen. By the time of McCarthy's visit, this commercial viability and the anticipated gentrification of the surrounding midtown area had failed to materialise, and there were few shoppers to be seen. In addition, the video wall itself had stopped working, visibly deteriorating like many other elements of the mall's 'festive' architecture. Yet instead of dismissing Birnbaum's project, McCarthy proposes that it might be read as a 'battered monument to postmodernity',[28] embodying the unstable relationship 'between places and flows in contemporary geographies of capital'.

Unlike *Hole in Space*, the critique Birnbaum articulates in her video wall was not premised upon the potential of communication technologies. In fact the work was concerned not with an analysis of media policy or practice, but with the conditions of urban destruction and renewal. In addition, if artists such as Galloway and Rabinowitz could be said to reiterate the myths of immediacy and liveness commonly attributed to television, while at the same time highlighting its limitations as an actually-existing technology of communication at that moment, *Rio Videowall* tended to undercut these myths. As McCarthy points out, Birnbaum's artwork 'ironized the eternal present of TV news, diminishing the latter's pretensions to realness, liveness, and immediacy with the more "live", more "real-time", more "present-tense" image of the shopper in the mall'.[29] Significantly, the 'live' figure of the shopper also operated in tension with a different image: that of the empty landscape produced, and erased, through successive processes of urban renewal and speculative development.

Even though it was not concerned with preserving the memory of a particular place, *Rio Videowall* actually fulfilled a memorial role of a different sort, by functioning as a monument to the forces that shaped its own production and decay. In my view, the recent works cited at the outset of this chapter are marked by a related, yet much more self-conscious, emphasis on memorialisation. It is true that only Hirschhorn explicitly frames his work as a monument (one of a series focusing on the ideas of philosophers), although even he disavows conventional usage of this term. I argue, however, that all of these recent works engage with the form and function of the monument, often through the development of complex connections between the sites of production, exhibition and histories of broadcasting. Although some of my examples encompass national or local television transmissions, these artists are wholly unconcerned with the technological or social potential of broadcasting. Instead they articulate the persistence of broadcasting as a powerful, albeit sometimes fraught, signifier of the public sphere.

Histories and Theories of Broadcasting in Practice

Susan Philipsz's sound installation *You Are Not Alone* was commissioned by Modern Art Oxford and first presented in 2009 at the Radcliffe Observatory, now part of Green Templeton College at Oxford University. It was also installed two years later, in a slightly different form, for a period of several days in the atrium of Haus des Rundfunks as part of the Berlin Gallery Weekend in April 2011.[30] In this work, Philipsz drew attention to the persistence of sound in time through the form of the radio interval signal. These signals are short musical sequences, originating in the 1920s and 30s when broadcast radio schedules often featured lengthy pauses. Intended to function as recognisable musical signatures enabling listeners to identify stations while tuning, interval signals were generally played before the commencement of transmission and during breaks. Although they have not vanished entirely, the majority of the sequences gathered by Philipsz during the course of her research were produced many decades ago.

Rather than focusing her research on interval signals of historical significance,[31] Philipsz instead focused on the musical qualities of the sequences, noting that despite their varied form and origination, many were characterised by 'a sort of chime, like wind chimes, that can sound really beautiful—distant and melancholy'.[32] She recorded herself playing these

Above: Kutluğ Ataman, *Küba*,
2005 Commissioned and Produced
by Artangel.

Above: Katya Sander,
Was ist Öffentlichkeit?, 2004,
(What is Publicness?).
Image courtesy of the artist.

sequences on a vibraphone, a percussive instrument related to the xylophone, with a vibrating effect that can be controlled and sustained, producing a four channel recording. This was broadcast from separate FM transmitters located in the tower of Modern Art Oxford, across the city to receivers located in the Observing Room on the second floor of the Radcliffe Observatory. In this room, which once housed scientific machinery, the transmissions were relayed to visitors through four speakers, positioned beside the large windows that look out over the city. Experiencing the work in this context, Joerg Heiser was reminded of popular melodies while also being prompted to speculate upon more sinister uses of radio technology, through his suggestion that secret code information might have been hidden within interval signals during the Cold War era.[33] In a practical sense, *You Are Not Alone* transformed the Observing Room into a kind of 'listening station', focused on sounds rather than distant images. But Philipsz also proposed a conceptual parallel between the telescope and radio, by invoking Marconi's notion that 'sounds once generated never die', but rather 'continue to reverberate as sound waves across the universe'.[34] This notion of endless reverberation cast the Radcliffe Observatory as a kind of time machine, which might enable imaginative transport to earlier moments in the history of scientific thought.

This 'time machine' quality was even more apparent at Haus des Rundfunks, where Philipsz's sound piece was installed over a period of several days in April 2011.[35] Although the building remains in use as part of a complex belonging to Rundfunk Berlin-Brandenburg (RBB), it has gradually acquired the role of an unofficial monument to broadcasting in Germany. Designed by Hans Poelzig and opened in 1931 (a year before the completion of BBC Broadcasting House in London), the upper floors of the atrium now house architectural models and documentary panels detailing the building's central role in German social and political history. Early utopian aspirations for the medium of radio as a technology of public communication are suggested both by its luminous interior and its carefully crafted brick exterior, which suggests substance rather than spectacle. These aspirations were, however, rapidly overtaken by the rise of National Socialism and, following Hitler's ascent to power, 'Reichsender Berlin' acquired a new function, eventually becoming the wartime Broadcasting Headquarters of Greater Germany. At the end of the war Haus des Rundfunks was liberated by Russian troops and even though it was located in the British sector, it remained physically segregated from the rest of West Berlin, surrounded by barbed wire and manned by armed Soviet guards until 1956. It then housed the station Sender Freies Berlin from 1957 to 2003, which was to prove important in the early history of artists' television.[36]

In response to this charged context, Philipsz reconfigured *You Are Not Alone* so that the sound sequence opened with a vibraphone version of the final signal transmitted in 1990 from the East German station Radio Berlin International (located in former East Berlin) and ended with a version of the Sender Freies Berlin signal from 1975. By locating both the transmitter and receiver signals within the same atrium space, Philipsz also hinted at the dual identity and purpose of Haus des Rundfunks, as both a site of transmission and a place in which music was frequently performed in front of a live audience. As demonstrated by the architectural models, the building was designed around a large auditorium, located immediately behind the atrium, and images of live performances feature prominently in the documentary panels that detail its history. These images confirm the symbolic significance of Haus des Rundfunks as a space of public gathering in which crowds assembled, serving as audiences both for live entertainment and for political propaganda. The mediating presence of these crowds, audible to those listening at home, would have been integral to the perception of 'live broadcasting' during the 1930s and 40s, and the creation of a sense of shared time and space. But the purpose of an interval signal is far less closely bound to these notions of liveness and presence, since it is open-ended rather than reciprocal. By drawing attention to a mode of communication that preceded the propagandistic use of radio, *You Are Not Alone* amplified the hopeful, even somewhat utopian, vision of broadcasting articulated in the architecture of Haus des Rundfunks.

My next example, *Radio Ballet*, was realised by LIGNA—a group of three media theorists and radio practitioners, Ole Frahm, Michael Hüners and Torsten Michaelsen, who have been associated with the non-profit radio station Free Broadcaster Combine, Hamburg, since the late 1990s. First performed in the main train station of Hamburg in May 2002 and repeated in Leipzig Hauptbahnhof in June 2003, the work was devised as a response to the privatisation of these spaces, which since the mid-1990s have been managed by the private company Deutsche Bahn. Like many of the major train stations in German cities, the Hamburg and Leipzig stations are centrally located and incorporate large shopping areas that remain open on Sundays, unlike the majority of German retail spaces. Consequently, they tend to serve as sites of social gathering for young people, as well as busy thoroughfares for shoppers and travellers: microcosms of urban life in which activity is overseen by privatised security forces rather than the police.

Radio Ballet attempted to highlight the constraints on public gathering in these spaces by inviting around 500 radio listeners to enter the station, bringing with them small cheap, portable radios and earphones. They tuned into a radio programme that consisted of 'choreography suggesting permitted and forbidden gestures (to beg, to sit or lie down on the floor etc.)' and also incorporated 'reflections on the public space and on the Radio Ballet itself'.[37] When Deutsche Bahn became aware of the planned event they attempted to secure a court order to prevent it from proceeding. Ultimately, however, the court determined that since it was not a gathering or a demonstration, but rather a 'dispersion' or 'distribution' of radio listeners, the event could proceed. *Radio Ballet* seeks to transpose (and perhaps transform) private experience into collective physical performance, a strategy that some commentators have critiqued as reminiscent of the mass spectacle often favoured by fascist and communist regimes, or more apolitical forms of collective performance organised via social media.[38]

It is clear from stills and videos documenting the event in Leipzig station that the choreography of *Radio Ballet* produced striking visual compositions. But it is important to emphasise that the participants did not rehearse or practices their responses, and they were free to move through the train station, rather than aligning their bodies in relation to each other. Instead, by carrying radios, wearing headphones, and performing movements likely to elicit the attention of security staff, they identified themselves to each other and to passersby. As may already be apparent, LIGNA drew upon Brecht's ideas on broadcasting, as articulated in 'Radio as a Means of Communication'.[39] In this text, Brecht argues for direct collaboration between theatre and radio performances in the public realm, proposing that radio could both transmit 'choruses' to the theatre, and also publicly broadcast the activities of the audiences engaging in, or responding to, collective performances. As only the 'choreography' was actually transmitted, *Radio Ballet* did not illustrate Brecht's thinking by establishing a two-way connection between theatre and broadcast audiences. But the fact that the transmissions incorporated commentaries and reflections on the space and performance clearly signals an interest in the communicative potential of radio. In some respects, this work gestured toward the limits of radio as it is currently often experienced, but it acquired much of its force from the visibility of a 'dispersion of listeners' bound together in a physical space, engaging in an activity that did not involve material consumption.

Museums, Monuments and TV Transmissions

The next two works are linked by an interest in the monument as both a material artefact and a focus for political and social discourse, and by a direct engagement with the production of television. *State Britain* (2007) by Mark Wallinger is the title of an installation in the Duveen Galleries at Tate Britain, for which the artist received a Turner Prize nomination.[40] Conceived specifically for this setting, the work consisted of a full-size recreation of the protest camp established by the peace campaigner Brian Haw on Parliament Square, opposite the Palace of Westminster in 2001. Growing in size over a five-year period, this assemblage of materials served as an unofficial yet prominent anti-war monument, focusing on UK foreign policy in relation to Afghanistan and Iraq. Wallinger's version was described as an exact replica of the encampment, and included '600 weather-beaten banners, photographs, peace flags and messages from well-wishers, […] the makeshift tarpaulin shelter and tea-making area, [and a] profusion of hand-painted placards and teddy bears wearing peace-slogan t-shirts'.[41] The form and title of *State Britain* was a pointed response to the passing of the Serious Organised Crime and Police Act in the UK. This legislation prohibits 'unauthorised demonstrations' within a one kilometre radius of Parliament Square, and it resulted in the removal of much of Haw's protest camp on May 23, 2006. The form of *State Britain* specifically drew attention to the fact that part of Tate Britain actually falls within this one mile radius, marked by a line of tape running through the gallery building and the installation itself.

As is customary in the lead-up to the award of the Turner Prize, each one of the four artists nominated in 2007 was the subject of a short profile video, which was presented as part of the *Three Minute Wonder* series broadcast by Channel 4 in a fixed weekday primetime slot (at 7.55pm). Significantly, the video devoted to Wallinger did not focus on the works actually presented as part of the *Turner Prize 2007* exhibition, held at Tate Liverpool. Instead, it featured documentary video of the *State Britain* installation at Tate, punctuated by still images of Haw's protest camp in situ, and night-time video footage of police disassembling it in 2006. As the officers calmly load the banners, flags and photographs into a container, Haw can be heard off-camera shouting at them 'You criminals […] Which one of you has children?', while the sounds of onlookers and the distant tolling of bells, perhaps emanating from 'Big Ben', can be heard in the background. This footage is intercut with material shot in Tate Britain, including sedate tracking shots past the installation, details of photographs, placards and attentive visitors perusing the display. In the video's closing minute, another act of disassembly takes place as gloved museum workers carefully de-install Wallinger's installation, packing each element and finally removing the black tape that runs across the floor, marking the edge of the control zone.

Even though Wallinger was credited as co-director and co-producer (with Emily Dixon) of the *Three Minute Wonder* video, it cannot be readily defined as an integral component of *State Britain*, not least because of the fact that as a TATE Media production, it clearly served a promotional function in relation to the Turner Prize exhibition. The *Three Minute Wonder* series is framed by Channel 4 as a platform for 'new talent', typically showcasing the work of young directors in addition to events like contemporary art exhibitions and fairs, in keeping with the channel's commitment to innovation and currency.[42] As part of a publicity campaign for the Turner Prize, Wallinger's video was linked to the temporality of the 'contemporary', but in terms of its form and documentary content (charting the removal of Haw's encampment and the disassembly of the *State Britain* installation) the video was strongly oriented toward the past, underscoring the museum's institutional responsibility to preserve and store, as well as display, material traces of history. By emphasising Wallinger's critique of the Serious Organised Crime and Police Act, the video also draws attention to important parallels between Tate Britain and Channel 4, as public cultural institutions that must be seen to operate independently from the government if they are to be regarded as legitimately and truly public.

Wallinger's work demonstrates the continued importance and viability of broadcasting in the production of the public sphere, so it should not be read as a memorialisation of television as public cultural form. Nonetheless, I would argue that the figure of the 'monument' is still pertinent to *State Britain*, for several reasons. Most obviously, Haw's encampment serves as a memorial to the victims of the Iraq War. Less obviously, *State Britain* also recalls Carol Duncan's description of the European public museum as a successor to the princely gallery, and a monument to processes of social and political struggle within an earlier era. Wallinger embraces this symbolic function, but at the same time he seems to acknowledge—through his insistence upon processes of disassembly and removal (in both the form of the installation and the content of the *Three Minute Wonder* video) that, as monuments, museums may be complicit in the erasure, as well as the preservation, of cultural memory.

My next example, Thomas Hirschhorn's *Bataille Monument*, developed for *documenta 11* in 2002, shared with *State Britain* a focus on processes of social assembly and material assemblage. Hirschhorn's work also involved the collaborative production of video, but in this instance realised by non-professionals, for transmission on a local television station. Conceived as part of an ongoing series of projects dedicated to philosophers,[43] *Bataille Monument* was located in the predominantly Turkish neighbourhood of Kannenberg, several kilometres away from the main *documenta 11* venues.[44] The monument was not a single structure but instead consisted of several temporary constructions, housing an exhibition about the work of Bataille, a library of texts, an *Imbiss* (snack bar), a makeshift TV studio, and a large sculpture in the form of a tree. Hirschhorn chose to work without professional assistants, technicians or art students, and instead paid an hourly wage to residents who were interested in constructing and operating the various components. Various activities loosely focused around the figure of Bataille were also organised at the site, including workshops led by invited writers and philosophers such as Christopher Fiat and Marcus Steinweg. But the project was not designed to emphasise academic expertise. Instead, Hirschhorn explicitly presented himself as 'a *fan* of Bataille', arguing that the 'fan' is not oriented toward the 'object of his love' and instead 'shares with other fans the fact of being a fan [...] Love is important, not the object of love'.[45]

More than just an assemblage of structures, the monument functioned as a setting for the production and circulation of texts in various media. So, for example, daily TV reports were produced for broadcast on a local cable channel for the duration of the exhibition. According to Hirschhorn, these television programmes 'had to have something to do with Georges Bataille, and to report on the housing complex, its residents, a worker or a visitor to the *Bataille Monument*'.[46] Some of the tapes, which were accessible to visitors as well as local TV viewers, replicate conventions associated with news programming, being loosely organised as reports, incorporating commentaries and interviews, whereas others are more informal accounts of everyday activities at the site—closer to amateur video diaries in terms of style and content. Importantly, however, Hirschhorn also integrated newer media into the project, in the form of webcams that were used to transmit images from the interior spaces of the monument to a website that provided information on the project. So *Bataille Monument* seems to have encompassed at least two different models of media production and distribution. While Hirschhorn's use of the community TV Studio/local transmission model recalls the heyday of guerrilla television and video activism, the use of more recent webcam technology is more closely associated with reality TV and surveillance culture.

Reflecting on the successes and failures of *Bataille Monument* two years after its completion, Hirschhorn expressed some doubts about the inclusion of the webcam images on the website, perhaps because they made remote access to the 'monument' too easy.[47] Although the monument was open to the public, it was located several kilometres away from the main exhibition venues. The only 'public' transport link was in fact a makeshift shuttle service consisting of four local Mercedes taxis, operating in two shifts, with each carrying up to four passengers: a strategy that seems intended to manage, or even reduce, the flow of visitors. The webcams may therefore have been a way of compensating for the relative inaccessibility of a project that was, after all, publicly-funded. Furthermore, while the use of webcams alongside much more explicitly local media, such as cable television, seems contradictory it is in keeping with Hirschhorn's hybrid model of public/private space. Just as 'fan culture' exists in tension with philosophical thought, the webcam operates as an addition to the local television transmission, and the shared taxi operates as a supplement to—or replacement for—mass transit. Through this hybrid model, Hirschhorn seemed to signal a dissolution of the public sphere, which has found expression in various forms, through the construction of public monuments, in the development of public service broadcasting and even, to some extent, in the establishment of mass transit systems.

Publicness in Question

I now turn to two final works, which share Hirschhorn's focus on the residents of specific communities, and also encompass a sculptural dimension; Kutluğ Ataman's *Küba* (2005) and Katya Sander's *Was ist Öffentlichkeit?* (2004). Unlike *Bataille Monument*, however, these later works are installations designed to be presented within multiple contexts, and I am specifically interested here in the version of *Küba* that was installed at a former postal sorting office in central London.[48] The work consists of an installation of 40 different television sets, generally somewhat antiquated, with each set placed in front of a single armchair to form the central component of a quasi-domestic viewing environment. Each television displayed a video of a monologue featuring a resident of Küba, an area of Istanbul that, according to the press release, has been 'home to nonconformists of diverse ethnicity, religion and political persuasion united in their defiant disregard for state control' since the 1960s.

The video monologues focus on the personal experiences of individual men and women, generally depicted in domestic settings and, as Adrian Searle noted in his review for *The Guardian*, 'each screen is a talking head, someone sitting at a kitchen table or in a cramped sitting-room, equipped for the most part with just the kind of old furniture we're sitting on.'[49] This description might suggest that *Küba* reinforced television's status as a 'domestic' medium but this reading is complicated by the fact that many of those delivering the monologues were Kurdish immigrants, who may or may not recognize Turkey as 'home'. As noted by Irit Rogoff, this work constitutes 'an alternative zone to "state experience"—that of deregulated experience' and the monologues communicate 'absolutely no unity of subject, thought and encompassing world'.[50] Here Rogoff is referring specifically to the fact that the 'village left behind' is not an object of nostalgia, or an imagined place of return, for Ataman's subjects. The videos, she argues, do not purport to offer knowledge about what it means to be a poor Kurdish migrant living in Istanbul, or about ghettoised ethnic communities in general. Instead the project addresses the 'limited categories and tropes that *we* think in.'[51]

Rogoff does not discuss the installation of the work in London or elsewhere, instead focusing exclusively on the content of the videos. Therefore she does not explain how the choice of site, or the evocation of western domesticity through antiquated TV sets and furniture, might operate in terms of 'deregulation'. But her concept of 'state experience' is nonetheless useful in understanding the form of the installation at the Sorting Office. She draws this concept from Deleuze and Guattari's critique of 'state philosophy', as a mode of thinking that is representational and analogical, founded upon a correspondence between 'the subject, its concepts and the objects in the world to which these concepts are applied'.[52] This bureaucratic 'fantasy of unity', she emphasises, is wholly at odds with the 'ruptures, fissures, chaotic disruptions and necessary mobilities' that characterise the world occupied by the residents of Küba. For those encountering the work in London, the sense of 'rupture and fissure' emphasised in Rogoff's account was not simply present within the content of the various video monologues. It also found expression in the materiality of the Sorting Office, which once formed part of the state-owned postal service, but is not longer in use. In order to actually reach Ataman's work, visitors to *Küba* had to enter the disused building and ascend to an upper floor, passing large pieces of equipment that were once used in the circulation of post, including huge metal chutes connecting the various stories. By presenting these somewhat antiquated TV viewing environments in such a post-Fordist setting, Ataman could be seen to evoke and perhaps also to critique the bureaucratic vision of unity which once informed the development of the public service broadcasting system—a vision that now seems irrevocably located in the past.[53]

My final example differs from all other projects discussed in this chapter because it is integrally and overtly concerned with 'publicness' as a concept. Katya Sander's *Was ist Öffentlichkeit?* is a two-part work produced at Kunstverein Munich within the context of DISPOSITIVE, a workshop series in which artists were invited to realise projects in collaboration with a group of people from the city. Sander's project consisted of an intervention into the built environment of the Munich Olympic Village (now used as student housing) and a single-channel video installation with an architectural component. The 1972 Olympic Games was significant for being one of first major events to be broadcast live across the globe and both the cohesive design and spatial organisation of the 'village' was intended, like all other buildings constructed for the competition, to facilitate this broadcast. Consequently the 'public gaze' formed an integral part of the architecture of the complex, even before members of the Israeli team were taken hostage, during the second week of the Munich games.

The 1972 Olympics is emblematic of a category that Daniel Dayan and Elihu Katz term the 'hijacked' media event, in which 'advocates of some revolutionary cause' seek to exploit media attention, requiring broadcasters to negotiate between the event as ceremony and as news.[54] Sander's project, however, was not primarily concerned with the phenomenon of the media event, or its role in structuring perceptions of collectivity. Instead she was interested in exploring how physical structures, and the forms of sociality that they invite and enable over time, can be shaped by the technological and institutional requirements of broadcasting at a given moment. Working with her collaborators, Sander spelled out the question "WAS IST ÖFFENTLICHKEIT?" (which can be translated either as "What is a public sphere?" or "What is publicness?") in large letters on the rooftops of several bungalows in the former Olympic village. These letters remained for the summer months and could be seen from the surrounding high-rise buildings.

Sander's video was shot from elevated locations, in order to suggest the perspective of a satellite, an urban planner or a tourist. She reiterated this vantage point in the installation, which involved a projection of the video onto the floor, surrounded by a wooden seating structure. The video opens with an ambiguous shot of a blue light moving through the sky, while a male voice speaks about the launch of Sputnik in October 1957: the first artificial earth satellite.[55] In the next shot, filmed directly from above, Sander and an older man

Above: Katya Sander, *Was ist*
Öffentlichkeit?, 2004 (What is Publicness?).
Installation view.
Image courtesy of the artist.

examine architectural plans and aerial photographs of the village, as he describes how the design was intended to facilitate live media coverage, to symbolise the concept of the 'global village'[56] and its associated ideas of simultaneity and immediacy. At other moments, television viewers are seen (also from above) watching what would appear to be recordings of the 1972 Games on an old-fashioned CRT monitor, fitted with an aerial.

Much of the remainder of the video, which includes both interviews and staged performances, tracks Sander, highly visible in a red jacket, carrying a microphone and again shot from above, as she poses the title question of her project to a mix of residents and visitors. The answers range from the mundane to the philosophical; many respondents link publicness to freedom and openness, but several make reference to notions of authority and regulation. For one respondent, for example, publicness is 'doing what you want without disturbing others', while for another publicness is associated with the image of a lecturer, in whose direction everyone looks. These interactions are rendered unsettling by the high camera angle, which the interviewees either ignore or fail to perceive. Suggesting the presence of a crane or high-powered lens, this aerial perspective amplifies the aesthetic (and ideology) of visibility articulated in the design of the Olympic Village. The question at the heart of *Was ist Öffentlichkeit?* eventually led Sander beyond the exterior of the Olympic Village. In a staged scenario toward the close of the video she actually enters a television studio and in another shot from above she poses her question to a newscaster. His response is no more satisfying that the others, since he simply states that publicness is simply 'what is visible'.[57]

Was ist Öffentlichkeit? differs from the other recent works discussed since, rather than focusing on privatisation and security (issues explored by LIGNA and Wallinger) it develops a more open-ended exploration of the televisual character of the built environment. Through her exploration of the Olympic complex as a physical prototype for the 'global village', Sander demonstrates that television has played a role in the formation of the built environment for many decades: since at least the early 1970s. In her video, the village functions like a microcosm of a 'televisual city', but its televisual character is not synonymous with the closure of public space or with the collapse of an idealised version of the 'polis'. Instead Sander approached the built environment of the Olympic Village as a stage that could be animated through temporary interventions performed for the camera, offering a counterpoint to the qualities of liveness, simultaneity and immediacy often emphasised by advocates of television as a utopian technology of communication.

Conclusion: Monuments to Broadcasting

Since at least the 1970s, artists engaging with the public realm have been interested in television, often focusing on its potential as a communications technology in projects ranging from media policy activism to participatory site-specific installations in heavily-trafficked urban spaces. In recent years, however, this 'potential' has acquired a new and different significance within the domain of European public art. In particular, the values associated with public service broadcasting now seem to figure as a point of reference—and also sometimes an object of critique—for artists who are not necessarily interested in either reforming television or in rendering it more accessible. Instead, many of these artists draw upon aspects of the history or theory of broadcasting to explore the changing form of public space.

I have argued that some of these works acquire a 'monumental' or memorialising function in relation to the ideals of public service broadcasting, or the public sphere. This is perhaps particularly pronounced in the installation of Susan Philipsz's *You Are Not Alone* in a site such as the Haus des Rundfunks in Berlin, where these ideals have been abandoned for several decades. Although Philipsz did not set out to examine the complex history of German broadcasting she alludes—through the form of the interval signal—to the utopian dimension of radio as a technology of communication. LIGNA also aims to mobilise a form of utopian thinking, but rather than responding to the ontology of the sound wave, their approach with a work like *Radio Ballet* is framed through reference to the history of radical political thought and practice. Mark Wallinger's *State Britain* installation functioned as a document of a political protest and its repression, underscoring the securitisation of public space. In addition, I would argue the form and scheduling of the *Three Minute Wonder* promotional video drew attention, perhaps unintentionally, to important continuities between the public museum and broadcaster as institutions that are (ideally) separate from the state.

In different ways, the projects of both Kutluğ Ataman and Thomas Hirschhorn propose new ways of thinking about the public sphere and its embodiment not just in public monuments, but also local television, communications infrastructure and mass transit systems. Both projects were attuned to the dynamism and flexibility of divisions between public and private space, emphasising the contradictions produced by these divisions. So even though the presentation of Ataman's *Küba* at the Sorting Office evoked a normative situation of domestic reception, it also questioned the stability of familial, national and state formations through its exploration of what Rogoff has termed 'de-regulation'. Hirschhorn's *Bataille Monument* used local television and online media to publicise the activities of Bataille 'fans'. But even though the project tacitly framed the monument as a site of social gathering and interaction, it seems to problematise this mode of publicness through its exploration of media and transport. Finally, Sander's *Was ist Öffentlichkeit?* reassessed the legacy of the 'global village' through the exploration of a physical environment designed to facilitate live media coverage. Rather than alluding to ideals and theories of the public sphere yet to be realised through broadcasting, however, it focused on the material traces of an earlier moment. Yet even though Sander's video is explicitly concerned with the history of broadcasting, it is not an attempt to recover or restore a utopian ideal. Instead, it is forcefully oriented toward the future, framing the concept of publicness as an unstable yet continually animating force.

Chapter Six

Talk Shows: Art Institutions and the Discourse of Publicness

The Kunstverein became a stage that offered the opportunity to revive memories, discussions and to create new perspectives in the spotlight. The well-attended and entertaining talk shows were filmed, quoting some of the stylistic clichés of well-known talk shows, edited and later shown on monitors on the stage in the exhibition space. [...] By being based on a format from everyday life they brought familiar mediation into play; that appeared to be popular with the Munich art audience.

Maria Lind, 'Telling Histories'[1]

The greenroom—the place where people hang out both before presenting on TV and afterward—frames TV live-ness with a nervous sense of the just-before and just-after and is, in fact, a perfect metaphor for TV's overdetermined, slippery, and refractive production of presence. 'Sitting in a greenroom ... thinking about how to present', as Gillick puts it in *Literally No Place*. [...] The greenroom is not just a space at the margins of live TV; it is actually the model for the televisual public sphere.

Ina Blom, *On the Style Site: Art, Sociality and Media Culture*[2]

Introduction: Talk Shows in Theory and Practice

Signifying both the 'everyday' and an overdetermined yet unstable form of 'presence', television played a complex role within the curatorial practices and discourses of the 2000s. This chapter explores several distinct (yet connected) intersections between television and art institutions during the 2000s, through reference to examples of artistic practice, curating and public programming. I focus on a number of projects in which television talk shows have provided a formal and cultural reference point for artists and curators seeking to explore the ideal of the public sphere and, in some instances, to validate the public role of the art institution as site of critique. In addition, my discussion engages with the art institution as a producer of television, identifying parallels and differences between projects developed during the 2000s and historical precedents, such as the cable TV shows developed by Long Beach Museum of Art (LBMA) in California during the 1980s. Finally, I examine formal and cultural aspects of public broadcasting that have been appropriated by curators and other professionals working in art institutions who seek to frame and promote the art museum as a model public sphere. The specific examples of practice discussed in depth are the exhibition *Telling Histories: an archive and three case studies* (Munich Kunstverein,

Above and next page: Stills from video documentation of Talk Shows, *Telling Histories: an archive and three case studies,* Munich Kunstverein, 2003. Courtesy of Søren Grammel and Kunstverein Munchen.

2003); the broadcast-inspired and currently ongoing Hammer Forum public discussions at the Hammer Museum, Los Angeles and Dora García's *KLAU MICH: Radicalism in Society Meets Experiment on TV*, commissioned for *dOCUMENTA (13)* in 2012 and realised over the course of 100 days. In addition, I briefly discuss a number of broadcast and online projects realised by European art institutions in the late 1990s and early 2000s such as Rooseum (Malmo, Sweden), the Contemporary Art Centre (Vilnius, Lithuania) and Arteleku (Donostia-San Sebastian, Northern Spain).[3]

These TV-themed projects form part of an array of publishing and commissioning strategies developed by European art centres, *Kunstvereine* and museums, which signalled an increased emphasis on self-reflexivity and discursivity, particularly with regard to the temporalities of exhibition-making and structures of institutional production, routinely described as 'New Institutional' practice. This term has been used to describe a range of practices and strategies developed in the late 1990s and mid 2000s by curators, directors and artists working in European public museums, art centres and associations. Broadly speaking, these strategies often involved moving away from traditional models of exhibition and toward participatory and discursive activities, sometimes by supporting artistic research through commissions and residencies. Writing in 2004, Claire Doherty identified New Institutionalism as 'the buzzword of current European curatorial discourse', describing it as 'a field of curatorial practice, institutional reform and critical debate concerned with the transformation of art institutions from within'.[4] Although there is no definitive list of 'new institutions', it is possible to identify multiple candidates for this title during the late 1990s and early 2000s. They include Platform Garanti Contemporary Art, Istanbul, the Museum of Contemporary Art in Oslo, the Contemporary Art Center in Vilnius, Kunsthalle Helsinki, Kunstverein Frankfurt (especially under the direction of Nicolaus Schafhausen), Palais de Tokyo in Paris (when directed by Nicolas Bourriaud and Jerome Sans) and BAK in Utrecht. Like Maria Lind, Charles Esche has contributed to the reconceptualisation of art institutional practice, in a succession of institutional roles.[5] Both Esche and Lind supported the development of long-term artistic research projects and at Munich Kunstverein, Lind established a network of practitioners designated as 'sputniks'. This term evoked both the notion of remote viewing and a sense of continual motion that was perhaps especially appropriate to an era defined by the emergence of highly mobile art professionals, whose activities were partly facilitated by the greater availability of cheap air travel.

This period was also marked by important changes in the communication technologies available to art institutions that, although somewhat self-evident, are worth noting. These changes included an increased emphasis on the use of websites to publicise art events, enabling geographically dispersed organisations to build and maintain this mobile community of international professionals. Websites could be used to host archive details of publications and events, providing extensive contextual information on discursive events and long-term projects. New mailing list services such as e-flux[6] also enabled the dissemination of information to this community more effectively than printed press releases. In conjunction with these developments, the practitioners associated with these new institutions were responding and generally seeking to engage critically with the instrumentalisation of culture in public policy. Although New Institutionalism has been extensively theorised,[7] its televisual dimension has received little attention. I am specifically interested in the possibility that television, in both online and broadcast form, may have functioned alongside publishing as a way for several so-called new institutions to cultivate remote, as well as local, audiences.

Accordingly, I revisit in this chapter the TV productions and related publishing initiatives of the late 1990s and early 2000s in order to understand how these institutional projects differed from earlier examples of 'museum television'. I also examine the continued significance of television talks for artists, curators and public programmers who seek to negotiate and legitimate the publicness of art institutions, in an era when the very notion of the public sphere is increasingly being called into question. Before proceeding to the exploration of specific examples, it is important to reiterate the significance of 'talk' as a point of connection between museums and broadcasting as two public cultural institutions. For Tony Bennett, the public museum is just one of many bourgeois formations that emerged to mediate between the state and the aristocratic court, on one hand, and the sphere of the family, on the other. The museum operated alongside various 'literary, artistic and cultural institutions' in which 'new forms of assembly, debate, critique and commentary were developed'.[8] These institutions included literary journals, philosophical societies, coffee houses as well as 'new cultural markets (academies, art galleries, salons)', which allowed the formative bourgeois public to be present to itself and, so to acquire self-consciousness. Differentiating his position from that of Habermas, especially with regard to 'social exclusiveness', Bennett frames the nineteenth-century museum as an exemplary space of self-display and self-regulation, integral to the production and maintenance of social hierarchies. For Bennett, the museum's capacity to act upon the social is not, however, restricted to a fixed set of techniques. Instead it is continually refashioned, functioning in recent decades, for example, as a 'differencing machine' with the potential to 'ameliorate conflicted racialized differences'.[9]

Dorothea von Hantelmann also emphasises the importance of the exhibition as 'flexible' format. She notes that, historically, public museums struggled to replicate the 'aesthetics of conversation and sociability' that had once marked the princely collection, because these aesthetics were 'now too time-consuming for a social class that worked, and whose life was more and more subject to a strict management of time'.[10] Television and radio talk shows clearly recall of some of the characteristics ascribed to bourgeois cultural institutions, in the sense that they function as (mediated) sites of assembly, debate, critique and commentary, yet they are routinely dismissed as sites of rational-critical discourse—in the Habermasian sense.[11] Writing in 1990, for example, Stephen Heath argues that television talk typically results in the production of representative as opposed to deliberative publics. As he points out, political and cultural representation were initially strongly linked in bourgeois conceptions of the subject, whose role was to 'be educated, socialized, cultured, indeed *acculturated*'.[12] But by the twentieth century, he argues, a more explicitly economic calculation had become apparent, as representation was reconfigured as 'a political fact and struggle *and* a market reality'.[13] While Heath suggests that residues of an address towards the 'citizen' persist in some broadcast contexts, he emphasise that this address forms part of more 'varied appeal' oriented toward the 'free subject plus state citizen plus socio-cultural being plus, more and more, consumer'.[14] Talk shows are very definitely *not* a remnant of the archaic address toward a 'citizen-viewer' in Heath's model, and instead exemplify the loss of the deliberative public sphere. He states:

> The true stars and symbols of television are talkers, instigators of ever more talk: Johnny Carson or Oprah Winfrey or Phil Donahue or Barbara Walters or…Television is meeting people over and over again [...] and talking over and over again (day in, day out, from *Good Morning America* through to Ted Koppel or David Letterman). Before all else we are treated to a permanent serial of the public for the public in a circle of proximation: if I watch for long enough, I will get to meeting and talking with everyone.[15]

So while certain forms of television talk might produce a sensation of proximity, according to Heath, this is simply an illusion of social connectedness, which is ultimately detrimental to the project of political representation.[16]

It is not my intention here to assess the merits or deficits of the talk show as a context for the performance of rational-critical deliberation. Instead, I argue that curators, artists and institutions have been drawn to the talk show precisely because its changing form serves to articulate important shifts in the public sphere. Although Heath does not seem to differentiate between hosts such as Phil Donahue and Oprah Winfrey, the late 1980s and early 1990s actually witnessed quite significant shifts in the form and economy of the US talk show. Jane Shattuc has charted these developments, noting that the 'general political commitment' evident in long-running shows such as *Phil Donahue* (1967–1996), while initially apparent in *Sally Jesse Raphael* (1983–2002), *The Oprah Winfrey Show* (1986–2011) and *Geraldo* (1987–1998), was eventually superseded by a new mode of daytime TV talk.[17] Rather than focusing on personal stories that connected to socio-political issues, a more recent generation of daytime hosts, including *Jerry Springer* (1991–), *Montel Williams* (1991–2008) and *Rikki Lake* (1993–2004), tended to emphasise and perhaps even encourage interpersonal conflict and were, as a consequence, much less bound to notions of the public sphere. Shattuc also notes that the newer shows were generally produced by independents rather than the main networks and tended to address a younger audience demographic than their predecessors. She suggests that their popularity attested to the power of 'youthful rule-breaking and renegade individualism in the face of the social regulation imposed not only by the identity politics of the 1990s, but also by the established shows of the 1980s'.[18] Shattuc emphasises the necessity of continual innovation within a fiercely competitive environment, and suggests that this drive for innovation contributed to the 'self-conscious gutting of the feminist notions of empowerment based on confession, testimony, and social conversion'.[19] Nonetheless, she acknowledges that 'at their best', the daytime talk shows that rose to prominence in the 1990s could offer empowerment in the form of 'an active, even aggressive "in your face" identity to people who have been represented either as victims or perverts by a dominant culture'.[20]

Talk Shows, Institutional Controversy and Critique

Several curators have engaged with the talk show as an exhibition theme or format.[21] For example, curator and critic Boris Groys presented *The Art Judgement Show* at Moderna Galerija in Ljubljana (2001) and at Roomade in Brussels (2002). Described as 'a television talk show', it was not televised or staged in front of a live audience and instead took the form of a video installation. This project was framed in the Roomade press release as a 'fascinating philosophical conversation', presented 'in an accessible form to the general public', involving a conversation between Groys and a group of students on the topic of 'whether today, "art" still has any relevance, whether it is significantly different from commercial pursuits such as advertising, design and popular music, and what criteria should be used in order to evaluate it'.[22] *The Art Judgement Show* may also have been an attempt to question—or at least make explicit—the power and celebrity status of the curator during this period, because Groys apparently modelled his persona as the presenter on the hosts of European and US shows, including *Arabella* (1994–2004, broadcast on the German channel ProSieben) and *The Oprah Winfrey Show* (1986–2011).

I am specifically interested, however, in curators and artists, who use TV talk show formats to reflect upon the form and structure of art institutions, a model exemplified by *Telling Histories: an archive and three case studies* (October 11—November 23, 2003). Curated by Maria Lind, Søren Grammel and with Ana Paula Cohen at Kunstverein Munchen in 2003, this project set out to examine three highly controversial exhibitions[23] presented at the Kunstverein since 1970, including Andrea Fraser's *Eine Gesellschaft des Geschmacks* from 1993 (translated as 'A Society of Taste'), to which I will return. *Telling Histories* included an archive of material relating to these three 'case studies', which was assembled and presented by artist Mabe Bethonico, and included catalogues, press clippings and exhibition files with contracts, lists of works and letters, which could be accessed via a computer. This archival material also formed the basis for three public discussions presented in an environment designed by Liam Gillick[24] and staged in the manner of a TV talk show. Grammel, who originated the talk show component of the exhibition, selected the guests and also took on the role of host. As evidenced by the video documentation, the set was relatively simple, with the guests seated on either side of the host, on a raised platform facing the audience. Several cameras were used, enabling close-ups and reaction shots of guests, and the video documentation of each event was edited for subsequent viewing within the gallery.

Writing in 2005, Lind emphasised her interest in the TV talk show as a 'format from everyday life', noting the importance of working with 'familiar forms of mediation'.[25] But Grammel, reflecting on *Telling Histories* some years later, offers a slightly more value-laden judgement of the talk show format and its relevance to the Munich context:

Looking at Munich with its saturated TV- and tabloid-based boulevard mentality, I chose the talk show as a metaphor for the phantom of mediation in general—or, to put it differently—a metaphor for the promises of the mediation industry. For this I chose the participants and trained for the role of a talk show host myself. For a while I analyzed the rhetorics and vocabulary of Sabine Christiansen—then the most well known talk show host in Germany.[26]

Grammel seems to envisage the transposition of TV conventions into the Kunstverein as way of representing the city's 'tabloid-based' mentality, implicitly framing the exhibition as a space for visitors to perform and display their awareness of the constructedness of television and the 'mediation industry'. This position might not have been shared by Gillick, however, since the latter's practice tends to question the very existence of a form of sociality that is *not* mediated. The place and question of mediation is discussed in Ina Blom's analysis of Gillick's practice, including his book *Literally No Place: Communes, Bars and Greenrooms* (2002), organised around the narratives of six nameless characters who are researching a utopian commune.[27]

Literally No Place is not intrinsically concerned with television as an institution or cultural technology, although Blom highlights a 'structural link between utopianism and TV culture that seems to run through Gillick's work',[28] which encompasses publications and architectural constructions installed in museums, galleries and public spaces. For Gillick, the commune and the television 'greenroom' form part of a larger assemblage of spaces that are associated with ideas of artistic creativity and sociality, but exist in a contradictory relation to each other. While both are to some extent associated with ideas of production the greenroom is also characterised by an ambiguous temporality, described by Blom:

> The greenroom (a term originally taken from the theater) is the liminal space where the participants in live TV shows wait before they go on camera and where they mingle afterward. It is a social space that frames televisual performance and thus also demarcates the shaped and edited nature of televisual real-time—the apparently spontaneous and unbroken flow of events that aligns TV time (as well as its artistic sidekick, video art) with lived temporality in general.[29]

By focusing on the greenroom as a liminal space, that typically exists off-camera,[30] Gillick proposes a social space that operates in tension with—and yet remains somehow bound to—televisual notions of immediacy and presence. Blom emphasises that while the ideal of 'presence' is continually evoked and promoted in television, it is an ideal that continually slips away, and the greenroom functions in Gillick's practice as one 'metaphor' for this slippage. Within this framework, the 'televisual public sphere' is no longer conceived as a privileged site for the performance of rational-critical discourse in the Habermasian sense. Instead, according to Blom, Gillick's work reveals the 'idealization of "discussion"' as both a component of 'the consensus-environment of post-corporate or post-industrial societies' and a value that is inherited from an earlier social moment—that of the utopian commune.[31]

The stage environment devised by Gillick for *Telling Histories* clearly relates to the assemblage of spaces and texts theorised by Blom, but there appears to be a tension between the logic of

Gillick's practice and the relationship between television and the gallery articulated in curatorial accounts of *Telling Histories*. The main difference in my view is that the curators of *Telling Histories* sought to retain the ideal of discussion. It is true that by turning the Kunstverein into a 'stage' they acknowledged the mediated character of sociality in the gallery, but through the self-conscious quotation of 'stylistic cliché' they *also* clearly addressed the gallery visitor as a rational-critical subject capable of recognising, and displaying their recognition of, this display of mediation. This reading is supported by Reesa Greenberg's analysis of *Telling Histories*, as one of several 'archival remembering exhibitions'. Emphasising that all three exhibitions 'remembered' in this show were controversial, she suggests that their memory was preserved as a form of validation for an institutional identity founded on 'transformational practices rather than the propagation of conformist ideas'.[32] Importantly, as Greenberg also notes, the project was actually framed in direct reference to a process of commemoration, since it coincided with the Kunstverein's 180th anniversary. The memories being revived in this project suggest that several forms of remembering were interwoven in *Telling Histories*: related to the history of the Kunstverein as institution, to the three earlier exhibitions (and related controversies) represented, and also to the content and form of the 'talk shows' which were encountered by visitors as both live events and video documentation.

Telling Histories also seemed to anticipate a broader process of 'remembering' and contextualising institutional critique on the part of artists and theorists, including Andrea Fraser, who in 2005 charted the process of transition towards what she termed 'an institution of critique'.[33] Writing a year later, Hito Steyerl also revisited this history: seeking to differentiate between different moments of institutional critique and theorise how these strategies function in relation to a changing conception of the public sphere, and altered conditions of labour and production. She argues that the first wave of critique 'challenged the authority which had accumulated in cultural institutions within the framework of the nation state'.[34] It was, she notes, premised upon the notion that the cultural institution could operate as a 'potential public sphere', which was 'implicitly national' and founded upon 'the model of representative parliamentarism'. By the 1990s, however, the cultural authority vested in the museum had begun to break down, like the Fordist economic model upon which it depended, and Steyerl goes on to chart the subsequent shift in criticism toward symbolic forms of representation; a move she sees as informed by cultural studies, feminism and postcolonial epistemologies. In Steyerl's account, this emphasis on the realm of the symbolic is integrally linked to, and perhaps reflective of, the emergence of a politics of identity and the attendant fragmentation of both public spheres and markets. With the third phase, however, critique was symbolically integrated into the institution, or rather 'on the surface of the institution without any material consequences within the institution itself or its organisation'.[35] Steyerl's point here is that while museums began to display or perform criticality in various ways, the conditions of labour for those engaged in this performance—such as artists and independent curators—became increasingly precarious. As a result, in her rather bleak formulation, integration 'into the institution' was followed by integration 'into representation' and, thus finally, 'into precarity'.

Steyerl's analysis clearly raises important issues with regard to practices and histories of institutional critique, including those articulated in exhibitions such as *Telling Histories*. As already noted, Fraser's 1993 project for Munich Kunstverein (then directed by Helmut Draxler) was entitled *Eine Gesellschaft des Geschmacks* and it developed a quasi-sociological analysis of the Kunstverein structure from the perspective of an 'outsider', albeit one authorised by the institution, since it was developed in cooperation with nine members of the Kunstverein's Board of Directors.[36] Fraser interviewed board members, posing questions such as 'Do you own art objects? What service do you think the Kunstverein provides in Munich?'. Interestingly, her research identified 'international prestige' as an important focus for several interviewees, signalling that they valued their position within a cultural and social network that extended beyond Munich and Germany. Transcripts of the answers were presented in the catalogue and also edited to form an audio collage, played in the gallery alongside a display of 25 works of art owned by board members, exhibited without the specific details of artists or owners.

Following *Eine Gesellschaft des Geschmacks*, Fraser realised another project with Helmut Draxler, this time within a different German institutional context,[37] entitled *Services: Conditions and Relations of Project Oriented Artistic Practice*. This was an exhibition and working group focusing on the concept of art as a 'service' and it addressed, amongst other issues, the changing institutional and economic context of artistic production.[38] Fraser has continued to explore related issues of creative production since the 1990s, sometimes engaging directly with conditions of precarious labour within the cultural economy. Yet even though her work articulates an acute consciousness of curatorial and institutional practice, it is not necessarily immune to the dynamics of integration highlighted by Steyerl. Here I am referring to the fact that although *Telling Histories* framed *Eine Gesellschaft des Geschmacks* as an important historical precedent for non-conformist practice at Munich Kunstverein, it also implicitly integrated Fraser's approach into a genealogy of institutional self-reflection.[39]

More generally, it can be argued that the late 1990s and early 2000s witnessed a new emphasis on the art institution as a site of visible *production* on the part of curators, artists and public programmers. Noah Horowitz, for example, suggests that organisations such as Palais de Tokyo in Paris built their reputations through the constant commissioning of new work. At the same time, he seeks to differentiate the mode of practice exemplified by Palais de Tokyo from what he terms the 'event-driven conflation of museum management and cultural tourism', noting that the latter results in the promotion of 'destination art', in which the 'act of *seeing* art is complemented, even eclipsed, by the touristic experience of *being there*'.[40] He also situates BALTIC, which opened in 2003 in a converted flour mill in Newcastle-Gateshead, within the production-oriented as opposed to event-oriented category. But, writing in 2004, Claire Doherty offers a quite different perspective on this organisation, claiming that, even though it was promoted as a production-centred space through symposia, publications and artists' studios, it is primarily a conventional exhibition space.[41] Even if BALTIC never actually put a new institutional agenda into practice, however, the rhetoric around production—combined with the physical transformation of the former flour mill into an art factory—has a symbolic value, especially for those seeking to promote the discourse of culture-led urban regeneration.

Remote Audiences and New Publics: Art Institutions as Broadcasters and Publishers

The drive toward highly visible production, manifest in many so-called 'New Institutions', can also be read as a response to the museum's loss of cultural authority, reflecting the fragmentation of public spheres and markets. According to Simon Sheikh, the bourgeois subject was historically constituted through 'interlinked process of self-representation and self-authorization', and cannot be understood in isolation from its 'cultural self-representation as a public'.[42] As already noted, museums and journals enabled this process, allowing the bourgeois public to become *visibly* present to itself. But in the era of 'post-public' fragmentation these traditional modes of bourgeois self-representation have changed, displaced by what Sheikh describes as a neo-liberal discourse of 'consumer groups, as segments of a market with particular demands and desires to be catered to, and to be commodified'.[43] He also emphasises that these ongoing processes of fragmentation and segmentation have 'direct consequences for art's spaces, be they bourgeois or otherwise inclined, in terms of public funding (always the main tool of cultural policies)'.[44] At stake here is the fact that publicly-funded art institutions typically derive and secure some, if not all, of their resources through their engagement with local constituencies, and so must satisfy the demands of local funding authorities or other 'stakeholders'. At the same time, as evidenced by Fraser's interactions with the board members of Kunstverein Munchen and the 'destination art' dynamics theorised by Horowitz, art institutional practices are also often dictated by the desire to address constituencies located elsewhere.

During the 2000s, broadcasting, webcasting and publishing became increasingly important as ways to develop and manage these disparate constituencies. Reflecting upon her experience as director of Munich Kunstverein (in 2006), Lind actually used a media industries framework to analyse the art economy and its relations of scale, suggesting that 'MoMA, Tate Modern and some other institutions have more in common with big media companies like Channel 4 [...] in how they operate, while small institutions like Kunstvereine would have more in common with a little publisher or a little record label or a little research institute somewhere'.[45] The publishing analogy is perhaps particularly significant because serial publications such as journals were favoured by many so-called new institutions. Reflecting in

Next pages: Poster for CAC TV, 2004.
Courtesy of Contemporary Art Centre
(CAC), Vilnius.
Designer: Povilas Utovka.

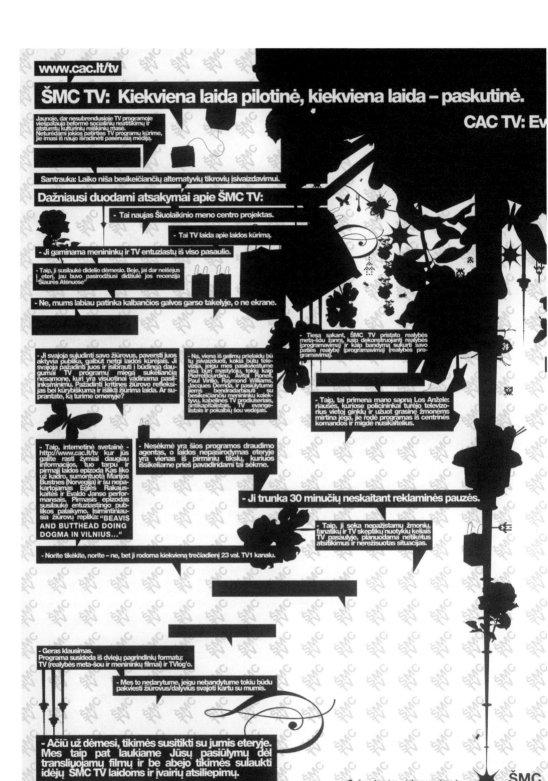

www.cac.lt/tv

ery program is a pilot. Every program is the final episode.

Log-Line: An amorphous group of social misfits and cultural outcasts are handed the reigns of a fledgling television program. Not having any experience in making television, they decide to re-invent the medium.

Synopsis: A time-slot for imagining alternate realities.

Frequently Given Responses:

- It is a new project of the Contemporary Art Centre, Vilnius.

- It is a TV program about making a TV program.

- It is produced by artists and television enthusiasts worldwide.

- Yes, this reminds me of a dream I had during the L.A. Riots in which the police were carrying television sets instead of guns. And instead of threatening people with lethal force, they induced them into a strange slumber by zapping them with programs from central command.

- Well, one possible premise would be to imagine what kind of television could be produced if we were to invite a group of thinkers (i.e., Pierre Bourdieu, Avital Ronell, Paul Virilio, Raymond Williams, Jacques Derrida) to collaborate with a rotating cast of artists, cable-access producers, anti-capitalists, tele-evangelists, and day time talk show hosts.

- Yes, the obligatory website plug, http://www.cac.lt/tv where you can find much more including The First Episode: Behind The Scenes (featuring the unforgetable performances of Egle Rakauskaite and Evaldas Jansas as well as editing by Maria Bustnes), which premiered in Lithuania in October and received a number of enthusiastic reactions including the famous: "BYVIS IR TESLAGALVIS FILMUOJA DOGMĄ VILNIUJE..."

- Good question. The show consists of two basic formats: the broadcast version including a showcase of artists films, games and devices and TVlog

- We would not be doing it if we did not think that it would in fact be an invitation to the viewers/participants to dream together.

- No, we prefer talking heads being inside the soundtrack instead of on the screen.

- Yes, the interest has been surprising. In fact, it had its official review of 1500 words before it went to an editing room.

- It lasts 30 minutes minus a commercial break.

- Believe it or not, it airs once a week on TV1, a commercial TV channel in Lithuania.

- Failure is the underwriter of this program, and cancellation is one of several goals we have before we can call this a success.

- Yes, it follows the adventures of strangers, fans and TV-sceptics inside TV-land through planned accidents and unscripted actions.

- Actually, it introduces the genre of reality meta-show both as a deconstruction of the format of reality (programming) and as an attempt to create one's own reality (programming) (reality-programming).

- It dreams of turning audience members and spectators into an active public possibly even producers. It dreams of inducing wakefulness and tapping into the inherent power of the multitude to counter the sleep inducing nonsense that often passes as entertainment. Activating the creativity and critical skills of the viewer while still remaining watch-able. You know what we mean?

- Thanks, we truly are hoping to meet you online or on air. We also look forward for your suggestions for films as well as ideas and proposals for the CAC TV.

email: tv@cac.lt

2006 upon commonalities between art institutions headed by formerly independent curators, Alex Farquharson noted the pervasiveness of journal-publishing. He cites examples such as *Drucksache* published by Munich Kunstverein, the *Zeitung* published by Shedhalle in Zurich, *Interviu* (from CAC Vilnius), *L'Ed* (from CAC Bretigny, outside Paris), *Kiasma* (from Kiasma in Helsinki), and *Zehar* from Arteleku in Spain.[46]

Farquharson suggests that these journals—several of which have long since ceased publication—enabled the integration of multiple strands of programming, sometimes also functioning as discrete platforms for the parallel exploration of ideas, in the form of interviews and commissioned essays. Implicitly acknowledging the primacy of geographically dispersed peer-based communities over local readers, he notes that these publications enabled communication beyond the venue, 'with a second, remote audience that in some cases is more receptive than their local constituency.'[47] This remote audience is not necessarily bound to a fixed physical place but, as I have suggested earlier, rather conceived as highly mobile, continually 'on the move'. In a critical history of the culture of curating, Paul O'Neill emphasises the specific role played by nomadic curators as 'mediators, or intermediary agents' both within given exhibition contexts and within the 'superstructure of the international cultural economy'.[48] In the first part of the 2000s, serial publications offered one way for these mobile and dispersed audiences to engage with curatorial programmes unfolding over extended periods of time.[49] Unlike exhibition catalogues, journal-style publications may also have been especially attractive to curators because they occupy an especially privileged place in theories and histories of the public sphere, as evidenced by the work of Habermas and others who have engaged with his thinking.

Michael Warner, for example, draws upon the history of journals such as *The Spectator* in order to theorise public and counterpublic formations. He differentiates between the public conceived through reference to a 'social totality [such as] the nation, the commonwealth, the city, the state or some other community',[50] or articulated in the form of a 'concrete audience, a crowd witnessing itself in visible space, as with a theatrical public'. Instead he focuses on a third sense of publicness, much more directly relevant to serial publication; 'a kind of public that comes into being only in relation to texts and their circulation' and is self-organised through discourse, rather than through an external framework. This form of publicness is especially dependent upon the 'concatenation of texts through time'.[51] Warner notes the specific importance of feedback loops, such as those produced through the publication of readers' letters, for example, even if, in the case of *The Spectator*, some of these 'readers' may also have been the writers and publishers.[52] He is also interested in the emergence of what he terms 'talk value', understood in terms of a new, creative and distinctly modern mode of power, and associated with a 'projective' mode of discourse.

This orientation or projection toward a future moment means that public discourse functions as 'an engine for (not necessarily progressive) social mutation',[53] contributing in some contexts to the formation of counterpublics—whereby dominated or subordinate groups seek to re-create themselves *as* public. While I am not suggesting that journals such as Munich Kunstverein's *Drucksache* contributed to the articulation of 'counterpublics' (since they did not necessarily emanate from or address constituencies with a subordinate social status), these publications played an important role in the projective discourse of curators and artists associated with New Institutionalism. In particular, the journals contributed to the emergence of a form of publicness distinct from—and perhaps at odds with—both the 'social totality' signified by nation or city and the 'concrete audience' visible to itself within the space of the gallery.

In parallel with these publishing activities, Farquharson cites three specific examples of 'in-house television as art work and curatorial medium' [54]: Superflex's television productions at Rooseum in Malmo (2001–2002), CAC TV at the Contemporary Art Centre, Vilnius (2004–2007) and also Arteleku TV, at Arteleku in Donostia-San Sebastian, Northern Spain. Arteleku TV was an internet TV channel set up in 2003, which operated until the late 2000s and aimed to 'support artistic creation for the Internet and the construction of new flows of information'.[55] The Danish artists' group Superflex developed an array of webcasting projects as part of their *Superchannel* project. In an interview from 2001, Charles Esche framed this project as a way of extending the institution's engagement with local communities, citing webcast projects developed in the suburbs of Malmo.[56] While this aspect of the project is certainly important, Superflex's involvement in the Rooseum programme also facilitated the development of links with other art institutions, located in Liverpool, Leipzig and also Thailand.[57] Unlike the other examples cited by Farquharson, the programmes produced by CAC TV were devised not for the web but for transmission on commercial television. Developed in response to a proposition from a Lithuanian broadcaster, and produced by curator Raimundas Malasauskas, the project was informed by precedents such as Chris Burden's *TV commercials* (1974–77) and numerous ventures by Andy Warhol.[58] Programmes were transmitted on the Channel TV1, at 11 pm on Wednesday evenings over a three-year period, with episodes also available for viewing on the CAC website.

In an outline addressed to 'future sponsors' of the 'Public CAC TV Draft Concept', the producers list a number of goals, which include 'creating a TV genre that does not exist yet in Lithuanian television, developing critical skills of TV audience, deconstructing fundamentals of intellectual infotainment, exploring the field of open-source (reality) programming and self-regulation [through the] genre of the Reality meta-show'.[59] This 'meta-show' was to be broadcast monthly, with more frequent transmissions of artists' film and video. The first episode of the monthly show resembles a surreal video diary or an absurd road movie, documenting the preparations for a party to be held in the presence of a Macau ape, who is first collected from a circus encampment. The purpose of the party remains unclear but the confused participants are continually assured that the programme will be broadcast on Lithuanian television, a strategy that usually secures their cooperation.

CAC TV is cited by Sally O'Reilly in a 2006 article on artists' television in the *Financial Times*. She notes that the producers were given 'total autonomy' and simply delivered programmes to the television centre on DVD, 'without being censored or even previewed by the station',[60] implicitly framing this level of trust as unusual. Yet CAC TV was never conceived as either a disruption or intervention, but rather as a long-term partnership with the specified goal of developing the critical skills of TV audience over time, suggesting a

Above: *CAC TV Reality Metashow*, episode 1, 2004. Courtesy of Contemporary Art Centre (CAC), Vilnius.

conscious (albeit light-hearted) continuation of the traditional bourgeois project of self-formation. Of the various examples cited by O'Reilly, CAC TV is the only television show to be produced by an art institution. Yet there are important precedents for this approach, such as the cable TV programmes produced by Long Beach Museum of Art (LBMA) in California during the 1980s.

Founded in the 1950s, and located in a building that was formerly a private home, LMBA's relatively small gallery spaces were well-suited to the screening of single-channel monitor works. It was one of the first US museums to establish a video art department, established in 1974 and including specialists such as David A. Ross and, subsequently, Kathy Rae Huffman (from 1976–1983).[61] The museum's first foray into cable television was in May 1977, with a performance event called *Douglas Davis: Two Cities, A Text, Flesh, and the Devil,* which took place simultaneously in Santa Monica and San Francisco, in a collaboration between LBMA and the art department of California State University Long Beach. During this period, museum staff were also involved in the development of a new building, which was initially supposed to include a cable television studio facility as part of its infrastructure. This facility was partly inspired by Ross's experience of working at the independent video studio Art/Tapes/22 in Florence (Italy),[62] but the plans for a new building at Long Beach were ultimately shelved, prompting his departure as curator.

In 1980, the existing LBMA video studio was upgraded to broadcast quality with assistance from the Rockefeller Foundation and the National Endowment for the Arts (NEA). Two years later, the museum also collaborated with New York University, UCLA and the University of Iowa to produce *The Arts for Television.* This was a three-hour, one-off live cable TV programme, linking artists in New York, Long Beach and Iowa City, featuring contributions from curators such as John Hanhardt and Barbara London, and artists such as Nancy Buchanan, Chris Burden, Jaime Davidovich, Mike Kelley and Michael Smith. This event was documented by Davidovich for inclusion in an episode of his own Manhattan-based cable programme, *The Live! Show,* to which I will return.[63] Around this time, the museum also hosted a conference called *Shared Realities,* which brought artists, curators and the developers of new cable TV services together to explore the future of 'art as TV'. It was followed by the LBMA's first regular cable TV show, also called *Shared Realities* (1983).

During the 1980s LBMA also established a television production grant programme for California-based video artists, called *Open Channels,* with the support of the local cable industry, which ran from 1986 until 1995 and included cable operators, artists and curators as jurors.[64] The works produced as part of Open Channels included Paul McCarthy's *Family Tyranny/Cultural Soup* (1987), shot in a set constructed in the three-camera studio of Alhambra Cable.[65] The Museum also produced an 18-part series of short works by video artists called *Video Viewpoints* (1987–89) and arts television programmes such as *Art Off the Wall* and *Arts Revue,* also for cable. These initiatives were developed alongside a programme of exhibitions that often engaged directly with television, including shows such as *Tele-visions: Channels for Changing TV* (1991), curated by Michael Nash and featuring works by David Lynch and Mark Frost, Martha Rosler and Paper Tiger Television and Antonio Muntadas.

Reflecting upon the significance of LBMA's engagement with television, Gloria Sutton suggests that it was one of several organisations seeking to establish 'new institutional models' for the collection, preservation, circulation, and exhibition of visual art during the 1970s and 80s'.[66] She also emphasises that despite its limited financial resources, the museum adhered to traditional museological models, differentiating it from 'more overtly anti-institutional and artist-centered aims' of organisations such as Franklin Furnace and The Kitchen. So rather than adopting an 'alternative' organisational structure, LBMA instead 'sought to radically recast the museum itself and expand its reach through television'.[67] For Sutton, LBMA functions not only as a significant venue for media-art production in the late 1970s and early 80s, but also as a 'model [...] which radically challenged the expectations of an art museum as a repository'.[68] Sutton emphasises that Nam June Paik, whose practice was the focus of the first exhibition which David Ross curated at LBMA, was a highly influential figure in the development of Ross's concept of the 'museum as medium'.[69] Ross, following Paik, considered that the museum of the future would have to be a 'television channel, among other things',[70] and that artists would eventually be able to sidestep the infrastructure of the museum and engage with audiences directly.

The museum's activities as a cable producer were, however, also partly modelled upon the work of another artist: Jaime Davidovich. Huffman points out that LBMA's early interest in cable coincided with the founding of New York's Cable SoHo, a collaboration between a group of New York-based organisations including The Kitchen, Anthology Film Archives and Franklin Furnace, and individuals such as Davidovich, Gregory Battcock and Douglas Davis. As the group's first programme director, Davidovich established a broadcasting base with the public access station Manhattan Community TV and founded the non-profit Artists Television Network, with funding from the NEA and the New York State Council for the Arts. He also produced and starred in his own regular cable programme, *The Live! Show* (1979–1984),[71] appearing sometimes in the guise of his alter ego 'Dr Videovich'. Claiming that he could cure viewers of their addiction to television, this TV 'doctor' may have been partly inspired by the growing prominence of Dr Ruth Weistheimer, the host of a NBC radio phone-in show called *Sexually Speaking*, who soon became a fixture on network talk shows before landing her own cable show.[72] Davidovich was clearly responding to the rise of lifestyle-driven commercial cable programming, by creating opportunities for his audience to enage with this altered media environment, sometimes directly addressing the viewers as *consumers* though tele-shopping style sequences.

In the early 1980s, Davidovich was invited to LBMA to present a selection of 'SoHo TV' cablecasts in the gallery, and during this time he made a video work called *The Gap* (1981/2) in the museum's newly-established broadcast studio, exploring the question 'what is art?'. According to Huffman, this work re-ignited the museum's interest in producing its own cable TV programming and his 'easy, confident' approach to presentation provided direct inspiration for the *Shared Realities* show.[73] As implied by its title, *The Gap* addressed the disconnection between contemporary art institutions and other spaces of cultural consumption. With a running time of 26 minutes, it was framed as an evening news-style 'special episode' of *The Live! Show* with Davidovich in the role of an investigative reporter searching for 'art' in a local shopping mall and in the museum. He first wanders around the mall commenting on displays as though they might be artworks, occasionally engaging bemused sales staff in conversation about kitsch objects, before returning to the museum, to observe and question visitors in interactions that appear more obviously staged. While Davidovich's own approach communicates a fascination with the changing forms of commercial television—and their associated modes of address and consumption—curators such as Ross and Huffman seem to have viewed television as a cultural (and social) form that could both extend the functions of the museum and inform its reinvention.

The LBMA does not seem to have been widely cited as a precedent for the TV shows produced by so-called New Institutions. Nonetheless there are many parallels with newer organisations, particularly given LBMA's emphasis on commissioning and producing works for circulation well beyond the physical space of the museum. In addition, as Sutton makes clear, the museum's engagement with cable TV was just one element of a much broader project of institutional self-critique. Given the influence of Paik's thinking, it could be that LBMA's project of self-critique was at least partly technologically-determined, yet this is also somewhat true of subsequent 'museum TV' ventures involving webcasting, such as Superflex's *Superchannel*.[74] In my view, the main connection between these different institutional formations lies in their shared use of television to both question and confirm the significance of the museum as public space. Rather than emphasising the co-presence of gallery visitors and artworks, or the representation of the social totality of the nation or city through collections of objects organised into narratives of national progress, these institutions favoured more multi-faceted understanding of publicness, produced and articulated through publishing and broadcasting. So, just as the LBMA programme emphasised the distribution and dissemination of art works through cable transmission, organisations such as Munich Kunstverein sought to constitute new publics through the continual production and circulation of texts, including serialised publications. Similarly, CACTV videos were encountered not only on Lithuanian television but also in various other art institutions, extending the art centre's programme beyond the national context.

It would be misleading, however, to suggest that so-called New Institutions were wholly uninterested in the concrete audiences who were physically present to each other in the gallery. In fact, Claire Doherty has argued that several British galleries and art centres consistently framed the museum as a site of social gathering, often through discursive events that required people to be physically present to each other.[75] *Telling Histories* also involved the temporary transformation of the Kunstverein into a stage for presentations in front of a live audience, albeit in a form that questioned televisual discourses of presence and liveness. In recent years, these disparate modes of publicness—dispersed and physically present to each other—have arguably become more intertwined, because it has become much easier to webcast live events taking place in galleries, and to access online content, such as conference blogs, while sitting in a wireless-equipped art spaces. As a result visitors attending a gallery talk or discussion might at the same time form part of a larger audience accessing the event via the web. This does not necessarily mean, however, that the various categories of publicness specified by Warner have collapsed into each other. Instead I would argue they remain important in the production of symbolic value, and in the legitimation of art spaces as recognisably public institutions.

Museums, Journalistic Public Spheres and Radicalism on TV

My next example is not a curatorial initiative but rather an aspect of the public programming developed at the Hammer Museum in Los Angeles. Although it cannot be defined as an example of 'museum television', the Hammer Forum nonetheless draws heavily upon the form and content of public current affairs broadcasting. While it is not a 'New Institution' in the sense already discussed, the Hammer Museum has sought to review and revise aspects of its institutional structure during the 2000s, and to reconfigure its relationship to its audience, which includes a considerable number of local residents. Writing in 2010, the museum's director Ann Philbin outlined the specific challenges presented by the demands of the 'experience economy',[76] which requires art institutions to compete with—and yet articulate their difference from—shopping malls and theme parks. I am especially interested in the role played by broadcasting in the museum's Public Program, particularly the ongoing series of current affairs-themed talks entitled the Hammer Forum (2004–).[77]

The Hammer Forum consists of a series of public discussions, usually held monthly in the museum's Billy Wilder Theater, focusing on topical issues such as environmental concerns, gay marriage and the role of commercial media in the democratic political process. Admission is free and the discussions (which are also webcast and archived online) typically involve presentations by one or two speakers, followed by questions from the audience. The Forum is moderated by the journalist and broadcaster Ian Masters, host of the radio show *Background Briefing*, which deals primarily with political issues and is broadcast on KPFK 90.7 FM. It is a listener-supported (as opposed to advertising-dependent) radio station that forms part of the left-leaning California-based Pacifica Radio network. Masters's long-standing experience as a radio host is strongly emphasised in publicity for the Forum, and he is often introduced at the start of the discussions as a BBC-trained journalist, an association that seems symbolically as well as professionally significant because of the BBC's history and international prominence as a public service broadcaster. He and Claudia Bestor (Director of Public Programs at the Hammer) work together on the identification of possible speakers, who are usually confirmed several months in advance of the Forum event, and a news-related theme is often explored over a series of public sessions. It is worth noting that the origins of the Hammer Forum lie partly in the huge public attention generated by a public talk delivered by Gore Vidal in March 2003, prior to the US bombing of Iraq.[78] Following this event, museum staff recognised that there was a local interest in discursive events focusing explicitly on politics. As the museum is not a broadcaster or social media website, excessively topical material can actually result in costs to the institution, since

Above: Billy Wilder Theater, Hammer
Museum, Los Angeles (venue for
Hammer Forum events).
Photo by Todd Cheney.
Courtesy of the Hammer Museum.

they are charged by the server for very large volumes of downloading.[79] So the programme promotes in-depth exploration of issues that are topical but not necessarily headline news. The 2011–2012 programme, for example, included several sessions on the theme of the 'American Dream' as well as a session on November 19, 2011 entitled 'Political Persuasion' addressing the role of demographic research in the 2012 US Presidential election campaign, featuring two 'veteran campaign strategists', both of whom critiqued the divisive, and often highly emotive, use of television advertising in recent election campaigns.

The Hammer museum does not currently gather detailed demographic information on the Forum attendees, but anecdotal evidence gathered by museum staff suggests that events attract a mix of museum members, listeners to Ian Masters's radio show, UCLA students and also specific interest groups targeted by the Public Program staff in relation to specific issues. Forum events are free, but ticketed, and attendees receive a calendar detailing forthcoming exhibitions and public programmes. Since 2011, the Hammer's communications department have also produced a short presentation about the Museum's activities, which plays in the theatre before the discussion begins. Surprisingly, however, there is no attempt to directly link the Forum topics with the exhibition or event calendar. Instead, Bestor emphasises that the aim of the event is to offer a physical space for audiences, most of them LA residents, to engage with each other and to pose unscripted questions to experts such as policy-makers. So even though the events are webcast, and legitimated through reference to internationally situated broadcast institutions (such as the BBC), the Hammer Forum reiterates the significance of the museum as a localised space of social gathering and public visibility. In terms of its content, the Hammer Forum addresses many of the problems of social and political participation posed by the fragmentation and segmentation of the bourgeois public sphere. But it offers a response to this situation that is clearly at odds with *Telling Histories*. Rather than engaging with the celebrity-driven talk show, as a familiar form of 'mediation', the Hammer Forum instead invokes the authority and seriousness of public radio, a form of broadcasting that enjoys a relatively high cultural status and legitimacy in the US.

This direct focus on current affairs and political participation is not especially representative of the Museum's overall programming, but there are some points of connection between the Hammer Forum and aspects of the Museum's Public Engagement programme, directed by Allison Agsten. Established in 2009, this initiative has focused on the inclusion of artists' perspectives in new audience-engagement initiatives, and in the museum's institutional planning processes. It is supported by a grant from the James Irvine Foundation, a philanthropic organisation that, in addition to funding arts programmes, also supports public policy initiatives intended to promote democracy in California.[80] In 2010, for example, the Hammer Public Engagement programme included a version of a project called *Libros Schmibros* by David Kipen, which consists of a hybrid lending library and second-hand bookshop. Originally established in the LA neighbourhood of Boyle Heights (where Kipen lives), *Libros Schmibros* aimed to improve local reading resources by offering books to local residents for one dollar. A temporary 'branch' was set up in the Hammer Museum's lobby gallery, again offering one dollar books to locals, and also functioning as a social space with public readings and other events. In one sense this project reiterated the museum's 'public service' role, but rather than working with a relatively well-established model of the (broadcast) public sphere, the emphasis here was on the exploration of a distinctive hybrid model of public and private space, with both social and commercial functions.

My final example, Dora García's *KLAU MICH: Radicalism in Society Meets Experiment on TV* (2013), is an artwork rather than a curatorial or public programming initiative, even though it incorporates a curatorial dimension through the selection of participants and contributors. Devised for *dOCUMENTA (13)*, it was an installation and performance work consisting of a series of weekly discussions (held in the Ständehaus exhibition venue) between invited guests, and performed on a stage in an environment designed to resemble the set of a magazine-style talk show—*Die Klau Mich Show*. Open rehearsals were held each week and on each Friday the show was presented in front of a public audience and transmitted live via the local Kassel community TV channel Offener Kanal. Rehearsal documentation, images of the set and recordings of the transmissions are also presented online.[81] All of these elements seem to have been equally significant for García, who describes the work as 'a television talk show [...] a permanent theater rehearsal that can be followed in real time every day online, and a video and blog archive'.[82]

Die Klau Mich Show included a significant German language element but the first instalment—recorded and transmitted on June 8, 2012 during the preview week of *dOCUMENTA (13)*—was conducted primarily in English with bilingual hosts and predominantly English-speaking guests. It also featured a 'warm-up presenter', who outlined the format and also introduced a group of performers identified as a 'professional audience'. Numbering approximately ten adults of various ages, these 'professionals' occupied a specially designed bank of seating located at right angles to the stage, on the same level as the general audience. The group included several people whose movements and speech suggest that they might have experienced emotional disorders or mental illness (although this was not clearly specified) and in addition to leading the applause, this 'professional audience' addressed the general audience at various moments, delivering scripted lines and presenting the closing credits.

The title of *Die Klau Mich Show* refers to a 1968 publication by Rainer Langhans and Fritz Teufel which gives an account of their failed prosecution as political radicals accused of inciting arson in protest against the Vietnam war. Accordingly, the show was characterised by a vaguely 'retro' aesthetic, with the set design and the furnishings all recalling the late 1960s. Consumer objects from this period were also displayed on the set and the show included vague references to outmoded technologies, most notably when one of the participants played a record on a turntable. As the presenters and the professional audience were not costumed to suggest an earlier moment, it appears that there was no attempt to precisely reconstruct a 1960s television show, and the technology used by the crew also bore no relation to the history of television. Instead García simply employed modes of presentation associated with television (and theatre) to explore the social history of the anti-psychiatry movement and its relevance to artistic practice and popular culture during the 1960s and 70s.

The first instalment of *Die Klau Mich Show* featured guests, who had been active in this movement, reflecting upon the ideas of R. D. Laing, the importance of the squatting movement, events such as the 1966 Destruction in Art symposium and the Dialectics of Liberation congress in 1967, both of which took place in London. Their discussions explored the anti-psychiatry and counter-institutional movements, through reference to archival material and personal recollection. In addition to the discussion, the show included a monologue drawn from Beckett's play *Happy Days* (1961), performed by a woman seated on the upper level of the set, and a screened excerpt from the 1967 documentary *Anatomy of Violence* directed by Peter Davis, featuring footage from the Dialectics of Liberation congress. But, even though the format seemed designed to bring these disparate cultural reference points into contact with each other, there was little attempt to further develop these interconnections through further discourse or analysis in this instalment of the show. Instead the tone and content of the presenter's responses remained neutral, even banal, suggesting that aspects of the interaction had been rehearsed or even scripted. It is worth recalling that García was one of several artists who collaborated with curator Chus Martinez on the exhibition *Are You Ready for TV?* at MACBA in Barcelona.[83] But rather than engaging primarily with television as a cultural or artistic form in its own right (as in the MACBA show), García's project for *dOCUMENTA (13)* used aspects of televisuality to explore histories and legacies of radicalism and anti-institutionalism.

There are obvious connections between the strategies of rehearsal and staging employed in *Die Klau Mich Show* and the exploration of mediation developed in *Telling Histories*, and clearly both projects were concerned with histories of non-conformist practices. But while Cohen, Grammel and Lind were solely interested in past controversies associated with the Kunstverein's exhibition programme, García's project was framed as a much more expansive exploration of social radicalism, extending beyond the gallery. Significantly, like the talk show component of *Telling Histories*, *Die Klau Mich Show* was designed and staged to resemble a celebrity talk show rather than a current affairs programme. Yet even

Next page: Dora García: *KLAU MICH: Radicalism in Society Meets Experiment on TV*, 2012, TV set sculpture, performance, live and Internet TV, www.dieklaumichshow.org. All images courtesy Dora García, Commissioned and produced by dOCUMENTA (13) with the support of Acción Cultural Espanola (AC/E); Ramon Llull Institute, promoting Catalan Culture abroad; Aktion Mensch; Art to be; Centro Jose Guerrero; Fonds Cantonal d'art contemporain Republique et canton de Geneve; 3 bis f centre d'art—Aix-en-Provence; Galerie Michel Rein, Paris; Hessisches Ministerium fur Wissenschaft und Kunst; Kulturamt der Stadt Kassel; Kadist Art Foundation Collection.
Photo: Klau Mich Team.

Above: Dora García: *KLAU MICH: Radicalism in Society Meets Experiment on TV*, 2012.

Above: Dora García: *KLAU MICH: Radicalism in Society Meets Experiment on TV*, 2012.

though García mimicked the stylistic attributes of this 'low cultural' form, I would argue that her project was premised upon a different, and more traditionally authoritative, model of the broadcast public sphere. In fact, she explicitly stated her intention to 'recover the atmosphere of true public debate and new forms of narrative, experimental theater and means of challenging the audience that were once to be found on public-access television'.[84] Here García seems to both consign the broadcast public sphere to the past and imply that 'true public debate' (or at least its atmosphere) can be temporarily recovered or reproduced through artistic performance. Her project confirms the continued importance of television talk for artists and curators seeking to explore the changing form of the public sphere and also to question, or sometimes validate, the publicness of contemporary art institutions.

Although he acknowledges that the notion of the public sphere, manifest in the form of the public-as-nation, might never have been anything more than a projection,[85] Simon Sheikh has argued that the 'public' is still routinely imagined to be located inside a model of the social bound up with the modern nation-state. Consequently, he cautions against 'nostalgic returns to bygone conceptions of the public and spaces of production'.[86] This warning seems especially pertinent to *Die Klau Mich Show* because it draws upon aspects of television talk show form that are clearly 'outmoded', predating the transformations of the early 1990s. Ultimately, however, García does not idealise the talk show as a representative public sphere, or present a wholly open space of public discussion and debate. Instead, the scripted movements and speech of the so-called 'professional audience' serve to emphasise the symbolic role that these performers play within the show, clearly framing the televisual public sphere as representative rather than deliberative.

Conclusion

In this chapter, I have explored the relationship between television and the 'publicness' of the art institution, focusing on several projects in which museums and exhibition are envisaged and framed as important spaces in which to explore the changing form of the broadcast public sphere. Sometimes, the televisual public sphere is staged in order to be lamented or critiqued, but other projects articulate a more open-ended fascination with television talk. My discussion has also highlighted continuities and differences between older and newer modes of 'museum TV' production, through reference to the history of cable television production by the Long Beach Museum of Art and later projects such as CAC TV, Arteleku TV and the work of Superflex. In the case of LBMA, cable TV shows served both as a means to extend the museum's activities of producing and exhibiting video and as an integral component in a much broader process of self-reflection concerning the current and future role of the art institution. Like LBMA, newer institutions such as the Contemporary Art Centre in Vilnius responded to the opportunities presented by the proliferation of new television services. But the various modes of museum TV (whether in the form of online or broadcast production) that emerged in the 2000s were also shaped by concerns over the fragmentation and segmentation of audiences, including those traditionally addressed by public museums.

Turning to the exhibition projects, I have argued (through reference to Reesa Greenberg's account of the 'archival remembering exhibition') that *Telling Histories* drew upon the form of the daytime talk show in order to reassert the history and legacy of the Kunstverein model, while at the same time underscoring the non-conformist identity of this particular institution. In addition, I argue that *Telling Histories* counters the concept of the 'greenroom' as upholding the values of immediacy, presence and liveness that have tended to figure prominently in accounts of the televisual public sphere. These values do persist, however, in the Hammer Museum's Hammer Forum, a project that derives its legitimacy from symbolic association with public radio, rather than commercial TV talk. Dora García's *Die Klau Mich Show,* in contrast, seems to stage a fusion of entertainment talk show formats and the social radicalism attributed to the history of public access television. While all of these projects could perhaps be said to exploit the symbolic capital that remains associated with publishing and broadcasting, this does not mean they necessarily articulate an uncritical investment in the Habermasian notion of the bourgeois public sphere. Instead they communicate a more ambivalent fascination with the forms of publicness that have emerged to take the place of this historical model.

Chapter Seven

Production on Display: Television, Labour and
Contemporary Art

More and more young artists whose practices fall under the rubric of 'poststudio' today tend to conceive of producing a work as does a film director. Rarely do they fully determine its technical presentation (since this generally lies outside their area of competence and requires specialists hired for the task); and rarely can they preview it (since they lack adequate studio space or equipment to test it in private).

Lynne Cooke, 'In Lieu of Higher Ground'[1]

[…] cultural producers are, from one point of view, very powerful. They constitute a relatively small number of people who have the capacity to communicate to many others; in some cases, literally to millions of people. Combined with the prestige attached to artistry and knowledge, this gives cultural workers influence, recognition and occasionally prestige and glamour, at least relative to nearly all other workers earning similar wages. […] However, there is an important qualification to be made. Such power and prestige is of course distributed very unequally, both *between* different media organizations, and between different creative workers *within* the same media organization.

David Hesmondhalgh and Sarah Baker, 'Creative Work and
Emotional Labour in the Television Industry'[2]

Introduction: Economies of Art and Television

In April 2012, members of the Occupy Museums group announced their intention to hold a day-long demonstration at the opening of the inaugural Frieze Art Fair New York (May 10–13, 2012), in protest against the fair's use of nonunionised labour and the 'financialisation of art'. Frieze co-founder Amanda Sharp responded to this threat by suggesting that the protestors failed to understand the contemporary art economy, implying that it was reality television that had somehow misled them:

In America there is a more politicised awareness of inequality between class and wealth. At the same time, more people have decided that art can be a career. They've seen art reality TV shows and they think they can make a career purely out of their work. That's an unrealistic expectation so a lot more people feel disenfranchised.[3]

Above: Alan Kane, Life Class: *Today's
Nude*, 2009. Commissioned by
Artangel and the Jerwood Charitable
Foundation.

Above: LuckyPDF's James Early
and Chloe Sims at *Remote Control*,
Institute of Contemporary Arts, 2012.
Photographer: Victoria Erdelevskaya.
Courtesy LuckyPDF & Institute of
Contemporary Arts.

Significantly, Sharp does not actually dispute the fact that the art world is characterised by inequality. But she seems to imply that television is somehow just as exploitative as the art fair, since it misrepresents the 'reality' of artistic labour. Taking Sharp's observation as a starting point, this chapter seeks to examine the various ways in which television figures in the display and representation of contemporary art production, both within and beyond the gallery. My discussion is primarily concerned with reality TV shows which are focused on art and artists, as well as a range of TV-related artworks—including video installations and performative events—realised since the mid-2000s. I also draw attention to important shifts in the relationship between artists and television workers since the 1970s, through reference to activist video groups associated with the guerrilla television movement in the US.

The first section of the chapter considers the art reality TV show as an important site for the public display and performance of artistic labour, focusing on shows produced for US and British television, such as *Art School* (2005), *Artstar* (2006), *School of Saatchi* (2009) and *Work of Art: The Next Great Artist* (2010–).[4] Some of these shows feature artists as contestants, competing for an award that will contribute to their professional advancement. In other instances, the art school figures as an important setting for interactions between 'students' and 'teachers', in which the artists are set various challenges in order to demonstrate their professional aptitude, which require them to build and maintain interpersonal relationships with peers and also with teachers and mentors. The second section of this chapter explores continuities between the art reality TV show and modes of contemporary art practice, through the analysis of projects realised within art world contexts (such as galleries and fairs), by two London-based artists groups (LuckyPDF and Auto Italia South East) and by LA-based practitioners with professional experience of reality TV production (Alexis Hudgins and Lakshmi Luthra). While LuckyPDF consciously deploy strategies of promotion associated with reality television in their projects, emphasising the importance of publicity (and celebrity) within the contemporary art economy, Auto Italia South East invoke a history of experimentation and innovation associated with an earlier era of television production, in order to develop an exploration of labour and collaboration in art practice. In contrast, Hudgins and Luthra focus directly on contemporary reality TV aesthetics, using an LA gallery as an experimental space in which to stage and observe television performance and production practices over three days. The third and final section of the chapter focuses on three moving image artworks realised for gallery contexts, by Christian Jankowski, Gerard Byrne and Maya Schweizer, all of which involve the collaboration of television workers, such as actors, presenters, camera operators and comedy writer-performers.[5]

Considered together, the projects developed by LuckyPDF, Auto Italia South East, Hudgins and Luthra, Jankowski, Byrne and Schweizer point toward a pervasive fascination on the part of contemporary artists with practices and conditions of television work. This fascination may be linked to the increased visibility of artists in reality TV shows, but (with the possible exception of Hudgins and Luthra) these artists are not necessarily interested in developing a critique of reality television, or in countering its (mis)representation of artistic labour. Instead, most of these artists develop a more open-ended exploration of production and labour practices within the television industry. For Jankowski, reality television has served as an important source for familiar scenarios and scripts, which can be transposed to contemporary art production contexts, and in the process ostensibly disrupt its established hierarchies and conventions of representation. But his interest in television and its associated modes of labour extends well beyond reality genres, suggesting a more expansive interest in TV performance. Similarly expansive in his interests, Gerard Byrne is also attuned to the specificity of TV, theatre and film performance styles, but equally emphasises the material culture and institutional history of television production environments. Schweizer's practice also responds to aspects of site and location, but her work *Before the Rehearsal* (2009) is closer to a documentary than the other examples discussed, involving the observation of a group of underemployed performers rehearsing their scripts and promotional strategies.

For some of these artists, and for the Auto Italia South East group in particular, the television studio is envisaged as a site of collaborative production, whether located in the past or present, and valued because it seems to offer a potential counterpoint to the contemporary condition of precarious, and often highly individualised, artistic labour. But others, including Schweizer, Jankowski and LuckyPDF, explore modes of televisual performance which extend beyond the studio into various aspects of everyday life: through practices of rehearsal, staging and publicity that are just as likely to be encountered in domestic spaces, art galleries or online. Through their exploration of television production and performance—both in front of and behind the camera—these artists draw attention to distinctions, parallels and interconnections between the labour of artists and television workers.

Video Activism and the TV Industry

The current generation of artists is not the first to observe and examine the practices of television workers, as evidenced by the work of guerrilla television collective Videofreex. Their tape *Process Video Revolution* documents the making of a WNET/13 TV show about video collectives in April 1971.[6] Instead of participating in a discussion with members of other activist groups, the bearded and casually-dressed 'Freex' move around the television studio, recording the activities of the clean-shaven and smartly dressed TV camera operators, only to be told that 'you can't shoot in the studio'. When they persist, one of the studio crew (possibly a floor manager) approaches and states in vaguely threatening tones: 'this is a union shop. You can't do that here'. As interlopers in the broadcast studio who refused to put down their own cameras and fulfil their assigned role as TV show guests, the Videofreex clearly represented a threat to the established order. By observing the production practices of the studio crew, they were also making the 'hidden' knowledge of TV production public.

Process Video Revolution communicates an interest in the technology and industrial 'process' of broadcast television production, which is also apparent in the work of other activist groups from this period, most notably TVTV. Led by Michael Shamberg (who was later to become established as a commercial film and TV producer), TVTV initially aimed

Above: Auto Italia South East, *Auto Italia LIVE: Double Dip Concession*, 2012, live broadcast from the ICA, London, as part of the exhibition *Remote Control*.
Courtesy: Auto Italia South East, London; photograph: Ryan McNamara.

Above: Alexis Hudgins and Lakshmi
Luthra *Reverse Cut*, 2010.
Courtesy of the artists.
Photograph: April Totten.

to offer an alternative to commercial production and distribution. But, as Deirdre Boyle demonstrates, the group gradually abandoned the aim of operating outside commercial and public networks and instead sought to develop an 'exemplary' practice that would—at least in theory—help to change the television industry from within.[7] In terms of production, TVTV was initially successful in involving large number of collaborators in ostensibly 'heterarchical' practices of decision-making, developing an approach, often event-oriented, to project development, shooting and editing. So tapes such as *Four More Years* (1972), a documentary about the Republican convention, were produced with resources drawn from an array of individuals and collectives. Some of these resources may have been freely donated, but several TVTV camera operators aspired to work in professional film or television production and were therefore willing to provide unpaid (but credited) labour to achieve this goal.

Stylistically, TVTV productions were characterised by an emphasis on 'behind-the-scenes' activity then largely absent from network news, often featuring casual interviews with (and candid shots of) TV camera operators and reporters. David Joselit comments approvingly on the strategy of interviewing celebrity correspondents such as Dan Rather in *Four More Years* (1972), suggesting that it exploited and exposed the 'feedback loop of television news'.[8] Although many of those involved in these productions were motivated by a critique of the media industry, these shots of network professionals were also intended to secure public attention, and hopefully access to broadcast distribution. TVTV crews could not hope to compete with the network news teams, in terms of resources or speed of production, so they needed to differentiate their approach and this was achieved through the development of a signature style. *Four More Years* and *The World's Largest TV Studio* (1972) both offered an insider's view of production conventions, whilst explicitly framing them as media spectacles.

Unlike the broadcast technicians who responded with hostility to the Videofreex in 1971, the network crews covering the Republican and Democratic conventions of 1972 do not seem to have regarded the TVTV crews as a threat. In fact, as John Caldwell points out, TVTV's low-tech approach, involving 'existing light shooting, handheld camerawork, unedited conversational takes, and extreme portability [...] beckoned politicos and media personages alike to let down their guard'.[9] Boyle, however, situates the rise of guerrilla television within the context of a changing news production culture, associated with the introduction of smaller and cheaper 'Electronic News Gathering' (ENG) network crews during this period.[10] Citing the critical success of TVTV productions,[11] she points out that productions such as *Four More Years* and *The World's Largest TV Studio* were favourably compared to network coverage of the conventions, with one reviewer (in the *San Francisco Chronicle*) even claiming:

These kids, crawling around with their hand cameras, did such a fantastic job that in New York, a top CBS exec called a meeting of his convention staff to grump 'Our network spent more on coffee than these kids did to cover both conventions and they did a better job'.[12]

Caldwell, however, states that 'hardly anyone saw [*Four More Years*] at least in terms of network numbers', simply because groups such as TVTV lacked a viable distribution system. Emphasising that broadcasters largely ignored the possibilities of portable tape in favour of a different aesthetic of 'liveness', he points out that if mainstream audiences did encounter the TVTV production it was many months after the convention, via 'a handful of PBS affiliate stations or later yet at museums'.[13] Yet even if guerrilla television producers could not hope to offer an economically viable alternative to the commercial networks, it is clear that TVTV regarded depictions of the process and performance of television work as both an integral component of their critique of the media industry, and a means of securing critical attention—if not large-scale audiences.

The subsequent history of TVTV is marked by a continued focus on media spectacles and celebrity, particularly *TVTV Looks at the Oscars* (1976), one of several works involving scripted performance.[14] Structured around the broadcast of the 1975 Academy Actress award, it features actress and comedian Lily Tomlin in a dual role. Nominated for her performance in *Nashville*, Tomlin appears both as herself and as a fictional Middle-American woman watching the ceremony at home with her dog, in the company of a television crew—to whom she addresses various comments and criticisms about the show, before eventually falling asleep on her couch. *TVTV Looks at the Oscars*, which was shot in colour with much higher production values than the earlier convention tapes, does not actually include any footage of the Academy Award ceremony and instead consists mainly of the scripted sequences and interviews with various nominees before, during and after the event. These nominees include Verna Fields (editor of *Jaws*), actress Lee Grant (nominated for *Shampoo*), Steven Spielberg (waiting anxiously in his production office to hear news about *Jaws*), Michael Douglas, Jack Nicholson and Ken Kesey, who were all interviewed separately in relation to a dispute over *One Flew Over the Cuckoo's Nest* (nominated for multiple awards). This structure was used to emphasise the uneven distribution of wealth and power in Hollywood; Kesey is pictured doing manual labour and Fields is depicted as an ordinary worker leaving her modest suburban home to the cheers of family, neighbours and friends. In contrast, Douglas is shown on a ski slope and clearly framed as 'Hollywood royalty'.

The sequences featuring Lee Grant are especially significant, in terms of TVTV's stance as an 'alternative' media producer, because she recounts her experience as a theatre actress who was blacklisted during the McCarthy years. Her nomination is consequently framed as a kind of belated compensation for the fact that she was precluded from working professionally for several years. Although *TVTV Looks at the Oscars* offers a highly engaging account of Hollywood 'behind the scenes', it is ultimately difficult to discern a specific critique of the media industry in this work, beyond the references to Ken Kesey and the adaptation of *One Flew Over the Cuckoo's Nest*. But the presence of this countercultural icon was significant and deliberate, not least because it affirmed TVTV's own 'outsider' position in relation to Hollywood. Ultimately *TVTV Looks at the Oscars* should be regarded as the outcome of a collaboration between (activist) artists and film and television workers which potentially benefited both parties. By participating in this project, Tomlin could symbolically dissociate

Above: Alexis Hudgins and Lakshmi
Luthra *Reverse Cut*, 2010.
Courtesy of the artists.
Photograph: April Totten.

Above: Alexis Hudgins and Lakshmi
Luthra *Reverse Cut*, 2010.
Courtesy of the artists.
Photograph: April Totten.

herself from Hollywood spectacle and Shamberg could present himself as a media industry outsider while at the same time developing connections within this industry.[15]

Changing Conditions of Art and Media Production

Unlike TVTV, the contemporary artists cited at the outset of this chapter are not motivated by the desire to establish careers within the film and television industry. Nor, as I have already noted, are they necessarily concerned with reforming commercial television, or securing access to broadcast distribution. Instead, these artists (particularly Jankowski and Byrne) have incorporated formal strategies and production techniques associated with commercial film and television into their practices. In addition, they often employ, or collaborate with, production personnel working in the media industry, including cinematographers and actors. This does not mean that boundaries between contemporary art, television economies and production cultures have simply collapsed. Instead, I would argue that artists sometimes seek to work with media industry personnel or production contexts such as TV studios precisely in order to emphasise differences between these economies and cultures: either to generate symbolic capital or to highlight changes in artistic production and labour practices.

These changes may be linked to developments in art practice since the 1990s, noted by Lynne Cooke, within the context of a discussion of exhibition-making. Writing in 2007, she suggests that artists now often operate like film directors, working with a range of hired specialists.[16] As a result of this approach, artworks are often literally unavailable for viewing or testing in advance. Instead, she suggests, artists or curators often only encounter the artwork in its 'definitive guise' at the moment of the exhibition's inauguration. In this 'poststudio' economy, the curator is required to operate not only as commissioner but also as 'host' of an institutional environment that is increasingly shaped by the economic logic of the 'experience economy';[17] facilitating interactions between artist, work and institution, acting as a 'producer' who provides resources, and above all as a publicist who 'stage-manages the exhibition as event'. While Cooke's account raises many important issues, I am specifically interested in the analogy that she proposes between the artist-curator dynamic and the director-producer relation in the film industry. This analogy may not be wholly accurate, but it speaks to a perception of changing professional roles and responsibilities within the art world. More recently, Paul O'Neill has charted the emergence of the curator as artist (or author) within contemporary art discourse, noting that this shift has been perceived by some as 'detrimental to contemporary art'.[18] He proposes that resistance to the 'curator-as-artist' is founded, in some cases, upon 'a kind of nostalgia for the perceived certainty of the fixed division of labor between artist, curator, and critic' seen as characteristic of an earlier moment: a position which may involve rejection of the actual diversity of curatorial practices that have emerged 'beyond the museum structure'[19] since the 1960s. Yet even if it is misleading to frame the history of contemporary art in terms of the secure division of artistic and curatorial labour, there is little doubt that professional roles and hierarchies are *perceived* to have changed.

Above and Next page: Christian Jankowski,
Tableau Vivant TV, 2010. Video, 31:42 min,
16:9, PAL, colour, sound, English.
Courtesy of the artist and Lisson Gallery.

Definitions of artistic work and authorship are also open to contestation within the media industries, but are likely to be more frequently governed and regulated through reference to copyright law. As Matt Stahl has argued, in an analysis of copyright and collective bargaining in the media industries: property and authorship rights are allocated unevenly, as evidenced by the distinctions that exist between 'above the line' and 'below the line' workers. The latter group are typically characterised as technical workers and unlikely to benefit from the compensations systems offered to 'creatives', which include personal service contracts (overwriting minimum scale payments) and residuals.[20] Stahl points out that privilege and distinction in relation to authorship 'do not *reflect* observable, noncontroversial differences in creativity, but [rather] serve to *produce* and/or *sustain* particular (im)balances of power'.[21] So, for example, copyright law can be used to protect the rights of a corporation, which can be identified as the author under the 'work for hire' doctrine, whilst even freelance workers (as opposed to contracted employees) can be required to give up their rights as authors—a situation routinely encountered by animators and graphic designers.

Stahl's analysis is attuned to significant shifts in labour relations and industrial hierarchies, wrought in part by the introduction of new digital technologies from the early 2000s onwards. These developments have also been theorised by John Caldwell who notes that 'decades-old, union-regulated, technically standardized, mentor-managed workflow assignments are crumbling in favor of untested, non-union, nonstandardized manufacturer-managed workflow assignments'.[22] The new workflows are, according to Caldwell, no longer managed by a 'coalition of labour groups, guilds, unions, technologists, and studios' but rather by manufacturers of cameras and other technologies, who promote their own distinct and diverse workflows. This changing environment has given rise to fears and experiences of underemployment for workers with traditional skills, articulated in 'worker blowback', a term that describes a range of practices, such as the production and dissemination of online content, as a means of negotiating and managing a changing labour environment. This worker-generated content (including blog posts and contributions to online trade forums) is used to re-establish 'long-standing forms of industrial legitimacy', to articulate 'intercraft contention', or to expand professional contacts and find new clients.[23]

Caldwell's discussion of worker-generated material focuses on trade websites such as *ReelExchange*, where below-the-line film and video craft workers market themselves by uploading demo reels, pitches and bios. Caldwell's discussion also includes posts to sites maintained by professional organisations such as the Society of Operating Cameramen. One such post warns against camera operators that have not come up 'through the ranks' but are instead 'discovered' by producers and brought to the set, having learned their craft in independent and low-budget sectors. This distrust of outsiders forms part of a long-standing resistance to 'the DIY ethos preached in many art and film schools', which 'produces edgy "artists" who mock and disregard long-protected union camera department assignments'.[24] While this type of anxiety is not new, Caldwell is specifically interested in the use of social media networks to manage changing models of labour organisation. Citing ethnographer Andreas Wittel, he describes the emergence of 'networked sociality', in which technology-based

Above: Gerard Byrne: *A man and a woman make love,*
2012, Parallel projections of synchronized video material.
All images courtesy Gerard Byrne, Lisson Gallery, London;
Green on Red Gallery, Dublin; Galerie Nordenhake, Berlin,
Stockholm, Commissioned and produced by dOCUMENTA
(13) with the support of Viglietta Matteo SpA, Fossano.

Above: Gerard Byrne: *A man and a woman make love,*
2012, Parallel projections of synchronized video material.
All images courtesy Gerard Byrne, Lisson Gallery, London;
Green on Red Gallery, Dublin; Galerie Nordenhake, Berlin,
Stockholm, Commissioned and produced by dOCUMENTA
(13) with the support of Viglietta Matteo SpA, Fossano.

cultural activities substitute for actual community for independent professionals in the creative industries'.[25] These activities serve as a means of making and preserving bonds between workers, and are also characterised (in Caldwell's formulation) as 'reflexive'. It is precisely by 'circulating highly reflexive forms among themselves' that workers affirm and promote their understanding of the industry. More precisely, through 'narratives of self-affirmation' they verify and communicate their ability 'to do the one thing required of any professional in film and tv: successfully, and repeatedly, negotiate one's own value'.[26] This skill is also crucial for artists and curators. As I will argue through reference to the work of LuckyPDF, Auto Italia South East and the collaboration between Hudgins and Luthra, artists also routinely circulate 'highly reflexive forms' as a means of affirming their professional skill and ability. But for artists, these forms may actually constitute their principle professional output, unlike the skills set theorised by Caldwell.

While artists and television workers are rarely considered together in theorisations of labour or production culture, there are commonalities between these cultures. For example, many professional artists also work as studio assistants, so they defer rights to authorship in certain contexts and defend them in others. Stahl also makes the important point that some media industry workers have publicly promoted themselves as 'natural authors' precisely in order to preserve their rights within a context of technological change, citing the 2007–2008 strike by members of the Writers Guild of America (WGA).[27] His analysis demonstrates the economic value of *public* perception, particularly during a period of changing labour practices. In my view, issues of perception are equally—if not more—important for contemporary artists, who are wholly or partially dependent upon public subvention, either directly in the form of grants and public commissions, or indirectly through the prestige conferred by association with publicly-funded museums. But, unlike the US television workers discussed by Caldwell and Stahl, contemporary artists (particularly those in receipt of public funding) also often need to frame their work as a contribution to the social and cultural life of a city or nation.

Just as media industry employees have traditionally belonged to unions, guilds or other organisations that safeguard workers' rights, contemporary artists have also organised and campaigned in many contexts for their rights as cultural workers. Yet professional artistic practice is rarely contingent upon membership to a union or representative organisation in quite the same way as it might be for many below-the-line media workers. In addition, artists have repeatedly been cast as exemplary figures of flexible, precarious and self-exploitative work practice, with some theorists also proposing that the 'artistic critique' of employment has been wholly absorbed and deployed in management culture since the 1960s.[28] Andrea Fraser suggests that because artists often value flexibility over security and come from middle-class backgrounds, which discourage them from seeing themselves as labour,[29] they may be resistant to conventional modes of labour organisation. But there are signs that in the post-2008 era, contemporary artists are more willing to view—and publicly present—themselves as workers in the hope of preserving or restoring state subventions for artistic practice. They are also more likely to emphasise goals and objectives shared with other contemporary art practitioners/workers such as curators and critics, and with arts professionals in other disciplines. These strategies are apparent in the various campaigns and lobbying groups established by art workers to combat reductions in funding, and to counter neo-liberal agendas regarding culture.[30]

Some arts organisations have also responded to this altered economic and political environment by trying to secure or restore public support for artists through the use of strategies that have been successfully deployed in other labour struggles, including those that have little to do with authorship or conventional definitions of creativity. For example, in June 2012 the Utrecht-based organisation Casco—Office for Art, Design and Theory— organised a workshop led by a union organiser associated with the successful *Justice For Janitors* campaign developed in the US.[31] The workshop was a practical attempt to share this model of organisation and campaigning with artists and designers, and it was especially interesting for its focus on the need to secure the involvement of independent 'allies', whose support added legitimacy to the workers' struggles. In addition, CASCO is one of many organisations involved in the formation of cross-institutional alliances, which serve as a means of sharing resources and achieving organisational goals. These alliances include the 'Cluster Network', linking a number of small visual arts organisations, including CASCO, CAC Brétigny (France), CA2M in Madrid, the Israeli Centre for Digital Art in Holon, Les Laboratories D'Aubervilliers in Paris, The Showroom (London), Tensta Konsthall (Sweden) and Zavod P.A.R.A.S.I.T.E. in Ljubljana.[32]

As this short comparison of art and media production cultures indicates, art and television workers use broadly similar strategies to negotiate and manage a shifting labour environment, even if the factors shaping their production environments may differ. It is also important to emphasise that these two spheres of employment are increasingly interconnected. For many decades artists have supported themselves, and their practices, by working in the film and television industries. Since the 1990s, however, artists have also increasingly engaged the paid services of *film and television workers*, such as actors, cinematographers or even producers. Here I am not referring to feature films directed by artists for theatrical distribution but to rather more modest situations in which an artist hires a professional cinematographer to shoot a moving image work for exhibition and distribution as an art object, or casts a professional actor known for their work in film and television productions.

In such situations, artists may appear to occupy a more powerful position than television workers, since they operate as employers. But in practice, artists may also compete to secure the services of a sought-after cinematographer or performer, often engaging with these film and television workers as collaborators, and restructuring their production to facilitate the schedules of these 'employees'. So while some of these projects may have substantial budgets by art world standards, they are unlikely to secure the involvement of prominent collaborators on purely financial grounds. Instead it would be accurate to frame these works as the outcome of a complex exchange of symbolic capital, not unlike that involved in the production of *TVTV Looks at the Oscars,* in which artists and film and television workers both potentially stand to benefit from association with the project. One final related development is worth citing before turning to art reality TV, and this is the use of television production environments, such as TV studios, as shooting locations and (less frequently) as exhibition spaces for contemporary art installations.[33] Such works do not necessarily involve the participation of television workers, yet nonetheless speak to a fascination, anticipated in the Videofreex tape *Process Video Revolution*, with the material culture, and social environment, of TV production in contemporary art culture.

Artists as Performers and Contestants in Reality TV

Just as artists have sought to collaborate with television workers, and to deploy television production environments as the settings for artworks, television producers have gravitated toward art studios and colleges as settings for TV shows, including *Artstar* (2006) and *Work of Art: The Next Great Artist* (2010–) in the US, and *Art School* (2005) and *School of Saatchi* (2009) in the UK. It is also possible to identify alternatives to the art reality TV format within the British context, such as the Artangel-produced *Life Class: Today's Nude* (2009), a project by the artist Alan Kane that took the form of a televised drawing class. Kane's project focused on the teaching and learning of traditional fine art skills, whereas I am primarily interested in shows that engage with the labour and economy of contemporary art production, which typically involves the modelling of non-traditional skills.

   Artstar, produced by Gallery HD (a high-definition channel available on the Dish Network) was an eight-episode show conceived partly by Jeffrey Deitch, then a SoHo art dealer. As might be expected, the show was not entirely focused upon demonstrations of artistic ability, and Deitch was specifically interested in how 'telegenic' participants could project 'personality', a quality he perceived as necessary for market success:

> It's not that different from the way we look at artists who we want to get involved in the gallery. It's the whole personality. And generally people who, in their way, have a very distinct personality are often the more interesting artist.[34]

Deitch's focus on 'telegenic' artists is well known—as director of LA Museum of Contemporary Art (since 2010) he has been criticised for his tendency to favour celebrity-themed shows, such as a retrospective devoted to Dennis Hopper's work as an artist, and an exhibition curated by James Franco.[35] While *Artstar* was fairly explicit in its thematization of celebrity, several British art reality shows have been framed as 'educational', even if this is sometimes a thinly-disguised cover for the familiar 'fish out of water' strategy common in casting shows. *Art School* was a BBC Two series produced by Endemol (known for originating the *Big Brother* format) that aired in September 2005. Hour-long episodes were broadcast five days a week at 6 pm over two weeks, following five 'celebrities' as they attended a two-week art course, run in conjunction with Chelsea College of Art and Design. The participants included British TV newscaster John Humphrys, former TV presenter Ulrika Jonsson and

Above: Gerard Byrne: *A man and a woman make
love*, 2012, Parallel projections of synchronized
video material. All images courtesy Gerard Byrne,
Lisson Gallery, London; Green on Red Gallery,
Dublin; Galerie Nordenhake, Berlin, Stockholm,
Commissioned and produced by dOCUMENTA (13)
with the support of Viglietta Matteo SpA, Fossano.

Above: Maya Schweizer, *Before the Rehearsal*, 2009.
Courtesy of the artist.

Above: Maya Schweizer, *Before the Rehearsal*, 2009.
Courtesy of the artist.

comedian Keith Allen, and the show was promoted by the BBC as an 'entertaining and informative series', in keeping with the public service ethos, which sought to 'demystify some aspects of contemporary art'.[36]

Four years after *Art School*, Channel 4 broadcast an art project by Alan Kane that was much more explicitly educational in its objectives, and far less indebted to the reality genre. *Life Class: Today's Nude* was commissioned and produced for Channel 4 by Artangel (in collaboration with the Jerwood Foundation) and it was supported by the National Lottery through Arts Council England.[37] Daily half-hour drawing classes were broadcast on Channel 4 at 12.30 pm from Monday July 6 until Friday July 10, 2009. The classes, led by tutors that included critic John Berger and artist Gary Hume, provided insights into the techniques of figurative drawing and were broadcast from various locations. In addition, for several weeks in advance of the broadcast, Artangel organised temporary drop-in life drawing classes in various locations across London and also in Manchester, Bristol, Southampton and Glasgow. Framed as an extension of Kane's ongoing practice of 'democratising the production and dissemination of art and culture', the show was relatively traditional in terms of its focus on skills. Berger's participation as tutor also invoked a much earlier intersection between art and television; the BBC series *Ways of Seeing* (1972), which directly addressed the relationship between vision, representation and structures of power.

Life Class was followed, however, by the most overtly art market-oriented reality TV production within the British context to date: *School of Saatchi*, which was broadcast on BBC Two in November–December 2009 as four hour-long episodes. The show was structured around the (absent) figure of Charles Saatchi, described on the BBC website as 'the powerful art world kingmaker behind the Brit Art revolution'. Fully embracing the role of kingmaker, Saatchi guided the proceedings from 'behind the scenes', directing a selection panel that consisted of artist Tracey Emin, critic and broadcaster Matthew Collings, art collector Frank Cohen and Barbican curator Kate Bush. The first episode featured works by 12 unknown artists, chosen to present works for Saatchi to view (off screen) through an open submission process. Based on this presentation, six of these artists—mostly recent graduates or currently art students—were invited to enjoy 'the bounties of [Saatchi's] patronage for ten weeks in his art studio'. The remaining episodes were organised around a series of tasks and exercises vaguely resembling art school projects but the skills being imparted or modelled through this process were somewhat different from those promoted in *Life Class,* as the 'students' were often rewarded with attention and approval when they rejected guidance or twisted the rules.

Meanwhile, in the US, *Artstar* has been followed by yet other art-themed reality TV show—the US cable channel Bravo's *Work of Art: The Next Great Artist*. Launched in 2010, and developed by Sarah Jessica Parker's production company, this show focuses on the 'discovery' and promotion of artists in the early stages of their careers. While not explicitly educational in its structure, it nonetheless presents its participants (a mix of graduates and artists without formal qualifications) with tasks that are vaguely reminiscent of art school projects. The show also involves the participation of powerful artworld 'mentors' such as Simon de Pury, the chairman of Phillips de Pury auction house, with equally prominent figures as 'judges', such as the experienced and influential art critic Jerry Saltz. Unlike music or dance-based reality TV contests, art-themed shows tend *not* to be organised around viewer participation and voting. Instead, the focus is primarily on judgements and evaluations performed by art world insiders, and on endorsements by established art institutions such as museums or auction houses. For example, the Brooklyn Museum hosts a solo exhibition that is awarded to the winner of *Work of Art: The Next Great Artist*, along with $100,000 in prize money. This association has generated some controversy but it has also served to publicise the Museum's programming.[38]

As already noted at the outset of this chapter, art world professionals such as Amanda Sharp have accused art reality TV shows of fuelling unrealistic expectations and it is certainly true that few of the artists 'launched' in this way have achieved the fame of early winners of *Pop Idol* or *X Factor*, for example. Nonetheless, art reality TV shows articulate a shift in the televisual display of artistic labour and 'skill', particularly when compared to projects such as Alan Kane's *Life Class*. Through their quasi-educational settings and scenarios, shows like *Work of Art* and *School of Saatchi* teach competing artists, and by extension viewers, that professional success as a contemporary artist is no longer bound up with craft skill[39] or even wholly dependent upon the aesthetic or conceptual merit of the artworks produced. Instead, the interactions between artists, mentors and judges in these shows serve to emphasise the overarching significance of professional networking, while also suggesting that traditional modes of legitimation (such as the award of an exhibition in a public museum) may be determined by institutional requirements for media coverage and publicity.[40]

In addition to 'teaching' transformations in artistic skill, art reality TV shows function as exemplary sites for the public performance and display of affective labour, through their emphasis on networking and publicity. This concept, often theorised alongside related notions of 'immaterial labour' and 'precarity' (particularly within the context of autonomist Marxism), draws attention to the specificity of labour involving human contact and interaction, performed in contexts that range from healthcare to service and cultural industries. According to Michael Hardt and Antonio Negri, affective labour is often valued because it can result in the production of social networks and communities involving cooperation and collaboration.[41] For cultural industries theorists such as David Hesmondhalgh and Sarah Baker, however, the work of Hardt and Negri lacks sufficient empirical engagement with specific labour environments and also tends to overstate the 'nature and extent of transformation in contemporary labour'.[42] They argue instead for a more focused empirical analysis of artistic and creative work 'in what is still the most important media (and therefore cultural) industry of all: television', and their approach also emphasises the importance of *symbolic power*.[43] This symbolic power is founded in part upon a 'fundamental asymmetry between producers and receivers' that confers prestige and glamour upon cultural workers, albeit unevenly distributed.[44]

Countering what they see as 'Hardt and Negri's blithe assertions about cooperation in immaterial and affective labour', Hesmondhalgh and Baker demonstrate, through their empirical analysis of researchers and producers working on a British TV talent show (*Show*

Us Your Talent, broadcast by the BBC in 2007), that 'additional pressures are borne by these workers because of their particularly strong need to maintain good working relations in short-term project work, a need generated by the importance of maintaining contacts in order to secure future employment'.[45] In order to theorise these pressures, Hesmondhalgh and Baker turn to the seminal research which sociologist Arlie Hochschild developed in relation to the 'emotional labour' expended by workers in service industries, who were required to 'induce or suppress feeling in order to sustain the outward countenance that produces the proper state of mind in others'.[46] Here, Hochschild is referring to the fact that such workers often need to exhibit a particular emotional state in order to elicit a response from customers or clients that will serve the needs of their employer. Hochschild's research is an important point of reference in Laura Grindstaff's analysis of US TV talk shows, also cited by Hesmondhalgh and Baker. Grindstaff's research highlights various strategies used to cultivate the forms of self-expression around which talk shows are structured. She notes that production workers were routinely required to manage the responses of the talk show guests through their own performance of emotional labour, thereby ensuring that strong emotions would be visible on screen at the appropriate moment.[47]

In their study of *Show Us Your Talent* (2007) made by a London-based independent production company for the BBC, Hesmondhalgh and Baker focus on the emotional labour routinely performed by the show's researchers, both in their relations with the talent show contributors whose emotions and expectations they had to manage, and in their relations with co-workers, from whom they hope to secure further employment. Hesmondhalgh and Baker conclude that pressure to deliver high quality, and reputation-building work—even in contexts where production resources are declining—'impacts on the individual's ability to do emotional labour', while at the same time 'building one's reputation hinges upon the management of emotions'.[48] Since their emphasis is on employment and labour within the cultural industries, Hesmondhalgh and Baker do not discuss the emotional or affective labour expended by the TV show contestants, instead focusing exclusively on the research and production staff. Yet reality TV shows involving competitive performance by professionals (such as artists) also involve emotional labour on the part of the contestants, in terms of the management of interpersonal relationships. Just as the researchers and production workers involved in shows such as *Work of Art* need to manage their interactions with contestants and co-workers, in order to secure future work opportunities, artists competing to be '*The Next Great Artist*' must cultivate professional and personal relationships with art world mentors and judges.

Performing Televisual Labour at Art Fairs and Exhibitions

As already suggested, art reality TV shows are both endorsed by some art world insiders, who participate as judges and mentors, and dismissed by others as inauthentic or misleading in their representation of the art economy. Yet even if reality TV shows are not wholly reliable as a source of information about artistic labour and art careers, they have served as an important cultural reference point for several contemporary art practitioners engaging with issues of artistic labour, performance and skill. The London-based art group LuckyPDF (James Early, John Hill, Ollie Hogan and Yuri Pattison), for example, have frequently used television formats to explore, and sometimes amplify, the promotional character of art discourse. Their projects include a 'TV show' produced for the Frieze Art Fair in 2011, featuring 50 artists who were invited to show and produce new work.[49] More recently, LuckyPDF have developed the parodic *School of Global Art*, which promises to take students 'on a journey to the cusp of a new era in learning'.[50]

School of Global Art was launched during a programme of talks and events accompanying the exhibition *Remote Control* at the Institute of Contemporary Arts, London in April 2012. An 'enrolment booth' in the gallery offered membership and a 'welcome pack of essays' to prospective students in exchange for their personal data, and the event also included a publicity stunt involving reality TV star Chloe Sims, from *The Only Way is Essex* (2010), famous for her plastic surgery and extravagant lifestyle. Sims was led on a tour of the *Remote Control* show and her responses to works, by artists such as Michelangelo Pistoletto, were duly reported in promotional coverage of the event:

> It's something that I'm interested in as in my day-to-day work I have to negotiate reality and created fictions. [The Pistoletto work] is also a mirror, both for the viewer and as a metaphor, it's both art and I can check my make-up in it, and that is very practical.[51]

It is clear that LuckyPDF do not distinguish between art fairs and publicly-funded art galleries as institutional sites, and rather than seeking to operate 'outside' publicity-driven media industries they take publicity as their content. This is not an original strategy—it is obviously indebted to artists such as Warhol. But rather than citing art historical precedents LuckyPDF seem to propose the highly constructed public personas created by reality TV stars such as Chloe Sims as models for artistic performance.

In contrast, the London-based group Auto Italia South East (Kate Cooper, Amanda Dennis and Richard John Jones) cite a variety of art historical references in the development of their multi-episode TV show *Auto Italia LIVE* (2010–). Like LuckyPDF, they contributed to the programme of *Remote Control*, staging and shooting a special episode—*Auto Italia LIVE: Double Dip Concession* (2012)—in the ICA Theatre. As with previous iterations of this project, the show performed before a studio audience and 'broadcast over the internet',[52] framing their show as means of re-engaging with the history of 'experimental' television:

> Produced collaboratively by artists, *Auto Italia LIVE* aims to reclaim a space within the television format that has increasingly lost its experimental aspect. [...] Questioning the demise of risk taking in mainstream cultural programming within the history of British Television, the project aims to provoke discussion and challenge how artists might work together [...] examining how dialogues are negotiated and tested within this unique context.[53]

'Liveness' is signified in *Auto Italia LIVE* partly through the evocation of familiar TV formats involving talk and music performance shows, but also through the performance styles of presenters, who frequently address the camera. There are also occasional technical glitches (such as delays in playback of pre-recorded elements) and the choreographed actions of cameras and performers are at times rehearsed on screen, especially in episode two, *Cosmosis* (2011).

There are certainly echoes here of older TV formats involving a live audience, ranging from the 1950s game shows to more recent performance-based shows such as BBC2's *Later With Jools Holland* (1992–), characterised by highly mobile camerawork and 'in-the-round' staging. The most overt and consistent articulation of liveness can, however, be found in the display of the cast, crew and audience, particularly in the three earlier episodes shot in Auto Italia's warehouse-like studio. During *Cosmosis* and episode three, *C2C P2P* (2011), for example, the camera repeatedly pans and sometimes lingers over large groups of (predominantly young) people gathered around the mixing desk or arranged around the set. It could be argued that this emphasis on the technology of production is simply a way to invoke earlier moments in the history of live television, involving novel and innovative technologies such as, for example, satellite transmission.[54] But rather than exhibiting the technology of television production for its own sake, *Auto Italia LIVE* uses the aesthetic of 'live' TV production to display the social resources that are associated with, and necessitated by, the practice of collaborative artistic production. Significantly, this project was developed and resourced with public funding (from the Arts Council of England) as part of a broader process of investigation into 'issues of copyright and collective authorship', intended to result in documents detailing 'best practice for commissioning on Digital Media platforms'. Even if these documents have not yet been produced (somewhat ironically due to lack of time—a condition of precarious labour),[55] the *Auto Italia LIVE* series makes collaboration highly visible through the onscreen presence of cast and crew and the performative presentation of lengthy credit lists.[56]

LuckyPDF and Auto Italia South East both envisage exhibitions as settings for the appropriation and staging of televisual performance: whether for the purposes of generating publicity or as a means of intensifying and displaying artistic collaboration. Some artists, however, are more interested in the gallery as a space for the critical analysis of television and its characteristic modes of labour. In August 2010, Alexis Hudgins and Lakshmi Luthra collaborated on *Reverse Cut*, a three-day installation at the Los Angeles gallery Las Cienegas Projects, transforming this space into a fully functioning reality television set and studio, open to the public 24 hours a day for three days.[57] Hudgins (an artist and at that time an MFA student at University of California) has extensive professional experience of producing and directing reality TV shows, and she was especially interested in examining conventions such as the '180-degree rule'. This rule dictates camera position, and is used to establish continuity in the filmic space, creating a stable position from which to view the action, encouraging emotional identification with those on screen. The project was presented as a quasi-anthropological attempt to examine the 'wall of technology', connecting and separating the cast and crew, by crossing the 180 degree line in a 'reverse cut'.

Gallery visitors were invited to enter the control room and see professional crews at work behind the scenes, and could also be escorted onto the set by a production assistant in order to observe the five-member cast being filmed. The cast living space was fitted with surveillance cameras and microphones transmitting to the control room and camera operators were primed to 'catch stories', which could be directed via walkie-talkie radios. *Reverse Cut* was not devised to be broadcast or webcast and the activities of the cast could only be viewed in the gallery, either from the control room or though guided 'walk-throughs' led by crew members. Hudgins and Luthra were also specifically interested in involving participants (as cast or crew) who had professional experience of reality TV production, and in creating a discursive forum for them to reflect upon the project. Six months after the exhibition, they organised a public event entitled *Reverse Cut Wrap Party* at the Mandrake Bar in Culver City, a popular venue in the gallery district, in which cast members, crew and gallery visitors were invited to reflect on the project.[58]

There are important distinctions in terms of resourcing between *Reverse Cut*, an artist-funded project (involving an artist who was also an MFA candidate), and the LuckyPDF launch event, which was commissioned and facilitated by the ICA. As Noah Horowitz has pointed out, certain forms of art practice (including video and 'experiential' artworks) are supported by dealers and gallerists because they are perceived as resistant to commercialization, functioning as a 'loss leader'[59] that enhances credibility. According to this logic, projects such as *School of Global Art* and *Reverse Cut* both have a potential market value, even if this value is not immediately apparent in terms of sales. LuckyPDF's collaboration with Chloe Sims arguably also served a straightforward promotional function, as it generated publicity for *Remote Control*. Hudgins and Luthra, in contrast, seem to have been less interested in mobilising the glamour or prestige of the television industry for the purposes of generating publicity.

In some respects, *Reverse Cut* calls to mind the worker-generated content theorised by Caldwell, not least because it provided Hudgins, who is a television worker as well as an artist, with an opportunity to actively articulate her own professional experience as producer and director, without infringing confidentiality (or intellectual property) agreements. But at the same time, the project very clearly privileged physical community, with informal gatherings in galleries and bars in place of the technologically-mediated sociality emphasised in Caldwell's account of 'worker blowback'. For this reason, I would argue that even though *Reverse Cut* clearly drew upon professional knowledge and networks acquired by Hudgins within the television industry, it was not necessarily motivated by the Hudgins and Luthra's need to negotiate their own value within this industry. Instead, it functioned as a way to secure symbolic capital (and in Hudgins's case, formal accreditation) within the art *education* field.

Staging and Observing Television Work

Christian Jankowski has produced a great many primarily single channel videos that either involve the collaboration of television workers (as actors, presenters, or in various production roles) or derive their structure from TV formats. In some instances, an impending exhibition dictates the logic of Jankowski's interaction with television workers, serving as both the context and the content of a video work, which may function as a component of the exhibition or circulate independently of this context. These concerns are evident in the early work *Telemistica* (1999), in which he consults TV fortune-tellers by phone to ask for advice on the artwork he is making for the Venice Biennale. These TV mystics offer encouragement and reassurance about this work, without realising that they are participating in its production. Similarly, in *The Perfect Gallery* (2010), Jankowski 'hires' interior designer Gordon Whistance, known for appearances on the British home improvement show *Changing Rooms* (1996–2004) to speedily renovate the Pump House Gallery in South London. The gallery is presented as the site of Jankowski's forthcoming solo show, but Whistance is apparently unaware of the fact that the newly-renovated empty gallery will be the artwork. The video documents his progress as he conducts rapid research on gallery design and agonises, somewhat unconvincingly, over whether he can realise the project and please the artist.

Jankowski has also devised makeover projects that require the participation of art workers, rather than TV performers, such as *Dienstbesprechung (Briefing)* (2008). This video documents the experiences of the staff of the Kunstmuseum Stuttgart who were required by Jankowski to swap roles for a period of several weeks, prior to the opening of his solo show at the museum. Although the new roles were apparently dictated by a lottery system, they tended to involve dramatic shifts in power and expertise. So, for example, the director changed places with a technician, the curator took on the job of the security guard and the funding manager was replaced by a caretaker. Since Jankowski hired a promotional media company to document the preparations for the exhibition (without apparently informing them of the role changes), the video offers only a partial view of the project. As Burkhard Meltzer notes,[60] *Dienstbesprechung* is not a particularly self-reflexive work, in part because it reveals little about the negotiations that presumably occurred between the artist and the museum in advance of the exhibition. Consequently it cannot be read as an attempt to expose or critique established hierarchies within the art world.

In subsequent works, however, Jankowski has placed greater emphasis on his own position as a performer, both in front of and behind the camera. Devised for the Sydney Biennale 2010, *Tableaux Vivant TV* (2010) consists of a series of location 'reports' conducted by television journalists, broadcast in advance of the Biennale, which focus on various milestones in the realisation of Jankowski's project. These reports exist as publicity for the exhibition (and Jankowski) but instead of featuring the usual TV-friendly action shots they are conducted in front of live 'tableaux vivants', in which key players, such as the artist, the administrative team and the artistic director David Elliot, are depicted in a moment of artificial stillness. The various TV presenters standing in front of these static scenes use various strategies to inject a sense of excitement and animation. For example, in one sequence Jankowski is depicted sitting alone looking out to sea, frozen in a moment of highly choreographed reflection, while the cameras look on and the TV presenter speculates about his innermost thoughts and hopes.

At another moment, the television cameras move through a production office in which the administrators and curators involved in the realisation of the Biennale are also frozen in motion. This sequence is particularly significant since it requires the (presumably already overworked) production staff to perform in yet another capacity, helping to realise an artwork by pausing their usual activity. In contrast to the video component of *Dienstbesprechung*, which might readily be mistaken for a documentary account of a participatory art project, *Tableaux Vivant TV* is both unsettling and formally distinctive. By choreographing and artificially pausing the action that serves as the content of each reportage sequences, Jankowski both makes explicit and subtly confounds the convention strategies used to publicise artistic and curatorial work. Again, however, this strategy does not suggest a critique of the television industry, but rather a more open-ended fascination with both the peculiar, mutable quality of artistic labour and with television as one of several stages upon which these forms of labour are frequently performed.

My next example, Gerard Byrne's multi-channel video installation *A man and a woman make love* (2012), is largely unconcerned with the theme of artistic labour. Nonetheless, it incorporates a depiction of television work, conducted in a broadcast TV studio environment, that remains pertinent to my discussion. Produced for *dOCUMENTA (13)*, this work presents a television drama based upon a 'script' that (largely in keeping with Byrne's usual practice) is drawn from the published transcription of a conversation. The source in this instance is a conversation about eroticism between a group of surrealists including André Breton, which took place in January 1928, and was published in the May 1928 issue of *La Révolution Surréaliste*. A reconstruction of this event is staged in the form of a TV drama performed by an all-male cast of professional actors and shot with multiple cameras in a purpose-built set in the studios of the Irish public service broadcaster Raidió Telefís Éireann (RTÉ). Although the lighting and camerawork are broadly consistent with television drama production, the action was performed for the camera as a series of continuous live takes, which were subsequently edited.[61] In addition, although the set design and costuming convincingly suggest the 1920s, the actors deliver their lines in Irish accents, and the transposition from transcription to script produces stilted and unnatural dialogue. This sense of artifice is heightened by the fact that 'Breton' continually addresses the others by surname, blandly requesting responses from all to a series of questions about sexual preferences.

Byrne's work was exhibited as an installation, incorporating five projections onto a dispersed series of eight propped slabs, which function as screens.[62] In addition, the action is organised into a number of separate sequences presented across the various screens, loosely recalling the 'chapters' found in commercial DVD releases so that, in order to view the work in full, the exhibition visitor is required to move around the gallery, potentially missing certain sequences. The television drama shot by the RTÉ studio cameras (in standard definition) is also interspersed with additional 'behind-the-scenes footage' shot in HD, which depicts the camera operators at work on the studio floor and the producers in the control booth. At other moments, the television drama is shown playing on TV sets in pubs and family homes, apparently unobserved in several of these spaces. For example, in one sequence the drama plays on a television set in a domestic living room, while teenage girls are visible in the background, sitting at a computer screen. As a result, many of the most attentive observers of 'television' in *A man and a woman make love* would seem to be the studio personnel engaged in its production and, by implication, the artist overseeing the shoot.

References to television are not new in Byrne's practice. For example, earlier installation works such as *New Sexual Lifestyles* (2003) and *1984 and beyond* (2005–7) owe certain aspects of their staging to television, and particularly to the cult late night show *After Dark*, broadcast on Channel 4 in 1987–97, celebrated for its relatively unstructured discussion of contemporary cultural themes. In addition, Byrne shot part of an earlier work, *Subject* (2009), in a television studio located on the Brutalist campus of the University of Leeds, making use of outdated TV technology and sets in the staging of his exploration of the material and social history of this institution, an important institutional site of cultural studies research in the 1950s and 1960s.[63] Byrne's subsequent work, *A Thing is a hole in a thing it is not* (2010), also features a direct reference to broadcasting history as it includes audio drawn from a 1964 radio talk show featuring Dan Flavin, Donald Judd and Frank Stella. Considered together, these works underscore Byrne's interest in the material architecture of antiquated radio and television studios. But *A man and a woman make love* actually marks a significant departure since it was produced with the collaboration of a functioning broadcaster. As such it engages—albeit somewhat obliquely—with the contemporary institutional context of television production.

The final work in my discussion, Maya Schweizer's *Before the Rehearsal*, was realised without the involvement of a broadcaster. Despite its relatively modest form, as a single-channel video work with a running time of 16 minutes, it brings into focus several of the themes that have recurred throughout my study. They include the issues of representation that have been raised, especially within the US context, by the form of television genres such as 'progressive' sitcoms and confessional talk shows, the modes of self-exploitation widely associated with reality TV and social media, and the performance of emotional and affective labour in the cultural industries. I am also drawn to this work because Schweizer does not purport to analyse the situation that she observes, or to resolve the contradictions that her video reveals.

Shot in Los Angeles, while Schweizer was on residency in the city, *Before the Rehearsal* depicts the comedy sketch group Slow Children Crossing rehearsing elements of their television show in two different domestic spaces, and discussing strategies of self-marketing. Formed in 2006, and including mainly African-American writer-performers, this group describes itself as promoting a 'take-no-prisoners' approach to humour, dealing with subjects such as 'politics, race, sex, slavery, celebrities'.[64] The video developed as a relatively spontaneous response to Schweizer's interaction with this group of aspiring television workers, and they participated in its production as a networking strategy. Schweizer was invited to record several of the group's rehearsals and meetings, in return for copies of the master tapes, which Slow Children Crossing could then potentially use for promotional purposes.

The members of Slow Children Crossing consciously and continually present themselves to each other (and to Schweizer's camera) as savvy media professionals, in command of every aspect of their brand, despite the relatively limited material resources that seem available to them. So *Before the Rehearsal* features fragments of scripted performances, followed by moments of feedback and self-critique, in which the performers rapidly shift between the characters they are playing and other modes of equally constructed self-presentation. In these interactions, they demonstrate their knowledge of marketing opportunities offered by social media and discuss their individual personas as group members rather than characters, in the course of planning a reality-style video about themselves, which might be modelled on reality TV shows such as *Survivor*, *The Real World* and *The Real Housewives of Orange County*. The video culminates with a shot of several group members watching an old clip of (then Presidential candidate) Barack Obama dancing with Ellen DeGeneres on her TV show. As several of the performers casually mime Obama's moves, it is unclear whether this is a moment of relaxation, research or even the beginning of yet another rehearsal. Schweizer's open-ended conclusion also underscores the fact that, while they may be watching this old video clip on a social media website rather than a TV set, these aspiring performers continue to interact with each other, and to structure their professional and personal identities, through reference to television.

Conclusion

For many decades, artists have been drawn toward television production environments, whether seeking to observe, intervene or collaborate in the practices of broadcasting institutions and television workers. For many of the activist video makers associated with the guerrilla television movement in the US, broadcast networks were viewed as hierarchical corporate structures to be challenged, circumvented or—in the case of TVTV—subverted and reformed from within. While early Videofreex tapes such as *Process Video Revolution* document a confrontation between Portapak-wielding activists and network employees, other collectives developed a different approach to the television worker, more attuned to the publicity value of network newscasters and Hollywood stars. Through 'behind the scenes' coverage of spectacular media events, in *Four More Years*, *The World's Largest TV Studio* and *TVTV Looks at the Oscars*, TVTV producers such as Michael Shamberg presented themselves as outsiders to the media industry, while at the same time trading upon the celebrity appeal of industry insiders in the hope of gaining access to broadcast distribution networks.

Although collaborative approaches to production have remained important for many artists engaging with television, the context of production for artists' moving image has changed significantly since the 1970s. Rather than seeking to gain access to broadcast infrastructures, the contemporary artists discussed in this chapter are more likely to work with broadcasting institutions towards the realisation of projects for gallery exhibition, or to employ film and television workers such as actors, cinematographers and producers. Yet the need for publicity remains an important (even increasingly significant) consideration in the art economy, as evidenced by the proliferation of art reality TV shows involving professional artists, curators and critics, and the establishment of partnerships between broadcasters and art institutions such as the Brooklyn Museum. For some artists, including LuckyPDF, reality TV stardom functions as a resource for artists and institutions seeking publicity. In contrast, Auto Italia South East are drawn toward an earlier moment in the history of television, when the TV studio could be imagined as a site of collaborative experimentation and innovation. Meanwhile, for artists who are also TV workers, such as Alexis Hudgins, the gallery serves as a valuable physical, social and conceptual space in which practices of television production can be restaged for the purposes of critique.

Other artists, such as Christian Jankowski, draw exhibition and television production processes into proximity with each other in order to explore practices that are particular to these disparate production worlds, working with—but also distorting—conventionalised modes of 'behind the scenes' publicity. Gerard Byrne's work, on the other hand, is more specifically focused upon the material, institutional and social architecture of the television studio, although as part of his expansive investigation of television's cultural history and legacy, it encompasses an exploration of labour practices. In contrast, Maya Schweizer is drawn toward the poststudio environment inhabited by underemployed writer-performers, who aspire to work in television and collaborate in the continual production of personal and public personas that evolve in conjunction with the changing forms of television and social media. In diverse ways, these contemporary works all contest the notion that the art economy is exceptional, highlighting commonalities as well as differences in the negotiation of ceaselessly changing contexts of art and television production.

Conclusion: Contemporary Art After Television

At the outset of this study, I suggested that *documenta 11* marked the beginning of a shift in the imagining of television in contemporary art culture, with works such as Black Audio Film Collective's *Handsworth Songs* and Stan Douglas's *Suspiria* signalling a new emphasis on retrospection in the place of reform. In the years since 2002, television's position as a dominant cultural form has been called into question within many contexts but it continues to function as an important resource for artists, curators and art institutions. Television's status as 'resource', rather than object of reform, finds expression in the thirteenth instalment of Documenta, reflected in works such as Dora García's *Die Klau Mich Show* and in Gerard Byrne's *A man and a woman make love*. But *dOCUMENTA (13)* also includes another work that engages with the history and institutional context of television, and highlights its importance, as well as its circumscription, as a public form: *Muster* (Rushes) (2012) by Clemens von Wedemeyer.

Muster is one of the most ambitious moving image projects realised for *dOCUMENTA (13)*, existing in two forms, as a three-channel HD installation (at the Hauptbahnof venue) and as a single-channel version with a running time of 81 minutes, produced with financial support from 3Sat, a publicly-funded cultural television channel run by the German broadcaster ZDF.[1] The feature-length version was broadcast on 3Sat within the context of a *Fernseh-Finissage*, or television-closing, marking the exhibition's final weekend.[2] The German word *Muster* can be translated to mean 'patterns' or 'samples', but when interpreted as 'rushes' it is much more explicitly linked to the critical evaluation of material generated as part of a filmic production process. Given this self-conscious concern with evaluation, as well as its prominence as a project devised both for gallery exhibition and broadcast, *Muster* offers a useful vantage point from which to review both the specific conclusions of this study and the broader project of integrating television and art histories.

Von Wedemeyer's work was shot at Breitenau, a location described by curator Carolyn Christov-Bakargiev as the 'ghostly other' to Kassel.[3] Once the site of a twelfth-century Benedictine monastery, Breitenau has fulfilled many functions during its long history. Following the Reformation, several of the monastery buildings were repurposed and the church initially became a storehouse. In the nineteenth century it housed a prison, but part of the building was also reopened as the village church. This church continued to hold services throughout the era of National Socialism, with the prison serving as a work re-education camp and a concentration camp. After World War Two, Breitenau remained a place of detention, functioning as the site of a reform school for girls. In this role it was one of several such institutions critiqued by journalist Ulrike Meinhof in a series of articles, which she followed with a script for a television film set in a reform school. The film's title, *Bambule* (1970), is slang for a generally non-violent form of prison protest. Shortly before the scheduled broadcast of *Bambule*, however, Meinhof's career as a journalist came to a dramatic end when she helped Andreas Baader, arrested for a politically-motivated arson attack on a department store, to escape from prison. Marked as the work of a terrorist, *Bambule* was not shown on German television until 1994, years after the reform school institutions it critiqued had closed.

In *Muster*, the making of Meinhof's film is transposed from Berlin, where it actually occurred, to the reform school in 1970s Breitenau. This reimagining of Meinhof's film constitutes one of three specific moments in the long history of the complex explored by von Wedemeyer. The other moments are the liberation of prisoners at Breitenau in 1945 by a group of American soldiers, accompanied by a filmmaker (a role played by the artist and researcher Angela Melitopoulos), and a visit by a group of students in 1994, who view film footage relating to the concentration camps and a tape of *Bambule*, one day after its delayed broadcast on German television. These three moments are linked both by the location and by several actors who reappear in different guises in multiple timelines.[4] So, for example, Melitopoulos plays not only the documentary filmmaker in 1945 but also an unidentified woman introducing *Bambule* to the students in 1994. Another actor plays a prisoner at Breitenau in 1945 and a student in 1994 encountering a performance by *Die Fremden* (The Strangers), a band known in the Kassel-Göttingen region for songs critiquing normative German society. A different actor appears as the interpreter accompanying the US forces, the director of *Bambule* in 1970, and the educator showing the students around the complex 24 years later. Finally, the lead actress in *Bambule* reappears as a student in the 1994 timeline.

By casting the same performers in different roles, von Wedemeyer draws attention to processes of forgetting, as well as remembering. The structure of the work, in both its multi- and single-screen versions, serves to emphasise both repetition and miscommunication. All three timelines involve flawed attempts by individuals to communicate aspects of their experience. So, in 1945, the interpreter cannot fully understand the testimony of the French-speaking prisoner who witnessed a mass execution of prisoners. Then in 1970 the director of *Bambule* refuses to allow the reform school residents to play themselves, despite their protests, and in 1994 the educator leading the tour around Breitenau struggles to engage some of the students with his account of its complex history. As suggested by this summary, the narrative structure of *Muster* is highly complex. The three timelines are intercut in the single channel edit, so that the action continually shifts between 1945, 1970 and 1994. But in the installation version, which involves projections onto a three-screen structure, the three timelines are spatially separate and visitors must move around the structure to view the work in full.

Most importantly, *Muster* derives its complex temporal structure from the delayed broadcast of Meinhof's *Bambule*. The relationship between transmission and (mis)communication is suggested in a key scene set during the production of the film in the 1970 timeline. A group of female extras are seated in the church at Breitenau, waiting for the shoot to begin, but as the camera tracks to the left it becomes clear that their comments are temporally out of synch. One girl points out that the film is being made by Ulrike Meinhof, but she cautions that 'no one is allowed to say, people would think it was about terrorism'. Another responds 'What's Meinhof's link with terrorism?', only to be told by others, 'she went underground', and then 'Rubbish, not yet. She's a journalist. She has to go underground to free Baader'. This is just one of many points in the complex narrative of *Muster* in which timelines converge, so that action and events ostensibly belonging to different historical moments appear to intersect and overlap.

Muster also engages with the loaded institutional context of Documenta, as a privileged setting for the exploration of history and memory in German society.[5] Christov-Bakargiev's *dOCUMENTA (13)* was not the first iteration of the exhibition to focus on the events that occurred at Breitenau during the National Socialist era. In 1982, a slide show and documentary material exploring the evidence and occlusion of war crimes at this site, developed by the historian Gunnar Richter with Project Group Breitenau, was presented as part of Joseph Beuys's Free International University at *documenta 7*. This presentation contributed to the founding of the Breitenau Memorial in 1984 (directed by Richter), which figures obliquely within *Muster* through the display of material artefacts from the era of the camps, such as identity cards and logbooks, which are presented to the camera for inspection one by one. The relationship between *documenta 7* and Project Group Breitenau is also acknowledged in *dOCUMENTA (13)*, through the re-presentation of the slide show and documentary material in a small structure at Karlsaue Park, one of the main venues in Kassel.

Muster also invites comparison with earlier Documenta projects engaging with television history, most notably Douglas's 2002 work *Suspiria*. As noted in my introduction to this study, Douglas's *Suspiria* incorporated a live feed from cameras installed in the Octagon, which could be viewed by day at the Museum Fridericianum and by night on local television. *Muster*, by contrast, was devised to be exhibited first as an installation work by visitors to *dOCUMENTA (13)*, and subsequently in broadcast form. Despite this important difference, both Douglas and von Wedemeyer establish links between the exhibition space and production locations that are historically significant and located outside the centre of Kassel. Both works also propose connections between their respective sites of production and television—framing the latter as a somewhat problematic object of cultural memory and history. But while Douglas draws attention to the ways in which aspects of the history of broadcast technology are accidently (and temporarily) preserved in NTSC television, von Wedemeyer focuses on a charged moment in the institutional history of German broadcasting, where the role of the state circumscribed television's limits as a platform for social and political critique.

Through its highly reflexive exploration of television history, *Muster* seems to reiterate the turn toward retrospection highlighted in the opening chapter of this book, 'Sets, Screens and Social Spaces: Exhibiting Television'. Referencing a range of TV-themed exhibitions

Above: Clemens von Wedemeyer, *Muster
(Rushes)*, 2012, 3-channel synchronized
HD film installation, color, sound, 3 screens:
280 x 500 cm, 3 x 27 min., Installation at
dOCUMENTA(13), Kassel, 2012
Courtesy: Galerie Jocelyn Wolff, Paris,
KOW Berlin.
Photo: Clemens v. Wedemeyer / VG
BildKunst Bonn.

realised since the mid-2000s, this chapter charted both a renewal of curatorial interest in television and the emergence of a retrospective approach to its exhibition in contemporary art contexts. My research identified an array of curated presentations, from scholarly art historical surveys to in-depth analyses of specific themes and more experimental ventures, which together underscored the importance of the gallery as a space in which to reflect upon the history of television both as a cultural form, and also as an object of artistic critique and exploration.

Although von Wedemeyer does not engage with the TV genres explored in Chapter Two, 'Quality Television and Contemporary Art: Soaps, Sitcoms and Symbolic Value', *Muster* closely approximates the production values of television drama. Like Phil Collins, von Wedemeyer uses various formal strategies, including 'studio-made alienation effects'[6] such as back projection, to dissociate his work from more standardised forms of television drama. Nonetheless, the formal reflexivity displayed in this work offers a point of connection with contemporary 'quality' television, as theorised in this chapter. Significantly, *Muster* differs from most of the works discussed in Chapter Two, in that it was actually produced with the support of a broadcaster and devised in order to viewed on television. The partnership between 3Sat and *dOCUMENTA (13)*, promoted through scheduled events such as the *Fernseh-Finissage*, also seems specifically devised to confer distinction upon the cultural television channel, affirming the claims made by Newman and Levine with regard to the role that art institutions might play in legitimating certain forms of television.[7] But this conferral of distinction occurred within a very particular cultural and political context, while other cross-institutional collaborations between broadcasters and museums are likely to be shaped by different agendas.

Throughout Chapter Three, 'Reality TV, Delegated Performance and the Social Turn', I drew attention to the prevalence of non-professional performers in contemporary art, whether appearing as themselves or in assigned roles. *Muster* very specifically addresses the role of performance within the context of projects animated by social and political critique, and also touches upon the ideology underpinning the Method school of acting. At one point during the 1970 sequence, the lead actress in *Bambule* questions the director about the decision to use professional performers, instead of the reformatory inmates, and he responds by stating 'a station guard can play himself but a reformatory girl can't. It's not an occupation'. Leaving the set, the actress then appears to walk side by side with another version of herself—this time dressed as a 'real' inmate who accuses the production team of making a film for their 'own glory'. At another moment, she plays the part of a student in 1994, who attempts to develop a connection to the former inmates by lying down in one of the cells, only to be rebuked by the educational tour guide.

Given its sustained focus on practices of remembering as well as forms of erasure and occlusion, *Muster* clearly has much in common with the contemporary works discussed in Chapter Four, 'European Television Archives, Collective Memories and Contemporary Art', several of which reflect upon television's role in the articulation, or elision, of collective memory. Von Wedemeyer even incorporates a fragment of the television film *Bambule*.

Above: A prisoner (Tómas Lemarquis)
recalls the mass murder at the Fulda hill.
Film still, Clemens von Wedemeyer,
Muster, 2012. © VG BildKunst Bonn.

Above: A movie is being made in the brig.
Film still, Clemens von Wedemeyer,
Muster, 2012. © VG BildKunst Bonn.

Rather than being shown directly, however, this footage is reflected as a screen image in the eye of one viewer, slumped over the television set. But while the works discussed in Chapter Four explore interconnections between broadcast archives and aspects of personal and familial memory, *Muster* places even greater emphasis on the physical and material relics relating to the history of Breitenau and the National Socialist era, when the collection of the Breitenau foundation is presented to the camera for inspection.[8]

Like many of the works discussed in Chapter Five, 'Monuments to Broadcasting: Television and Art in the Public Realm', *Muster* is also concerned with memorialisation, and with the contested history and status of television as a public cultural form. But von Wedemeyer is actually dealing with a physical site, and production location, that is formally recognised as a memorial. In addition, far from exploring the privatisation of public space and culture, the production of *Muster*—involving a partnership between 3Sat and *dOCUMENTA (13)*—actually demonstrates the extent to which television continues to function within certain privileged contexts as a platform for contemporary art. In Chapter Six, 'Talk Shows: Art Institutions and the Discourse of Publicness', I highlighted the importance of television, and particularly the talk show, as a resource for curators, artists and art institutions seeking to assert or reconfigure the publicness of contemporary art. While it would be highly misleading to categorise Christov-Bakargiev's curatorial approach in terms of an extension of 'New Institutionalism', *dOCUMENTA (13)* did incorporate an engagement with the history of Documenta, as evidenced by the citation of Project Group Breitenau's inclusion in *documenta 7*. Given the focus on serial publication noted in Chapter Six, it also worth recalling that Christov-Bakargiev's exhibition was preceded by the publication of 100 numbered books (100 Notes—100 Thoughts) including one by von Wedemeyer, incorporating Meinhof's original script for *Bambule*.[9]

Finally, like many of the installation and performance works referenced in Chapter Seven, 'Production on Display: Television, Labour, and Contemporary Art', *Muster* clearly articulates a fascination with practices and processes of production. But the directors, camera operators and actors observed during the making of *Bambule* clearly differ from the 'real' television workers depicted by artists such as Gerard Byrne and Christian Jankowski. Perhaps more importantly, it could also be argued that *Muster* is equally focused upon practices of media consumption, not least because the teenage visitors to Breitenau are repeatedly depicted watching film and television, and listening to music. Consequently von Wedemeyer's project does not neatly illustrate my analysis. Instead, like many of the contemporary works discussed in this study, it proposes new ways of thinking about the relationship of television to art practice.

Embarking upon the research that led eventually to *TV Museum*, I had a sense that television was beginning to rival cinema as an object of artistic memory and perhaps also nostalgia. As my research progressed, however, it became increasingly clear that histories and practices of television production interest artists in part because they can inform analysis of changes in the cultural economy of contemporary art. This means that exploring 'the televisual' is not simply an articulation of nostalgia for a diminished cultural form or a way for artists, curators and institutions to generate symbolic value or publicity, even though TV-themed projects might sometimes fulfil this function. Television may in fact remain important to artists, curators and art institutions because its characteristic forms and modes of production can be utilised to imaginatively adopt a position that is symbolically 'outside' the culture of contemporary art. At the same time, it could be argued that it also offers us a new way of seeing—from a televisual distance—those aspects of art culture that are sometimes obscured by proximity.

Notes

Notes to Introduction

1. Andreas Huyssen, *Twilight Memories: Marking Time in a Culture of Amnesia* (London: Routledge, 1995), 32.
2. Huyssen, 33.
3. Volker Pantenburg, '1970 and Beyond. Experimental Cinema and Art Spaces,' in *Screen Dynamics: Mapping the Borders of Cinema*, ed. Gertrude Koch, Volker Pantenburg, Simon Rothöhler (Vienna: Austrian Film Museum and SYNEMA—Gesellschaft für Film und Medien, 2012), 91.
4. Douglas Gordon, cited by Pantenburg, 90. The interview, conducted by David Sylvester, is published in *Douglas Gordon*, ed. Russell Ferguson (Cambridge: MIT Press, 2002), 152–173.
5. Georgina Born examines the history of Channel 4 in 'Strategy, Positioning and Projection in Digital Television: Channel Four and the Commercialization of Public Service Broadcasting in the UK,' *Media, Culture & Society* 25 (2003): 773–799. See also Simon Blanchard and David Morley, *What's This Channel Four?: An Alternative Report* (London: Comedia, 1982) and Rod Stoneman, 'Sins of Commission,' *Screen* 33, no. 2 (Summer 1992): 127–144.
6. Lynn Spigel, 'Our TV Heritage: Television, The Archive, and The Reasons for Preservation,' in *A Companion to Television*, ed. Janet Wasko (Oxford: Blackwell Publishing, 2010), 67–102.
7. Sean Cubitt, *Timeshift: On Video Culture* (London and New York: Routledge, 1991).
8. Erika Balsom, *Exhibiting Cinema in Contemporary Art* (Amsterdam: Amsterdam University Press, 2013), 137.
9. Balsom, 138.
10. Balsom, 140. Gordon's recollections are cited by Amy Taubin, '24 Hour Psycho,' in *Spellbound: Art and Film*, ed. Ian Christie and Philip Dodd (London: BFI Publishing, 2006), 70.
11. Balsom, 142.
12. See Maeve Connolly, 'Temporality, Sociality, Publicness: Cinema as Art Project,' *Afterall* 29 (2012): 4–15.
13. Gordon's work featured in numerous exhibitions related to the centenary of cinema, including *Spellbound: Art and Film* at the Hayward Gallery (1996), *Art and Film Since 1945: Hall of Mirrors* at the Museum of Contemporary Art in Los Angeles (1996) and *Scream and Scream Again: Film in Art* at Museum of Modern Art Oxford (1996). For a review of

Spellbound in the context of other cinema-themed exhibitions, see Douglas Fogle, 'Cinema is Dead, Long Live the Cinema', *Frieze* 29 (1996): 32.

14. In addition to the previously cited publications by Erika Balsom and Volker Pantenburg, see also various contributions to Tanya Leighton and Pavel Buchler (eds), *Saving the Image: Art After Film*, (Glasgow and Manchester: Centre for Contemporary Arts and Manchester Metropolitan University, 2003) and Tanya Leighton (ed) *Art and the Moving Image: A Critical Reader*, (London: Tate Publishing and Afterall, 2008). See also Mike Sperlinger and Ian White (eds), *Kinomuseum: Towards an Artists' Cinema*, (Cologne: Verlag der Buchhandlung Walther Konig, 2008), Catherine Fowler, 'Remembering Cinema "Elsewhere": From Retrospection to Introspection in the Gallery Film', *Cinema Journal* 51.2 (2012), 26–45; and my own book *The Place of Artists' Cinema: Space, Site and Screen* (Bristol and Chicago: Intellect and Chicago University Press, 2009).

15. See Jean-Christophe Royoux, 'Mobile TV: le lieu des récits entrecroisés', *Homo Zappiens Zappiens* (Rennes: Presses Universitaires de Rennes 2, 1998). Le Consortium [Accessed June 1, 2013] http://leconsortium.fr/expositions-exhibitions/pierre-huyghe/.

16. There are some important exceptions, particularly amongst French critics. See Benjamin Thorel, *Telle est la Télé: L'art Contemporain et la télévision* (Paris: Editions Cercle d'Art, 2006).

17. See John Thornton Caldwell, *Televisuality: Style, Crisis, and Authority in American Television* (New Brunswick, NJ: Rutgers University Press, 1995) 25–27. Caldwell notes the importance of Raymond Williams's elaboration of flow as an important reference point in the development of 'glance theory' (by John Ellis among others). The main texts cited by Caldwell are Marshall McLuhan, *Understanding Media: The Extensions of Man* (New York: McGraw-Hill, 1964), John Ellis, *Visible Fictions: Cinema, Television, Video* (London: Routledge and Kegan Paul, 1982) and Raymond Williams, *Television: Technology and Cultural Form* (New York: Schocken, 1975). Interestingly, as Caldwell points out, McLuhan's own model actually emphasised the active viewer response elicited by the low-resolution image, 'necessitated by the need to give conceptual closure to video's mosaiclike imagery'.

18. Caldwell, 26.

19. Caldwell, 28. For a valuable discussion of televisual liveness, McLuhan and satellite broadcasting see Lisa Parks, *Cultures in Orbit: Satellites and the Televisual* (Durham and London: Duke University Press, 2005), 21–46. See also Jane Feuer, 'The Concept of Live Television: Ontology as Ideology', in *Regarding Television: Critical Approaches—An Anthology*, ed. E. Ann Kaplan (Frederick, Md.: University Publications of America, 1983), 12–22 and William Kaizen, 'Live on Tape: Video, Liveness and the Immediate', in *Art and the Moving Image: A Critical Reader*, ed. Tanya Leighton, London: Tate Publishing in Association with Afterall Books, 2008), 269–272.

20. Caldwell, 29.

21. Caldwell, 29.

22. Martha Rosler, 'Video: Shedding the Utopian Moment', in *Illuminating Video: An Essential Guide to Video Art*, ed. Doug Hall and Sally Jo Fifer (New York: Aperture Foundation in association with Bay Area Video Coalition, 1990), 31.

23. Jay David Bolter and Richard Grusin, *Remediation: Understanding New Media* (Cambridge, MA: MIT Press, 2000).

24. Parks, 12.
25. Lynn Spigel, *TV by Design: Modern Art and the Rise of Network Television* (Chicago: University of Chicago Press, 2008) 8–9. John Wyver, 'TV Against TV: Video Art on Television,' *Film and Video Art*, ed. Stuart Comer, (London: Tate Publishing, 2009), 1 25–26.
26. The other 'moments' cited by Wyver include *The Medium is the Message* (1969) produced by the public station WGBH in Boston and *Fernsehgalerie* (1969–70), the 'television gallery' initiated by Gerry Schum through a broadcast anthology of short works entitled *Land Art* films on Sender Freies Berlin, various other projects produced by Schum, including Jan Dibbets's *TV as a Fireplace*, broadcast as the closing transmission for eight nights on WDR3, and David Hall's *TV Interruptions*, made with Scottish TV (with funding from the Scottish Arts Council) and broadcast during the Edinburgh Festival. For an insightful discussion of the US context, focusing on the work of the National Center for Experiments in Television, see Kris Paulsen, 'In the Beginning, There was the Electron,' *X-TRA Contemporary Art Quarterly* 15, no. 2 (2012): 56–73.
27. Noah Horowitz, *Art of the Deal: Contemporary Art in a Global Financial Market* (Princeton and Oxford: Princeton University Press, 2011), 33.
28. Horowitz, 26–86. See also Paul Ryan's detailed analysis of the development of institutional supports for video art in 'A Genealogy of Video,' *Leonardo* 21, no. 1 (1988): 39–44.
29. This term is drawn from Marina Turco, cited by Wyver, 126. See Marina Turco, 'Changing history, changing practices: an instance of confrontation between video art and television in the Netherlands,' *E-view*, no. 2 (2004). E-view Journals [Accessed June 1, 2013] https://ojs.uvt.nl/.
30. On Kovacs, see Spigel, *TV by Design*, 178–212 and on *The Gracie Allen and George Burns Show* and *I Love Lucy* see Lynn Spigel, *Make Room for TV: Television and the Family Ideal in Postwar America* (Chicago: University of Chicago Press, 1992), 136–180. See also Caldwell, 23.
31. Caldwell, 75.
32. Milly Buonanno, *The Age of Television: Experiences and Theories*, trans. Jennifer Radice (Bristol and Chicago: Intellect and University of Chicago, 2008) 12.
33. Buonanno, 20–21. The John Ellis text cited is *Seeing Things*, (London: I.B. Tauris, 2000).
34. Buonanno, 21.
35. Philip Auslander, *Liveness: Performance in a Mediatized Culture*, Second edition (Oxon: Routledge, 2008), xii.
36. Spigel, cited by Auslander, 18. The Spigel text referenced is *Make Room for TV: Television and the Family Ideal in Postwar America*.
37. Auslander, 18. Italics in original.
38. Auslander, 184.
39. The show evolved from a series of live events at Brooklyn-based Louis V E.S.P. contemporary art gallery and festivals such as Index in New York. For details on E.S.P. TV, see Whitney Kimball, 'Artists are on TV! This Time, Not For Bravo Money,' *Art Fag City*, August 23, 2012 [Accessed June 1, 2013] http://www.artfagcity.com/2012/08/23/artists-are-on-tv-this-time-not-for-bravo-money/. Thanks to Mark Cullen and Gavin Murphy of Pallas Projects for drawing my attention to the work of E.S.P. TV.

40. Venues include Millennium Film Workshop in New York, General Public in Berlin and Pallas Projects in Dublin. Details on E.S.P. TV production and exhibition practices were provided by Victoria Keddie via email, March 19, 2013.

41. Mike Sperlinger, 'Looking Back: Film,' *Frieze* 136 (2011), 24.

42. Colin Perry, 'TV Makeover,' *Art Monthly* 352 (2011–2012): 11.

43. Perry, 13.

44. For a full synopsis, see *BFI Screenonline* [Accessed June 1, 2013] http://www.screenonline .org.uk/film/id/441093/.

45. Black Audio Film Collective was formed in 1982 and four years later, following the production of *Handsworth Songs* (which was broadcast on Channel 4) it was enfranchised as a Workshop group under the terms of the Workshop Agreement. For a discussion of the Collective's relationship to broadcasting see John Akomfrah, interviewed by Margaret Dickinson, *Rogue Reels: Oppositional Film in Britain 1945–1990*, London: BFI, 1999), 312.

46. Stan Douglas, 'Suspiria,' in *Stan Douglas—Past Imperfect—Works 1986-2007*, ed. Iris Dressler and Hans. D. Christ (Ostfildern: Hatje Cantz Verlag, 2007), 207.

47. Douglas, 207. The broadcast seems to have been originally intended for transmission on the French-German public television channel ARTE. See Stan Douglas, 'Suspiria,' in *Documenta 11_Platform 5: Exhibition Venues*, ed. Documenta and Museum Fridericianum (Ostfildern: Hatje Cantz 2002), 39.

48. See Max Dawson, 'Home Video and the "TV Problem": Cultural Critics and Technological Change,' *Technology and Culture* 48 (2007): 524–549.

49. Amy Holdsworth, *Television, Memory and Nostalgia* (New York: Palgrave Macmillan, 2011).

50. See for example various contributions to *Television Studies After TV: Understanding Television in the Post-Broadcast Era*, ed. Graeme Turner and Jinna Tay (London and New York: Routledge, 2009). See also Lynn Spigel, 'Introduction,' in *Television After TV: Essays on a Medium in Transition*, ed. Lynn Spigel and Jan Olsson (Durham, NC: Duke University Press, 2004): 1–34; Lynn Spigel, 'TV's Next Season?,' *Cinema Journal* 45, no. 1 (2005): 83–90, and Amy Holdsworth, ' "Television Resurrections": Television and Memory,' *Cinema Journal* 47, no. 3 (2008): 137–144.

51. Perry, 14.

52. See David Joselit, *Feedback: Television Against Democracy* (Cambridge, MA and London: The MIT Press, 2007).

53. For an insight into the imagining of differences between European and North American artists' television see Reinhard Braun and Kathy Rae Huffman, 'Television/Art/Culture: Reinhard Braun in Conversation with Kathy Rae Huffman,' *Changing Channels: Art and Television 1963–1988*, ed. Museum Moderner Kunst Stiftung Ludwig Wien and Matthias Michalka (Cologne: Verlag der Buchhandlung Walther König, 2010), 87–124.

54. Michael Z. Newman and Elana Levine, *Legitimating Television: Media Convergence and Cultural Status* (New York and London: Routledge, 2012). See also Perry, 14.

55. See B. Joseph Pine II, and James H. Gilmore, *The Experience Economy: Work is Theatre & Every Business is a Stage* (Boston, MA: Harvard Business School Press, 1999), 2.

56. Horowitz, 87–142.

57. The first part of the exhibition, 'The Game and the Players', focused upon the objectives of artists and exhibition makers, engaging with the museum as an environment for production and presentation. The second ('Time Machines') examined a range of museum models from the past, while the third ('The Politics of Collecting/The Collecting of Politics') dealt with acquisition practices. My discussion draws upon press materials, accessible on the museum's website, and on a visit to *Play Van Abbe* Part 4, followed by conversations with curators Christiane Berndes and Annie Fletcher at the Van Abbemuseum, on August 9, 2011.

58. There are parallels, for example, with the language used by marketing specialists such as Peter Gomori (Marketing Manager at Tate Modern) to profile exhibition visitors. Gomori specifically used terms such as 'Aficionados, Actualisers, Sensualists, Researchers, Self-improvers, Social Spacers' to describe visitors, in a presentation entitled 'Innovation in Audience Development in the Visual Arts', at the symposium *Here and Now: Visual Arts Audiences in Ireland*, Temple Bar Gallery and Studios, Dublin, May 18, 2011.

59. A video featuring director Charles Esche and providing information on the research process, was also included in the exhibition (at a distance from the entrance area) and visitors to the upper galleries could also experience a 'reloaded' version of part two of Play Van Abbe, providing further context.

60. This work can be viewed in full on Ressler's website http://www.ressler.at/what_is_democracy_film/ [Accessed June 1, 2013].

61. Pierre Bourdieu, *Distinction: A Social Critique of the Judgement of Taste*, trans. Richard Nice (London: Routledge, 1984); Pierre Bourdieu, *The Field of Cultural Production: Essays on Art and Literature*, ed. Randal Johnson (Cambridge: Polity Press, 1993); Pierre Bourdieu, *The Rules of Art: Genesis and Structure of the Literary Field* (Stanford: Stanford University Press, 1996).

62. John Thornton Caldwell, *Production Culture: Industrial Reflexivity and Critical Practice in Film and Television*. Durham and London: Duke University Press, 2008. See also various contributions to *Production Studies: Cultural Studies of Media Industries*, ed. Vicki Mayer, Miranda J. Banks and John Thornton Caldwell (New York and London: Routledge, 2009).

63. Caldwell, *Production Culture*, 2.

64. There have, however, been various important attempts to organise art workers in the past. See Julia Bryan-Wilson, *Art Workers, Radical Practice in the Vietnam War Era*. Berkeley: University of California Press, 2009.

65. Jürgen Habermas, *The Structural Transformation of the Public Sphere: An Inquiry into a Category of Bourgeois Society*, trans. Thomas Burger with the assistance of Frederick Lawrence (Cambridge: Polity Press, 1989). For critical responses to the work of Habermas, which have informed contemporary art practice see Oskar Negt and Alexander Kluge. *Public Sphere and Experience: Toward an Analysis of the Bourgeois and Proletarian Public Sphere*, trans. Peter Labanyi, Jamie Owen Daniel and Assenka Oksiloff (Minneapolis: University of Minnesota Press, 1993), Chantal Mouffe, 'Artistic Activism and Agonistic Spaces', *Art & Research: A Journal of Ideas, Context and Methods* 1, no. 2 (2007): 1–5, and Jodi Dean, 'Democracy: A Knot of Hope and Despair', *e-flux Journal* 39 (2012) [Accessed June 1, 2013] http://www.e-flux.com/journal/democracy-a-knot-of-hope-and-despair/.

66. Samuel Weber, *Mass Mediauras: Form, Technics, Media* (Palo Alto: Stanford University Press, 1996), 124–125.
67. This retrospective turn responds to widely-publicised changes in broadcast technology, as evidenced by the fact that *Remote Control* (at the Institute of Contemporary Arts, London in 2012) was timed to coincide with the switchover from analogue to digital broadcasting in the London region.
68. See Claire Bishop, 'Outsourcing Authenticity? Delegated Performance in Contemporary Art,' in *Double Agent*, edited by Claire Bishop and Silvia Tramontana (London: ICA, 2009), 110–125.
69. Jerome Bourdon, 'Some Sense of Time: Remembering Television,' *History & Memory* 15, no. 2 (2003): 5–35.
70. Anna McCarthy, *Ambient Television: Visual Culture and Public Space*. Duke University Press, 2001; Malcolm Miles, 'Critical Spaces: Monuments and Changes,' in *The Practice of Public Art*, ed. Cameron Cartiere and Shelly Willis (Routledge: London and New York, 2008), 66–90.
71. See David Hesmondhalgh and Sarah Baker. 'Creative Work and Emotional Labour in the Television Industry,' *Theory, Culture & Society* 25, no. 7/8 (2008): 97–118; John Caldwell, Thornton, 'Worker Blowback: User-Generated, Worker-Generated, and Producer-Generated Content within Collapsing Production Workflows,' in *Television as Digital Media*, ed. James Bennett and Niki Strange (Durham and London: Duke University Press, 2011), 283–310.

Notes to Chapter 1

1. Samuel Weber, *Mass Mediauras: Form, Technics, Media*, (Palo Alto: Stanford University Press, 1996), 124–125. Italics in original.
2. Ina Blom, *On the Style Site: Art, Sociality and Media Culture* (Berlin and New York: Sternberg Press, 2007), 87.
3. Anna McCarthy, 'From Screen to Site: Television's Material Culture, and Its Place,' *October* 98, Autumn (2001): 93. For a different perspective on the relationship between television and place, see Meghan Sutherland, 'On the Grounds of Television,' in *Taking Place: Location and the Moving Image*, ed. John David Rhodes and Elena Gorfinkel, Minneapolis and London: University of Minnesota Press, 2011), 339–362.
4. McCarthy, 93.
5. McCarthy, 95.
6. McCarthy emphasises that television's emergence, in commercial form, coincided with the 'golden age' of Fordism in the US. She notes that television advertising played a crucial role in the rise of national brands and retailing chains, which were integral to the 'Fordist wage contract' and also often took the place of local businesses, contributing to a loss of regional specificity. See McCarthy, 96.
7. McCarthy, 96.
8. McCarthy, 99.
9. My focus here is on exhibitions in art museums and galleries rather than displays in television or film museums, such as those discussed by Amy Holdsworth in *Television, Memory and Nostalgia*, (New York: Palgrave Macmillan, 2011), 127–148.

10. See Christine Mehring, 'TV Art's Abstract Starts: Europe, c.1944–1969,' *October* 125 (2008): 29–64.

11. Andreas Huyssen, *Twilight Memories: Marking Time in a Culture of Amnesia* (London: Routledge, 1995), 33.

12. Huyssen, 34.

13. Lisa Parks, *Cultures in Orbit: Satellites and the Televisual* (Durham and London: Duke University Press, 2005) 34. See also Thomas Elsaesser, 'Digital Cinema: Delivery, Event, Time,' in *Cinema Futures: Cain, Abel or Cable? The Screen Arts in the Digital Age*, ed. Thomas Elsaesser and Kay Hoffman (Amsterdam: Amsterdam University Press, 1998), 201–222.

14. Weber, 126.

15. Weber, 126.

16. John Thornton Caldwell, *Televisuality: Style, Crisis, and Authority in American Television* (New Brunswick, NJ: Rutgers University Press, 1995), 11.

17. Tony Bennett, 'Civic Laboratories: Museums, Cultural Objecthood, and the Governance of the Social', *Cultural Studies* 19, no. 5 (2005): 521–547.

18. It should be noted that some aspects of the relationship between art and television *were* historicised prior to this recent retrospective turn. For example, in 1979–1980, Gerry Schum's *Videogalerie—Fernsehgalerie* toured to numerous venues, and in 1982 Wulf Herzogenrath curated *Videokunst in Deutschland 1963–1982* (1982) at Kölnischer Kunstverein in Cologne. In 1987, Kathy Rae Huffman and Dorine Mignot curated *The Arts for Television*, organised by the Los Angeles Museum of Contemporary Art and the Stedelijk Museum in Amsterdam. But this was primarily an exhibition about television as a venue for the arts, including theatre, literature, dance and music. See Kathy Rae Huffman, 'Seeing is Believing: The Arts on TV,' in *The Arts for Television*, ed. Kathy Rae Huffman and Dorine Mignot (Los Angeles and Amsterdam: Los Angeles Museum of Contemporary Art and Stedelijk Museum, 1987), 8–16.

19. My discussion of 'Remote Control' incorporates material revised from Maeve Connolly 'Televisual Objects: Props, Relics and Prosthetics,' *Afterall* 33 (2013), 66–77. This chapter also includes material revised from Maeve Connolly, 'Staging Mobile Spectatorship in the Moving Image Installations of Amanda Beech, Philippe Parreno, and Ryan Trecartin/Lizzie Fitch,' in *Display und Dispositif*, ed. Ursula Frohne, Lilian Haberer and Annette Urban (Munich: Wilhelm Fink, forthcoming, 2014).

20. One could also cite *Forbidden Love: Art in the Wake of Television Camp*, conceived by Simon Denny, Kathrin Jentjens and Anja Nathan-Dorn at Kölnischer Kunstverein, Cologne, September – December 2010, and *Channel TV* (2010), a collaboration between Kunstverein Harburger Bahnhof, Hamburg, CNEAI, Chatou, Paris and Halle für Kunst, Lüneburg. In addition to exhibitions and related discursive events, this project included an eight-hour programme of moving image work, broadcast in Paris, Hamburg and Lüneburg, and a publication realised in collaboration with the multilingual journal *Multitudes* entitled *Art TV Clash*, published in Autumn 2010. See also Kris Paulsen's insightful review of the exhibition California Video at the Getty Center, Los Angeles in 2008, 'California Video,' *X-TRA Contemporary Art Quarterly* 11.1 (2008) http://x-traonline.org/article/california-video/ (Accessed June 1, 2013).

21. It is also possible to cite US curatorial projects that focus on experimental and innovation practices by television producers (as distinct from artists) such as *Change the Channel: WCVB-TV 1972–1982*, curated by Gary Fogelson and Michael Hutcherson at Apex Art, New York (2011).

22. Several shows also explored the significance of television within specific histories and cultures of artistic production, such as *TV Gallery* curated by Dunja Blažević at Gallery Nova, Zagreb (2007); *Fast and Loose: My Dead Gallery*, curated by the artists group The Centre of Attention at Fieldgate Gallery, London (2006), which included histories of several London-based projects and spaces with a focus on television, such as the Arts Lab and NeTWork 21 pirate TV station. Within the US, the graduating class of the California College of the Arts Graduate Program in Curatorial Practice curated a show at the CCA Wattis Institute for Contemporary Arts, San Francisco, exploring the history of the now-defunct gallery La Mamelle/ART COM, known for its engagement with TV and multimedia; *God Only Knows Who the Audience Is: Performance, Video, and Television Through the Lens of La Mamelle/ART COM* (2011).

23. Blom, 85. Rather than engaging specifically with questions of affect or attention associated with the shift from productive to postproductive capitalism, however, Paik often invoked 'anticommercialist' forms of exchange (such as barter) and interaction (such the festival) that preceded commodity capitalism. See Sook-Kyung Lee, 'Videa 'n' Videology: Open Communication,' in *Nam June Paik*, ed. Sook-Kyung Lee and Susanne Rennert (London: Tate Publishing, 2010), 33.

24. Blom, 86.

25. The programme focused on developments since the end of World War Two, featuring images of bombed cities and culminating with footage of Adenauer's state visit to the White House. See Andrew S. Weiner, 'Memory under Reconstruction: Politics and Event in Wirtschaftswunder West Germany,' *Grey Room* 37 (2009): 98. See also the brief discussion of this work in Benjamin H.D. Buchloh, 'Readymade, Photography, and Painting in the Painting of Gerhard Richter,' in *Neo-Avantgarde and Culture Industry: Essays on European and American Art from 1955 to 1975* (Cambridge: MIT Press, 2000), 365–404.

26. Dan Graham, 'Art as Design/Design as Art,' in *Dan Graham: Beyond*, ed. Bennett Simpson and Chrissie Iles (Los Angeles and Cambridge, MA: The Museum of Contemporary Art and MIT Press, 2009), 272.

27. Graham, 272.

28. Anna McCarthy, *Ambient Television: Visual Culture and Public Space* (Duke University Press, 2001).

29. Dan Graham interviewed by Benjamin Buchloh, 'Four Conversations: December 1999–May 2000,' *Dan Graham, Works 1965–2000*, ed. Marianne Brouwer (Düsseldorf: Richter Verlag, 2001), 78.

30. Blom, 57.

31. Noah Horowitz also notes the establishment of several new institutions (such as BALTIC), in which boundaries between exhibition spaces and social spaces, such as cafes and book shops, were deliberately blurred. Noah Horowitz, *Art of the Deal: Contemporary Art in a Global Financial Market* (Princeton and Oxford: Princeton University Press, 2011), 129.

32. Blom, 74.
33. Blom, 75.
34. Roberta Smith, 'A Channel-Surfing Experience with Beanbag Chairs and Gym,' *The New York Times*, April 25, 1997, C22.
35. Smith, C22.
36. Smith, C22.
37. Her review communicates a strong resistance to the reconfiguration of the museum around self-conscious relaxation, perhaps pointing toward distinctions between US and European contexts of reception. See Tim Griffin's discussion of the issue of cultural difference in the reception of *theanyspacewhatever* at the Solomon R. Guggenheim Museum, New York (2008), in 'Postscript: The Museum Revisited,' *Artforum* 48, no. 9 (2010): 330.
38. Shamberg's (unsigned) review was published in *Time*, May 30, 1969, 74.
39. Michael Shamberg and Raindance Corporation, *Guerrilla Television* (New York: Holt, Rinehart and Winston, 1971). For a discussion of Shamberg and Raindance Corporation, see David Joselit, 'Tale of the Tape,' *Artforum* 40, no. 9 (2002): 152–57.
40. Press Release for *Home Sweet Home*, Witte de With, Rotterdam January 24, 1998 – March 22, 1998 [Accessed June 1, 2013] http://www.wdw.nl/event/home-screen-home/.
41. This section includes material (significantly revised) from Maeve Connolly, 'Staging Television: James Coleman's *So Different…and Yet*,' *Mousse Magazine* 27 (2011): 160–165.
42. Benjamin Buchloh, 'Memory Lessons and History Tableaux: James Coleman's Archaeology of Spectacle,' in *James Coleman* (Barcelona: Fundació Antoni Tàpies, 1999), 70.
43. Buchloh, 69.
44. Jean Fisher, '*So Different…and Yet*,' in *James Coleman* (Dublin: Irish Museum of Modern Art, 2009), 35–47. Fisher extends and revises this chronology in her text 'So Different … and Yet,' *James Coleman*, (Madrid: Museo Nacional Centro de Arte Reina Sofia, 2012), 164-169.
45. Fisher, 36. The castle was the site of Coleman's performance *guaiRE: An Allegory* (1985), also featuring Fouéré. For a discussion of this work see Luke Gibbons, 'Narratives of No Return: James Coleman's guaiRE,' *Transformations in Irish Culture* (Cork: Cork University Press in association with Field Day, 1996), 129–133.
46. Fisher, 36.
47. Fisher, 38.
48. Fisher, 41.
49. The show opened at the Hatton Gallery (February 28 – April 5, 2008), before touring to Cornerhouse in Manchester (June 13 –August 10, 2008). My discussion is informed by Sarah Cook's presentation to students on the MA in Visual Arts Practices, Institute of Art, Design & Technology, Dublin, in April 2008, as well as documentation of the exhibition.
50. Sarah Cook and Kathy Rae Huffman, 'Curatorial Statement,' *Broadcast Yourself*, 2008 [Accessed June 1, 2013] http://www.broadcastyourself.net/.
51. Documentation of artworks, and a conference at BALTIC that accompanied the project can be found at http://www.swansong.tv/ [Accessed June 1, 2013]. See also the discussion of *TV Swansong* in Beryl Graham and Sarah Cook, *Rethinking Curating: Art After New Media* (Cambridge, MA: MIT Press, 2010), 255.
52. Dan Fox, 'TV Swansong,' *Frieze* 68 (2002): 124.

53. For a discussion of display and exhibition strategies used in broadcasting museums, such as such as the National Media Museum in Bradford, England (formerly the National Museum of Photography, Film and Television) see Amy Holdsworth, *Television, Memory and Nostalgia* (New York: Palgrave Macmillan, 2011), 127–148.

54. Matthias Michalka, 'Introduction,' *Changing Channels: Art and Television 1963–1988*, ed. Museum Moderner Kunst Stiftung Ludwig Wien and Matthias Michalka (Cologne: Verlag der Buchhandlung Walther König, 2010), 11.

55. Matthias Michalka, personal interview conducted at MUMOK, November 21, 2011.

56. Kathy Noble, 'Art and TV,' *Metropolis M* no. 5 (October–November 2010). Metropolis M [Accessed June 1, 2013] http://metropolism.com/magazine/2010-no5/in-verzet-tegen-het-troostkijken/english.

57. Described in the exhibition guide as an experimental television project, twm.macba.cat was available during the exhibition, but somewhat difficult to navigate due to the lack of an obvious index.

58. New texts were published every two weeks during the show, and a PDF of the full catalogue can be downloaded from http://www.macba.cat/en/essay-are-you-ready-for-tv [Accessed June 1, 2013].

59. See Sean Cubitt, 'Grayscale Video and the Shift to Color,' *Art Journal* 65.3 (2006), 49.

60. Cathode ray tube (CRT) was the technology used in the first television sets to be commercialised and the most common until the late 2000s, when it was supplanted by flat-screen technology.

61. For example, in *Television After TV: Essays on a Medium in Transition*, ed. Lynn Spigel and Jan Olsson (Durham, NC: Duke University Press, 2004) and more recently in *Television as Digital Media*, ed. James Bennett and Niki Strange (Durham and London: Duke University Press, 2011).

62. For a discussion of the museum within the context of new media, see Graham and Cook, 21–50.

63. Here I am referring both to the widespread use of video sharing websites (such as Vimeo) by artists and also to curated online platforms such as Vdrome, which was initiated by the Italian publisher *Mousse* and is presented in partnership with the artists' moving image agency LUX. For details see http://www.vdrome.org/about.html [Accessed June 1, 2013].

Notes to Chapter 2

1. Lynn Spigel, *TV by Design: Modern Art and the Rise of Network Television* (Chicago: University of Chicago Press, 2008), 249–250. Italics in original.

2. Michael Z. Newman and Elana Levine, *Legitimating Television: Media Convergence and Cultural Status* (New York and London: Routledge, 2012), 2–3.

3. Spigel notes frequent references to television in pop art and its precursors, 257. See also Christine Mehring, 'TV Art's Abstract Starts: Europe, c.1944–1969,' *October* 125 (2008): 29–64, and Martha Rosler, 'Video: Shedding the Utopian Moment,' in *Illuminating Video: An*

Essential Guide to Video Art, ed. Doug Hall and Sally Jo Fifer (New York: Aperture Foundation in association with Bay Area Video Coalition, 1990), 30–50 [Originally published in *Block*, Winter 1985/86]. See also Marita Sturken, 'Paradox in the Evolution of an Art Form: Great Expectations and the Making of a History,' in *Illuminating Video: An Essential Guide to Video Art,* ed. Doug Hall and Sally Jo Fifer (New York: Aperture Foundation in association with Bay Area Video Coalition, 1990), 101–121.

4. Spigel, 8–9. See also John Wyver, John Wyver, 'TV Against TV: Video Art on Television,' *Film and Video Art*, ed. Stuart Comer, (London: Tate Publishing, 2009), 122–131.
5. Spigel, 9. See David Antin, 'Video: The Distinctive Features of the Medium,' in *Video Culture: A Critical Investigation*, ed. John Hanhardt (1975; reprinted, Rochester, NY: Peregrine Smith Books, 1986), 148–166.
6. Spigel, 8.
7. Spigel, 9.
8. David Joselit, *Feedback: Television Against Democracy* (Cambridge, MA and London: MIT Press, 2007), 21. For a useful critical response to Joselit's book, see Andrew S. Weiner, 'Changing Channels: Broadcast Television, Early Video, and the Politics of Networked Media,' *Qui Parle* 16, no. 2 (2008): 133–145.
9. Joselit, 25.
10. Joselit, 41.
11. Elsewhere, however, Joselit has addressed the representation (and co-option) of counter-cultural rhetoric and media critique in network television. See Joselit, 'Yippie Pop: Abbie Hoffman, Andy Warhol, and Sixties Media Politics,' *Grey Room* 8 (2002): 62–79. See also Todd Gitlin, *The Whole World is Watching* (Berkeley: University of California Press, 1980).
12. Spigel, 249.
13. John Thornton Caldwell, *Televisuality: Style, Crisis, and Authority in American Television* (New Brunswick, NJ: Rutgers University Press, 1995), 253.
14. Caldwell, 255.
15. Caldwell, 158.
16. Newman and Levine, *Legitimating Television: Media Convergence and Cultural Status* (New York and London: Routledge, 2012).
17. Newman and Levine examine differences between the traditional multi-camera sitcom and newer single camera sitcoms, 59–79.
18. John Thornton Caldwell, *Production Culture: Industrial Reflexivity and Critical Practice in Film and Television* (Durham and London: Duke University Press, 2008), 1.
19. Newman and Levine, 152.
20. Newman and Levine, 8. The key references cited with regard to nineteenth and early twentieth-century art forms are Lawrence W. Levine, *Highbrow Lowbrow: The Emergence of Cultural Hierarchy in America*, (Cambridge, MA: Harvard University Press, 1988) and Paul DiMaggio, 'Cultural Boundaries and Structural Change: The Extension of the High Culture Model to Theater, Opera, and the Dance, 1900–1940,' *Cultivating Differences: Symbolic Boundaries and the Making of Inequality*, edited by Michèle Lamond and Marcel Fournier. (Chicago: University of Chicago Press, 1992), 21–57.
21. Newman and Levine, 47.

22. My discussion of Mellors's *Ourhouse* is revised from Maeve Connolly, 'Televisual Objects: Props, Relics and Prosthetics,' *Afterall* 33 (2013): 66–77, which also features discussion of TV-themed works by Shana Moulton, and Ryan Trecartin and Lizzie Fitch. This chapter could be extended to include works by many other contemporary artists who have borrowed from TV soaps, sitcoms, and serialised dramas, including Moulton, Trecartin & Fitch, Alex Bag and Christian Jankowski.

23. Colin Perry, 'TV Makeover,' *Art Monthly* 352 (2011–2012): 13.

24. Newman and Levine, 8.

25. Carol Duncan, *Civilizing Rituals: Inside Public Art Museums* (London and New York: Routledge, 1994), 26. See also Dorothea von Hantelmann's discussion of exhibitions and museums in *How to Do Things With Art: What Performativity Means in Art* (Zurich and Dijon: JRP Ringier and Les Presses du Réel, 2010), 8–21.

26. Duncan, 49.

27. Duncan, 53–54. Miriam Hansen also notes that the 'American variant' of the bourgeois public sphere 'never possessed quite the same degree of autonomy as its European prototypes'. See Hansen, 'Early Silent Cinema: Whose Public Sphere?,' *New German Critique* 29 (1983): 155.

28. Duncan, 57. Italics in original.

29. Duncan, 57.

30. Duncan, 56.

31. Tony Bennett, *The Birth of the Museum: History, Theory, Politics* (Oxon and New York: Routledge, 1995), 31.

32. Tony Bennett, 'Habitus Clivé: Aesthetics and Politics in the Work of Pierre Bourdieu,' *New Literary History* 38, no. 1 (2007): 219.

33. For a more expansive exploration of these issues see Toby Miller, *The Well-Tempered Self: Citizenship, Culture and the Postmodern Subject* (Baltimore and London: John Hopkins University Press, 1993).

34. Pierre Bourdieu, cited by Bennett, 'Habitus Clivé,' 202.

35. Bennett, 'Habitus Clivé,' 204. Italics added.

36. Bennett, 'Habitus Clivé,' 214.

37. Bennett, 'Habitus Clivé,' 222.

38. Bennett, 'Habitus Clivé,' 215. See also Jacques Rancière, 'The Emancipated Spectator,' *Artforum* 45, no. 7 (2007): 271–280.

39. Nielsen ratings are the audience measurement system developed by the Nielsen Company, with the aim of determining the size and composition of the television programming audience in the US. For a critical analysis of the ratings system, see Eileen R. Meehan, 'Why We Don't Count: The Commodity Audience,' *Logics of Television*, ed. Patricia Mellencamp (London and Bloomington: BFI and Indiana University Press, 1990), 117–137.

40. Laurie Ouellette, *Viewers like You?* (New York: Columbia University Press, 2002) 2.

41. Ouellette, 3.

42. Ouellette, 4.

43. Ouellette, 158.

44. This programme preceded the BBC arts-based television documentary series *Omnibus*, which was broadcast between 1967 and 2003.

45. Ouellette, 159.
46. Ouellette, 163.
47. Anna McCarthy, *The Citizen Machine: Governing by Television in 1950s America* (New York and London: New Press, 2011), 24–25.
48. McCarthy, 25. Italics added.
49. McCarthy, 39.
50. This term refers to the, now relatively common, practice of addressing broadcasts toward specific (often demographically defined) segments of the audience, rather than the general public.
51. Spigel, 28.
52. Spigel, 151.
53. Spigel, 153.
54. Spigel notes that MoMA exhibited ads as exemplars of US design, 176.
55. Rosalind Krauss, 'The Cultural Logic of the Late Capitalist Museum,' *October* 54 (1990): 427–441.
56. Newman and Levine, 22.
57. McCarthy, 253.
58. Newman and Levine, 25.
59. Boyle notes that the film was screened at Chicago Film Festival, and so would have been seen by an audience outside Minnesota. Deirdre Boyle, *Subject to Change: Guerrilla Television Revisited* (New York and Oxford: Oxford University Press, 1997), 123.
60. Jonathan Bignell, 'Seeing and Knowing: Reflexivity and Quality,' in *Quality TV: Contemporary American Television and Beyond*, ed. Janet McCabe and Kim Akass (London: I.B. Tauris, 2007) 167–169.
61. Bignell, 162.
62. Newman and Levine, 2–3.
63. Derek Kompare, 'Publishing Flow : DVD Box Sets and the Reconception of Television,' *Television and New Media* 7, no. 4 (2006): 335–360.
64. Production details are drawn from email correspondence with Fiona Macdonald, September 19, 2012, and http://www.fionamacdonald.com.au/index.php?/projects/museum-emotions/ [Accessed June 1, 2013].
65. Coincidentally, *Melrose Place* had already served as the focus of a three year (1995–98) art project realised by GALA Committee, a collaboration between the artist Mel Chin, students and faculty at University of Athens, Georgia ('GA') and the California Institute of the Arts ('LA') and the show's producers and set decorator. Over two seasons, GALA Committee produced over 150 'site-specific objects' for incorporation into the show's sets, often including imagery or textual material relating to social or political themes raised obliquely (but not addressed directly) in *Melrose Place* plotlines, including environmental concerns, global conflict, crime and violence, gender and sexual health issues. The collaboration was initiated by Chin in response to an invitation (extended in 1995) to produce work for the exhibition *Uncommon Sense* at Geffen Contemporary, LA MoCA in 1997. For this show, GALA Committee produced *In The Name of The Place*, an installation featuring a *Melrose-*style set, complete with a selection of objects and videos of several episodes. See Yilmaz Dziewior, 'GALA Committee,' *Artforum* 33.10 (2000): 193–194.

66. For details see Sarah Browne and Gareth Kennedy, 'Episode 306: Dallas, Belfast,' in *SPACE SHUTTLE: Six Projects of Urban Creativity and Social Interaction*, ed. Peter Mutschler and Ruth Morrow (Belfast: PS², 2007): 15–21.

67. Browne and Kennedy, 19.

68. See, for example, Ien Ang, *Watching Dallas: Soap Opera and the Melodramatic Imagination*, trans. Della Couling, (London and New York: Methuen, 1985).

69. Caldwell, 61.

70. Caldwell, 62–63.

71. Lynn Spigel, *Make Room for TV: Television and the Family Ideal in Postwar America* (Chicago: University of Chicago Press, 1992), 99–135. Interestingly, *Window on the World* was also the title of a late 1940s TV show on the Dumont Network, which included a section featuring newsreel clips, accompanied by a humorous commentary. See Caldwell, 23–24.

72. *The Magic Window* was exhibited alongside *Vertical Roll* (1972) by Joan Jonas and *The Amazing Bow Wow* (1976) by Lynda Benglis in *TV Honey: Desiree Holman with Lynda Benglis and Joan Jonas*, curated by Larry Rinder at the Silverman Gallery, San Francisco, October 11 – November 10, 2007.

73. Joselit, 26.

74. Lynn Spigel, 'Our TV Heritage: Television, The Archive, and The Reasons for Preservation,' in *A Companion to Television*, ed. Janet Wasko (Oxford: Blackwell publishing, 2010), 86.

75. Spigel, 'Our TV Heritage,' 87.

76. Ara H. Merjian, 'TV Honey, Silverman Gallery,' *Artforum.com*, November 2, 2007 [Accessed June 1, 2013] http://www.artforum.com/print.php?id=18867&pn=picks&action=print.

77. Press release, 'Phil Collins: *soy mi madre*,' Victoria Miro Gallery, November 24 –December 18, 2009.

78. For a discussion of the global circulation of telenovelas see John Sinclair, 'Latin America's Impact on World Television Markets,' in *TV: Understanding Television in the Post-Broadcast Era*, ed. Graeme Turner and Jinna Tay (London and New York: Routledge, 2009), 141–148.

79. Adriana Estill, 'Closing the Telenovela's Borders: "Vivo Por Elena's" Tidy Nation,' *Chasqui* 29, no. 1 (2000): 82.

80. Estill, 82.

81. Michéle Faguet, '*soy mi madre*: A Conversation Between Phil Collins and Michele Faguet,' *Celeste* Magazine 33 (2009) unpaginated.

82. Press release, Phil Collins: *soy mi madre*: Jane and Marc Nathanson Distinguished Artist in Residence Exhibition, August 9 – October 19, 2008.

83. Episodes of the series are typically shown alongside animatronic installations and sculptural objects, which sometimes appear on screen, forming part of a complex exploration of objecthood, signification and practices of naming. I discuss this aspect of *Ourhouse* elsewhere, in Connolly, 'Televisual Objects,' 66–77.

84. For a discussion of *Twin Peaks* in relation to 'quality television', see Newman and Levine, 42.

85. Gwendoline Christie, who is also credited as associate producer of several episodes, has a prominent role (as Brienne of Tarth) in the second series of the HBO drama *Game of Thrones* (2011).

86. While Mellors could be said to employ a 'co-production' model somewhat similar to that utilised in film and television industries, it is important to emphasise that his videos are not designed to be serialised on television, or mass distributed on DVD. From February 26 until March 8, 2013, however, the four completed episodes of *Ourhouse* were shown in sequence on Vdrome, a curated online platform. See http://www.vdrome.org/mellors.html [Accessed June 1, 2013].

87. Isabelle Graw, *High Price: Art Between the Market and Celebrity Culture* (Berlin and New York: Sternberg Press, 2009), 32. See Pierre Bourdieu, *The Rules of Art: Genesis and Structure of the Literary Field*, trans. Susan Emanuel (Stanford: Stanford University Press, 1996).

88. Graw, 23.

89. Graw, 148 argues that while engagement with the phenomenon of mass media celebrity enabled artists such as Warhol to negotiate a 'minority position', the position of the celebrity has now become normative. Warhol's work might also be read as critical response to *earlier* intersections between modernist art and mass culture, which (as Martha Rosler has noted) were especially pronounced in the U.S. context during the 1950s (Rosler, 41).

90. Graw, 43.

91. Instead of Bourdieu's designation of the art field as 'relatively autonomous', Graw argues for a notion of 'relative heteronomy' that takes account of art's structural alignment to other social systems, including those associated with cultural industries (particularly film and fashion), 147–148.

Notes to Chapter 3

1. Hito Steyerl, 'Is a Museum a Factory?', *e-flux journal* 7 (2009) [Accessed June 1, 2013] http://www.e-flux.com/journal/is-a-museum-a-factory/. This text is also included in Steyerl, *The Wretched of the Screen*, (Berlin: Sternberg Press, 2012), 60–76.

2. Anna McCarthy, *The Citizen Machine: Governing by Television in 1950s America* (New York and London: New Press, 2011), 255.

3. Claire Bishop, 'Outsourcing Authenticity? Delegated Performance in Contemporary Art,' in *Double Agent*, ed. Claire Bishop and Silvia Tramontana (London: ICA, 2009), 111. Bishop also develops her analysis of delegated performance in *Artificial Hells: Participatory Art and the Politics of Spectatorship* (London: Verso, 2012), 219–240, but my references are drawn from the 2009 text. For a valuable analysis of affect in relation to peformance in artists' video and reality television, see Catherine Fowler, 'Once more with feeling: Performing the self in the work of Gillian Wearing, Kutluğ Ataman and Phil Collins's, *Moving Image Review & Art Journal* 2, no.1 (2013): 10–24.

4. Tony Bennett, *The Birth of the Museum: History, Theory, Politics* (Oxon and New York: Routledge, 1995), 52.

5. Tony Bennett, 'Civic Laboratories: Museums, Cultural Objecthood, and the Governance of the Social,' *Cultural Studies* 19, no. 5 (2005): 528.

6. George Baker, 'The Storyteller: Notes on the Work of Gerard Byrne,' in *Gerard Byrne, Books, Magazines, and Newspapers,* ed. Nicolas Schafhausen (New York: Lukas & Sternberg, 2003): 40. See also Baker's contribution to Baker et al, 'Round Table: The Projected Image in Contemporary Art,' *October* 104 (2003): 71–96.

7. Baker's account of finance capitalism is informed by Fredric Jameson, 'The End of Temporality,' *Critical Inquiry* 29, no. 4 (2003): 703. See also Baker's discussion of Jameson in 'The Storyteller,' 73–80.

8. Baker, 'The Storyteller,' 41.

9. Steyerl draws upon Paul Virno's *A Grammar of the Multitude,* trans. Isabella Bertoletti, James Cascaito, and Andrea Casson (New York and Los Angeles: Semiotexte, 2004).

10. Steyerl, 'Is a Museum a Factory?'.

11. Bishop, 'Outsourcing Authenticity?', 111. Italics in original.

12. Bishop, 'Outsourcing Authenticity?', 118. Italics in original.

13. Bishop, 'Outsourcing Authenticity?', 114.

14. Masotta encouraged the performers to dress as poor people, so that they did not fully 'perform themselves'. Bishop, 'Outsourcing Authenticity?', 116.

15. Bishop, 'Outsourcing Authenticity?', 115. Her discussion also includes a landmark 1968 action by Graciela Carnevale, a work featured in the 2010 exhibition 'The Talent Show' curated by Peter Eleey at the Walker Art Center, Minneapolis, which explores continuities between artistic performance and reality TV. See Walker Art Center, 'The Talent Show', [Accessed June 1, 2013] http://www.walkerart.org/calendar/2010/the-talent-show.

16. Bishop, 'Outsourcing Authenticity?', 119.

17. Bishop , 'Outsourcing Authenticity?', 122.

18. Claire Bishop, 'Introduction: Documents of Contemporary Art,' in *Participation,* ed. Claire Bishop (Cambridge, MA and London: MIT Press and Whitechapel, 2006), 10–17. These works are cited in note 10, page 16.

19. Claire Bishop, 'The Social Turn,' *Artforum,* 44, no. 6 (2006): 178.

20. My discussion of delegated performance could be extended to include several other works by Collins, most notably *The Return of the Real* (2005–2007). Reality television is also an important point of reference for Christian Jankowski, whom I discuss in Chapter Seven, since his performers often have a professional relation to the role they are assigned. In addition, reality TV has served as an important point of reference for theatre/live art practitioners, as evidenced by Christoph Schlingensief's *Ausländer raus—Bitte liebt Österreich* (Foreigners Out—Please Love Austria) (2000). This *Big Brother*-style reality TV show took the form of a 'container camp' situated outside Vienna Opera House, in which 12 asylum-seekers were filmed live as they sought to win the sympathies of the public. The 'camp' was reconstructed and presented alongside documentation of Schlingensief's project, by Nina Wetzel and Matthias Lilienthal, at Haus der Kulturen der Welt, Berlin, as part of *Former West: Documents, Constellations, Prospects,* March 18–24, 2013. 'Big Brother' aesthetics also featured prominently in *QUIET: We Live in Public,* a participatory project conceived by Josh Harris, a dot-com entrepreneur and webcasting pioneer, in which over a hundred people lived communally in a windowless Manhattan 'bunker' for several weeks in December 1999, in the lead up to the Millennium. See Allen Salkin, 'For Him, the Web Was No Safety Net,'

New York Times, August 28, 2009. For an account from the perspective of a participant see Steven Kaplan's (untitled) blogpost to *The Thing*, 2009-09-1 [Accessed June 1, 2013] http://post.thing.net/node/2800.

21. McCarthy, *The Citizen Machine*, 84.
22. McCarthy, *The Citizen Machine*, 85.
23. McCarthy, *The Citizen Machine*, 86.
24. Anna McCarthy, "'Stanley Milgram, Allen Funt, and Me': Postwar Social Science and the "First Wave" of Reality TV', in *Reality TV: Remaking Television Culture* (second edition) ed. Susan Murray and Laurie Ouellette (New York and London: New York University Press, 2008), 32.
25. Amber Watts, 'Melancholy, Merit, and Merchandise: The Postwar Audience Participation Show', in *Reality TV: Remaking Television Culture* (second edition) ed. Susan Murray and Laurie Ouellette (New York and London: New York University Press, 2008), 302.
26. Watts, 306.
27. Watts, 314.
28. Su Holmes, "'An … Unmarried Mother Sat in a Wing-Backed Chair on TV Last Night … " BBC Television Asks Is This Your Problem? (1955–1957)', *Television & New Media* 9, no. 3 (2008): 176.
29. Holmes, 179.
30. Holmes, 178.
31. Holmes, 183.
32. Holmes, 180.
33. McCarthy, *The Citizen Machine*, 248.
34. Ralph Engelman, *Public Radio and Television in America* (Thousand Oaks, London and New Delhi: Sage Publications, 1996), 145.
35. 'Thomas Streeter, 'Blue Skies and Strange Bedfellows: The Discourse of Cable Television', in *The Revolution Wasn't Televised: Sixties Television and Social Conflict*, ed. Lynn Spigel and Michael Curtin (New York and London: Routledge, 1997), 222.
36. Streeter, 234. See also Laurie Ouellette, 'TV Viewing as Good Citizenship? Political Rationality, Enlightened Democracy and PBS', in *Television: Critical Concepts in Media and Cultural Studies vol IV*, ed. Toby Miller (London and New York: Routledge, 2003), 73–100.
37. John Thornton Caldwell, *Televisuality: Style, Crisis, and Authority in American Television* (New Brunswick, NJ: Rutgers University Press, 1995), 29.
38. David Joselit, 'Feedback', in *Changing Channels: Art and Television 1963–1988,* ed. Museum Moderner Kunst Stiftung Ludwig Wien and Matthias Michalka (Cologne: Verlag der Buchhandlung Walther König, 2010), 70. This text draws upon ideas discussed in Joselit's book *Feedback: Television Against Democracy* (Cambridge, MA and London: MIT Press, 2007).
39. Joselit, 'Feedback', 72.
40. Deirdre Boyle, *Subject to Change: Guerrilla Television Revisited* (New York and Oxford: Oxford University Press, 1997).
41. Boyle, 48–49. Boyle notes that Carpenter was specifically inspired by Highlander's 'each one, teach one' self-education model, intended as a rebuttal to missionary- and teacher-led systems.

42. Boyle, 51.
43. Boyle highlights regulatory changes introduced by the FCC 1974, which meant that CATV providers no longer had to provide locally originated programming, 139. Caldwell, however, notes that the guerrilla television 'revolution' was stymied by the fact that broadcasters simply refused to air half-inch tapes unless the content was particularly sensational, often rejecting them on the somewhat duplicitous grounds that they did not meet broadcast quality standards or were not in the public interest, 265.
44. Boyle, *Subject to Change*, 205. See also Christine Tamblyn's discussion of *America's Funniest Home Videos* in 'Qualifying the Quotidian: Artist's Video and the Production of Social Space,' in *Resolutions: Contemporary Video Practices*, ed. Michael Renov and Erika Suderberg (Minn.: Minnesota University Press, 1996) 13–28.
45. Laura Grindstaff, 'Self-Serve Celebrity: The Production of Ordinariness and the Ordinariness of Production in Reality Television,' in *Production Studies: Cultural Studies of Media Industries*, ed. Vicki Mayer, Miranda J. Banks and John Thornton Caldwell (New York and London: Routledge, 2009), 73. See also Jane M. Shattuc's analysis of the changing form of the daytime talk show in 'The Shifting Terrain of American Talk Shows,' in *A Companion to Television*, ed. Janet Wasko (Oxford: Blackwell Publishing, 2010), 324–336.
46. Grindstaff, 73.
47. These ideas are explored in Holmes, 186, and also in Shattuc, 334–335.
48. Arlie Russell Hochschild, *The Managed Heart: Commercialization of Human Feeling* (Berkeley: University of California Press 1983).
49. Laura Grindstaff, *The Money Shot: Trash, Class, and the Making of TV Talk Shows* (Chicago: University of Chicago Press, 2002).
50. David Hesmondhalgh and Sarah Baker, 'Creative Work and Emotional Labour in the Television Industry,' *Theory, Culture & Society* 25, no. 7/8 (2008): 108.
51. Hesmondhalgh and Baker, 108.
52. Bishop, 'Outsourcing Authenticity?,' 120.
53. McCarthy, *The Citizen Machine*, 246–47.
54. McCarthy, *The Citizen Machine,* 256.
55. McCarthy, *The Citizen Machine,* 257.
56. Watts, 301.
57. Watts, 317–318.
58. Laurie Ouellette and James Hay, *Better Living Through Reality TV: Television and Post-welfare Citizenship* (Malden, MA: Blackwell Publishing, 2008), 33.
59. Ouellette and Hay, 33.
60. Laurie Ouellette, '"Take Responsibility for Yourself": *Judge Judy* and the Neoliberal Citizen,' in *Reality TV: Remaking Television Culture* (second edition) ed. Susan Murray and Laurie Ouellette (New York and London: New York University Press, 2008), 223.
61. Ouellette, 'Take Responsibility for Yourself,' 228.
62. Ouellette, 'Take Responsibility for Yourself,' 232.
63. Ina Blom, *On the Style Site: Art, Sociality and Media Culture* (Berlin and New York: Sternberg Press, 2007); Nicolas Bourriaud, *Relational Aesthetics*, trans. Simon Pleasance and Fronza Woods (Dijon: Les Presses du Réel, 2002).

64. The work was initially presented under the title *EASY TV* in the exhibition 'Aperto' at Villeurbanne, Nouveau Musée, June 16 – September 23, 1995. For a discussion of this work within the context of Huyghe's practice, see Royoux, Jean-Christophe, 'Free-Time Workers and the Reconfiguration of Public Space: Several Hypotheses on the Work of Pierre Huyghe,' in *Saving the Image: Art After Film*, ed. Tanya Leighton and Pavel Buchler (Glasgow and Manchester: Centre for Contemporary Arts and Manchester Metropolitan University, 2003), 180–200.

65. Claire Bishop, 'The Social Turn,' *Artforum*, 44, no. 6 (2006): 178.

66. Olivier Bardin, 'Olivier Bardin: Interview by Pierre Huyghe and Hans-Ulrich Obrist,' trans. Teresa Bridgeman, in *The Fifth Floor: Ideas Taking Space*, ed. Peter Gorschlüter (Liverpool: Liverpool University Press and Tate Liverpool, 2009), 74.

67. Bardin, 75. Bardin's involvement in *Mobile TV* is also discussed, alongside related works such as Fabrice Hybert's presentation for the French Pavilion at Venice Biennale 1997, by Benjamin Thorel in *Telle est la Télé: L'art Contemporain et la télévision* (Paris: Editions Cercle d'Art, 2006), 38–41.

68. Superflex website, *Superchannel* description [Accessed June 1, 2013] http://www.superflex .net/tools/superchannel//2.

69. See Alan Dunn, 'Who Needs a Spin Doctor? Part Two,' *Art of Encounter: Engage* 15 (2004) [Accessed June 1, 2013] http://www.engage.org/engage-journal.aspx.

70. Superflex website, *Superchannel/Tenantspin* [Accessed June 1, 2013] http://superflex.net/ activities/2002/05/01/superchannel_-_tenantspin/image/2#g.

71. This exhibition included many familiar elements of Tiravanija's practice, encompassing practical demonstrations of skills and activities within the gallery, furnished to suggest a bar with a juke box and pool tables. By this point, Tiravanija was well known for presenting 'stations' of various sorts, and he went on to develop several projects that parallel aspects of the Superchannel model. They include *Qualsiasi (tv)*, translated as *Whatever (tv)* (2004), realised at the art gallery Base/Progetti per l'Arte, located in the San Niccolò district of Florence, and involving design students from the Università IUAV di Venezia. This was followed by *Untitled* (2005) *(the air between the chain-link fence and the broken bicycle wheel)* at the Guggenheim Museum, New York, which featured a low-power transmitter, TV receiver and a display of texts on US governmental regulation of television transmission.

72. *Tenantspin* is one of several examples of community television highlighted in *Reaktio,* a series of books published by the Finnish Institute of London. See Minna Tarkka, 'Interview: Superflex', *Reaktio* no. 2: *TV Like Us*, edited by Hannah Harris (London: Finnish Institute of London, 2012), 42–47. The publication can be downloaded from The Finnish Institute of London, [Accessed June 1, 2013] http://www.finnish-institute.org.uk/en/articles/ 56-reaktio-2. Thanks to Samuel Mercer for this reference.

73. Dunn, 'Who Needs a Spin Doctor? Part Two.'

74. See Patrick Fox, 'New Adventures Online, Case tenantspin, Liverpool,' *Reaktio* no. 2: *TV Like Us* edited by Hannah Harris (London: Finnish Institute of London, 2012), 52–64. Fox was previously Collaborations & Engagement Programme Manager at FACT, with responsibility for *tenantspin* amongst other projects.

75. Emily Keaney, 'Culture and Civil Renewal—The Human Face of Regeneration,' *Regeneration: Engage* 17 (2005). Engage [Accessed June 1, 2013] http://www.engage.org/engage-journal .aspx.

76. Apichatpong Weerasethakul, 'Annotated Filmography,' in *Apichatpong Weerasethakul*, ed. James Quandt (Vienna: Austrian Film Museum and SYNEMA—Gesellschaft für Film und Medien, 2009), 225–226.

77. Press release, *Polish Pavilion at the Venice Biennale*, June 2005. E-flux [Accessed June 1, 2013] http://www.e-flux.com/announcements/artur-zmijewski/.

78. McCarthy, 'Stanley Milgram, Allen Funt, and Me,' 41.

79. While *Self Made* received a (limited) theatrical distribution, *Bully* was first shown in the UK, alongside various other gallery installation works by the artist, as part of *Gillian Wearing*, Whitechapel Art Gallery, London, March 28 –June 17, 2012.

80. My discussion is informed by viewing the second night of the performance at Hebbel am Ufer theatre, as well as an installation version of the work presented at *This Unfortunate Thing Between Us: Phil Collins*, Void Gallery, Derry (November 13, 2012 – January 11, 2013). This section includes material revised from Maeve Connolly, 'Unfortunate Things,' *Artes Mundi 5 2012: Wales International Visual Art Exhibition and Prize* (Cardiff: Artes Mundi, 2012), 50–55.

81. Kay Richardson and Ulrike H. Meinhof, *Worlds In Common?: Television Discourse in a Changing Europe* (London: Routledge, 1999).

82. Collins is well known for a long-standing interest in pop music and the mise-en-scene of *This Unfortunate Thing Between Us* at the Hebbel am Ufer theatre included a live in-house band featuring Welsh musician Gruff Rhys and North Wales surf group Y Niwl.

83. Caldwell, *Televisuality*.

84. All aspects of the performance were in fact filmed and the work now exists in the form of an edit determined by Collins, which retains some of the content left out by the TV director.

85. Thomas Elsaesser, 'Discipline through Diegesis: The Rube Film between "Attractions" and "Narrative Integration",' in *The Cinema of Attractions Reloaded*, ed. Wanda Strauven (Amsterdam: Amsterdam University Press, 2006), 205–226.

86. Elsaesser, 213.

87. Elsaesser, 213.

88. Elsaesser, 220. Elsewhere, Elsaesser has suggested that the Rube category might be extended to include films—and also installation works—that relate to later changes in the moving image dispositive. Here I am referring to his keynote lecture, 'The Cinematic Dispositif After Film: Purification, Saturation of Mutual Interference,' presented at *Display/Dispositif: Aesthetic Modes of Thought*, organised by Ursula Frohne, Lilian Haberer and Annette Urban, Kunsthistorisches Institut, University of Cologne, 10 May 2012.

89. Thomas Elsaesser, 'The Mind-Game Film,' in *Puzzle Films: Complex Storytelling in Contemporary Cinema*, ed. Warren Buckland (Oxford: Wiley-Blackwell, 2009), 38.

90. Elsaesser, 'The Mind-Game Film,' 34. The Deleuze text referenced is 'Postscript on the Societies of Control,' *October* 59 (1992): 3–7.

Notes to Chapter 4

1. This chapter is an expanded and revised version of my article 'European Television Archives, Collective Memories and Contemporary Art,' *The Velvet Light Trap 71* (2013): 47–58. Copyright ©2013 by the University of Texas Press. All rights reserved.
2. Mary Ann Doane, 'Information, Crisis, Catastrophe,' in *Logics of Television*, ed. Patricia Mellencamp (London and Bloomington: BFI and Indiana University Press, 1990), 234–235.
3. Amy Holdsworth, *Television, Memory and Nostalgia* (New York: Palgrave Macmillan, 2011), 4.
4. Lynn Spigel, 'Our TV Heritage: Television, The Archive, and The Reasons for Preservation,' in *A Companion to Television*, ed. Janet Wasko (Oxford: Blackwell Publishing, 2010), 67.
5. Spigel, 91. An intriguing counterpoint to this fantasy of accumulation is offered by the work of Dominic Gagnon, an artist who preserves online materials that might otherwise become inaccessible, in a trilogy of video works assembled from censored YouTube clips, which were uploaded by amateur videographers and then anonymously flagged as 'inappropriate' by other users. The trilogy consists of RIP in *Pieces America* (2009), featuring content by male-only YouTube users, *Pieces and Love All to Hell* (2011), which includes only material posted by women, and *BIG KISS GOODNIGHT: Joetalk100 and the Holy Spirit against the New World Order* (2012), focusing on the video posts of a single individual.
6. General Idea (AA Bronson, Felix Partz, Jorge Zontal) developed a more open-ended exploration of television as a ceremonial form, through an array of performances, exhibitions, videos, and publications often framed as rehearsals, plans or remnants of the 'Miss General Idea' pageant. Several of their videos, such as *Pilot* (1977) and *Test Tube* (1979), are also modelled after TV entertainment or news magazine shows. See Gabrielle Moser, 'Exhibition-Making with Ghosts: The 1984 Miss General Idea Pavilion,' *Fillip* 11 (2010). Fillip Magazine [Accessed June 1, 2013] http://fillip.ca/content/the-1984-miss-general-idea-pavilion.
7. Eva Kernbauer, 'Establishing Belief: Harun Farocki and Andrei Ujica, Videograms of a Revolution,' *Grey Room* 41 (2010): 72–87.
8. See Margaret Morse's discussion of this work in 'News as Performance,' *Virtualities: Television, Media Art and Cyberculture* (Bloomington, Indiana: Indiana University Press, 1998), 60–62, and Benjamin Young, 'On Media and Democratic Politics: Videograms of a Revolution,' in *Harun Farocki: Working on the Sight-lines*, ed. Thomas Elsaesser (Amsterdam: Amsterdam University Press, 2004), 245–260.
9. Stan Douglas, 'Evening,' in *Stan Douglas—Past Imperfect—Works 1986-2007*, ed. Iris Dressler and Hans. D. Christ (Ostfildern: Hatje Cantz Verlag, 2007), 194.
10. Douglas, 193. Italics in original.
11. Douglas, 194. See also Todd Gitlin, *The Whole World is Watching* (Berkeley: University of California Press, 1980).
12. Craig Allen, 'Discovering "Joe Six Pack" Content in Television News: The Hidden History of Audience Research, News Consultants, and the Warner Class Model,' *Journal of Broadcasting & Electronic Media* 49.4 (2005): 376.
13. Allen, 364.
14. Allen, 364.

15. Allen, 372.
16. See Erika Balsom, *Exhibiting Cinema in Contemporary Art* (Amsterdam: Amsterdam University Press, 2013), 107–147, Mark Godfrey 'The Artist as Historian', *October* 120 (2007): 140–172, and also Maeve Connolly, *The Place of Artists' Cinema: Space, Site and Screen*, (Bristol and Chicago: Intellect and University of Chicago Press, 2009): 130–143.
17. My discussion of Tsivopoulos's work is drawn (in revised form) from Maeve Connolly, 'Cinematic Space, Televisual Time and Contemporary Art', *Critical Quarterly*, 54, no. 3 (2012): 31–45.
18. The footage shows young men armed with swords and shields, costumed to suggest ancient Greece. The specific historical (or mythological) events being re-enacted or referenced are not specified in Tsivopoulos's film.
19. Email exchange with Tsivopoulos, October 2012. See also Hilde de Bruijn, 'The Real The Story The Storyteller', *SMART Papers: Stefanos Tsivopoulos: 'The Real The Story The Storyteller'*, ed. Thomas Peutz (Amsterdam: Smart Project Space, 2010), 6–7. Smart Project Space [Accessed June 1, 2013] http://www.smartprojectspace.net/pdf_papers/100911story.pdf.
20. Jay David Bolter, and Richard Grusin. *Remediation: Understanding New Media* (Cambridge, MA: MIT Press, 2000).
21. Jerome Bourdon, 'Some Sense of Time: Remembering Television', *History & Memory* 15, no. 2 (2003): 6.
22. Bourdon, 6.
23. Doane, 234–235. It is also worth noting that, even prior to Doane's formulation, artists had been drawn to explore the relationship between television, death and memory. See Marita Sturken, 'The Politics of Video Memory: Electronic Erasures and Interruptions,' in *Resolutions: Contemporary Video Practices*, ed. Michael Renov and Erika Suderberg (Minn.: Minnesota University Press, 1996), 1–12.
24. Daniel Dayan and Elihu Katz, *Media Events: The Live Broadcasting of History* (Cambridge: Harvard University Press, 1992).
25. For a related exploration of media events and their limits in relation to the production of publics see Daniel Dayan, 'The Peculiar Public of Television', *Media, Culture & Society* 23 (2001): 743–765.
26. Bourdon, 32.
27. Bourdon, 9.
28. Joseph W. Slade and Leonard J. Barchak, 'Public Broadcasting in Finland: Inventing a National Television Programming Policy', *Journal of Broadcasting & Electronic Media* 33, no. 4 (1989): 356.
29. But even though funded primarily by license fees, the public broadcaster Yleisradio was from the outset required to lease time (20 hours a week in 1989) to a private company, which could in turn resell a small percentage for advertising. Consequently, the public stations TV1 and TV2 promoted imported commercial programming and advertising also formed a part of the schedule. Slade and Barchak also note that satellite television (retransmitted by private cable companies) was also available in 20% of Finnish households by late 1980s, 365.
30. Jukka Kortti, 'Multidimensional Social History of Television: Social Uses of Finnish Television from the 1950s to the 2000s', *Television & New Media* 12, no. 4 (2011): 313.

31. Zala Volcic, "'The Machine that Creates Slovenians": The Role of Slovenian Public Broadcasting in Re-affirming and Re-inventing the Slovenian National Identity,' *National Identities* 7, no. 3 (2005): 292.

32. Volcic, 294.

33. Volcic, 295.

34. Bourdon, 19.

35. See Paddy Scannell, *Radio, Television and Modern Life: A Phenomenological Approach* (Cambridge, MA and Oxford, Blackwell, 1996).

36. Bourdon, 26.

37. Holdsworth, 4.

38. *Family* was modelled on the US series *An American Family* (1972).

39. Holdsworth, 21.

40. John Beeson, 'Laura Horelli's "The Terrace",' *Art Agenda*, December 14, 2011. Art Agenda [Accessed June 1, 2013] See http://www.art-agenda.com/reviews/.

41. See www.bojanfajfric.net [Accessed June 1, 2013].

42. Sirkka Moeller, 'All Creatures Great and Small: The 57th International Short Film Festival Oberhausen,' *Senses of Cinema* 59, June 23, 2011. Senses of Cinema [Accessed June 1, 2013] http://sensesofcinema.com/2011/festival-reports/all-creatures-great-and-small-the-57th-international-short-film-festival-oberhausen/.

43. Karen Rosenberg, 'A Show Is All Cyber, Some of the Time,' *The New York Times*, October 21, 2010, The New York Times [Accessed June 1, 2013] http://www.nytimes.com/2010/10/22/arts/design/22free.html.

44. Aleksandra Domanović, personal interview, Berlin, September 2, 2011.

45. See www.aleksandradomanovic.com and www.nineteenthirty.net [Accessed June 1, 2013].

46. Holdsworth, 4.

47. John Caughie, 'Mourning Television: The Other Screen,' *Screen* 5, no. 4 (2010): 421. For an exploration of related issues focusing on television studies in the US, see Elana Levine, 'Teaching the Politics of Television Culture in a Post-Television Era,' *Cinema Journal* 50, no. 4 (2011): 177–182.

48. Caughie, 421.

Notes to Chapter 5

1. Malcolm Miles, 'Critical Spaces: Monuments and Changes,' in Cameron Cartiere and Shelly Willis (eds), *The Practice of Public Art*, (Routledge: London and New York, 2008), 77.

2. Anna McCarthy, *Ambient Television: Visual Culture and Public Space* (Duke University Press, 2001), 121.

3. Television is explicitly framed as a public platform, which has been 'lost' to contemporary art, by Branka Ćurčić in a discussion of the exhibition *TV Gallery*, curated by Dunja Blažević in 2007 and presented at various venues in Belgrade, Sarajevo, Zagreb and Novi Sad as part of the project 'Political practices of (post)Yugoslav Art'. See Branka Ćurčić, 'Television as a

Symbol of Lost Public Space,' *European Institute for Progressive Cultural Policies*, December 12, 2007 [Accessed June 1, 2013] http://transform.eipcp.net/correspondence/1197491434# redir#redir.

4. For the concept of the public sphere see Jürgen Habermas, *The Structural Transformation of the Public Sphere: An Inquiry into a Category of Bourgeois Society*, trans. Thomas Burger with the assistance of Frederick Lawrence (Cambridge: Polity Press, 1989). See also Oskar Negt and Alexander Kluge. *Public Sphere and Experience: Toward an Analysis of the Bourgeois and Proletarian Public Sphere*, trans. Peter Labanyi, Jamie Owen Daniel and Assenka Oksiloff (Minneapolis: University of Minnesota Press, 1993).

5. It is also possible to identify 'broadcast'-themed projects that respond to the privatised space of the personal computer. *Field Broadcast*, developed by Rebecca Birch and Rob Smith in 2010, is described as 'a live broadcasting network/project/platform/contraption that enables artists to make artworks that forge a direct link between the place they are broadcasting from and their audience'. By downloading custom-built software via an internet connection, *Field Broadcast* viewers are alerted—via a loud 'ping'—to the imminent transmission of an artwork, as it is produced live in a remote (often rural) location. The transmissions are intermittent and unscheduled—they can occur at any moment within a specified timeframe—usually a period of several weeks. My discussion is informed by Rebecca Birch's 'Field Montage' presentation at Central Saint Martins/LUX Student Symposium, *LUX/ICA Biennial of Moving Images*, Institute of Contemporary Arts, London, May 27, 2012. Field Broadcast [Accessed June 1, 2013] http://www.fieldbroadcast.org/about.html.

6. I discuss various projects curated by the Artangel Trust for 'Spectacolour' lightboards in Maeve Connolly, 'Artangel and the Changing Mediascape of Public Art,' *Journal of Curatorial Studies* 2, no. 2 (2013): 196–217.

7. McCarthy, 140.

8. McCarthy, 4.

9. McCarthy, 5.

10. McCarthy, 121.

11. McCarthy, 121.

12. Pierre Nora, 'Between Memory and History: *Les Lieux de Mémoire*,' trans. Marc Roudebush, *Representations* 26, (Spring 1989): 7–8.

13. Antony Gormley has, however, produced a public art work with a broadcast component for a particularly loaded public space. *One & Other* (2009) was a temporary commission realised for Trafalgar Square's 'empty' Fourth Plinth. Framed as 'collective portrait of humanity', it offered a physical and virtual platform for 'people from every walk of life, and every corner of the UK' to spend an hour alone on the plinth, over a period of 100 days in July–October. 2400 people were chosen from a total of 35,000 applicants, and publicity for the project emphasised the broadly equal participation of men and women, aged between 16 and 84, with a range of occupations that included 'lorry drivers and teachers, Morris dancers and lawyers, students and nudists'. The project addressed both the physical audience gathered in the square and those following via the web or edited highlights broadcast on Sky Arts television (a commercial, subscription-based service). Rather depressingly, the plinth was surrounded by a highly visible safety net, designed to catch falling objects and

bodies—a continual reminder of the fact that reality TV-style 'celebrity' is often dependent upon displays of self-destructive behaviour. For details on the commissioning context, see Greater London Authority [Accessed June 1, 2013] http://www.london.gov.uk/fourthplinth/commissions.

14. Miles, 77.

15. Carol Duncan, *Civilizing Rituals: Inside Public Art Museums* (London and New York: Routledge, 1994), 53–54.

16. Su Holmes identifies the arrival of commercial competition as a factor in the development of a short-lived BBC show focused on the problems of viewers. See Holmes, "'An … Unmarried Mother Sat in a Wing-Backed Chair on TV Last Night …" BBC Television Asks Is This Your Problem? (1955–1957),' *Television & New Media* 9, no. 3 (2008): 176.

17. Deirdre Boyle, *Subject to Change: Guerrilla Television Revisited* (New York and Oxford: Oxford University Press, 1997).

18. These initiatives were documented in the exhibition on the history of CAVS, entitled 'The Future Archive,' curated by Uta Meta Bauer, Neue Berliner Kunstverein, Berlin, June 30 – July 29, 2012. See also Kathy Rae Huffman, 'Video Art: What's TV Got To Do With It?,' in *Illuminating Video: An Essential Guide to Video Art,* ed. Doug Hall and Sally Jo Fifer (New York: Aperture Foundation in association with Bay Area Video Coalition, 1990), 82.

19. The activist-oriented cable channel Paper Tiger TV actually developed out of the *Communications Update* series (in 1981). See Ralph Engelman, *Public Radio and Television in America* (Thousand Oaks, London and New Delhi: Sage Publications, 1996), 261.

20. Lisa Parks, *Cultures in Orbit: Satellites and the Televisual* (Durham and London: Duke University Press, 2005), 171.

21. Gloria Sutton, 'Playback: Reconsidering the Long Beach Museum of Art as a Media Art Center,' in *Exchange and Evolution: Worldwide Video Long Beach 1974–1999,* ed. Kathy Rae Huffman (Long Beach: Long Beach Museum of Art, 2011), 126–127.

22. Ann-Sargent Wooster, 'Reach Out and Touch Someone: The Romance of Interactivity,' in *Illuminating Video: An Essential Guide to Video Art,* ed. Doug Hall and Sally Jo Fifer (New York: Aperture Foundation in association with Bay Area Video Coalition, 1990), 285. My discussion is also informed by Andrew Weiner, 'Vanishing Mediators: The Televised Event and the Politics of Emergent Video,' presented as part of the panel *Art and the Televisual,* chaired by Aviva Dove-Viebahn, College Art Association, Los Angeles, February 12, 2010.

23. For a discussion of several projects realised for Times Square, New York, see Patricia C. Phillips, 'Temporality and Public Art,' *Art Journal* 48, no. 4 (1989): 331–335.

24. McCarthy, 240. This project was marked by disagreements over the use and ownership of the video wall, documented by Birnbaum in 'The Rio Experience: Video's New Architecture Meets Corporate Sponsorship,' in *Illuminating Video: An Essential Guide to Video Art,* ed. Doug Hall and Sally Jo Fifer (New York: Aperture Foundation in association with Bay Area Video Coalition, 1990), 189–204.

25. McCarthy, 241.

26. McCarthy, 243.

27. McCarthy, 243. Italics in original.

28. McCarthy, 249.
29. McCarthy, 243.
30. This section is revised from Maeve Connolly, 'Reverberations in Time and Space,' *Susan Philipsz—Ten Works: 2007-2013*, ed. James Lingwood and Brigitte Franzen (Cologne: Koenig Books, 2014), 84–87.
31. Some are also associated with cultural and political contexts that now resonate with historical significance, such as Radio Normandie in 1939, Mother Vietnam in 1971 and Serb Republic Radio in 1993.
32. Susan Philipsz, 'You Are Not Alone,' in *Susan Philipsz: You Are Not Alone*, ed. Michael Stanley (Oxford: Modern Art Oxford, 2010), 7.
33. Joerg Heiser, 'Lullabies for Strangers,' in *Susan Philipsz: You Are Not Alone*, ed. Michael Stanley (Oxford: Modern Art Oxford, 2010), 20.
34. Philipsz, 7.
35. Philipsz's project was scheduled to coincide with the 'Berlin Gallery Weekend 2011,' an annual event intended to promote the city's contemporary art economy, which includes private galleries.
36. Sender Freies Berlin broadcast Gerry Schum's *Land Art* on April 15, 1969. See Christine Mehring, 'TV Art's Abstract Starts: Europe, c.1944–1969,' *October* 125 (2008): 62.
37. LIGNA, 'Radio Ballet: Exercise in lingering not according to the rules,' Ligna website [Accessed June 1, 2013] http://ligna.blogspot.de/2009/12/radio-ballet.html.
38. These concerns are explored in a workshop on Radio Ballet, facilitated by Jelena Vesic, documentation of which was published in *Variant* magazine. See Vesic et al, 'Miraculous Mass Communication: Radioballet by LIGNA,' *Variant* 31 (2008): 5–7. See also Erik Granly Jensen, 'Collective Acoustic Space—LIGNA and Radio in the Weimar Republic (Brecht, Benjamin),' in *Radio Territories*, ed. Erik Granly Jensen and Brandon LaBelle (Los Angeles and Copenhagen: Errant Bodies Press, 2007), 154–169.
39. Bertolt Brecht, 'Radio as a Means of Communication: A Talk on the Function of Radio,' *Screen* 20, no. 3–4 (1979): 24–28.
40. See Adrian Searle, 'Wallinger deserved to win the Turner prize,' *The Guardian*, December 4, 2007.
41. The press release notes that each component of the peace camp has been 'painstakingly sourced and replicated for the display'. Press release, Mark Wallinger, *State Britain*, Duveens Commission, Tate Britain, January 15 – August 27, 2007. Tate Britain [Accessed June 1, 2013] http://www.tate.org.uk/whats-on/tate-britain/exhibition/mark-wallinger-state-britain.
42. Broadcasts are often developed and timed to coincide with events in the contemporary art calendar, such as the Turner Prize exhibition and the Frieze Art Fair. In addition, slots are sometimes awarded to artists working with the moving image, such as the winner of the Jarman Prize.
43. The earlier works in the series included *Spinoza Monument* in Amsterdam's red light district, 1999, and *Deleuze Monument*, in a suburban neighbourhood of Avignon, 2000. The fourth monument was meant to have been dedicated to Antonio Gramsci, but seems to have been supplanted by *24hr Foucault*, at Palais de Tokyo, Paris in 2004.

44. Carlos Basualdo, 'Bataille Monument, Documenta 11, 2002,' in *Thomas Hirschhorn* (London: Phaidon, 2004), 104. Basualdo also notes that Hirschhorn was initially interested in finding a location close to the site of a previous work for Documenta 7 in 1982; *7,000 (7,000 Oaks)* by Joseph Beuys, 101.

45. Thomas Hirschhorn, interviewed by Craig Garrett, 'Philosophical Battery,' *Flash Art* 238 (2004): 90–93.

46. Thomas Hirschhorn, 'Bataille Monument,' in *Contemporary Art: From Studio to Situation*, ed. Claire Doherty (London: Black Dog Publishing, 2004), 141. The videos emanating from the TV Studio were broadcast each day and also available to view at the 'monument' for the duration of Documenta 11. My discussion is informed by viewing copies of the tapes sourced, by request, from Hirschhorn's studio.

47. Hirschhorn, 'Bataille Monument,' 143. This strategy would appear to run counter to Bataille's own thinking, particularly as theorised by Sven Lütticken, which emphasised the role of secrecy (and secret societies) in the production of public spheres. See Lütticken, 'Secret Publicity: The Avant-Garde Repeated,' *Secret Publicity: Essays on Contemporary Art* (Rotterdam and Amsterdam: Nai Publishers and Fonds BKVB, 2005), 21–41.

48. This presentation of the work was produced by the UK public art agency Artangel and installed at The Sorting Office, New Oxford Street, London from March–June 2005. *Küba* was first shown at the Carnegie Museum of Art, Pittsburgh in 2004, and it has also been exhibited at various other venues, including Thyssen-Bornemisza Art Contemporary (T-B A21) in Vienna, Theater der Welt, Stuttgart, and the Museum of Contemporary Art, Sydney.

49. Adrian Searle, 'Talking Heads,' *The Guardian*, March 29, 2005.

50. Irit Rogoff, 'De-Regulation: With the Work or Kutlug Ataman,' *Third Text* 23, no. 1 (2009): 178.

51. Rogoff, 178. Italics in original.

52. Rogoff, 177. The Deleuze and Guattari text cited is *A Thousand Plateaus: Capitalism and Schizophrenia*, trans. Brian Massumi (Minneapolis: University of Minnesota Press, 1987).

53. It is worth noting that, until the late 1960s, the British postal service was operated by the General Post Office, the same Government department involved in the early establishment of the British Broadcasting Company during the 1920s.

54. Daniel Dayan and Elihu Katz, *Media Events: The Live Broadcasting of History* (Cambridge, MA and London: Harvard University Press, 1992), 72.

55. The term 'sputnik' also has a specific resonance within the context of Kunstverein Munchen programme under Maria Lind's direction, discussed further in Chapter Six.

56. For a discussion of Marshall McLuhan's concept of the 'global village' in relation to satellite broadcasting, see Parks, 21–45.

57. The figure of the newscaster is explored more fully in Sander's subsequent multi-channel video work *Televised I: the Anchor, the I, and the Studio* (2006), briefly discussed in Maeve Connolly, 'Studio Spaces,' *Frieze* 155 (2013): 208–212.

Notes to Chapter 6

1. Maria Lind, 'Telling Histories: Archives/Spatial Situation/Case-studies/Talkshows/ Symposium,' in *Curating with Light Luggage: Reflections, Discussions and Revisions*, ed. Liam Gillick and Maria Lind (Munich: Kunstverein München and Revolver, 2005), 102. This text is included in *Selected Maria Lind Writing*, ed. Brian Kuan Wood (New York: Sternberg Press, 2010), 309–324, but my references are drawn from the earlier publication.

2. Ina Blom, *On the Style Site: Art, Sociality and Media Culture* (Berlin and New York: Sternberg Press, 2007), 146–147.

3. This chapter focused specifically on television talk, but many artists have used radio talk to explore issues of publicness. Daniel Jewesbury's *Exchange 2000* (1999–2000), realised for *Manifesta 3* in Ljubljana, consisted of four radio receivers broadcasting a discussion between six people who talk about issues such as immigration, racial prejudice, multiculturalism and national affiliation. The content initially seems unrehearsed but is revealed to be scripted when participants begin to talk in different languages. For details see the *Manifesta 3* website [Accessed June 1, 2013] http://www.manifesta.org/ manifesta3/a_dani.html. Garrett Phelan has also produced numerous works for radio. In *Black Brain Radio* (2006), a radio and installation work realised with Temple Bar Gallery and Studios and the Irish Museum of Modern Art (IMMA), Dublin, he used his own voice to reprocess material culled from an array of sources, in order to explore the processes through which values and ideas enter society. For details see the IMMA http://www.imma .ie/en/page_134278.htm.

4. Claire Doherty, 'The Institution is Dead! Long Live the Institution! Contemporary Art and New Institutionalism,' *Art of Encounter: Engage* 15 (2004). Engage [Accessed June 1, 2013] http://www.engage.org/engage-journal.aspx.

5. Esche was Director of Tramway Gallery, Glasgow, 1993–1997, co-founder of The Modern Institute in Glasgow in 1998, Director of Rooseum in Malmo, 2000–2004, and is currently Director of Van Abbemuseum in Eindhoven.

6. Established in January 1999 by New York-based artists Anton Vidokle and Julieta Aranda, e-flux distributes what it calls a 'news digest' to 70,000 visual art professionals on a daily basis. Organisations pay significant fees to post information to this list, which is tightly curated. E-flux announcements always include a link to the organisation's website, and are the main means of promoting contemporary art activities internationally. See the section 'About e-flux' at http://www.e-flux.com/about/ [Accessed June 1, 2013].

7. See, for example, various contributions to *Art and its Institutions: Current Conflicts, Critique and Collaborations*, ed. Nina Möntmann (London: Black Dog Publishers, 2006).

8. Tony Bennett, *The Birth of the Museum: History, Theory, Politics* (Oxon and New York: Routledge, 1995), 25.

9. Tony Bennett, 'Civic Laboratories: Museums, Cultural Objecthood, and the Governance of the Social,' *Cultural Studies* 19, no. 5 (2005): 536.

10. Dorothea von Hantelmann, '30 July 2010 – 22 October 2010,' *Philippe Parreno: Films 1987–2010*, ed. Karen Marta, Kathryn Rattee, Zoe Stillpass (London and Cologne: Serpentine Gallery and Koenig Books, 2010), 87.

11. Habermas identifies rational-critical debate and discussion, enabled by the new civic institutions that emerged in the eighteenth century, as central to the development of the bourgeois public sphere. His research also demonstrates the significance of social spaces where newspapers were shared, which were often more easily accessed by men than women. Jürgen Habermas, *The Structural Transformation of the Public Sphere: An Inquiry into a Category of Bourgeois Society*, trans. Thomas Burger with the assistance of Frederick Lawrence (Cambridge: Polity Press, 1989).

12. Stephen Heath, 'Representing Television', in *Logics of Television*, ed. Patricia Mellencamp (Bloomington and London: BFI and Indiana University Press, 1990), 272–273. Italics in original.

13. Heath, 273. Italics in original.

14. Heath, 275.

15. Heath, 276.

16. As Heath notes, this aspect of television talk was also identified earlier by Stanley Cavell. See Stanley Cavell, 'The Fact of Television', in *Video Culture: A Critical Examination*, ed. John G. Hanhardt (Layton, UT: Peregrine Smith Books/Visual Studies Workshop Press, 1986), 192–218.

17. This 'general political commitment' was apparent in a focus on then current social and political issues, rather than (for example) on interpersonal disputes. See Jane M. Shattuc, 'The Shifting Terrain of American Talk Shows', in *A Companion to Television*, ed. Janet Wasko (Oxford: Blackwell Publishing, 2010), 324.

18. Shattuc, 325.

19. Shattuc, 325. See also Laura Grindstaff's discussion of the confessional mode in 'Self-Serve Celebrity: The Production of Ordinariness and the Ordinariness of Production in Reality Television', in *Production Studies: Cultural Studies of Media Industries*, ed. Vicki Mayer, Miranda J. Banks and John Thornton Caldwell, (New York and London: Routledge, 2009), 71–86.

20. Shattuc, 334.

21. It is worth noting that the exhibition *Talk Show* (6 May – 31 May 2009) curated by Will Holder, in collaboration with Richard Birkett and Jennifer Thatcher, at the Institute of Contemporary Arts, London, actually took the act of human speech—rather than television talk—as its theme. It did, however, include an event by artist Stephen Sutcliffe, presenting material from his archive of TV interviews and talk shows. Sutcliffe's work also featured in *Talking Heads*, curated by Claire Feeley at IMOCA, (Dublin) in February 2010. Although more specifically concerned with moving image work, this show focused on the talking head as a filmic and televisual convention across a wide range of genres. For details see http://the.imoca.ie/opening/talking-heads/.

22. Roommade is no longer in operation but the press release for this show can be found at http://amsterdam.nettime.org/Lists-Archives/nettime-bold-0109/msg00308.html.

23. The three exhibitions were *Poetry Must Be Made by All! Transform the World!* from 1970, *Dove Sta Memoria* (Where is memory) by Gerhard Merz from 1986 and *Eine Gesellschaft des Geschmacks* (A society of taste) by Andrea Fraser from 1993.

24. Lind had previously curated the exhibition 'What If: Art on the Verge of Architecture and Design' (Moderna Museet, Stockholm, 2000) in which Gillick was invited to participate as

'a "filter" through which the artworks would take shape in the design and layout'. See Paul O'Neill, *The Culture of Curating and the Curating of Culture(s)* (Cambridge, MA: MIT Press, 2012), 118.

25. Lind, 102.

26. Søren Grammel, 'A Series of Acts and Spaces', *On Curating* 8 (2011): 35 [Accessed June 1, 2013] http://www.on-curating.org/documents/oncurating_issue_0811.pdf.

27. Liam Gillick, *Literally No Place: Communes, Bars and Greenrooms* (London: Book Works, 2002).

28. Blom, 147.

29. Blom, 132. Elsewhere, Maria Lind and Hito Steyerl use the term 'greenroom' to define an ancillary area where discussion is not 'on stage', but derives 'concentration and rigour' from proximity to the stage. See Lind and Steyerl, 'Introduction: Reconsidering the Documentary and Contemporary Art', in *The Greenroom: Reconsidering the Documentary and Contemporary Art*, ed. Lind and Steyerl (New York: Sternberg Press and Center for Curatorial Studies, Bard College, 2008), 26.

30. Gillick does not seem to be specifically interested in the strategy of broadcasting 'live' from the greenroom, a technique widely used by shows such as *Friday Night with Jonathan Ross* (2001–2010), which regularly featured interactions with guests in a backstage waiting area.

31. Blom, 146.

32. Reesa Greenberg, 'Archival Remembering Exhibitions', *Journal of Curatorial Studies* 1, no. 2 (2012): 159–177.

33. For an exploration of the evolution of this term see Andrea Fraser, 'From the Critique of Institutions to an Institution of Critique', *Artforum* 44, no. 1 (2005): 279.

34. Hito Steyerl, 'The Institution of Critique', *European Institute for Progressive Cultural Policies*, January 2006. EIPCP Transversal Project [Accessed June 1, 2013] http://eipcp.net/transversal/0106/steyerl/en.

35. Steyerl, 'The Institution of Critique'.

36. Lind, 97–98.

37. The project was presented at Kunstraum der Universität Luneburg, January 29 – February 20, 1994.

38. Andrea Fraser, 'What's Intangible, Transitory, Mediating, Participatory, and Rendered in the Public Sphere? Part 1 (1996)', in *Museum Highlights: The Writings of Andrea Fraser*, ed. Alexander Alberro (Cambridge, MA: MIT Press, 2005), 47–53.

39. For a provocative account of the loss of artistic authorship and agency in contemporary art see Anton Vidokle, 'Art Without Artists?', *e-flux journal* 16 (2010) [Accessed June 1, 2013] http://www.e-flux.com/journal/art-without-artists/.

40. Noah Horowitz, *Art of the Deal: Contemporary Art in a Global Financial Market* (Princeton and Oxford: Princeton University Press, 2011), 129. Italics in original.

41. Doherty, 'The Institution is Dead! Long Live the Institution! Contemporary Art and New Institutionalism'.

42. Simon Sheikh, 'In the Place of the Public Sphere? Or, the World in Fragments', *European Institute for Progressive Cultural Policies*, (EIPCP) Republicart Project, June 2004 [Accessed June 1, 2013] http://republicart.net/disc/publicum/sheikh03_en.htm.

43. Simon Sheikh, 'In the Place of the Public Sphere?.' For a discussion of challenges facing many New Institutions by the late 2000s, see Nina Möntmann, 'The Rise and Fall of New Institutionalism: Perspectives on a Possible Future,' *European Institute for Progressive Cultural Policies* (EIPCP) Transversal Project, August 2007 [Accessed June 1, 2013] http://eipcp.net/transversal/0407/moentmann/en.

44. Segmentation is also a concern for theorists of broadcasting. See, for example, Elihu Katz, 'And Deliver Us From Segmentation,' *Annals of the American Academy of Political and Social Science* 546 (1996): 22–33.

45. Maria Lind, in Roger M. Buergel et al 'Curating with Institutional Visions,' in *Art and its Institutions: Current Conflicts, Critique and Collaborations,* ed. Nina Möntmann (London: Black Dog Publishers, 2006), 39.

46. Alex Farquharson, 'Bureaux de Change,' *Frieze* 101 (September 2006): 156–159.

47. Farquharson, 158.

48. O'Neill, 73.

49. It is also important to note that some 'new institutions' also sought to engage with local visitors who could make repeat visits. For example, Lind's programme at Munich Kunstverein included a retrospective of Christine Borland's work (in 2002–2003) involving eight projects presented in the form of 'stations,' over a period of 14 months in various parts of the building.

50. Michael Warner, 'Publics and Counterpublics,' *Public Culture* 14 (2002): 49–50. See also Michael G. Ketcham, *Transparent Design: Reading, Performance, and Form in the Spectator Papers* (Athens: University of Georgia Press, 1985).

51. Warner, 62.

52. Warner, 70–71.

53. Warner, 81.

54. Farquharson, 157.

55. Although its main focus was to promote Arteleku activities via the web, this form of production is nonetheless explicitly described by Arteleku staff as 'broadcasting.' Email correspondence with Maitane Otaegi, Arteleku, January 25, 2012.

56. Charles Esche, interviewed by Mats Stjernstedt, 'Rooseum Director Charles Esche on the Art Center of the 21st Century,' www.*artforum*.com, December 7, 2001 [Accessed June 1, 2013] http://artforum.com/index.php?pn=interview&id=1331.

57. See, for example, the discussion of Superflex and Liverpool-based *tenantspin* in Chapter Three.

58. Details of sources and references can be found in 'Public CAC TV Draft Concept,' October 20, 2004 [Accessed June 1, 2013] http://www.cac.lt/tv.

59. CAC TV, 'Public CAC TV Draft Concept'. Thanks to Tessa Giblin for her assistance in accessing documentation of CAC TV.

60. Sally O'Reilly, 'Do not adjust your set,' *Financialtimes.com*, October 6, 2006 [Accessed June 1, 2013] http://www.ft.com/cms/s/0/9b457392–537a-11db-8a2a-0000779e2340.html#ixzz1gSCMXf8I.

61. LUX Blog, 'The California State of Mind: an interview with Glenn Phillips,' posted by Anne Colvin on 06/09/11 [Accessed June 1, 2013] http://www.lux.org.uk/blog/california-state-mind-interview-glenn-phillips.

62. Kathy Rae Huffman, 'Exchange and Evolution: Worldwide Video Long Beach 1974–1999,' *Exchange and Evolution: Worldwide Video Long Beach 1974–1999*, ed. Kathy Rae Huffman (Long Beach: Long Beach Museum of Art, 2011), 13.

63. The conference was organised by Hans Breder at the University of Iowa, Oct. 20–23, 1982, and it is discussed by Carl Loeffler (one of the participants) in 'Performing Post-Performancist Performance or the Televisionist Performing Televisionism,' in *Give Them the Picture: An Anthology of La Mamelle/ART COM*, ed. Liz Glass, Susannah Magers, and Julian Myers (San Francisco: California College of the Arts, 2011), 100–103.

64. Huffman, 18.

65. Nancy Buchanan, 'Remembered Excerpts from the Long Beach Museum of Art,' *Exchange and Evolution: Worldwide Video Long Beach 1974–1999*, ed. Kathy Rae Huffman (Long Beach: Long Beach Museum of Art, 2011), 32.

66. Gloria Sutton, 'Playback: Reconsidering the Long Beach Museum of Art as a Media Art Center,' in *Exchange and Evolution: Worldwide Video Long Beach 1974–1999*, ed. Kathy Rae Huffman (Long Beach: Long Beach Museum of Art, 2011), 123.

67. Sutton, 123.

68. Sutton, 125.

69. Ross, cited by Sutton, 122. During the late 1970s and early 80s, Paik figured prominently in art institutional broadcasts such as the *documenta 6* satellite telecast in 1977, a 30-minute live transmission from Kassel to more than 25 countries, with performances by Joseph Beuys, Douglas Davis as well as Paik and Charlotte Moorman. Paik's own *Good Morning Mr. Orwell* (broadcast on New Year's Day in 1984) also used satellite to link New York, San Francisco and Paris with the explicit aim of countering Orwell's dystopian vision of the future.

70. Sutton, 123.

71. My discussion is informed by Sarah Johnson Montross's insightful analysis of Davidovich's practice in '"We Must Build Our Theaters in the Air": Jaime Davidovich and Public-Access Cable Television,' paper presented at the College Art Association conference, Los Angeles, February 25, 2012. See also the history of the Artists Television Network, *Experimental TV Center*, http://experimentaltvcenter.org/artists-television-network [Accessed June 1, 2013].

72. 'Dr Ruth' made several successful appearances on the *David Letterman Show* before becoming the host of her own cable TV show (on Lifetime) in 1982.

73. Kathy Rae Huffman, 'Exchange: A Screening Event,' *Exchange and Evolution: Worldwide Video Long Beach 1974–1999*, ed. Kathy Rae Huffman (Long Beach: Long Beach Museum of Art, 2011), 113–114.

74. Superflex's involvement with television is discussed in more detail in Chapter Three.

75. Doherty, 'The Institution is Dead!,' 2004. More recently, in a text that reflects upon the mixed legacy of New Institutionalism, Sven Lütticken articulates a deep scepticism with regard to discursive events built around high profile curatorial celebrity-figures who draw large audiences. See Sven Lütticken, 'Once More on Publicness: A Postscript to *Secret Publicity*,' *Fillip* 12 (2010): 86–91.

76. See also Ann Philbin's discussion of the Hammer Museum, 'The Museum Revisited,' *Artforum* 48, no. 10 (2010): 298–299.

77. My discussion is informed by interviews conducted at the Hammer Museum with Claudia Bestor, and her colleague Camille Thoma, on February 22, 2013.
78. Hilarie M. Sheets, 'Armand Hammer's Orphan Museum Turns Into Cinderella in Los Angeles,' *The New York Times*, arts section, October 6, 2004.
79. Christian Sandvig notes that server issues often limit the public reach of small organisations, in Sandvig, 'The Structural Problems of the Internet for Cultural Policy,' in *Critical Cyberculture Studies*, ed. David Silver and Adrienne Massanari (New York: NYU Press, 2006), 110.
80. My discussion is informed by Allison Agsten's contribution to *Curating and Education*, a panel organised by Independent Curators International, College Art Association conference, February 23, 2012, and by an interview with Agsten, conducted following her presentation. Anne Ellegood, Senior Curator at the Hammer, also spoke about the museum's public and educational programmes at a seminar in the Science Gallery, Dublin on October 16, 2010. For a review of this event see Anne Lynott, 'Productive Reflection,' *Visual Artists Newssheet*, March/April 2011 [Accessed June 1, 2013] http://visualartists.ie/articles/van-marchapril-2011-productive-reflection/.
81. Full details of the shows and participants can be found at www.dieklaumichshow.org [Accessed June 1, 2013]. My discussion is based upon information drawn from the website and my attendance at the public recording of the first transmission, during the press preview at *dOCUMENTA (13)* on June 8, 2012.
82. *Klau Mich: Radicalism in society meets experiment on TV*: An introduction to the project by Dora García, www.dieklaumichshow.org [Accessed June 1, 2013].
83. See also Dora García, 'Absurdity in Prime Time,' *Are You Ready for TV?* exhibition catalogue, (Barcelona: MACBA, 2010), 26–36.
84. Dora García, *Klau Mich: Radicalism in society meets experiment on TV*: An introduction to the project, www.dieklaumichshow.org [Accessed June 1, 2013].
85. Simon Sheikh, 'Publics and Post-Publics: The Production of the Social,' *Open 14: Art as a Public Issue* (2008): 34.
86. Sheikh, 36.

Notes to Chapter 7

1. Lynne Cooke, 'In Lieu of Higher Ground,' in *Questions of Practice: What Makes a Great Exhibition?*, ed. Paula Marincola (Chicago: University of Chicago Press, 2007), 33.
2. David Hesmondhalgh and Sarah Baker, 'Creative Work and Emotional Labour in the Television Industry,' *Theory, Culture & Society* 25.7/8 (2008): 102. Italics in original.
3. Amanda Sharp, quoted in Edward Helmore, 'London Frieze braves backlash to fly the flag of British culture in Manhattan,' *The Guardian*, April 28, 2012.
4. Other examples of US art reality TV include Bravo's *Gallery Girls* (2012–), focusing on aspiring gallery workers rather than artists. Thanks to Volker Pantenburg for drawing my attention to this show. The French-German (publicly-funded) arts channel ARTE has also developed an artist-focused show, *Tous pour l'art/Alles für die Kunst*, scheduled for late 2012. Thanks to Sophia Graefe for this reference.

5. My discussion of 'television workers' in contemporary art could be extended to include Katya Sander's *Televised I: the Anchor, the I and the Studio* (2006) and Liz Magic Laser's *In Camera* (2012) as both involve the participation of television news producers. For a brief discussion of both works, within the context of an overview of TV studio spaces in contemporary art, see Maeve Connolly, 'Studio Spaces,' *Frieze* 155 (2013): 208–212. Several artists have also developed projects in collaboration with telenovela actors including Phil Collins (whose video *soy mi madre* is discussed in Chapter Two), Christian Jankowski—who worked with the cast and crew of a Televisa telenovela to produce *Crying for the March of Humanity* (2012) and Wendelien van Oldenborgh, whose film *Bete & Deise* (2012) features a well-known Brazilian actress, activist and politician.

6. Videofreex had specific reasons to be sceptical about network interest in video collectives because of prior experience of the failed CBS 'Now Project.' See Deirdre Boyle, *Subject to Change: Guerrilla Television Revisited* (New York and Oxford: Oxford University Press, 1997), 17–25.

7. Boyle charts the rise and fall of TVTV in several chapters, detailing Shamberg's growing interest in Hollywood production, 172–189.

8. David Joselit, *Feedback: Television Against Democracy* (Cambridge, MA: MIT Press, 2007), 99.

9. John Thornton Caldwell, *Televisuality: Style, Crisis, and Authority in American Television* (New Brunswick, NJ: Rutgers University Press, 1995), 271.

10. Boyle, 109.

11. Boyle, 45.

12. *San Francisco Chronicle* reviewer (Herb Caen) cited by Boyle, 63.

13. Caldwell, 272.

14. Boyle, 179. In 1976, TVTV also produced *Super Bowl*, with scripted performances by Christopher Guest and Bill Murray. Both had contributed as writers and performers to the pilot of *Saturday Night Live* (1975), an important point of reference for TVTV. *Superbowl* may also have anticipated the rise of the 'mockumentary' form, as exemplified by *This is Spinal Tap* (1984), written by Guest and, according to Boyle, produced by a former TVTV worker (Karen Murray). See Boyle, 187.

15. Tomlin also contributed to other artist-produced projects around this time, such as Collisions (1976), also featuring Dan Ackroyd. See Fred Barzyk, cited by Kathy Rae Huffman in'Video Art: What's TV Got To Do With It?', *Illuminating Video: An Essential Guide to Video Art*, ed. Doug Hall and Sally Jo Fifer, (New York: Aperture Foundation in association with Bay Area Video Coalition, 1990), 85.

16. Cooke, 33.

17. Cooke, 33, notes the influence of B. Joseph Pine II and James H. Gilmore's, *The Experience Economy: Work is Theatre & Every Business is a Stage* (Boston, MA: Harvard Business School Press, 1999).

18. Paul O'Neill, *The Culture of Curating and the Curating of Culture(s)* (Cambridge, MA: MIT Press, 2012), 122.

19. O'Neill, 123.

20. Residuals are supposed to compensate creative workers for the loss of labour associated with reruns of TV shows, which take the place of new productions. See Matt Stahl, 'Privilege

and Distinction in Production Worlds: Copyright, Collective Bargaining and Working Conditions in Media Making,' in *Production Studies: Cultural Studies of Media Industries*, ed. Vicki Mayer, Miranda J. Banks and John Thornton Caldwell (New York and London: Routledge, 2009), 58–59.

21. Stahl, 65. Italics in original.

22. John Thornton Caldwell, 'Worker Blowback: User-Generated, Worker-Generated, and Producer-Generated Content within Collapsing Production Workflows,' in *Television as Digital Media*, ed. James Bennett and Niki Strange, (Durham and London: Duke University Press, 2011), 295–296.

23. Caldwell, 'Worker Blowback,' 297. Worker-generated content operates alongside 'user-generated content' and 'producer-generated content,' which includes, for example, stealth marketing techniques, in which employees pose as online fans to create buzz and gossip. See Caldwell, 'Worker Blowback,' 302.

24. Caldwell, 'Worker Blowback,' 302.

25. Caldwell, 'Worker Blowback,' 306. The text cited is Andreas Wittel, 'Toward a Network Sociality,' *Theory, Culture and Society* 18, no. 6 (2001): 51–77.

26. Caldwell, 'Worker Blowback,' 306.

27. Stahl, 60.

28. See Luc Boltanski and Eve Chiapello, *The New Spirit of Capitalism*, trans. Gregory Elliott (London and New York: Verso, 2007).

29. Andrea Fraser, 'A Museum is not a business. It is run in a business-like fashion,' *Art and its Institutions: Current Conflicts, Critique and Collaborations,* ed. Nina Möntmann (London: Black Dog Publishers, 2006), 94.

30. See, for example, the work of the National Campaign for the Arts, in Ireland (http://ncfa.ie/) and Haben und Brauchen, in Berlin, (http://www.habenundbrauchen.de/en) [Accessed June 1, 2013].

31. My discussion is informed by the experience of attending a workshop on labour organisation, which formed part of the exhibition *I Can't Work Like This*, Casco—Office for Art, Design & Theory, Utrecht, 1 May – 23 June 2012. Casco [Accessed June 1, 2013] http://www.cascoprojects.org/?entryid=490.

32. Cluster Network was formed in June 2011 to facilitate internal and public exchange of knowledge about the member institutions, and also to establish further collaborations between them. For details see http://www.clusternetwork.eu/index.php [Accessed June 1, 2013]. Some of these organisations are also involved in more local networks and The Showroom, for example, is part of 'Common Practice,' an alliance of small publicly-funded organisations based in London, including Afterall, Chisenhale Gallery, Electra, Gasworks, LUX, Matt's Gallery, Mute Publishing and Studio Voltaire. For details see http://www.commonpractice.org.uk/ [Accessed June 1, 2013] In addition, a number of European private collectors involved in the production and exhibition of art, including La Maison Rouge (Paris) and Magazin 3 (Stockholm), have established an alliance entitled Foundation of Arts for a Contemporary Europe, to extend their activities through shared ventures in areas such as programming, publications and public relations. See Jeffrey Kastner, 'New Foundations,' *Artforum* 48, no. 10 (2010): 314–319.

33. See Maeve Connolly, 'Studio Spaces', *Frieze* 155 (2013): 208–212.

34. Deitch quoted in Randy Kennedy, '*Artstar* on Gallery HD: The Art World Tries Realism (the TV Kind),' *New York Times*, May 28, 2006.

35. Edward Helmore, 'LA aesthetes fight pop-art billionaire,' *The Observer*, July 22, 2012.

36. Press release, *Art School*, August 10, 2005 [Accessed June 1, 2013] http://www.bbc.co.uk/pressoffice/pressreleases/stories/2005/08_august/10/art.shtml.

37. For press coverage of this project see Artangel [Accessed June 1, 2013] http://www.artangel.org.uk//projects/2009/life_class/press_coverage/press_coverage.

38. Karen Rosenberg, 'A Museum Show as a TV Contest Prize,' *The New York Times*. August 18, 2010. The New York Times [Accessed June 1, 2013] http://www.nytimes.com/2010/08/19/arts/design/19abdi.html?

39. See John Roberts, *The Intangibilities of Form: Skill and Deskilling in Art After the Readymade* (London and New York: Verso, 2008).

40. Isabelle Graw, *High Price: Art Between the Market and Celebrity Culture* (Berlin and New York: Sternberg Press, 2009).

41. For a critique of Hardt and Negri, see David Hesmondhalgh and Sarah Baker, 'Creative Work and Emotional Labour in the Television Industry,' *Theory, Culture & Society* 25, no. 7/8 (2008): 99.

42. Hesmondhalgh and Baker, 100.

43. Hesmondhalgh and Baker, 101.

44. Hesmondhalgh and Baker, 103.

45. Hesmondhalgh and Baker, 104.

46. Hochschild, cited by Hesmondhalgh and Baker, 108. See Arlie Russell Hochschild, *The Managed Heart: Commercialization of Human Feeling* (Berkeley: University of California Press 1983).

47. Laura Grindstaff, *The Money Shot: Trash, Class, and the Making of TV Talk Shows* (Chicago: University of Chicago Press, 2002).

48. Hesmondhalgh and Baker, 113.

49. *Live from Frieze Art Fair this is LuckyPDFTV* included elements of performance, news and chat, introduced by guest presenters. Visitors could attend open rehearsals and live recordings in the project studio or watch the 'action' on screens located around the fair.

50. LuckyPDF, *School of Global Art*, press release, http://schoolofglobalart.org/#about [Accessed June 1, 2013].

51. Sims, cited by LuckyPDF artist James Early in 'LuckyPDF invite reality TV star to critique ICA show,' *Phaidon*, April 3, 2012 [Accessed June 1, 2013] http://de.phaidon.com/agenda/art/events/2012/april/03/luckypdf-invite-reality-tv-star-to-critique-ica-show/.

52. Links to all episodes can be found on the Auto Italia South East website [Accessed June 1, 2013] http://autoitaliasoutheast.org/projects/auto-italia-live-episode-1-talking-objects-in-space/.

53. Press release for *Auto Italia LIVE Episode 1: Talking Objects in Space*, September 24, 2011. Auto Italia website [Accessed June 2013] http://autoitaliasoutheast.org/projects/auto-italia-live-episode-1-talking-objects-in-space/ [Accessed June 1, 2013].

54. See Lisa Parks, 'Satellite Spectacular: One World and the Fantasy of Global Presence,' *Cultures in Orbit: Satellites and the Televisual* (Durham and London: Duke University Press, 2005), 21–46.

55. My discussion is informed by email correspondence with Kate Cooper of Auto Italia South East, July 12, 2012. The group's website does, however, include commissioned texts on the theme of labour, such as Marina Vischmidt's *'Counter (Re-)Productive Labour,'* posted on the Auto Italia South East website, April 4, 2012 [Accessed June 1, 2013] See http://autoitaliasoutheast.org/blog/news/2012/04/04/counter-re-productive-labour/.

56. In addition, Auto Italia South East communicate their central position within a social network that extends beyond the physical confines of the studio, most effectively in the 'advertisements' featured in episode three, which included a short promotional message for another London-based artists collective, called The Haircut Before the Party.

57. My discussion is informed by email correspondence with Alexis Hudgins, in addition to the press release, 'Alexis Hudgins and Lakshmi Luthra: Reverse Cut,' Las Cienegas Projects, posted August 2, 2010. See also http://alexishudgins.com/Reverse-Cut-Wrap-Party-2011 and http://lascienegasprojects.wordpress.com/2010/08/02/alexis-hudgins-and-lakshmi-luthra/ [Both accessed June 1, 2013].

58. Details of this event, including a transcript, were provided by Alexis Hudgins, email correspondence, July 2012.

59. Noah Horowitz, *Art of the Deal: Contemporary Art in a Global Financial Market* (Princeton and Oxford: Princeton University Press, 2011), 23.

60. Burkhard Meltzer, 'Christian Jankowski, Kunstmuseum Stuttgart,' trans. Nicholas Grindell, *Frieze* 120 (2009): 146–147.

61. My discussion is informed by personal interviews with Gerard Byrne, on August 8, 2012, and with David McKenna at RTÉ, on October 26, 2012.

62. My discussion of the installation relates to the presentation of this work in 'Gerard Byrne: A state of neutral pleasure,' January 17 – March 8, 2013, Whitechapel Gallery, London.

63. For a more detailed discussion of *Subject* see Maeve Connolly, 'Architecture, Television, Archaeology: Gerard Byrne's *Subject,* 2009,' *Images or Shadows: Gerard Byrne,* ed. Pablo Lafuente (Dublin: Irish Museum of Modern Art, 2011), 71–90.

64. For further details see Slow Children Crossing [Accessed June 1, 2013] http://www.slowchildrenxing.com/about/.

Notes to Conclusion

1. Available to television viewers throughout Germany, Austria and Switzerland, the channel is designated as one of *dOCUMENTA (13)*'s 'media partners.'

2. This event, which included broadcasts of *The Refusal of Time* (2012) by William Kentridge and *Continuity* (2012) by Omer Fast, took place on September 15, 2012 and the works could also be viewed in full on the 3Sat website. Although the 'television-closing' was framed as a special event, the alignment of broadcast and 'festival' schedules is not unprecedented in

German cultural television, since this type of programming often includes transmissions of live theatre and music events. This was not the first Documenta to include a significant broadcast element—in 1977, the sixth instalment of the exhibition (often described as the 'media Documenta') included a 30-minute live international satellite telecast from Kassel, transmitted to more than 25 countries. For an overview of television and media art in Documenta see Rudolf Frieling, 'Form Follows Format: Tensions, Museums, Media Technology and Media Art,' *Media Art Net*, 2004 [Accessed June 1, 2013] http://www .medienkunstnetz.de/themes/overview_of_media_art/museum/.

3. Carolyn Christov-Bakargiev, 'The dance was very frenetic, lively, rattling, clanging, rolling, contorted, and lasted for a long time,' *dOCUMENTA (13): Catalogue 1/3, The Book of Books*, ed. documenta und Museum Fridericianum (Ostfildern: Hatje Cantz, 2012), 36. See also Bert Rebhandl, 'Clemens von Wedemeyer: The Site Creates Simultaneity,' *Mousse Magazine* 34 (2012): 118–125.

4. This strategy loosely recalls the casting of Deborah Kerr in Michael Powell and Emeric Pressburger's wartime epic *The Life and Death of Colonel Blimp* (1943), where she appears in several roles, appearing at different moments in history.

5. See, for example, Andrew S. Weiner's discussion of Documenta in 'Memory under Reconstruction: Politics and Event in Wirtschaftswunder West Germany,' *Grey Room* 37 (2009): 99–107, and Walter Grasskamp, 'For example, *Documenta*, or, How is History Produced?,' trans. Rebecca Pates, in *Thinking About Exhibitions*, ed. Reesa Greenberg, Bruce Ferguson, Sandy Nairne (London and New York: Routledge, 1996), 67–78.

6. Eva Scharrer, 'Clemens von Wedemeyer,' *dOCUMENTA (13): Catalogue 3/3, The Guidebook*, ed. documenta und Museum Fridericianum (Ostfildern: Hatje Cantz, 2012), 374.

7. Michael Z. Newman and Elana Levine, *Legitimating Television: Media Convergence and Cultural Status* (New York and London: Routledge, 2012), 47.

8. In addition to a blanket, plate and spoon, they include photographs, identity passes and a number of logbooks filled with entries.

9. Clemens von Wedemeyer, *Bambule: The Script*. Series: dOCUMENTA (13): 100 Notes – 100 Thoughts No. 092, (Ostfildern: Hatje Cantz, 2012). Published in German and English. This publication includes an introduction by von Wedemeyer, Meinhof's original script and also an epilogue written by her daughter Bettina Röhl, exploring the motivations for the campaign against the reform schools.'

References

Allen, Craig. 'Discovering "Joe Six Pack" Content in Television News: The Hidden History of Audience Research, News Consultants, and the Warner Class Model.' *Journal of Broadcasting & Electronic Media* 49, no. 4 (2005): 363–382.

Ang, Ien. *Watching Dallas: Soap Opera and the Melodramatic Imagination*. Translated by Della Couling. London and New York: Methuen, 1985.

Antin, David. 'Video: The Distinctive Features of the Medium.' In *Video Culture: A Critical Investigation*, edited by John Hanhardt, 148–166. Rochester, NY: Peregrine Smith Books, 1986.

Auslander, Philip. *Liveness: Performance in a Mediatized Culture*, 2nd ed. Oxon: Routledge, 2008.

Baker, George et al. 'Round Table: The Projected Image in Contemporary Art.' *October* 104 (2003): 71–96.

Baker, George. 'The Storyteller: Notes on the Work of Gerard Byrne.' In *Gerard Byrne, Books, Magazines, and Newspapers*, edited by Nicolas Schafhausen, 7–96. New York: Lukas & Sternberg, 2003.

Balsom, Erika. *Exhibiting Cinema in Contemporary Art*. Amsterdam: Amsterdam University Press, 2013.

Bardin, Olivier. 'Olivier Bardin: Interview by Pierre Huyghe and Hans-Ulrich Obrist.' Translated by Teresa Bridgeman. In *The Fifth Floor: Ideas Taking Space*, edited by Peter Gorschlüter, 72–76. Liverpool: Liverpool University Press and Tate Liverpool, 2009.

Basualdo, Carlos. 'Bataille Monument, Documenta 11, 2002.' In *Thomas Hirschhorn*, 96–108. London: Phaidon, 2004.

Beeson, John. 'Laura Horelli's "The Terrace".' *Art Agenda*, December 14, 2011. Art Agenda. [Accessed June 1, 2013] http://www.art-agenda.com/reviews/.

Bennett, James and Niki Strange eds. *Television as Digital Media*. Durham and London: Duke University Press, 2011.

Bennett, Tony. *The Birth of the Museum: History, Theory, Politics*. Oxon and New York: Routledge, 1995.

Bennett, Tony. 'Civic aboratories: Museums, Cultural Objecthood, and the Governance of the Social.' *Cultural Studies* 19, no. 5 (2005): 521–547.

Bennett, Tony. 'Habitus Clivé: Aesthetics and Politics in the Work of Pierre Bourdieu.' *New Literary History* 38, no. 1 (2007): 201–228.

Bignell, Jonathan. 'Seeing and Knowing: Reflexivity and Quality.' In *Quality TV: Contemporary American Television and Beyond*, edited by Janet McCabe and Kim Akass, 158–170. London: I.B. Tauris, 2007.

Birnbaum, Dara. 'The Rio Experience: Video's New Architecture Meets Corporate Sponsorship.' In *Illuminating Video: An Essential Guide to Video Art*, edited by Doug Hall and Sally Jo Fifer, 189–204. New York: Aperture Foundation in association with Bay Area Video Coalition, 1990.

Bishop, Claire. 'Introduction: Documents of Contemporary Art.' In *Participation*, edited by Claire Bishop, 10–17. Cambridge, MA and London: MIT Press and Whitechapel, 2006.

Bishop, Claire. 'The Social Turn.' *Artforum* 44, no. 6 (2006): 178–183.

Bishop, Claire. 'Outsourcing Authenticity? Delegated Performance in Contemporary Art.' In *Double Agent*, edited by Claire Bishop and Silvia Tramontana, 110–125. London: ICA, 2009.

Bishop, Claire. *Artificial Hells: Participatory Art and the Politics of Spectatorship*. London: Verso, 2012.

Blanchard, Simon and David Morley. *What's This Channel Four?: An Alternative Report*. London: Comedia, 1982.

Blom, Ina. *On the Style Site*: *Art, Sociality and Media Culture*. Berlin and New York: Sternberg Press, 2007.

Boltanski, Luc and Eve Chiapello. *The New Spirit of Capitalism*. Translated by Gregory Elliott. London and New York: Verso, 2007.

Bolter, Jay David, and Richard Grusin. *Remediation: Understanding New Media*. Cambridge, MA: MIT Press, 2000.

Born, Georgina. 'Strategy, Positioning and Projection in Digital Television: Channel Four and the Commercialization of Public Service Broadcasting in the UK.' *Media, Culture & Society* 25 (2003): 773–799.

Bourdieu, Pierre. *Distinction: A Social Critique of the Judgement of Taste*. Translated by Richard Nice. London: Routledge, 1984.

Bourdieu, Pierre. *The Field of Cultural Production: Essays on Art and Literature*, edited by Randal Johnson. Cambridge: Polity Press, 1993.

Bourdieu, Pierre. *The Rules of Art: Genesis and Structure of the Literary Field*. Translated by Susan Emanuel. Stanford: Stanford University Press, 1996.

Bourdon, Jerome. 'Some Sense of Time: Remembering Television.' *History & Memory* 15, no. 2 (2003): 5–35.

Bourriaud, Nicolas. *Relational Aesthetics*. Translated by Simon Pleasance and Fronza Woods. Dijon: Les Presses du Réel, 2002.

Boyle, Deirdre. *Subject to Change: Guerrilla Television Revisited*. New York and Oxford: Oxford University Press, 1997.

Braun, Reinhard, and Kathy Rae Huffman. 'Television/Art/Culture: Reinhard Braun in Conversation with Kathy Rae Huffman.' In *Changing Channels: Art and Television 1963–1988*, edited by Museum Moderner Kunst Stiftung Ludwig Wien and Matthias Michalka, 87–124. Cologne: Verlag der Buchhandlung Walther König, 2010.

Brecht, Bertolt. 'Radio as a Means of Communication: A Talk on the Function of Radio.' *Screen* 20, no. 3–4 (1979): 24–28.

Browne, Sarah, and Gareth Kennedy. 'Episode 306: Dallas, Belfast.' In *SPACE SHUTTLE: Six Projects of Urban Creativity and Social Interaction*, edited by Peter Mutschler and Ruth Morrow, 15–21. Belfast: PS², 2007.

Bryan-Wilson, Julia. *Art Workers, Radical Practice in the Vietnam War Era*. Berkeley: University of California Press, 2009.

Buchanan, Nancy. 'Remembered Excerpts from the Long Beach Museum of Art.' *Exchange and Evolution: Worldwide Video Long Beach 1974–1999*, edited by Kathy Rae Huffman, 26–35. Long Beach: Long Beach Museum of Art, 2011.

Buchloh, Benjamin H.D. 'Memory Lessons and History Tableaux: James Coleman's Archaeology of Spectacle.' In *James Coleman*, 51–75. Barcelona: Fundació Antoni Tàpies, 1999.

Buchloh, Benjamin H.D. 'Readymade, Photography, and Painting in the Painting of Gerhard Richter.' In *Neo-Avantgarde and Culture Industry: Essays on European and American Art from 1955 to 1975*, 365–404. Cambridge: MIT Press, 2000.

Buchloh, Benjamin H.D. 'Four Conversations: December 1999–May 2000.' In *Dan Graham, Works 1965–2000*, edited by Marianne Brouwer, 69–84. Düsseldorf: Richter Verlag, 2001.

Buergel, Roger M. et al. 'Curating with Institutional Visions.' In *Art and its Institutions: Current Conflicts, Critique and Collaborations*, edited by Nina Möntmann, 28–59. London: Black Dog Publishers, 2006.

Buonanno, Milly. *The Age of Television: Experiences and Theories*. Translated by Jennifer Radice. Bristol and Chicago: Intellect and University of Chicago, 2008.

Caldwell, John Thornton. *Televisuality: Style, Crisis, and Authority in American Television*. New Brunswick, NJ: Rutgers University Press, 1995.

Caldwell, John Thornton. *Production Culture: Industrial Reflexivity and Critical Practice in Film and Television*. Durham and London: Duke University Press, 2008.

Caldwell, John Thornton. 'Worker Blowback: User-Generated, Worker-Generated, and Producer-Generated Content within Collapsing Production Workflows.' In *Television as Digital Media*, edited by James Bennett and Niki Strange, 283–310. Durham and London: Duke University Press, 2011.

Caughie, John. 'Mourning Television: The Other Screen.' *Screen* 5, no. 4 (2010): 410–421.

Cavell, Stanley. 'The Fact of Television.' In *Video Culture: A Critical Examination*, edited by John G. Hanhardt, 192–218. Layton, UT: Peregrine Smith Books / Visual Studies Workshop Press, 1986.

Christov-Bakargiev, Carolyn. 'The dance was very frenetic, lively, rattling, clanging, rolling, contorted, and lasted for a long time.' In *dOCUMENTA (13): Catalogue 1/3, The Book of Books*, edited by documenta und Museum Fridericianum, 30–45. Ostfildern: Hatje Cantz, 2012.

Connolly, Maeve. *The Place of Artists' Cinema: Space, Site and Screen*. Bristol and Chicago: Intellect and Chicago University Press, 2009.

Connolly, Maeve. 'Staging Television: James Coleman's *So Different … and Yet*.' *Mousse Magazine* 27 (2011): 160–165.

Connolly, Maeve. 'Architecture, Television, Archaeology: Gerard Byrne's *Subject, 2009*.' *Images or Shadows: Gerard Byrne*, edited by Pablo Lafuente, 71–90. Dublin: Irish Museum of Modern Art, 2011.

Connolly, Maeve. 'Temporality, Sociality, Publicness: Cinema as Art Project.' *Afterall* 29 (2012): 4–15.

Connolly, Maeve. 'Unfortunate Things.' *Artes Mundi 5 2012: Wales International Visual Art Exhibition and Prize*, Cardiff: Artes Mundi, 2012, 50–55.

Connolly, Maeve. 'Cinematic Space, Televisual Time and Contemporary Art.' *Critical Quarterly* 54 no. 3 (2012): 31–45.

Connolly, Maeve. 'European Television Archives, Collective Memories and Contemporary Art.' *The Velvet Light Trap* 71 (2013): 47–58.

Connolly, Maeve. 'Studio Spaces.' *Frieze* 155 (2013): 208–212.

Connolly, Maeve. 'Televisual Objects: Props, Relics and Prosthetics.' *Afterall* 33 (2013): 66–77.

Connolly, Maeve. 'Artangel and the Changing Mediascape of Public Art.' *Journal of Curatorial Studies* 2, no. 2 (2013): 196–217.

Connolly, Maeve. 'Staging Mobile Spectatorship in the Moving Image Installations of Amanda Beech, Philippe Parreno, and Ryan Trecartin/Lizzie Fitch.' In *Display und Dispositif*, edited by Ursula Frohne, Lilian Haberer and Annette Urban. Munich: Wilhelm Fink (forthcoming, 2014).

Connolly, Maeve. 'Reverberations in Time and Space.' *Susan Philipsz—Ten Works, 2007–2013*, edited by James Lingwood and Brigitte Franzen 84–87. (Cologne: Koenig Books, 2014).

Cooke, Lynne. 'In Lieu of Higher Ground.' In *Questions of Practice: What Makes a Great Exhibition?*, edited by Paula Marincola, 32–43. Chicago: University of Chicago Press, 2007.

Cubitt, Sean. *Timeshift: On Video Culture.* London and New York: Routledge, 1991.

Cubitt, Sean. 'Grayscale Video and the Shift to Color.' *Art Journal* 65. 3 (2006): 46–49.

Ćurčić, Branka. 'Television as a Symbol of Lost Public Space.' *European Institute for Progressive Cultural Policies*, December 12, 2007. [Accessed June 1, 2013] http://transform.eipcp.net/corr espondence/1197491434#redir#redir.

Dawson, Max. 'Home Video and the "TV Problem": Cultural Critics and Technological Change.' *Technology and Culture* 48 (2007): 524–549.

Dayan, Daniel, and Elihu Katz. *Media Events: The Live Broadcasting of History.* Cambridge: Harvard University Press, 1992.

Dayan, Daniel. 'The Peculiar Public of Television.' *Media, Culture & Society* 23 (2001): 743–765.

Dean, Jodi. 'Democracy: A Knot of Hope and Despair.' *e-flux Journal* 39 (2012). [Accessed June 1, 2013] http://www.e-flux.com/journal/democracy-a-knot-of-hope-and-despair/.

de Bruijn, Hilde. 'The Real The Story The Storyteller.' *SMART Papers: Stefanos Tsivopoulos: 'The Real The Story The Storyteller'*, edited by Thomas Peutz, 6–7. Amsterdam: Smart Project Space, 2010. [Accessed June 1, 2013] http://www.smartprojectspace.net/pdf_papers/100911story. pdf.

Deleuze, Gilles and Felix Guattari. *A Thousand Plateaus: Capitalism and Schizophrenia.* Translated by Brian Massumi. Minneapolis: University of Minnesota Press, 1987.

Deleuze, Gilles. 'Postscript on the Societies of Control.' *October* 59 (1992): 3–7.

Dickinson, Margaret. *Rogue Reels: Oppositional Film in Britain 1945–1990.* London: BFI, 1999.

DiMaggio, Paul. 'Cultural Boundaries and Structural Change: The Extension of the High Culture Model to Theater, Opera, and the Dance, 1900–1940.' *Cultivating Differences: Symbolic Boundaries and the Making of Inequality*, edited by Michèle Lamond and Marcel Fournier, 21–57. Chicago: University of Chicago Press, 1992.

Doane, Mary Ann. 'Information, Crisis, Catastrophe.' In *Logics of Television*, edited by Patricia Mellencamp, 234–235. London and Bloomington: BFI and Indiana University Press, 1990.

Doherty, Claire. 'The Institution is Dead! Long Live the Institution! Contemporary Art and New Institutionalism.' *Art of Encounter: Engage* 15 (2004). [Accessed June 1, 2013] http://www.engage.org/engage-journal.aspx.

Douglas, Stan. 'Suspiria.' In *Documenta 11_Platform 5: Exhibition Venues, Catalogue*, edited by Documenta and Museum Fridericianum, 39. Ostfildern-Ruit: Hatje Cantz 2002.

Douglas, Stan. 'Evening.' In *Stan Douglas—Past Imperfect—Works 1986-2007*, edited by Iris Dressler and Hans. D. Christ, 193–194. Ostfildern: Hatje Cantz Verlag, 2007.

Douglas, Stan. 'Suspiria.' In *Stan Douglas—Past Imperfect—Works 1986-2007*, edited by Iris Dressler and Hans. D. Christ, 206–208. Ostfildern: Hatje Cantz Verlag, 2007.

Duncan, Carol. *Civilizing Rituals: Inside Public Art Museums.* London and New York: Routledge, 1994.

Dunn, Alan. 'Who Needs a Spin Doctor? Part Two.' *Art of Encounter: Engage* 15 (2004). [Accessed June 1, 2013] http://www.engage.org/engage-journal.aspx.

Dziewior, Yilmaz. 'GALA Committee.' *Artforum* 33, no. 10 (2000): 193–194.

Ellis, John. *Visible Fictions: Cinema, Television, Video.* London: Routledge and Kegan Paul, 1982.

Ellis, John. *Seeing Things.* London: I.B. Tauris, 2000.

Elsaesser, Thomas. 'Digital Cinema: Delivery, Event, Time.' In *Cinema Futures: Cain, Abel or Cable? The Screen Arts in the Digital Age*, edited by Thomas Elsaesser and Kay Hoffman, 201–222. Amsterdam: Amsterdam University Press, 1998.

Elsaesser, Thomas. 'Discipline through Diegesis: The Rube Film between "Attractions" and "Narrative Integration".' In *The Cinema of Attractions Reloaded*, edited by Wanda Strauven, 205–226. Amsterdam: Amsterdam University Press, 2006.

Elsaesser, Thomas. 'The Mind-Game Film.' In *Puzzle Films: Complex Storytelling in Contemporary Cinema*, edited by Warren Buckland, 13–42. Oxford: Wiley-Blackwell, 2009.

Engelman, Ralph. *Public Radio and Television in America.* Thousand Oaks, London and New Delhi: Sage Publications, 1996.

Esche, Charles. 'Rooseum Director Charles Esche on the Art Center of the 21st Century.' *artforum.com*, December 7, 2001. Artforum.com. [Accessed June 1, 2013] http://artforum.com/index.php?pn=interview&id=1331.

Estill, Adriana. 'Closing the Telenovela's Borders: "Vivo Por Elena's" Tidy Nation.' *Chasqui* 29, no. 1 (2000) 75–87.

Faguet, Michéle. '*soy mi madre*: A Conversation Between Phil Collins and Michéle Faguet.' *Celeste* Magazine 33 (2009). Unpaginated.

Farquharson, Alex. 'Bureaux de Change.' *Frieze* 101 (September 2006): 156–159.

Feuer, Jane. 'The Concept of Live Television: Ontology as Ideology.' In *Regarding Television: Critical Approaches—An Anthology*, edited by E. Ann Kaplan, 12–22. Frederick, Md.: University Publications of America, 1983.

Fisher, Jean. '*So Different ... and Yet.*' In *James Coleman*, 35–47. Dublin: Irish Museum of Modern Art, 2009.

Fisher, Jean. 'So Different ... and Yet.' In *James Coleman*, edited by Dorothea von Hantelmann and Jean Fisher, 164-169.

(Madrid: Museo Nacional Centro de Arte Reina Sofia, 2012).

Fogle, Douglas. 'Cinema is Dead, Long Live the Cinema.' *Frieze* 29 (1996): 32.

Fowler, Catherine. 'Remembering Cinema "Elsewhere": From Retrospection to Introspection in the Gallery Film.' *Cinema Journal* 51, no. 2 (2012): 26–45.

Fowler, Catherine. 'Once more with feeling: Performing the self in the work of Gillian Wearing, Kutluğ Ataman and Phil Collins's, *Moving Image Review & Art Journal* 2, no. 1 (2013): 10–24.

Fox, Dan. 'TV Swansong.' *Frieze 68* (2002): 124.

Fox, Patrick. 'New Adventures Online, Case tenantspin, Liverpool.' *Reaktio* no. 2: *TV Like Us*, edited by Hannah Harris, 52–64. London: Finnish Institute of London, 2012.

Fraser, Andrea. 'From the Critique of Institutions to an Institution of Critique.' *Artforum* 44, no. 1 (2005): 278–293, 322.

Fraser, Andrea. 'What's Intangible, Transitory, Mediating, Participatory, and Rendered in the Public Sphere? Part 1 (1996).' In *Museum Highlights: The Writings of Andrea Fraser*, edited by Alexander Alberro, 47–53. Cambridge, MA: MIT Press, 2005.

Fraser, Andrea. '"A Museum is not a business. It is run in a business-like fashion".' In *Art and its Institutions: Current Conflicts, Critique and Collaborations*, edited by Nina Möntmann, 86–99. London: Black Dog Publishers, 2006.

Frieling, Rudolf. 'Form Follows Format: Tensions, Museums, Media Technology and Media Art.' *Media Art Net*, 2004. *Media Art Net*, 2004. [Accessed June 1, 2013] http://www.medienkunstnetz.de/themes/overview_of_media_art/museum/.

García, Dora. 'Absurdity in Prime Time.' In *Are You Ready for TV?* exhibition catalogue, 26–36, Barcelona: MACBA, 2010.

Gibbons, Luke. 'Narratives of No Return: James Coleman's guaiRE.' In *Transformations in Irish Culture*, 129–133. Cork: Cork University Press in association with Field Day, 1996.

Gillick, Liam. *Literally No Place: Communes, Bars and Greenrooms*. London: Book Works, 2002.

Gitlin, Todd. *The Whole World is Watching*. Berkeley: University of California Press, 1980.

Godfrey, Mark. 'The Artist as Historian.' *October* 120 (2007): 140–172.

Gordon, Douglas. 'Interview with Douglas Gordon.' In *Douglas Gordon*, edited by Russell Ferguson, 152–173. Cambridge, MA: MIT Press, 2002.

Graham, Beryl and Sarah Cook. *Rethinking Curating: Art After New Media*. Cambridge, MA: MIT Press, 2010.

Graham, Dan. 'Art as Design/Design as Art.' In *Dan Graham: Beyond*, edited by Bennett Simpson and Chrissie Iles, 267–276. Los Angeles and Cambridge, MA: The Museum of Contemporary Art and MIT Press, 2009.

Grammel, Søren. 'A Series of Acts and Spaces.' *On Curating* 8 (2011): 33–38. [Accessed June 1, 2013] http://www.on-curating.org/documents/oncurating_issue_0811.pdf.

Granly Jensen, Erik. 'Collective Acoustic Space—LIGNA and Radio in the Weimar Republic (Brecht, Benjamin).' In *Radio Territories*, edited by Erik Granly Jensen and Brandon LaBelle, 154–169. Los Angeles and Copenhagen: Errant Bodies Press, 2007.

Grasskamp, Walter. 'For example, *Documenta*, or, How is History Produced?' Translated by Rebecca Pates. In *Thinking About Exhibitions*, edited by Reesa Greenberg, Bruce Ferguson, Sandy Nairne, 67–78. London and New York: Routledge, 1996.

Graw, Isabelle. *High Price: Art Between the Market and Celebrity Culture*. Berlin and New York: Sternberg Press, 2009.

Greenberg, Reesa. 'Archival Remembering Exhibitions.' *Journal of Curatorial Studies* 1, no. 2 (2012): 159–177.

Griffin, Tim. 'Postscript: The Museum Revisited.' *Artforum*, 48, no. 9 (May 2010). 329–335.

Grindstaff, Laura. *The Money Shot: Trash, Class, and the Making of TV Talk Shows*. Chicago: University of Chicago Press, 2002.

Grindstaff, Laura. 'Self-Serve Celebrity: The Production of Ordinariness and the Ordinariness of Production in Reality Television.' In *Production Studies: Cultural Studies of Media Industries*, edited by Vicki Mayer, Miranda J. Banks and John Thornton Caldwell, 71–86. New York and London: Routledge, 2009.

Habermas, Jürgen. *The Structural Transformation of the Public Sphere: An Inquiry into a Category of Bourgeois Society*. Translated by Thomas Burger with the assistance of Frederick Lawrence. Cambridge: Polity Press, 1989.

Hansen, Miriam. 'Early Silent Cinema: Whose Public Sphere?' *New German Critique* 29 (1983): 147–184.

Heath, Stephen. 'Representing Television.' In *Logics of Television*, edited by Patricia Mellencamp, 267–302. Bloomington and London: BFI and Indiana University Press, 1990.

Heiser, Joerg. 'Lullabies for Strangers.' In *Susan Philipsz: You Are Not Alone*, edited by Michael Stanley, 11–33. Oxford: Modern Art Oxford, 2010.

Helmore, Edward. 'London Frieze braves backlash to fly the flag of British culture in Manhattan.' *The Guardian*, April 28, 2012.

Helmore, Edward. 'LA aesthetes fight pop-art billionaire.' *The Observer*, July 22, 2012.

Hesmondhalgh, David and Sarah Baker. 'Creative Work and Emotional Labour in the Television Industry.' *Theory, Culture & Society* 25, no. 7/8 (2008): 97–118.

Hirschhorn, Thomas. 'Bataille Monument.' In *Contemporary Art: From Studio to Situation*, edited by Claire Doherty, 133–148. London: Black Dog Publishing, 2004.

Hirschhorn, Thomas. Interviewed by Craig Garrett, 'Philosophical Battery.' *Flash Art* 238 (2004): 90–93.

Hochschild, Arlie Russell. *The Managed Heart: Commercialization of Human Feeling*. Berkeley: University of California Press 1983.

Holdsworth, Amy. '"Television Resurrections": Television and Memory.' *Cinema Journal* 47, no. 3 (2008): 137–144.

Holdsworth, Amy. *Television, Memory and Nostalgia*. New York: Palgrave Macmillan, 2011.

Holmes, Su. '"An…Unmarried Mother Sat in a Wing-Backed Chair on TV Last Night…" BBC Television Asks Is This Your Problem? (1955–1957).' *Television & New Media* 9, no. 3 (2008): 175–196.

Horowitz, Noah. *Art of the Deal: Contemporary Art in a Global Financial Market*. Princeton and Oxford: Princeton University Press, 2011.

Huffman, Kathy Rae. 'Seeing is Believing: The Arts on TV.' in *The Arts for Television*, edited by Kathy Rae Huffman and Dorine Mignot (Los Angeles and Amsterdam: Los Angeles Museum of Contemporary Art and Stedelijk Museum, 1987), 8–16.

Huffman, Kathy Rae. 'Video Art: What's TV Got To Do With It?' In *Illuminating Video: An Essential Guide to Video Art*, edited by Doug Hall and Sally Jo Fifer, 81–90. New York: Aperture Foundation in association with Bay Area Video Coalition, 1990.

Huffman, Kathy Rae. 'Exchange and Evolution: Worldwide Video Long Beach 1974–1999.' *Exchange and Evolution: Worldwide Video Long Beach 1974–1999*, edited by Kathy Rae Huffman, 10–25. Long Beach: Long Beach Museum of Art, 2011.

Huffman, Kathy Rae. 'Exchange: A Screening Event.' *Exchange and Evolution: Worldwide Video Long Beach 1974–1999*, edited by Kathy Rae Huffman, 113–116. Long Beach: Long Beach Museum of Art, 2011.

Huyssen, Andreas. *Twilight Memories: Marking Time in a Culture of Amnesia.* London: Routledge, 1995.

Jameson, Fredric. 'The End of Temporality.' *Critical Inquiry* 29, no. 4 (2003): 695–718.

Joselit, David. 'Tale of the Tape.' *Artforum* 40, no. 9 (2002): 152–57.

Joselit, David. 'Yippie Pop: Abbie Hoffman, Andy Warhol, and Sixties Media Politics.' *Grey Room* 8 (2002): 62–79.

Joselit, David. *Feedback: Television Against Democracy.* Cambridge, MA and London: MIT Press, 2007.

Joselit, David. 'Feedback.' In *Changing Channels: Art and Television 1963–1988*, edited by Museum Moderner Kunst Stiftung Ludwig Wien and Matthias Michalka, 67–78. Cologne: Verlag der Buchhandlung Walther König, 2010.

Kaizen, William. 'Live on Tape: Video, Liveness and the Immediate.' In *Art and the Moving Image: A Critical Reader*, edited by Tanya Leighton, 269–272. London: Tate Publishing in Association with Afterall Books, 2008.

Kastner, Jeffrey. 'New Foundations.' *Artforum* 48, no. 10 (2010): 314–319.

Katz, Elihu. 'And Deliver Us From Segmentation.' *Annals of the American Academy of Political and Social Science* 546 (1996): 22–33.

Keaney, Emily. 'Culture and Civil Renewal—The Human Face of Regeneration.' *Regeneration: Engage* 17 (2005).

Kennedy, Randy. '*Artstar* on Gallery HD: The Art World Tries Realism (the TV Kind).' *The New York Times*, May 28, 2006.

Kernbauer, Eva. 'Establishing Belief: Harun Farocki and Andrei Ujica, Videograms of a Revolution.' *Grey Room* 41 (2010): 72–87.

Ketcham, Michael G. *Transparent Design: Reading, Performance, and Form in the Spectator Papers.* Athens: University of Georgia Press, 1985.

Kimball, Whitney. 'Artists are on TV! This Time, Not For Bravo Money.' *Art Fag City*, August 23, 2012. [Accessed June 1, 2013] http://www.artfagcity.com/2012/08/23/artists-are-on-tv-this-time-not-for-bravo-money/.

Kompare, Derek. 'Publishing Flow: DVD Box Sets and the Reconception of Television.' *Television and New Media* 7, no. 4 (2006): 335–360.

Kortti, Jukka. 'Multidimensional Social History of Television: Social Uses of Finnish Television from the 1950s to the 2000s.' *Television & New Media* 12, no. 4 (2011): 293–313.

Krauss, Rosalind. 'The Cultural Logic of the Late Capitalist Museum.' *October* 54 (1990): 427–441.

Lee, Sook-Kyung. 'Videa 'n' Videology: Open Communication.' In *Nam June Paik*, edited by Sook-Kyung Lee and Susanne Rennert, 27–54. London: Tate Publishing, 2010.

Leighton, Tanya and Pavel Buchler, eds. *Saving the Image: Art After Film.* Glasgow and Manchester: Centre for Contemporary Arts and Manchester Metropolitan University, 2003.

Leighton, Tanya. 'Introduction.' In *Art and the Moving Image: A Critical Reader*, edited by Tanya Leighton, 7–40. London: Tate Publishing in association with Afterall, 2008.

Levine, Lawrence W. *Highbrow Lowbrow: The Emergence of Cultural Hierarchy in America.* Cambridge, MA: Harvard University Press, 1988.

Levine, Elana. 'Teaching the Politics of Television Culture in a Post-Television Era.' *Cinema Journal* 50, no. 4 (2011): 177–182.

Lind, Maria. 'Telling Histories: Archives/Spatial Situation/Case-studies/Talkshows/Symposium.' In *Curating with Light Luggage: Reflections, Discussions and Revisions*, edited by Liam Gillick and Maria Lind, 90–106. Munich: Kunstverein München and Revolver, 2005.

Lind, Maria, and Hito Steyerl. 'Introduction: Reconsidering the Documentary and Contemporary Art.' In *The Greenroom: Reconsidering the Documentary and Contemporary Art*, edited by Lind and Steyerl, 10–26. New York: Sternberg Press and Center for Curatorial Studies, Bard College, 2008.

Loeffler, Carl. 'Performing Post-Performancist Performance or the Televisionist Performing Televisionism.' In *Give Them the Picture: An Anthology of La Mamelle / ART COM*, edited by Liz Glass, Susannah Magers, and Julian Myers, 100–103. San Francisco: California College of the Arts, 2011.

Lütticken, Sven. *Secret Publicity: Essays on Contemporary Art.* Rotterdam and Amsterdam: Nai Publishers and Fonds BKVB, 2005.

Lütticken, Sven. 'Once More on Publicness: A Postscript to *Secret Publicity*.' *Fillip* 12 (2010): 86–91.

Lynott, Anne. 'Productive Reflection.' *VAN*: Visual Artists Newssheet, March 21, 2011. [Accessed June 1, 2013] http://visualartists.ie/articles/van-marchapril-2011-productive-reflection/.

Mayer, Vicki, Miranda J. Banks and John Thornton Caldwell, eds. *Production Studies: Cultural Studies of Media Industries.* New York and London: Routledge, 2009.

McCarthy, Anna. 'From Screen to Site: Television's Material Culture, and Its Place.' *October* 98, Autumn (2001): 93–111.

McCarthy, Anna. *Ambient Television: Visual Culture and Public Space.* Duke University Press, 2001.

McCarthy, Anna. '"Stanley Milgram, Allen Funt, and Me": Postwar Social Science and the "First Wave" of Reality TV.' In *Reality TV: Remaking Television Culture*, 2nd ed., edited by Susan Murray and Laurie Ouellette, 23–43. New York and London: New York University Press, 2008.

McCarthy, Anna. *The Citizen Machine: Governing by Television in 1950s America.* New York and London: New Press, 2011.

McLuhan, Marshall. *Understanding Media: The Extensions of Man.* New York: McGraw-Hill, 1964.

Meehan, Eileen R. 'Why We Don't Count: The Commodity Audience.' In *Logics of Television*, edited by Patricia Mellencamp, 117–137. London and Bloomington: BFI and Indiana University Press, 1990.

Mehring, Christine. 'Television Art's Abstract Starts: Europe circa 1944–1969.' *October* 125 (2008): 29–64.

Meltzer, Burkhard. 'Christian Jankowski, Kunstmuseum Stuttgart.' Translated by Nicholas Grindell, *Frieze* 120 (2009): 146–147.

Merjian, Ara H. 'TV Honey, Silverman Gallery.' *Artforum.com*, November 2, 2007. [Accessed June 1, 2013] http://www.artforum.com/print.php?id=18867&pn=picks&action=print.

Michalka, Matthias. 'Introduction.' In *Changing Channels: Art and Television 1963–1988*, edited by Museum Moderner Kunst Stiftung Ludwig Wien and Matthias Michalka, 11–13. Cologne: Verlag der Buchhandlung Walther Konig, 2010.

Miles, Malcolm. 'Critical Spaces: Monuments and Changes.' In *The Practice of Public Art*, edited by Cameron Cartiere and Shelly Willis, 66–90. Routledge: London and New York, 2008.

Miller, Toby. *The Well-Tempered Self: Citizenship, Culture and the Postmodern Subject.* Baltimore and London: John Hopkins University Press, 1993.

Moeller, Sirkka. 'All Creatures Great and Small: The 57th International Short Film Festival Oberhausen.' *Senses of Cinema* 59, June 23, 2011. [Accessed June 1, 2013] http://sensesofcinema. com/2011/festival-reports/all-creatures-great-and-small-the-57th-international-short-film-festival-oberhausen/.

Möntmann, Nina. 'Art and its Institutions.' In *Art and its Institutions: Current Conflicts, Critique and Collaborations*, edited by Nina Möntmann, 8–17. London: Black Dog Publishers, 2006.

Möntmann, Nina. 'The Rise and Fall of New Institutionalism: Perspectives on a Possible Future.' *European Institute for Progressive Cultural Policies* (EIPCP) Transversal Project, August 2007. [Accessed June 1, 2013] http://eipcp.net/transversal/0407/moentmann/en.

Morse, Margaret. *Virtualities: Television, Media Art and Cyberculture.* Bloomington, Indiana: Indiana University Press, 1998.

Moser, Gabrielle. 'Exhibition-Making with Ghosts: The 1984 Miss General Idea Pavilion.' *Fillip* 11 (2010). Fillip Magazine. [Accessed June 1, 2013] http://fillip.ca/content/the-1984-miss-general-idea-pavilion.

Mouffe, Chantal. 'Artistic Activism and Agonistic Spaces.' *Art & Research: A Journal of Ideas, Context and Methods* 1.2 (2007): 1–5.

Negt, Oskar, and Alexander Kluge. *Public Sphere and Experience: Toward an Analysis of the Bourgeois and Proletarian Public Sphere.* Translated by Peter Labanyi, Jamie Owen Daniel and Assenka Oksiloff. Minneapolis: University of Minnesota Press, 1993.

Newman, Michael Z., and Elana Levine. *Legitimating Television: Media Convergence and Cultural Status.* New York and London: Routledge, 2012.

Noble, Kathy. 'Art and TV.' *Metropolis M*, no. 5, October–November 2010. Metropolis M. [Accessed June 1, 2013] http://metropolism.com/magazine/2010-no5/in-verzet-tegen-het-troostkijken/english.

Nora, Pierre. 'Between Memory and History: *Les Lieux de Mémoire.*' Translated by Marc Roudebush. *Representations* 26, (Spring 1989): 7–24.

O'Neill, Paul. *The Culture of Curating and the Curating of Culture(s).* Cambridge, MA: MIT Press, 2012.

O'Reilly, Sally. 'Do Not Adjust Your Set.' *Financialtimes.com*, October 6, 2006. [Accessed June 1, 2013] http://www.ft.com/cms/s/0/9b457392–537a-11db-8a2a-0000779e2340.html#ixzz1gSCMXf8I.

Ouellette, Laurie. *Viewers like You?* New York: Columbia University Press, 2002.

Ouellette, Laurie. 'TV Viewing as Good Citizenship? Political Rationality, Enlightened Democracy and PBS.' In *Television: Critical Concepts in Media and Cultural Studies vol IV*, edited by Toby Miller, 73–100. London and New York: Routledge, 2003.

Ouellette, Laurie. "'Take Responsibility for Yourself": *Judge Judy* and the Neoliberal Citizen.' In *Reality TV: Remaking Television Culture*, 2nd ed., edited by Susan Murray and Laurie Ouellette, 223–242. New York and London: New York University Press, 2008.

Ouellette, Laurie and James Hay. *Better Living Through Reality TV: Television and Post-welfare Citizenship.* Malden, MA: Blackwell Publishing, 2008.

Pantenburg, Volker. '1970 and Beyond. Experimental Cinema and Art Spaces.' In *Screen Dynamics: Mapping the Borders of* Cinema, edited by Gertrude Koch, Volker Pantenburg, Simon Rothöhler, 78–92. Vienna: Austrian Film Museum and SYNEMA—Gesellschaft für Film und Medien, 2012.

Parks, Lisa. Cultures in Orbit: Satellites and the Televisual. Durham and London: Duke University Press, 2005.

Paulsen, Kris. 'California Video,' *X-TRA Contemporary Art Quarterly* 11.1 (2008) http://x-traonline.org/article/california-video/ (Accessed June 1, 2013).

Paulsen, Kris. 'In the Beginning, There was the Electron.' X-TRA Contemporary Art Quarterly 15. 2 (2012): 56–73.

Perry, Colin. 'TV Makeover.' *Art Monthly* 352 (2011–2012): 11–14.

Philbin, Ann. 'The Museum Revisited.' *Artforum* 48, no. 9 (2010): 298–299.

Philipsz, Susan. 'You Are Not Alone.' In *Susan Philipsz: You Are Not Alone*, edited by Michael Stanley, 7. Oxford: Modern Art Oxford, 2010.

Phillips, Patricia C. 'Temporality and Public Art.' *Art Journal*, 48, no. 4 (1989): 331–335.

Pine II, B. Joseph and James H. Gilmore. *The Experience Economy: Work is Theatre & Every Business is a Stage.* Boston, MA: Harvard Business School Press, 1999.

Rancière, Jacques. 'The Emancipated Spectator.' *Artforum* 45, no. 7 (2007): 271–280.

Rebhandl, Bert. 'Clemens von Wedemeyer: The Site Creates Simultaneity.' *Mousse Magazine* 34 (2012): 118–125.

Richardson, Kay and Ulrike H. Meinhof. *Worlds In Common?: Television Discourse in a Changing Europe.* London: Routledge, 1999.

Roberts, John. *The Intangibilities of Form: Skill and Deskilling in Art After the Readymade.* London and New York: Verso, 2008.

Rogoff, Irit. 'De-regulation: With the Work or Kutlug Ataman.' *Third Text* 23, no. 1 (2009): 165–179.

Rosenberg, Karen. 'A Show is All Cyber, Some of the Time.' *The New York Times*, October 21, 2010. The New York Times. [Accessed June 1, 2013] http://www.nytimes.com/2010/10/22/arts/design/22free.html.

Rosenberg, Karen. 'A Museum Show as a TV Contest Prize.' *The New York Times*, August 18, 2010. The New York Times. [Accessed June 1, 2013] http://www.nytimes.com/2010/08/19/arts/design/19abdi.html?_r=0.

Rosler, Martha. 'Video: Shedding the Utopian Moment.' In *Illuminating Video: An Essential Guide to Video Art*, edited by Doug Hall and Sally Jo Fifer, 30–50. New York: Aperture Foundation in association with Bay Area Video Coalition, 1990.

Royoux, Jean-Christophe. 'Mobile TV: le lieu des récits entrecroisés.' In *Homo Zappiens Zappiens*, Rennes: Presses Universitaires de Rennes 2, 1998.

Royoux, Jean-Christophe. 'Free-Time Workers and the Reconfiguration of Public Space: Several Hypotheses on the Work of Pierre Huyghe.' In *Saving the Image: Art After Film*, edited by

Tanya Leighton and Pavel Buchler, 180–200. Glasgow and Manchester: Centre for Contemporary Arts and Manchester Metropolitan University, 2003.

Ryan, Paul. 'A Genealogy of Video.' *Leonardo* 21, no. 1 (1988): 39–44.

Salkin, Allen. 'For Him, the Web Was No Safety Net.' *The New York Times*, August 28, 2009.

Sandvig, Christian. 'The Structural Problems of the Internet for Cultural Policy.' In *Critical Cyberculture Studies*, edited by David Silver and Adrienne Massanari, 107–118. New York: NYU Press, 2006.

Scannell, Paddy. *Radio, Television and Modern Life: A Phenomenological Approach.* Cambridge, MA and Oxford, Blackwell, 1996.

Scharrer, Eva. 'Clemens von Wedemeyer.' In *dOCUMENTA (13): Catalogue 3/3, The Guidebook*, edited by documenta und Museum Fridericianum, 374–375. Ostfildern: Hatje Cantz, 2012.

Searle, Adrian. 'Talking Heads.' *The Guardian*, March 29, 2005.

Searle, Adrian. 'Wallinger deserved to win the Turner prize.' *The Guardian*, December 4, 2007.

Shamberg, Michael, and Raindance Corporation. *Guerrilla Television.* New York: Holt, Rinehart and Winston, 1971.

Shattuc, Jane M. 'The Shifting Terrain of American Talk Shows.' In *A Companion to Television*, edited by Janet Wasko, 324–336. Oxford: Blackwell Publishing, 2010.

Sheets, Hilarie M. 'Armand Hammer's Orphan Museum Turns Into Cinderella in Los Angeles.' *The New York Times*, arts section, October 6, 2004.

Sheikh, Simon. 'In the Place of the Public Sphere? Or, the World in Fragments.' *European Institute for Progressive Cultural Policies*, June 2004. [Accessed June 1, 2013] http://republicart.net/disc/publicum/sheikh03_en.htm.

Sheikh, Simon. 'Publics and Post-Publics: The Production of the Social.' *Open 14: Art as a Public Issue* (2008): 28–36.

Sinclair, John. 'Latin America's Impact on World Television Markets.' In *Television Studies After TV: Understanding Television in the Post-Broadcast Era*, edited by Graeme Turner and Jinna Tay, 141–148. London and New York: Routledge, 2009.

Slade, Joseph W., and Leonard J. Barchak. 'Public Broadcasting in Finland: Inventing a National Television Programming Policy.' *Journal of Broadcasting & Electronic Media* 33, no. 4 (1989): 355–373.

Smith, Roberta. 'A Channel-Surfing Experience with Beanbag Chairs and Gym.' *The New York Times*, April 25, 1997, C22.

Sperlinger, Mike and Ian White, eds. *Kinomuseum: Towards an Artists' Cinema*, Cologne: Verlag der Buchhandlung Walther Konig, 2008.

Sperlinger, Mike. 'Looking Back: Film.' *Frieze* 136 (2011): 24.

Spigel, Lynn. *Make Room for TV: Television and the Family Ideal in Postwar America.* Chicago: University of Chicago Press, 1992.

Spigel, Lynn. 'Introduction.' In *Television After TV: Essays on a Medium in Transition*, edited by Lynn Spigel and Jan Olsson, 1–34. Durham, NC: Duke University Press, 2004.

Spigel, Lynn and Jan Olsson, eds. *Television After TV: Essays on a Medium in Transition.* Durham, NC: Duke University Press, 2004.

Spigel, Lynn. 'TV's Next Season?' *Cinema Journal* 45, no. 1 (2005): 83–90.

Spigel, Lynn. *TV by Design: Modern Art and the Rise of Network Television*. Chicago: University of Chicago Press, 2008.

Spigel, Lynn. 'Our TV Heritage: Television, The Archive, and The Reasons for Preservation.' In *A Companion to Television*, edited by Janet Wasko, 67–102. Oxford: Blackwell publishing, 2010.

Stahl, Matt. 'Privilege and Distinction in Production Worlds: Copyright, Collective Bargaining and Working Conditions in Media Making.' In *Production Studies: Cultural Studies of Media Industries*, edited by Vicki Mayer, Miranda J. Banks and John Thornton Caldwell, 54–67. New York and London: Routledge, 2009.

Steyerl, Hito. 'The Institution of Critique.' *European Institute for Progressive Cultural Policies*. January 2006. EIPCP Transversal Project. [Accessed June 1, 2013] http://eipcp.net/transversal/0106/steyerl/en.

Steyerl, Hito. 'Is a Museum a Factory?' *e-flux journal* 7 (2009). [Accessed June 1, 2013] http://www.e-flux.com/journal/is-a-museum-a-factory/.

Steyerl, Hito. *The Wretched of the Screen*, (Berlin: Sternberg Press, 2012).

Stoneman, Rod. 'Sins of Commission.' *Screen* 33: 2 (1992): 127–144.

Streeter, Thomas. 'Blue Skies and Strange Bedfellows: The Discourse of Cable Television.' In *The Revolution Wasn't Televised: Sixties Television and Social Conflict*, edited by Lynn Spigel and Michael Curtin, 221–242. New York and London: Routledge, 1997.

Sturken, Marita. 'Paradox in the Evolution of an Art Form: Great Expectations and the Making of a History.' In *Illuminating Video: An Essential Guide to Video Art*, edited by Doug Hall and Sally Jo Fifer, 101–121. New York: Aperture Foundation in association with Bay Area Video Coalition, 1990.

Superflex. Interviewed by Minna Tarkka. *Reaktio no. 2: TV Like Us*, edited by Hannah Harris, 42–47. London: Finnish Institute of London, 2012.

Sutherland, Meghan. 'On the Grounds of Television.' In *Taking Place: Location and the Moving Image*, edited by John David Rhodes and Elena Gorfinkel, 339–362. Minneapolis and London: University of Minnesota Press, 2011.

Sutton, Gloria. 'Playback: Reconsidering the Long Beach Museum of Art as a Media Art Center.' In *Exchange and Evolution: Worldwide Video Long Beach 1974–1999*, edited by Kathy Rae Huffman, 120–129. Long Beach: Long Beach Museum of Art, 2011.

Tamblyn, Christine. 'Qualifying the Quotidian: Artist's Video and the Production of Social Space.' In *Resolutions: Contemporary Video Practices*, edited by Michael Renov and Erika Suderberg, 13–28. Minn.: Minnesota University Press, 1996.

Taubin, Amy. '24 Hour Psycho.' In *Spellbound: Art and Film*, edited by Ian Christie and Philip Dodd, 68–75. (London: BFI Publishing, 1996).

Thorel, Benjamin. *Telle est la Télé: L'art Contemporain et la télévision*. Paris: Editions Cercle d'Art, 2006.

Turco, Marina. 'Changing history, changing practices: an instance of confrontation between video art and television in the Netherlands.' *E-view*, no. 2 (2004), https://ojs.uvt.nl/.

Turner, Graeme and Jinna Tay, eds. *Television Studies After TV: Understanding Television in the Post-Broadcast Era*. London and New York: Routledge, 2009.

Vesic, Jelena, et al. 'Miraculous Mass Communication: Radioballet by LIGNA.' *Variant* 31 (2008): 5–7.

Vidokle, Anton. 'Art Without Artists?' *e-flux journal* 16 (2010). [Accessed June 1, 2013] http://www.e-flux.com/journal/art-without-artists/.

Virno, Paul. *A Grammar of the Multitude.* Translated by Isabella Bertoletti, James Cascaito, and Andrea Casson. New York and Los Angeles: Semiotexte, 2004.

Vischmidt, Marina. '*Counter (Re-)Productive Labour*', posted on the Auto Italia South East website, April 4, 2012. [Accessed June 1, 2013] http://autoitaliasoutheast.org/blog/news/2012/04/04/counter-re-productive-labour/.

Volcic, Zala. '"The Machine that Creates Slovenians": The Role of Slovenian Public Broadcasting in Re-affirming and Re-inventing the Slovenian National Identity.' *National Identities* 7, no. 3 (2005): 287–308.

Von Hantelmann, Dorothea. *How to Do Things With Art: What Performativity Means in Art.* Zurich and Dijon: JRP Ringier and Les Presses du Réel, 2010.

Von Hantelmann, Dorothea. '30 July 2010–22 October 2010.' *Philippe Parreno: Films 1987–2010,* edited by Karen Marta, Kathryn Rattee, Zoe Stillpass, 85–92. London and Cologne: Serpentine Gallery and Koenig Books, 2010.

Von Wedemeyer, Clemens. *Bambule: The Script.* Series: dOCUMENTA (13): 100 Notes—100 Thoughts No. 092. Ostfildern: Hatje Cantz, 2012.

Warner, Michael. 'Publics and Counterpublics.' *Public Culture* 14, no. 1 (2002): 49–90.

Watts, Amber. 'Melancholy, Merit, and Merchandise: The Postwar Audience Participation Show.' In *Reality TV: Remaking Television Culture*, 2nd ed., edited by Susan Murray and Laurie Ouellette, 301–320. New York and London: New York University Press, 2008.

Weber, Samuel. *Mass Mediauras: Form, Technics, Media.* Palo Alto: Stanford University Press, 1996.

Weerasethakul, Apichatpong. 'Annotated Filmography.' In *Apichatpong Weerasethakul*, edited by James Quandt, 225–226. Vienna: Austrian Film Museum and SYNEMA—Gesellschaft für Film und Medien, 2009.

Weiner, Andrew S. 'Changing Channels: Broadcast Television, Early Video, and the Politics of Networked Media.' *Qui Parle* 16, no. 2 (2008): 133–145.

Weiner, Andrew S. 'Memory under Reconstruction: Politics and Event in Wirtschaftswunder West Germany.' *Grey Room* 37 (2009): 94–124.

Williams, Raymond. *Television: Technology and Cultural Form.* New York: Schocken, 1975.

Wooster, Ann-Sargent. 'Reach Out and Touch Someone: The Romance of Interactivity.' In *Illuminating Video: An Essential Guide to Video Art*, edited by Doug Hall and Sally Jo Fifer, 275–303. New York: Aperture Foundation in association with Bay Area Video Coalition, 1990.

Wittel, Andreas. 'Toward a Network Sociality.' *Theory, Culture and Society* 18, no. 6 (2001): 51–77.

Wyver, John. 'TV Against TV: Video Art on Television.' In *Film and Video Art*, edited by Stuart Comer, 122–131. London: Tate Publishing, 2009.

Young, Benjamin. 'On Media and Democratic Politics: Videograms of a Revolution.' In *Harun Farocki: Working on the Sight-lines*, edited by Thomas Elsaesser, 245–260. Amsterdam: Amsterdam University Press, 2004.

Index

Note: Page numbers in italics refer to illustrations, those followed by *n* to information in a note. Exhibitions, films and television programmes appear under their titles; works of art appear under the artist's name.